Big Girls
Do Cry

Deanna Boston

Books by Carl Weber

Up to No Good

Something on the Side

The First Lady

So You Call Yourself a Man

The Preacher's Son

Player Haters

Lookin' for Luv

Married Men

Baby Momma Drama

She Ain't the One (with Mary B. Morrison)

Carnegie Commission on Higher Education

Sponsored Research Studies

EDUCATION, INCOME, AND HUMAN BEHAVIOR
F. Thomas Juster (ed.)

AMERICAN LEARNED SOCIETIES
IN TRANSITION:
THE IMPACT OF DISSENT
AND RECESSION
Harland G. Bloland and Sue M. Bloland

ANTIBIAS REGULATION OF UNIVERSITIES:
FACULTY PROBLEMS AND THEIR SOLUTIONS
Richard A. Lester

CHANGES IN UNIVERSITY
ORGANIZATION, 1964–1971
Edward Gross and Paul V. Grambsch

ESCAPE FROM THE DOLL'S HOUSE:
WOMEN IN GRADUATE AND PROFESSIONAL
SCHOOL EDUCATION
Saul D. Feldman

HIGHER EDUCATION AND
THE LABOR MARKET
Margaret S. Gordon (ed.)

THE ACADEMIC MELTING POT:
CATHOLICS AND JEWS IN
AMERICAN HIGHER EDUCATION
Stephen Steinberg

LEADERSHIP AND AMBIGUITY:
THE AMERICAN COLLEGE PRESIDENT
Michael D. Cohen and
James G. March

THE ACADEMIC SYSTEM IN
AMERICAN SOCIETY
Alain Touraine

EDUCATION FOR THE PROFESSIONS
OF MEDICINE, LAW, THEOLOGY,
AND SOCIAL WELFARE
Everett C. Hughes, Barrie Thorne,
Agostino DeBaggis, Arnold Gurin,
and David Williams

THE FUTURE OF HIGHER
EDUCATION:
SOME SPECULATIONS AND
SUGGESTIONS
Alexander M. Mood

CONTENT AND CONTEXT:
ESSAYS ON COLLEGE EDUCATION
Carl Kaysen (ed.)

THE RISE OF THE ARTS ON THE AMERICAN
CAMPUS
Jack Morrison

THE UNIVERSITY AND THE CITY:
EIGHT CASES OF INVOLVEMENT
George Nash, Dan Waldorf, and Robert E.
Price

THE BEGINNING OF THE FUTURE:
A HISTORICAL APPROACH TO GRADUATE
EDUCATION IN THE ARTS AND SCIENCES
Richard J. Storr

ACADEMIC TRANSFORMATION:
SEVENTEEN INSTITUTIONS UNDER
PRESSURE
David Riesman and Verne A. Stadtman (eds.)

THE UNIVERSITY AS AN ORGANIZATION
James A. Perkins (ed.)

NEW DIRECTIONS IN LEGAL EDUCATION
Herbert L. Packer and Thomas Ehrlich abridged
and unabridged editions

WHERE COLLEGES ARE AND WHO ATTENDS:
EFFECTS OF ACCESSIBILITY ON COLLEGE
ATTENDANCE
C. Arnold Anderson, Mary Jean Bowman, and
Vincent Tinto

THE EMERGING TECHNOLOGY:
INSTRUCTIONAL USE OF THE COMPUTER
IN HIGHER EDUCATION
Roger E. Levien

A STATISTICAL PORTRAIT OF HIGHER
EDUCATION
Seymour E. Harris

THE HOME OF SCIENCE:
THE ROLE OF THE UNIVERSITY
Dael Wolfle

EDUCATION AND EVANGELISM:
A PROFILE OF PROTESTANT COLLEGES
C. Robert Pace

PROFESSIONAL EDUCATION:
SOME NEW DIRECTIONS
Edgar H. Schein

THE NONPROFIT RESEARCH INSTITUTE:
ITS ORIGIN, OPERATION, PROBLEMS, AND
PROSPECTS
Harold Orlans

THE INVISIBLE COLLEGES:
A PROFILE OF SMALL, PRIVATE COLLEGES
WITH LIMITED RESOURCES
Alexander W. Astin and Calvin B. T. Lee

AMERICAN HIGHER EDUCATION:
DIRECTIONS OLD AND NEW
Joseph Ben-David

A DEGREE AND WHAT ELSE?
CORRELATES AND CONSEQUENCES OF A
COLLEGE EDUCATION
*Stephen B. Withey, Jo Anne Coble, Gerald
Gurin, John P. Robinson, Burkhard Strumpel,
Elizabeth Keogh Taylor, and Arthur C. Wolfe*

THE MULTICAMPUS UNIVERSITY:
A STUDY OF ACADEMIC GOVERNANCE
Eugene C. Lee and Frank M. Bowen

INSTITUTIONS IN TRANSITION:
A PROFILE OF CHANGE IN HIGHER
EDUCATION
(INCORPORATING THE 1970 STATISTICAL
REPORT)
Harold L. Hodgkinson

EFFICIENCY IN LIBERAL EDUCATION:
A STUDY OF COMPARATIVE INSTRUCTIONAL
COSTS FOR DIFFERENT WAYS OF ORGANIZ-
ING TEACHING-LEARNING IN A LIBERAL
ARTS COLLEGE
Howard R. Bowen and Gordon K. Douglass

CREDIT FOR COLLEGE:
PUBLIC POLICY FOR STUDENT LOANS
Robert W. Hartman

MODELS AND MAVERICKS:
A PROFILE OF PRIVATE LIBERAL ARTS
COLLEGES
Morris T. Keeton

BETWEEN TWO WORLDS:
A PROFILE OF NEGRO HIGHER EDUCATION
Frank Bowles and Frank A. DeCosta

BREAKING THE ACCESS BARRIERS:
A PROFILE OF TWO-YEAR COLLEGES
Leland L. Medsker and Dale Tillery

ANY PERSON, ANY STUDY:
AN ESSAY ON HIGHER EDUCATION IN THE
UNITED STATES
Eric Ashby

THE NEW DEPRESSION IN HIGHER
EDUCATION:
A STUDY OF FINANCIAL CONDITIONS AT 41
COLLEGES AND UNIVERSITIES
Earl F. Cheit

FINANCING MEDICAL EDUCATION:
AN ANALYSIS OF ALTERNATIVE POLICIES
AND MECHANISMS
Rashi Fein and Gerald I. Weber

HIGHER EDUCATION IN NINE COUNTRIES:
A COMPARATIVE STUDY OF COLLEGES AND
UNIVERSITIES ABROAD
*Barbara B. Burn, Philip G. Altbach, Clark Kerr,
and James A. Perkins*

BRIDGES TO UNDERSTANDING:
INTERNATIONAL PROGRAMS OF AMERICAN
COLLEGES AND UNIVERSITIES
Irwin T. Sanders and Jennifer C. Ward

GRADUATE AND PROFESSIONAL EDUCATION,
1980:
A SURVEY OF INSTITUTIONAL PLANS
Lewis B. Mayhew

THE AMERICAN COLLEGE AND AMERICAN
CULTURE:
SOCIALIZATION AS A FUNCTION OF HIGHER
EDUCATION
Oscar Handlin and Mary F. Handlin

RECENT ALUMNI AND HIGHER EDUCATION:
A SURVEY OF COLLEGE GRADUATES
Joe L. Spaeth and Andrew M. Greeley

CHANGE IN EDUCATIONAL POLICY:
SELF-STUDIES IN SELECTED COLLEGES AND
UNIVERSITIES
Dwight R. Ladd

STATE OFFICIALS AND HIGHER EDUCATION:
A SURVEY OF THE OPINIONS AND
EXPECTATIONS OF POLICY MAKERS IN NINE
STATES
Heinz Eulau and Harold Quinley

ACADEMIC DEGREE STRUCTURES,
INNOVATIVE APPROACHES:
PRINCIPLES OF REFORM IN DEGREE
STRUCTURES IN THE UNITED STATES
Stephen H. Spurr

COLLEGES OF THE FORGOTTEN AMERICANS:
A PROFILE OF STATE COLLEGES AND
REGIONAL UNIVERSITIES
E. Alden Dunham

FROM BACKWATER TO MAINSTREAM:
A PROFILE OF CATHOLIC HIGHER
EDUCATION
Andrew M. Greeley

THE ECONOMICS OF THE MAJOR PRIVATE
UNIVERSITIES
William G. Bowen
(Out of print, but available from University Microfilms.)

THE FINANCE OF HIGHER EDUCATION
Howard R. Bowen
(Out of print, but available from University Microfilms.)

ALTERNATIVE METHODS OF FEDERAL
FUNDING FOR HIGHER EDUCATION
Ron Wolk
(Out of print, but available from University Microfilms.)

INVENTORY OF CURRENT RESEARCH ON
HIGHER EDUCATION 1968
Dale M. Heckman and Warren Bryan Martin
(Out of print, but available from University Microfilms.)

The following technical reports are available from the Carnegie Commission on Higher Education, 2150 Shattuck Ave., Berkeley, California 94704.

RESOURCE USE IN HIGHER EDUCATION:
TRENDS IN OUTPUT AND INPUTS, 1930–1967
June O'Neill

TRENDS AND PROJECTIONS OF PHYSICIANS
IN THE UNITED STATES 1967–2002
Mark S. Blumberg

MAY 1970:
THE CAMPUS AFTERMATH OF CAMBODIA
AND KENT STATE
Richard E. Peterson and John A. Bilorusky

MENTAL ABILITY AND HIGHER EDUCATIONAL
ATTAINMENT IN THE 20TH CENTURY
Paul Taubman and Terence Wales

AMERICAN COLLEGE AND UNIVERSITY
ENROLLMENT TRENDS IN 1971
Richard E. Peterson
(Out of print, but available from University Microfilms.)

PAPERS ON EFFICIENCY IN THE
MANAGEMENT OF HIGHER EDUCATION
*Alexander M. Mood, Colin Bell, Lawrence
Bogard, Helen Brownlee, and Joseph McCloskey*

AN INVENTORY OF ACADEMIC INNOVATION
AND REFORM
Ann Heiss

ESTIMATING THE RETURNS TO EDUCATION:
A DISAGGREGATED APPROACH
Richard S. Eckaus

SOURCES OF FUNDS TO COLLEGES AND
UNIVERSITIES
June O'Neill

NEW DEPRESSION IN HIGHER·
EDUCATION—TWO YEARS LATER
Earl F. Cheit

PROFESSORS, UNIONS, AND AMERICAN
HIGHER EDUCATION
*Everett Carll Ladd, Jr. and
Seymour Martin Lipset*

A CLASSIFICATION OF INSTITUTIONS
OF HIGHER EDUCATION

POLITICAL IDEOLOGIES OF
GRADUATE STUDENTS:
CRYSTALLIZATION, CONSISTENCY, AND
CONTEXTUAL EFFECT
Margaret Fay and Jeff Weintraub

FLYING A LEARNING CENTER:
DESIGN AND COSTS OF AN OFF-CAMPUS
SPACE FOR LEARNING
Thomas J. Karwin

THE DEMISE OF DIVERSITY?:
A COMPARATIVE PROFILE OF EIGHT
TYPES OF INSTITUTIONS
C. Robert Pace

The following reprints are available from the Carnegie Commission on Higher Education, 2150 Shattuck Avenue, Berkeley, California 94704.

ACCELERATED PROGRAMS OF MEDICAL EDUCATION, *by Mark S. Blumberg, reprinted from* JOURNAL OF MEDICAL EDUCATION, *vol. 46, no. 8, August 1971.**

SCIENTIFIC MANPOWER FOR 1970–1985, *by Allan M. Cartter, reprinted from* SCIENCE, *vol. 172, no. 3979, pp. 132–140, April 9, 1971.*

A NEW METHOD OF MEASURING STATES' HIGHER EDUCATION BURDEN, *by Neil Timm, reprinted from* THE JOURNAL OF HIGHER EDUCATION, *vol. 42, no. 1, pp. 27–33, January 1971.**

REGENT WATCHING, *by Earl F. Cheit, reprinted from* AGB REPORTS, *vol. 13, no. 6, pp. 4–13, March 1971.*

COLLEGE GENERATIONS–FROM THE 1930S TO THE 1960S, *by Seymour M. Lipset and Everett C. Ladd, Jr., reprinted from* THE PUBLIC INTEREST, *no. 25, Summer 1971.*

AMERICAN SOCIAL SCIENTISTS AND THE GROWTH OF CAMPUS POLITICAL ACTIVISM IN THE 1960S, *by Everett C. Ladd, Jr., and Seymour M. Lipset, reprinted from* SOCIAL SCIENCES INFORMATION, *vol. 10, no. 2, April 1971.*

THE POLITICS OF AMERICAN POLITICAL SCIENTISTS, *by Everett C. Ladd, Jr., and Seymour M. Lipset, reprinted from* PS, *vol. 4, no. 2, Spring 1971.**

THE DIVIDED PROFESSORIATE, *by Seymour M. Lipset and Everett C. Ladd, Jr., reprinted from* CHANGE, *vol. 3, no. 3, pp. 54–60, May 1971.**

JEWISH ACADEMICS IN THE UNITED STATES: THEIR ACHIEVEMENTS, CULTURE AND POLITICS, *by Seymour M. Lipset and Everett C. Ladd, Jr., reprinted from* AMERICAN JEWISH YEAR BOOK, *1971.*

THE UNHOLY ALLIANCE AGAINST THE CAMPUS, *by Kenneth Keniston and Michael Lerner, reprinted from* NEW YORK TIMES MAGAZINE, *November 8, 1970.*

PRECARIOUS PROFESSORS: NEW PATTERNS OF REPRESENTATION, *by Joseph W. Garbarino, reprinted from* INDUSTRIAL RELATIONS, *vol. 10, no. 1, February 1971.**

. . . AND WHAT PROFESSORS THINK: ABOUT STUDENT PROTEST AND MANNERS, MORALS, POLITICS, AND CHAOS ON THE CAMPUS, *by Seymour Martin Lipset and Everett C. Ladd, Jr., reprinted from* PSYCHOLOGY TODAY, *November 1970.**

DEMAND AND SUPPLY IN U.S. HIGHER EDUCATION: A PROGRESS REPORT, *by Roy Radner and Leonard S. Miller, reprinted from* AMERICAN ECONOMIC REVIEW, *May 1970.**

RESOURCES FOR HIGHER EDUCATION: AN ECONOMIST'S VIEW, *by Theodore W. Schultz, reprinted from* JOURNAL OF POLITICAL ECONOMY, *vol. 76, no. 3, University of Chicago, May/June 1968.**

INDUSTRIAL RELATIONS AND UNIVERSITY RELATIONS, *by Clark Kerr, reprinted from* PRO-CEEDINGS OF THE 21ST ANNUAL WINTER MEETING OF THE INDUSTRIAL RELATIONS RESEARCH ASSOCIATION, *pp. 15–25.**

NEW CHALLENGES TO THE COLLEGE AND UNIVERSITY, *by Clark Kerr, reprinted from Kermit Gordon (ed.),* AGENDA FOR THE NATION, *The Brookings Institution, Washington, D.C., 1968.**

PRESIDENTIAL DISCONTENT, *by Clark Kerr, reprinted from David C. Nichols (ed.),* PERSPEC-TIVES ON CAMPUS TENSIONS: PAPERS PREPARED FOR THE SPECIAL COMMITTEE ON CAMPUS TENSIONS, *American Council on Education, Washington, D.C., September 1970.**

STUDENT PROTEST—AN INSTITUTIONAL AND NATIONAL PROFILE, *by Harold Hodgkinson, reprinted from* THE RECORD, *vol. 71, no. 4, May 1970.**

WHAT'S BUGGING THE STUDENTS?, *by Kenneth Keniston, reprinted from* EDUCATIONAL RECORD, *American Council on Education, Washington, D.C., Spring 1970.**

THE POLITICS OF ACADEMIA, *by Seymour Martin Lipset, reprinted from David C. Nichols (ed.),* PERSPECTIVES ON CAMPUS TENSIONS: PAPERS PREPARED FOR THE SPECIAL COMMIT-TEE ON CAMPUS TENSIONS, *American Council on Education, Washington, D.C., September 1970.**

INTERNATIONAL PROGRAMS OF U.S. COLLEGES AND UNIVERSITIES: PRIORITIES FOR THE SEVENTIES, *by James A. Perkins, reprinted by permission of the International Council for Educational Development, Occasional Paper no. 1, July 1971.*

FACULTY UNIONISM: FROM THEORY TO PRACTICE, *by Joseph W. Garbarino, reprinted from* INDUSTRIAL RELATIONS, *vol. 11, no. 1, pp. 1–17, February 1972.*

MORE FOR LESS: HIGHER EDUCATION'S NEW PRIORITY, *by Virginia B. Smith, reprinted from* UNIVERSAL HIGHER EDUCATION: COSTS AND BENEFITS, *American Council on Education, Washington, D.C., 1971.*

ACADEMIA AND POLITICS IN AMERICA, *by Seymour M. Lipset, reprinted from Thomas J. Nossiter (ed.),* IMAGINATION AND PRECISION IN THE SOCIAL SCIENCES, *pp. 211–289, Faber and Faber, London, 1972.*

POLITICS OF ACADEMIC NATURAL SCIENTISTS AND ENGINEERS, *by Everett C. Ladd, Jr., and Seymour M. Lipset, reprinted from* SCIENCE, *vol. 176, no. 4039, pp. 1091–1100, June 9, 1972.*

THE INTELLECTUAL AS CRITIC AND REBEL: WITH SPECIAL REFERENCE TO THE UNITED STATES AND THE SOVIET UNION, *by Seymour M. Lipset and Richard B. Dobson, reprinted from* DAEDALUS, *vol. 101, no. 3, pp. 137–198, Summer 1972.*

COMING OF MIDDLE AGE IN HIGHER EDUCATION, *by Earl F. Cheit, address delivered to American Association of State Colleges and Universities and National Association of State Universities and Land-Grant Colleges, Nov. 13, 1972.*

THE NATURE AND ORIGINS OF THE CARNEGIE COMMISSION ON HIGHER EDUCATION, *by Alan Pifer, reprinted by permission of The Carnegie Commission for the Advancement of Teaching, speech delivered Oct. 16, 1972.*

THE DISTRIBUTION OF ACADEMIC TENURE IN AMERICAN HIGHER EDUCATION, *by Martin Trow, reprinted from* THE TENURE DEBATE, *Bardwell Smith (ed.), Jossey-Bass, San Francisco, 1972.*

THE POLITICS OF AMERICAN SOCIOLOGISTS, *by Seymour M. Lipset and Everett C. Ladd, Jr., reprinted from* THE AMERICAN JOURNAL OF SOCIOLOGY, *vol. 78, no. 1, July 1972.*

MEASURING FACULTY UNIONISM: QUANTITY AND QUALITY, *by Bill Aussieker and J. W. Garbarino, reprinted from* INDUSTRIAL RELATIONS, *vol. 12, no. 2, May 1973.*

PROBLEMS IN THE TRANSITION FROM ELITE TO MASS HIGHER EDUCATION, *by Martin Trow, paper presented at an Organization for Economic Co-operation and Development conference on mass higher education, June 1973.*

*The Commission's stock of this reprint has been exhausted.

Education, Income,
and Human Behavior

Education, Income, and Human Behavior

edited by *F. Thomas Juster*

with chapters by

Albert E. Beaton Isaac Ehrlich
Gilbert R. Ghez John C. Hause
Arleen Leibowitz Robert T. Michael
Jacob Mincer Sherwin Rosen
Lewis C. Solmon
Paul Taubman and *Terence Wales*
and *Paul Wachtel*

A Report Prepared for
*The Carnegie Commission on Higher Education
and the National Bureau of Economic Research
A Conference
of the National Bureau of Economic Research*

MCGRAW-HILL BOOK COMPANY

*New York   St. Louis   San Francisco
Düsseldorf   Johannesburg   Kuala Lumpur   London   Mexico
Montreal   New Delhi   Panama   Paris   São Paulo
Singapore   Sydney   Tokyo   Toronto*

The Carnegie Commission on Higher Education,
2150 Shattuck Avenue, Berkeley, California 94704,
and the National Bureau of Economic Research,
261 Madison Avenue, New York, New York 10016,
have sponsored preparation of this report as
part of a continuing effort to obtain and present
significant information for public discussion.
The views expressed are those of the authors.

EDUCATION, INCOME, AND HUMAN BEHAVIOR

This book was set in Vladimir by University Graphics, Inc.
It was printed and bound by The Maple Press Company.
The designers were Elliot Epstein and Edward Butler.
The editors were Nancy Tressel and Michael Hennelly
for McGraw-Hill Book Company and Verne A. Stadtman
and Sidney J. P. Hollister for the Carnegie Commission
on Higher Education. Audre Hanneman supervised preparation
of the index. Milton J. Heiberg supervised the production.

Library of Congress Cataloging in Publication Data

Juster, Francis Thomas, date
Education, income, and human behavior.

"A report prepared for the Carnegie Commission on
Higher Education."
"A Conference of the National Bureau of Economic Research."
1. College graduates—United States.   2.   Education,
Higher—Economic aspects—United States.   I.   Beaton,
Albert E.   II.   Carnegie Commission on Higher Education.
III.   National Bureau of Economic Research.   IV.   Title.
LB2424.J87   301.44'5   73-85442
ISBN 0-07-010068-3

1 2 3 4 5 6 7 8 9 MAMM 7 9 8 7 6 5

Contents

Contributors

Albert E. Beaton
Director
Office of Data Analysis Research
Educational Testing Service
Princeton, New Jersey
and Visiting Lecturer
Princeton University

Isaac Ehrlich
Assistant Professor of
Business Economics
University of Chicago
and Research Associate
National Bureau of Economic
Reserach

Gilbert R. Ghez
Assistant Professor of Economics
University of Chicago
and Research Associate
National Bureau of Economic
Research

John C. Hause
Professor of Economics
University of Minnesota
and Research Associate
National Bureau of Economic
Research

F. Thomas Juster
Program Director
Survey Research Center
University of Michigan
and Senior Research Staff
National Bureau of Economics
Research

Arleen Leibowitz
Visiting Assistant Professor
of Economics
Brown University
and Research Associate
National Bureau of Economic
Research

Robert T. Michael
Assistant Vice-President
National Bureau of Economic
Research
and Senior Research Staff
National Bureau of Economic
Research

Jacob Mincer
Professor of Economics
Columbia University
and Senior Research Staff
National Bureau of Economic
Research

Sherwin Rosen
Professor of Economics
University of Rochester
and Senior Research Associate
National Bureau of Economic
Research

Lewis C. Solmon
Associate Professor in Residence
UCLA School of
Education
and Executive Officer
Higher Education Research
Institute

Paul Taubman
Professor of Economics
University of Pennsylvania
and Senior Research Associate
National Bureau of Economic
  Research

Paul Wachtel
Professor of Economics
New York University
and Research Associate
National Bureau of Economic
  Research

Terence Wales
Associate Professor of Economics
University of British Columbia
and Research Associate
National Bureau of Economic
  Research

Foreword

by Clark Kerr, Chairman
Carnegie Commission on Higher Education

The precise measurement of the influence of educational attainment on behavior is one of the most important and sensitive issues facing decision makers in many areas of our society. From the private citizen who must decide how much to invest in higher education, to the government official who is charged with the planning and implementation of public policy, most of us are faced at one time or another with investment decisions regarding education.

In a recent Carnegie Commission publication, *Estimating the Returns to Education: A Disaggregated Approach,* Richard Eckaus warns that higher education may not "pay off" as much as we in the United States have traditionally assumed. He urges that no decision on the degree of educational "payoff" be made until a lot more hard evidence has been collected and evaluated. In making this recommendation, Eckaus not only calls for a closer look at one of the fundamental assumptions of American society, he also underlines the need for quantitative and qualitative judgments about the nature and extent of education's influence on human behavior.

Particularly timely, therefore, is this collection of essays edited by F. Thomas Juster, which maks a significant start toward providing the kind of evaluation Eckaus recommends.

The first group of essays in this wide-ranging book focuses on the direct financial returns to individuals, emphasizing in particular the degree to which educational attainment produces higher annual and lifetime earnings by increasing the value of time spent in the labor market. But these essays also examine such related questions as: Does the contribution of ability to income vary with the level of formal schooling and other factors, or is it independent of those factors? What specific types of formal schooling or ability influence earnings and how can they be measured? What are the effects of both formal schooling and informal training and learning on life-time earnings? In seeking answers to these and other questions, Mr. Juster and his colleagues have examined from several viewpoints how the development and investment of human skills and knowledge (human capital) determine differences in the level and time-profile of labor market earnings.

If education does enhance productivity in the job market, as this first group of essays suggests, it most likely influences behavior in other areas as well. Attitudes, values, and behavior, many have suggested, are significantly altered by education, but studies of the influence of educational attainment on these "noneconomic" aspects of human behavior have been largely subjective evaluations. The six essays in the second part of this book begin to replace these evaluations with empirical findings, looking at such traditionally "noneconomic" areas as fertility and family size, political attitudes, and participation in illegal activities.

This thorough and multifaceted book provides us with a substantial body of evidence that formal schooling repays, in the monetary as well as in the nonmonetary sense, both the individual who receives the education and the society as a whole. Moreover, these "payoffs" for educational attainment are not, as some have assumed, restricted to those with favorable family background or exceptionally high ability. F. Thomas Juster and his colleagues have thrown much-needed light on the highly complex relationship between higher education and human behavior.

June 1974

Foreword

by John R. Meyer, President
National Bureau of Economic Research

This book is the second published jointly by the Carnegie Commission on Higher Education and the National Bureau of Economic Research on the returns to investments in schooling. It contains two sets of essays written by NBER staff affiliates under the direction of F. Thomas Juster.

Both sets of essays are germane to the debate over the appropriate role of schooling as a social policy instrument for improving well-being. Well-being, in this context, can, or course, be defined in many, not necessarily mutually exclusive, ways: as enhancement of an individual's private ability to earn income; as a reduction in the general inequality of income in a society; or as an improvement in the general social and cultural milieu of a society.

Previous studies, at least those that have been quantitative in character, have largely concentrated on calculating the private returns realized by individuals from their personal investments in schooling (or, more formally, the augmentation of their own human capital). These calculations have focused mainly on determining the differential earnings, salaries, or wages received by individuals with different educational histories; the assumption has been that much of these observed differentials in earnings are attributable to the extra education. Needless to say, and as long recognized by those undertaking to make these measurements, many other factors, such as innate ability, preschool training, and on-the-job training, might also create earnings differentials.

The first set of essays in this volume is essentially concerned with measuring these private returns and, more particularly, with how to differentiate the contributions to income realized through education from those realized because of such other qualities as one's IQ, upbringing, or on-the-job experience.

Man, as has often been observed, does not live by bread alone. In the particular context of educational economics this has led to the observation that when an individual makes an investment in his own education, this is an act that is likely to benefit society as well as the individual. The educated person, in short, might be a better citizen, less prone to criminal activity, and a more effective contributor in the many civil and social roles that all of us assume outside our work places and, perhaps, in many activities not normally evaluated in market terms, such as the parental role in child upbringing. The expectation that these many social or other nonmarket benefits from education may often be large apparently underlies much of the public support for education in our and other societies. Even if these social advantages of education could not be identified, the educated person's economic benefits or contribution might extend well beyond those of the labor market: for example, into more enlightened and effective consumer or savings behavior.

A major difficulty in evaluating these and related arguments concerning the social, external, or non-labor market benefits of education is establishing their quantity. The second set of essays in this volume represents at least a beginning of such quantification. That is, these essays attempt to document some of the effects of education on savings behavior, on the propensity for illegal behavior, on fertility and family size, and on social, political, and economic attitudes.

Although these latter essays deal with their subjects quantitatively and adduce evidence of systematic relationships with schooling, no attempt is made to calculate an implied nonpecuniary "rate of return" to schooling. One reason is that it is not clear in all cases which effect should be labeled beneficial to the individual or to society. For example, less than complete consensus probably exists within any society, including our own, as to what is desirable fertility behavior—that is, the proper size for a typical family. Similarly, a higher savings rate may be deemed socially desirable by some and undesirable by others—and even individual views on this question may fluctuate with the economic or cyclical circumstances. In short, in judging the efficacy of schooling as an instrument for social policy, it may prove more difficult to select or agree upon the criteria for evaluation than to measure the actual influence.

Indeed, as the reader of these essays will quickly learn, the various contributors to this volume are hardly of one mind on these matters themselves. The authors and Mr. Juster held a series of meetings during the writing and revisions of the essays, sharing criticisms and suggestions, but they hardly came to full agreement among themselves on a number of issues. Several of these essays, in fact, deal with the same or similar questions, but from differing points of view and often with differing conclusions. The result is thus more in the nature of a conference volume than an integrated staff research report of the type more conventionally published by the National Bureau of Economic Research.

Accordingly, the Board of Directors of the National Bureau approved publication of these essays as a conference volume, which reflects the views of the respective authors, and which is exempted therefore from the rules governing submission of manuscripts for critical review and approval by the directors themselves. In short, this volume is offered as one more contribution, hopefully more quantitative, to the long-standing debate on the social and economic value of education, rather than as a definitive statement of quantitative findings about these issues.

June 1974

Relation of the National Bureau Directors to Publications Reporting Conference Proceedings

Since the present volume is a record of conference proceedings, it has been exempted from the rules governing submission of manuscripts to, and critical review by, the Board of Directors of the National Bureau.

(Resolution adopted July 6, 1948, as revised November 21, 1949, and April 20, 1968)

National Bureau of Economic Research

Education, Income, and Human Behavior

1. Education, Income, and Human Behavior: Introduction and Summary

by F. Thomas Juster

Precise quantification of the influence of educational attainment on human behavior is one of the most important and sensitive questions facing decision makers, whether they be private individuals concerned with their own resource allocation or government officials concerned with issues of public policy. The collection of chapters in this volume represents an attempt to provide some quantitative and qualitative judgments about the nature and extent of education's influence on behavior.

Economists have come to look on the process of formal schooling as reflecting an investment decision of those being educated and for society as a whole. Formal schooling requires an investment of student time in addition to direct monetary outlays for tuition and living expenses, and the influence of these schooling investments persists over an entire lifetime. Not only are occupational status and lifetime earnings strongly associated with education, but time of marriage and choice of marriage partner, family size, consumption and saving allocations, sociopolitical attitudes and values, use of leisure time and work-leisure choices, etc., are also likely to be influenced by the amount of investment in education.

Part One of the volume contains eight chapters that focus on direct financial returns to individuals. The main emphasis is on the analysis of differentials in salary or earnings rates, that is, on the degree to which educational attainment produces higher annual and lifetime earnings by increasing the value of time spent in the labor market. A subsidiary but important question is the way in which educational attainment influences the allocation of time between market and nonmarket activities, that is, the effect of education on labor force participation and on the way in which nonmarket time is allocated among alternative uses.

The analysis in this part of the volume provides the most precise documentation to date of the magnitude of direct financial returns to education. The rate-of-return estimates are obtained from sets of data in which it is possible to adjust, almost for the first time and certainly with greater precision than before, for the earnings impact of many important factors that both influence earnings and tend to be directly associated with education—measured (presumably innate) ability, family background, and so forth. The chapters in this part also examine the relation between investment in formal schooling and the shape of lifetime earnings profiles, the impact of differences in educational investments on the observed inequality in the distribution of earnings, and the role of educational differences among parents in producing educational differences in their children—possibly one of the most important mechanisms involved in the intergenerational transmission of earnings and the distribution of earnings.

The general theme of the chapters in this part is that differences in human skills and knowledge (human capital) are a major determinant of differences in the level and time profile of labor market earnings and that these differences in skills and knowledge are in turn determined by differences in human capital investments that range all the way from time spent by parents with preschool or school-age children, through time and resources used in formal schooling, to time invested in labor market learning experience. These investments cumulate through time, being very heavy in the early childhood and school-age years and tapering off at different points during the working lifetime. They are, of course, subject to depreciation and obsolescence, and they are a basic determinant of the lifetime earnings profile.

Part Two focuses on the nonmonetary returns to educational attainment. If education enhances productivity in the job market, it might also be expected to influence behavior in other areas as well, either because it affects the efficiency with which individuals combine available resources to achieve given objectives or because behavioral responses themselves depend systematically on factors associated with educational attainment. The chapters in this part cover a wide range. They examine the influence of educational attainment on traditional economic variables like consumption, saving, and the selection of investment portfolios; they also investigate a number of questions that have customarily been of more concern to social scientists other than economists, e.g., fertility and family size, participation in illegal activities, and a collection of social, political, and economic attitudes. The chapters in Part Two analyze a significant part of the possible nonmonetary returns to educational attainment and thus constitute a significant beginning to an analysis of the full range of returns that can be attributed to formal schooling.

For analytical convenience, the benefits (both positive and negative in principle) of educational attainment can be divided into *monetary* and *nonmonetary* returns and, within each of these broad classes, into *private* returns (those accruing to the individual being educated) and *social* returns (those that cannot be collected by the individual and thus accrue to society as a whole). This volume focuses mainly on the private monetary and nonmonetary returns, although a number of chapters provide insights into some of the social returns as well. Not surprisingly, the most unambiguous results relate to private returns and, within those, to monetary returns.

THE IMPACT OF EDUCATION ON EARNINGS The most easily measured and most often analyzed influence of educational attainment is its impact on earnings in the job market. A number of subquestions, important for both theoretical understanding and the formulation of public policies, can be distinguished:

1 What is the net influence of formal schooling in generating income differentials, as distinct from the combined influence of schooling and other variables that tend to be correlated with formal training, such as family background and mental ability?

2 Does the contribution of ability to income vary with the level of formal schooling and other factors, or is the influence of ability on earnings essentially independent of the levels of other variables?

3 What are the roles of less-formal kinds of education, such as learning on the job and parental training, in both the generation of earnings and the relation between formal schooling and earnings?

4 What specific types of formal schooling or ability, as opposed to rather general measures of both, influence earnings, and how can they be measured?

5 What are the effects of both formal schooling and informal training and learning on the time path of lifetime earnings and on the capital value (discounted present value) of earnings?

6 What is the role of formal schooling in explaining the distribution of both individual and family earnings and income, and have changes in the dis-

tribution of educational attainment over time increased or diminished earnings inequality?

7   What is the precise nature of the productivity-enhancing skills imparted by the process of formal education, and does all the observed earnings differential from education represent a return to higher skills?

Trends in Educational Attainment and Mental Ability

The chapters in Part One provide some answers to all these questions, although evidently better answers to some than to others. As a useful starting point, we can begin by examining the historical association between mental ability or IQ and formal schooling attainment. Over the past several decades in the United States the number of youngsters attending institutions of higher education has risen sharply. In the 1920s, less than 20 percent of the eligible population went on to receive more education; in the 1960s, close to 50 percent of the eligible population went on to do so.[1] What has been the impact of this huge increase in the proportion of college-bound students on the average quality of college students or on the ability of the average college freshman? Has this unprecedented expansion seriously diluted quality? Are students who entered college during the 1960s less well equipped to benefit from additional education than the much smaller numbers who matriculated during earlier decades?

A useful framework within which to analyze the historical relation between mental ability and educational attainment is to ask what would happen to the average ability of those entering college on the alternative assumptions that (1) colleges always exercised the maximum degree of selectivity in their admissions policy or (2) college admissions policies were based on random selection. As Figure 1-1 shows, if colleges always exercised the maximum degree of selectivity, i.e., admitted students in descending order of ability, starting with the most able until all available places were filled, an expansion in the proportion of the population attending college would necessarily be associated with a systematic decline in the average ability of entering freshmen. Such a policy would also, incidentally, necessarily result in a systematic decline in the average ability level of the population *not* entering college. For example, at the extreme at which only 1 percent of the population attends col-

[1] Interestingly enough, there is not much difference between the 1920s and the 1960s in the proportion of high school *graduates* going to college; the big difference between these periods is in the proportions of the eligible population that complete high school training.

FIGURE 1-1 *Illustrative relation between average ability and proportion of high school seniors attending college*

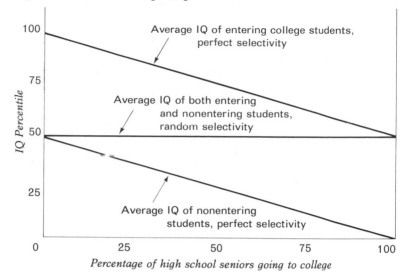

lege, only the most able students would be admitted, and average ability for entering freshmen would be in the 99th percentile, whereas average ability for the noncollege population would approximate average ability in the population as a whole. At the other extreme, at which almost everyone would be admitted to college, the average ability of entering freshmen would approximate the average for the population as a whole, and average ability for those (few) not entering college would be in the lowest (first) percentile. Thus, if colleges exercise maximum selectivity and the proportion of young people going to college increases, the average ability of entering freshmen must decline. On the other hand, if colleges admit students at random, average ability levels for both the college and noncollege populations would be equal to each other and to the population average and would be independent of the proportion going to college.

Those who feared that the great upsurge of postwar enrollments in colleges would lead to a deterioration in the average quality of students entering colleges must implicitly have had in mind a model in which college admission policies were highly selective. But Chapter 2, by Taubman and Wales, demonstrates conclusively that exactly the opposite has been true: Not only has there been no decline over time in the average ability of entering freshmen, but there has been a systematic tendency for average ability to increase. Much of the increase has resulted from an extremely rapid rise (from 50 percent to about 90 percent) in the proportion of the most able (upper tenth) high school seniors attending college and from almost as rapid an increase in the proportion of students in the upper quarter attending college. At the same time, the Taubman-Wales evidence indicates that the average ability of high school seniors not going to college has declined steadily over time. Thus, the average difference in ability between high school seniors entering and not entering college has steadily widened, from about 8 percentile points in the 1920s to approximately 27 in the 1960s.[2]

These results bear importantly on analysis of movements over time in the rates of return to different levels of educational attainment. Other things being equal, the rapid rise in the proportion of the labor force with higher educational attainment would be expected to reduce the financial returns to investment in higher education, but the strong secular increase in average ability for those receiving a college education would be expected to offset any tendency for rates of return to higher education to decline. Similarly, the declining proportion of the labor force with no more than a high school education would, other things being equal, be expected to result in higher returns to that level of educational attainment, but the declining average ability of non-college-bound high school seniors would tend to operate in the other direction. Hence, observed rates of return to college or high school training will not necessarily be inversely related to the changes in relative supply that have occurred over the last several decades, since changes in relative quality tend to work in the opposite direction.

Earnings and Educational Attainment

That additional amounts of formal schooling tend to be associated with additional earnings in the labor market is a widely documented and universally acknowledged fact. The magnitude of the earnings differential, however, and the rate of return to investment in formal

---

[2] Two facts should be kept in mind. First, in the data used here, ability is *defined* in such a way that the average cannot change over time—in effect, the measure discussed is actually relative ability. However, there is evidence, cited in the Taubman-Wales chapter, which suggests that absolute ability levels have in fact remained constant.

Second, the decline in average ability for non-college-bound students does not depend on the fact that the average for college-bound students has risen; as Figure 1-1 shows, it is perfectly possible for *both* averages to decline—and even likely that they would.

schooling are highly uncertain. Most studies show that rates of return to primary and secondary schooling are very high relative to returns on other forms of capital investment—a range of 20 to 30 percent or more is representative.[3] Estimates of returns to higher education tend to run somewhat lower, on the order of 10 to 15 percent for most studies. Yet it is rare to find estimates of returns to educational investment that account explicitly for all potentially important nonschooling influences on earnings. Hence, the estimated rates of return incorporate rough adjustments, if any, for the possible effects on earnings of variables such as ability, family background, and preschool investments by parents.

The chapters in this volume cover three subjects relating to the earnings return to formal schooling. The chapter by Mincer, "Education, Experience, and the Distribution of Earnings and Employment: An Overview," examines the role of formal schooling and of work experience in determining the observed distribution of labor market earnings at different points in the working lifetime. The chapters by Taubman and Wales, "Education as an Investment and a Screening Device"; Hause, "Ability and Schooling as Determinants of Lifetime Earnings, or If You're So Smart, Why Aren't You Rich?"; and Wachtel, "The Returns to Investments in Higher Education: Another View" represent attempts to estimate returns to formal schooling from samples of data in which explicit measures of variables like mental ability and family background are available.

The Mincer, Taubman and Wales, and Hause chapters are concerned almost entirely with the returns to investment measured in years of schooling. The Wachtel chapter involves a study of the effect of differences in the cost (and presumably quality) of formal schooling; Taubman and Wales also present some preliminary estimates of the earnings differentials associated with college quality differentials.[4]

---

[3] Estimates of rates of return to elementary school, although at the high end of this range, are subject to serious problems of both estimation and interpretation. There are no good data on forgone earnings for those who do not complete elementary schooling, although Fair Labor Standards legislation has probably increased rates of return by reducing the earnings opportunities of the very young. In addition, rates of return to elementary schooling are probably influenced by North-South differences in completion norms—traditionally six years for elementary school in the South and eight years in the North. I am indebted to Finis Welch for pointing out these considerations.

[4] Research at the National Bureau of Economic Research is under way on the question of returns to schooling quality. See the fifty-first *Annual Report* of the NBER.

The chapter by Leibowitz, "Education and the Allocation of Women's Time," examines differences, by education, in time spent in the care and training of preschool and school-age children, perhaps one of the principal ways that economic wealth (the capacity to produce income) is transmitted from one generation to the next. The final chapter in this part, "Measuring the Obsolescence of Knowledge," by Rosen, examines the question of how educational capital changes over an individual's lifetime, as it increases because of knowledge obtained in the labor market (learning) and depreciates because of obsolescence or physical wear and tear on the person in whom the educational capital is embodied.

Running through all these chapters is the common assumption that all investment in humans — taking the form of formal schooling, postschool learning and training in the labor market, or preschool learning and training at home — constitutes part of the accumulated stock of educational "capital" embodied in a person. Consequently, observed differences in the level, distribution, and lifetime profile of financial earnings realized by individuals in the market can, in considerable part, be explained by differentials among persons in their stocks of such capital. In effect, the underlying theme of these chapters is that individuals begin life with a certain amount of potential capital in the form of genetic endowment; they add to that capital throughout early childhood, school years, and the early working years; and they suffer deterioration or depreciation of that capital as their learning or training becomes outmoded or obsolescent. Further, the observed distribution of employment, wage rates, and occupation is determined largely within the framework of investment quantities and rates of return to these investments.

This is not to say that the only impact of human capital or of its formal schooling component is on observed market earnings and returns. Many would argue that the most significant impact of formal schooling is not on earnings at all, but on such diverse and diffuse variables as social and community behavior and responsiveness, efficiency in achieving welfare objectives within given financial constraints, and the development of constructive and cohesive attitudes, without which participatory government would function ineffectively or inequitably. Some of these other possible impacts of formal schooling on behavior are examined in the chapters in Part Two. In Part One, however, the focus is on direct monetary returns to formal schooling.

The conceptual framework of human capital accumulation proceeding through part of the working lifetime as well as in school is central to Jacob Mincer's chapter, "Education, Experience, and the Distribution of Earnings and Employment: An Overview." In fact, Mincer's earlier work constituted the first systematic analysis of the critical distinction between earnings as observed in the market and true earnings as reflected by the combination of observed market earnings and (unobservable) investment in learning.[5] The point is worth some additional emphasis. Modern human capital theorists recognize that the accumulation of embodied capital in humans extends far beyond the domain of formal schooling. Schooling was the earliest recognized and the most easily measured form of such investment and has therefore been given most attention by economists and other social scientists. But it is now recognized that additional capital is accumulated in the form of job market learning simultaneously with the earning of current income. Both the Mincer and the Rosen chapters, discussed later on, emphasize this aspect of the relation between human capital and lifetime earnings. In addition, as will be pointed out in connection with the Leibowitz chapter, it is beginning to be as widely recognized that preschool investments in children by parents, as well as continuing parental investments during schooling years, may represent a significant addition to the stock of human capital, although serious empirical investigation of that subject is just beginning.

Mincer's chapter is concerned mainly with the impact of educational and other human capital differences on the distribution of individual and family earnings, in regard both to the cross-sectional structure of earnings differentials and to changes in the structure over time. Basing his analysis on a human capital earnings function that is simple yet powerful in its ability to explain observed differences in earnings, Mincer finds that over 60 percent of the inequality in 1959 annual full-time earnings of white urban males can be attributed to differences in the distribution of investments in human capital. The distribution of formal schooling itself explains only about one-fourth of the total variance in income, while the distribution of postschooling investment explains perhaps another quarter. Differences in schooling costs for given numbers of years account for perhaps another 10 percent of observed inequality.

Since part of the variance in annual earnings is due to differences

---

[5] See his "On the Job Training," *Journal of Political Economy,* October 1962. (Supplement.)

in hours and weeks worked per year, and since some of this difference is systematically related to human capital differences, perhaps another 10 percentage points of income variance can be accounted for by systematic human capital differences in hours and weeks. Thus over 70 percent of normal or long-run income inequality can be attributed to differences in human capital stocks.

Mincer's chapter provides strong evidence for several propositions that are often a source of dispute among social scientists. The first is the significance of learning on the job as a source of both human capital investment and consequent future earnings; the second is whether the deceleration in earnings growth late in the working life represents a biological aging phenomenon or a conscious decision to reduce investments in additional learning, and hence future income, because the payoff period has shortened.

On the first point, if schooling investments were the only form of human capital investments, the correlation between years of schooling and earnings would be strongest in the early years of employment and would continuously decay over time. The observed pattern is that such correlations increase for about the first decade of working life and then tend to decline. The explanation suggested by Mincer is that the initial postschooling distribution of observed earnings reflects not true earnings, but the combination of observed market earnings plus earnings forgone by investing in learning opportunities. Since such investments will tend to increase observed market earnings through time, the distribution of observed earnings after a number of years of experience will better resemble the distribution of true (full) earnings immediately after the completion of schooling. Thus the schooling–observed earnings correlation should rise with experience, reaching a maximum before the first decade of earnings experience is completed, and then decline; this pattern is revealed in the empirical data.

On the second point, the question is whether chronological age or labor market experience provides a better explanation for observed earnings profiles. The answer yielded by the data is clear-cut: labor market experience is clearly the more powerful variable, and age has no influence on earnings once labor force experience has been accounted for.[6]

---

[6] The same point is forcefully documented in a recent study by B. Malkiel and J. Malkiel, "Male-Female Pay Differentials in Professional Employment" (1973). This study focuses mainly on sex differentials in earnings, and the difference between age and experience variables is especially strong for women.

The findings on the relation between schooling and the distribution of employment provide some valuable insights into a number of related questions. First, the pattern of labor force participation systematically differs by educational level. Males with more education evidently begin work later in life, but they also remain longer in the labor force; thus, the resulting differences by education in working lifetime are minimal. In effect, time spent in school before the start of the working life is roughly offset by additional time spent in the labor force at the close of the working life. For females, labor force participation rates are systematically higher as levels of formal schooling rise, with the interesting exception that participation rates are about the same for women with preschool or school-age children. Thus women with more education are more likely to be found in the labor force unless they have young children at home, in which case labor force participation is actually a little less likely —a finding discussed more fully in the Leibowitz chapter.

The explanation for these phenomena, in the case of women, probably lies more on the side of differences in labor supply functions than on the side of differences in labor demand functions. Differences in amounts of formal schooling imply differences in market productivity, but not necessarily the same kind of difference in productivity in the home or outside the market. Thus persons with more formal schooling and hence higher market wage rates will tend to substitute time spent in the market for time spent elsewhere, whether it be do-it-yourself chores about the house, cooking and cleaning, or housekeeping generally. In effect, observed differentials among educational groups in the amount of time spent in the labor force may result from the fact that those with more schooling, and hence higher market productivity, tend to substitute market for nonmarket time. Although one would expect that higher hourly and annual earnings would also result in a tendency to substitute leisure for working time, the net result of both effects together might well be that the more highly educated spend more time in the labor force. And, as mentioned earlier, the labor supply effects apply much more directly to women. The differential productivity argument is even more clearly applicable to women, among whom differences in labor force participation related to educational differences are much sharper.

The contribution of the Taubman-Wales and Hause chapters lies in their attempts to filter out from the observed (gross) returns to educational differences a measure of the influence on earnings of both mental ability and family background, thus arriving at a more truly "value-added" estimate of returns to formal schooling. The Taubman-Wales chapter analyzes this problem with the aid of two essentially new bodies of evidence. One comprises the unpublished detailed tabulations from a study of males who graduated from high school in 1938 and were surveyed in 1953 to determine earnings and education beyond high school.[7] Measures of both IQ and high school rank in class are available as proxies for ability. The sample contains unknown but possibly serious deficiencies, especially in terms of response bias. Nevertheless, the evidence from this sample suggests that only a slight bias exists in estimating returns to educational attainment when the ability variable is omitted from the analysis. However, ability is an important determinant of earnings in its own right.

Results using the other new sample are somewhat different. This sample, designated NBER-TH, was originally drawn in 1955 by Professors Thorndike and Hagen (Columbia Teachers College) from some 75,000 males who had taken a battery of United States Air Crew Aptitude Tests during the second half of 1943. The Thorndike-Hagen sample of some 10,000 was resurveyed by the NBER in 1969: data were obtained on earnings and occupational history, education, family background, nonmarket activities, and a variety of sociopolitical attitudes.[8]

In the NBER-TH sample, it turns out that the bias due to omission of ability ranges from 12 to 30 percent of the estimated gross returns, depending on the earnings period and on the interpretation of variables that could represent either parental or ability influences. The bias in estimated returns appears to be especially serious for those in the highest-ability classes—roughly the upper tenth of the ability distribution. Taubman and Wales also find that the relatively stronger influence of schooling on earnings for those in the upper end of the ability distribution is found only if some graduate training has been obtained.

The chapter by Hause provides a different view of the nonlinear or nonproportional influence of education on earnings. Hause is concerned primarily with the question of proper statistical specification of the relation between measured ability or IQ, formal school-

[7] The sample, originally obtained by Dael Wolfle and Joseph Smith, is described in "The Occupational Value of Education for Superior High School Graduates," *Journal of Higher Education,* vol. 27, pp. 201–213, 1956.

[8] The NBER-TH sample is described more fully in App. A.

ing attainment, and earnings. One common specification assumes that the dollar amount of earnings can be expressed as the sum of the effects of schooling attainment in years and IQ. But that specification implies that the effect of schooling on earnings is indepenent of IQ and, similarly, that the effect of IQ on earnings is independent of schooling; hence the return to additional schooling is no greater for those with high ability than for those with average or low ability. But the costs of additional schooling are likely to be higher for those with greater ability, since their forgone earnings are likely to be greater. Hence the arithmetic and linear specification implies that investment in schooling should be more profitable for those with low rather than high ability, a result contrary to observed investment patterns.

More appropriate specifications involve using either the relation between schooling, IQ, and the log of earnings — which implies a proportional effect of ability on dollar earnings (i.e., that *rates* of return are independent of ability) — or a specification that allows the effects of ability to depend on the level of formal schooling, but does not constrain the nature of the dependence. Using these alternatives, Hause reexamines the data originally obtained by D. C. Rogers from a Connecticut sample of high school graduates and also investigates data from Project Talent, the NBER-TH sample described above, and a set of Swedish data (Husén sample). He finds that the coefficient of ability in earnings functions, estimated for each schooling subgroup, tends to be a function of the level of formal schooling; that is, the returns to ability are relatively low for those with only a high school education and tend to rise as one examines subgroups with increasing amounts of formal schooling. These findings are consistent with a model in which ability and schooling interact to produce significantly higher incomes than would have been predicted by a linear combination of the two. The finding is significant, since it provides empirical support for what has been suspected by many for some time: that the rate of return to educational attainment is influenced by the level of basic ability and that the returns to those with one or more college degrees increase with the level of basic ability.

Evidence on the rate of return to investment in higher education is also found in the Taubman-Wales chapter. Such estimates use the observed-earnings differential between those with different amounts of schooling as the "return" and the costs of the extra schooling as the "investment": costs include both direct costs such as tuition and indirect costs such as forgone earnings. Correcting for the influence of ability and family background on earnings, the Taubman-Wales calculations indicate that social rates of return range, in real terms, from 11 percent for those with some college (but no degree) to around 2 percent for those with a Ph.D. degree. Rates of return for those with an undergraduate degree are about 8 percent, on the average. Private rates of return, which differ from social returns both because the direct investment (schooling) costs are usually subsidized and because the taxes paid on actual earnings tend to be proportionally higher than those on forgone earnings, tend to be somewhat larger. These range from 15 percent for those with some college (but no degree) to about 4 percent for those with a Ph.D.;[9] they are about 11 percent for those with an undergraduate degree.[10] These estimates of rates of return are a bit lower than previous ones, presumably because the data permit a more accurate correction for the impact of nonschooling variables, such as ability and family background, on earnings. Except at the graduate level, Taubman and Wales do not find that rates of return vary with ability, although the amount of schooling clearly does—being higher for those with greater ability.[11]

On the basis of evidence that is subject to considerable controversy, Taubman and Wales argue that these estimates represent probable upper limits to the augmentation of skills by higher education and reflect in part the fact that employers use educational at-

[9] These rates of return are of course direct monetary returns only. Thus the existence of significant nonmonetary returns, as is often alleged to be the case for Ph.D. holders, would imply relatively low observed monetary returns.

[10] There may be some downward bias in these rate-of-return estimates, stemming from the heavily entrepreneurial nature of the NBER-TH Air Force sample. Both high school graduates and college dropouts in the sample include a heavy proportion of independent business proprietors whose reported earnings presumably include a return to financial assets. Taubman and Wales find that the returns to college graduates are affected appreciably by the fact that the estimated forgone earnings include returns to financial assets, but they also find that the returns to "some college" are about the same as for college graduates after the appropriate adjustment.

[11] A priori, it is not at all obvious that rates of return to schooling will necessarily depend on ability. As Becker pointed out in his seminal essay on income distribution, demand *functions* for education may well depend on ability level, but whether price (rate of return) varies with ability depends on the supply functions (for investment funds) as well. To take one simple case, if everyone had access to funds for educational investments in unlimited amounts at a constant price, rates of return would be constant at the margin, and the quantity of education would vary with ability.

tainment as a relatively inexpensive screening device; that is, employers require a college degree for certain kinds of jobs on the grounds that this approach is more likely to be successful in identifying potentially productive employees or that it involves lower costs (at least for the employer, if not for society) than the use of alternative testing devices. In this interpretation, only part of the observed earnings differential reflects a return to the skills imparted by education; the remainder represents an "agency fee," which the employee gets because it is cheaper for employers to screen via a diploma than by independent measures of potential performance.[12]

This interpretation rests on evidence concerning the returns to educational differences *within* given occupational categories, since earnings differences due to education-related productivity differentials are most easily observed this way. Its controversial nature is due in part to the fact that very little of the within-occupation variance in earnings can be explained at all in the Taubman-Wales data, and hence a very large part of the total variation is due to causes which could not be identified and which might or might not be systematically associated with particular characteristics of the individuals involved. To the extent that the unidentified sources of variation in earnings within occupations are systematic rather than random, the observed effects of education on earnings could well be poor estimates of the true effects. On the other hand, the relatively modest ability of these equations to explain variance is equally characteristic of general earnings functions based on the sample used by Taubman and Wales; hence the empirical results are not necessarily unpersuasive.

The chapter by Paul Wachtel, "The Returns to Investments in Higher Education: Another View," represents one of the first attempts to relate future earnings returns to the quality as well as the quantity of schooling investments. For the most part, researchers have been limited to information on relatively simple measures of educational investment such as number of years completed, and have used these data to analyze the relation between schooling investments and future earnings. But there are marked differences among schools in the amounts of resources used, and there are correspondingly wide differences in the private costs (tuition, fees,

---

[12] By its very nature, the screening question is difficult to analyze empirically because productivity differentials are usually not observed directly, but are inferred from income differentials.

etc.) actually paid by those attending schools. The variation in resources used and private costs among schools is probably greater
for schools of higher education than for other institutions, since for
the most part schooling through the secondary level involves compulsion, public support for all costs, a commitment to minimum
standards, and a comparatively homogeneous curriculum — all of
which tend to reduce variability in resources. For higher education,
both private costs and resource costs can and do vary much more
widely. For example, private costs are often zero (full scholarship
aid), whereas the variation in resource costs between a school with
low faculty salaries and large classes and one with high faculty
salaries and small classes can be enormous.[13]

Wachtel's chapter examines the relation between cost differences
among institutions of higher education and the associated earnings
streams of graduates. Using a model that represents an elaboration
of the basic human capital earnings function discussed in the
Mincer chapter, he divides schooling investments into an indirect
(forgone earnings) and a direct (tuition expenditures) component.
Rates of return are estimated for each of these investment components and for investments adjusted for various assumptions
about part-time earnings that would tend to reduce forgone earnings. Adjustments are also made for tuition and living-cost subsidies allowed under post-World War II educational programs.

The results indicate that the rate of return on the total social
costs of educational investments for these World War II veterans
is relatively low compared with estimates from other studies:
Returns to undergraduate schooling are about 5 percent, and
allowance for part-time work increases the rate of return to just
under 7 percent. But if allowance is made for the tuition and living-
cost subsidies that would have been received by members of this
sample, private rates of return tend to be about the same as elsewhere — 10 percent or more. Returns to graduate training are markedly lower than those to undergraduate training, a result consistent
with other findings.

There is, however, a considerable difference between the returns

[13] Variation in the resource costs of schooling is primarily a function of variation
in faculty salaries and student-teacher ratios and of the correlation between
them. For elementary and secondary schools, the homogeneity of curricula
and the strength of teacher organization tend to reduce variation both in teacher-
pupil ratios and in salaries. Jencks reports that 30 of the 50 states spent between $600 and $880 per pupil in 1969–70 on the average, with the extremes
ranging from $1,237 to $438 (Jencks et al., 1972, p. 24).

to different investment components. Wachtel finds that the returns to the forgone earnings component of investment are very small once the direct investment component reflected by tuition fees or expenditures is accounted for: instead of 5 percent, rates of return are as low as 1 or 2 percent. However, there is a substantial return to direct investments, suggesting that higher-cost (and higher-quality?) institutions considerably enhance the incomes of their graduates. Rates of return on direct investments tend to run from 10 to 15 percent. A possible implication, which cannot really be tested with the data at hand, is that part-time attendance at institutions of higher education would yield substantially higher economic benefits than full-time attendance, since the forgone earnings investment, which yields a very small economic return in these data, would be greatly reduced. In effect, taking these results literally suggests that people could increase the overall rate of return to their educational investments by attending higher-cost (and presumably higher-quality) institutions on a part-time basis, thus increasing direct investment costs and reducing indirect ones.[14] However, there are no observations on differences in the returns for students with different combinations of direct and indirect investments, since the data do not enable us to distinguish part- or full-time college attendance.

The question of differential returns to those with different ability levels or socioeconomic backgrounds is also explored in Wachtel's chapter. He finds that the rate of return is positively associated with ability or IQ, and also with favorable socioeconomic background. Breaking the investment costs into indirect and direct components indicates that at least part of this differential is attributable to the fact that those with more ability or favorable socioeconomic backgrounds tend to get higher overall returns because they invest in higher-cost education and hence their indirect and direct investment costs are distributed differently.[15] That is, the overall rate of return to high ability or favorable socioeconomic

---

[14] An alternative interpretation is that the low return on forgone earnings reflects the high direct consumption benefit of full-time attendance at colleges and universities, which would (or might) be lost for part-time attendees.

[15] The conclusions here differ from those reported by Jencks (1972, p. 24), since these results imply that greater resource use produces a return in the form of higher eventual earnings for education beyond 12 years. Jencks argues, on the basis of indirect evidence, that there is no such effect for elementary and secondary schools. The results reported here, as well as in Jencks, standardize for other inputs besides schools.

background reflects the fact that the investments of these groups tend to be larger per year spent in school and that direct investments of this sort yield relatively high returns. Thus the interaction between ability and schooling observed in the chapter by Hause, for example, may in part reflect the inadequacy of schooling years as a measure of schooling investment.

On balance, what the Taubman-Wales, Hause, and Wachtel chapters suggest as reasonable estimates of the financial returns to investment in higher education are numbers significantly smaller than roughly comparable estimates of returns to physical capital investments. This is more clearly the case for estimates of social returns; the estimated private returns, when adjustments are made for the subsidization of investment costs, are only slightly less than returns to physical capital. On the other hand, none of these calculations includes either private nonmonetary returns to investment in schooling (some of which are examined below) or social monetary or nonmonetary returns. Although quantitative evidence is lacking, the analysis in Part Two suggests that these represent a significant addition to private financial returns.

In addition, of course, none of these estimates takes any account of the fact that the benefits of schooling include some direct consumption flows to those being educated, in addition to whatever investment returns will be obtained only in future years. What we tend to categorize as an "investment" in schooling really ought to be partitioned into a part that represents costs incurred for direct consumption benefits and a part that would be incurred only if the future returns were sufficiently high. Finally, although the private financial rates of return discussed above are significantly lower than the observed returns to investment in other forms of capital assets, they are not lower than the typical borrowing costs associated with such investments except (in the case of teachers, for example) where there is reason to suspect the existence of sizable private nonmonetary returns.

It is well to keep in mind that the rate-of-return estimates described above are still subject to potentially large uncertainties relating to the possible impact on earnings functions of factors excluded from the analysis. The earliest rate-of-return estimates were crude largely because they could not explicitly account for the impact of variables such as ability and family background, which are positively correlated with education and which add to earnings.

The estimates above remedy these particular deficiencies to a considerable extent and are thus much more net or "pure" estimates of the monetary return to educational investment. But we are still some distance from having the kind of income-generating function needed to identify the true net influence of educational attainment, since some of the important variables in a complete income function have yet to be taken into account.[16]

To illustrate, economists and other social scientists have recently begun to pay close attention to the possible role of preschool investments in children by parents, as it affects subsequent educational attainment. This question is examined in one of the chapters in this volume. Parental influences of this sort may also have effects on market productivity and earnings over and above any impact on school performance, and if so, returns to education can be affected. Although the results reported in this volume standardize for something called "family background," they do not account for the possible influence on earnings of different amounts of parental time spent with preschool or school-age children.

To show the potential importance of these kinds of factors, it is worth pointing out that cultural background as reflected by religious preference has a very powerful influence on observed earnings in both the Taubman-Wales and the Hause chapters. In the data sets used for both chapters, respondents were asked to report their religious preference as among Protestant, Catholic, Jewish, and other (including none). Taking account of family background factors like father's and mother's education and occupation, variables for both Jewish and Catholic religious preference have a significant (positive) impact on observed earnings (NBER-TH sample) relative to respondents reporting a Protestant preference. The Jewish religious preference variable also shows a significant impact on earnings in the Rogers sample.

Although the precise factors reflected in these religious preference variables are unknown, plausible hypotheses are that they reflect differences in the cultural background to which respondents were exposed during their formative years, or differences in the quantity or quality of parental time inputs, rather than differences

[16] In particular, we have not developed and tested models that permit returns to decline as average educational levels rise. The estimates discussed above relate to returns reflected by current incomes and hence past education; they do not necessarily predict future returns.

in specifically religious values or practices. The appropriate research stance seems clear. The existence of strong statistical differences in behavior patterns associated with religious preference variables—or, as in other studies, with variables reflecting race or sex—points toward the existence of forces whose influence needs to be better understood and more fully interpreted, rather than toward an inference of causal relationships from observed statistical associations.

Another interesting piece of evidence bearing on the same question, from the NBER-TH sample, is the strong influence on earnings of the education of the respondent's father-in-law. The basic data set contains information on the educational level of the respondent's wife as well as that of both his father and father-in-law. In regressions of earnings on sets of socioeconomic background variables, it was consistently true that the impact on the respondent's earnings of his father-in-law's educational level was much stronger than that of his father's educational level. The causal nexus involved in this relationship is not necessarily from education to earnings; for example, relatively successful men may tend to marry women from relatively high socioeconomic backgrounds, and such women would tend to have relatively highly educated parents. It is, of course, possible to hypothesize a chain of causation that runs in the opposite direction. The main point is that we have just begun to understand and investigate the full complexity of the income-generating function, and although the chapters in this volume make significant strides beyond results reported elsewhere, they are still some distance from providing a full understanding of the role of educational differences in the generation of income differences.

Education and Labor Force Participation

Arleen Leibowitz's chapter, "Education and the Allocation of Women's Time," is concerned primarily with the effect of women's (time) investment in children on the supply of their labor to the market. Leibowitz examines the relation between the labor supply of married women and their educational attainment, as well as the relation between education and specific types of nonmarket activities like housework and child care. A model of labor force supply is developed in which hours worked by married women are a function of husband's earnings, potential earnings rate as reflected by educational attainment, differential labor market productivity of husbands and wives as reflected by the difference in educational attainment, and the number and age distribution of children. The model specified that married women will enter the labor force when their productivity in the market exceeds their productivity at home, with the former estimated from educational level and the latter dependent on the number and age distribution of children. The basic argument is that the rearing and training of children is a relatively highly productive activity for married women and that their productivity in this activity is enhanced by formal schooling.

The results for labor supply are relatively clear-cut and largely consistent with the model's prediction. For younger women without children, weeks worked are greater as the level of education increases. The explanation advanced is that market productivity is higher, relative to home productivity, for more highly educated women: market productivity is strongly and positively associated with education, whereas home productivity is either unrelated or less strongly related to education. For women whose children are grown, labor force participation rates are also higher for those with more education, again for the same reason. But for women with young children of preschool or school age, the amount of labor supplied to the market is essentially independent of educational level, being roughly the same for all groups. Leibowitz also finds that, adjusting for the influence of the husband's wage rate, age, and other relevant variables, weeks worked by women with young children decline more sharply as the level of formal schooling increases, although declines set in for women of all educational backgrounds. Relating labor supply to the difference between productivity in the market and productivity in the home, these results suggest that the presence of young children in the home sharply increases productivity in the home relative to the market and that this effect is especially strong for women with higher levels of educational attainment.

Leibowitz next turns to an examination of data more directly related to productivity in the home. She examines three sets of time-use data[17] for married men and women that distinguish two types of activities in the home: those related to cleaning, cooking, and home maintenance generally and those directly related to child care.

The data indicate that there are systematic differences in the

---

[17] The data sets are the Cornell time-use study, the Purdue sample, and the sample of Parisian households.

distributions of time use for women with different educational backgrounds. There appears to be little aggregate difference in total amount of hours devoted to home production in all the above categories, but the distribution of time between home maintenance activities and child care varies sharply by educational level. Women with more education spend less time in activities related to home maintenance and considerably more time in activities related to child care. The same also appears to be true of the husbands of women in the sample; time spent with children is substantially higher for husbands with more highly educated wives.

The explanation suggested by Leibowitz is that with more education, women generally attempt to substitute both market goods and capital assets in performing home maintenance. That is, such women make greater use of capital equipment (washing machines, vacuum cleaners, etc.) and devote less of their own time to home maintenance. But in the care and training of children, women with more education apparently tend to regard the substitution of the time of others, or the use of purchased services, as less desirable than more intensive use of their own time, suggesting that they place a relatively higher value on the use of their time in child-raising activities.

The results reported in the Leibowitz chapter bear directly on the question of intergenerational transfers of wealth and also on the interpretation of the common finding that the private monetary returns to higher education are lower for women than for men. A decade ago intergenerational wealth transfers tended to be analyzed in terms of transfer of monetary or financial capital. It is now increasingly recognized that a major part of intergenerational wealth transfers are apt to consist of the accumulation of human capital in its broadest sense. What the Leibowitz chapter suggests is that an important role of the educational system is to increase the amount of educational capital not only among those being educated but in their offspring as well and that the second effect is especially important for the educational capital invested in women. Thus examination of differentials in market earnings for women may give a distorted picture of the true returns to educational investment, since a significant part of the total return accruing to female schooling may be in the subsequent buildup of skills, knowledge, etc., that they transmit to their own children. Although we still have a long way to go in understanding the nature and extent of this intergenerational transfer of human capital, the Leibowitz chapter represents a promising start.[18]

Earnings Profiles and Obsolescence

The last chapter in Part One is concerned more with the effects of postschool investment on earnings than with the effect of formal schooling. Rosen analyzes the relation between embodied knowledge at the completion of formal schooling, growth in knowledge through learning by experience in the labor market, depreciation-obsolescence rates on accumulated knowledge, and the lifetime profile of earnings. In Rosen's model, individuals implicitly purchase various combinations of current income and learning options in the labor market depending on their choice of occupation, and their decisions are made with the object of maximizing discounted lifetime earnings. Learning options are purchased by accepting jobs offering lower current income in return for the opportunity to invest in capital accumulation. The cost of learning varies with individual skills or abilities, and perhaps with the level of embodied knowledge reflected by formal schooling, as well as with the type of job chosen; the return depends on the length of working lifetime over which additional learning can yield income and on the rate of depreciation-obsolescence.

Thus individuals make sequential choices over a working lifetime. In the early years they tend to accept jobs carrying relatively large learning options and to switch to jobs with smaller or no learning options in their mature working years. These choices imply a path of net investment in knowledge following the completion of formal schooling: Net investment is positive during the early working years, reaches zero at some point, and eventually becomes negative toward retirement as capital stocks are allowed to run down.

It is not possible in the empirical work to distinguish between differences in learning efficiency among individuals and differences in depreciation-obsolescence rate; only the combined effect of both can be estimated from the available data on observed earnings. The evidence suggests that relative to depreciation-obsolescence rates, college graduates are as efficient and probably more efficient learners than high school graduates. Therefore, part of the observed

---

[18] Additional research in this area, now in process at the National Bureau of Economic Research, is described in the Bureau's fifty-first *Annual Report.*

differential in lifetime earnings between college and high school graduates may be due to the greater efficiency with which college graduates are able to accumulate knowledge, thus leading them to invest more in postschool training. This effect should be distinguished analytically from the simple fact that college graduates have higher lifetime earnings because of their larger investment in formal schooling; the learning efficiency gain can be thought of as adding to any differential due to greater knowledge or greater all-around ability.

In addition, the evidence can be used to indicate a lower limit for depreciation-obsolescence rates; this limit appears to be more severe (15 percent) for high school graduates than for college graduates (10 percent). Finally, Rosen finds no evidence of "vintage" effects of schooling on high school graduates[19]; that is, there is no evidence that high school graduates of several decades ago acquired less knowledge in high school than current high school graduates do. Considered in conjunction with the evidence in the Taubman-Wales chapter on changes over time in the average ability of high school seniors not going to college, Rosen's evidence on lack of vintage effects can be read as implying that "value added" in high schools has actually increased significantly over time. The Taubman-Wales data clearly indicate that the average ability of non-college-bound high school seniors has declined markedly over the last several decades. Hence if these same high school graduates end up being just as efficient learners as high school graduates in the past, it must be because the effectiveness of schools has increased sufficiently to offset the decline in student ability. Rosen's methodology can be tested adequately only with larger samples than have been available up to now, and his empirical conclusions must be viewed as tentative. More definitive tests will be permitted by analysis of the 1970 census samples that are now being made available to researchers.

THE IMPACT OF EDUCATION ON BEHAVIOR
The second set of chapters in this volume examines the impact of differences in educational attainment on a wide range of both economic and noneconomic behavioral variables. The distinction between the two is not sharply drawn; "economic" behavior refers simply to aspects of behavior that economists have conventionally been concerned with.

[19] Other investigators do find so-called vintage effects. For example, see Finis Welch (1972).

The first three chapters in Part Two examine the relation between education and consumption or saving behavior. In "Education and Consumption," Robert Michael examines the impact of formal schooling on the efficiency of consumption decisions. Next, Lewis Solmon, in "The Relation between Schooling and Savings Behavior: An Example of the Indirect Effects of Education," explores the effects of education both on aggregate savings behavior and on portfolio decisions involving the optimum form in which to hold savings. In "Education, the Price of Time, and Life-Cycle Consumption," Gilbert Ghez explores the life-cycle profiles of income and consumption and the association between these profiles and the level of educational attainment. The fourth chapter, "On the Relation between Education and Crime," by Isaac Ehrlich, explores the association between educational attainment and the propensity to participate in illegal or criminal activity. Next, Robert Michael, in "Education and Fertility," examines the impact of education on family size. Attention is given to the number of children, their distribution over the childbearing years, and their "quality" as reflected by the expenditure of both money and parental time. The final study, "The Influence of Education and Ability on Salary and Attitudes," by Albert Beaton, examines the relation between years of schooling and an extensive array of basically qualitative variables including parental education and occupation, perceived attitudes about the effectiveness of various aspects of formal schooling, voting behavior, general sociopolitical attitudes, and aptitude test scores.

As a group, the chapters in Part Two cover an important set of areas in which one might expect to find evidence of different behavior resulting from differentials in schooling levels and in which the benefits yielded by education are not measured directly in monetary terms. Much has been said and written about the effects of education in "improving" attitudes, values, and behavior. Little hard empirical analysis, however, has accompanied these judgments, which by and large can fairly be characterized as impressionistic. Although the studies reported in Part Two of this volume do not cover anything like the full range of potential nonmonetary benefits, and also do not have much to report on the benefits that accrue to society rather than to the individual being educated, they do constitute an important start in replacing casual impressions of the nonmonetary benefits of education with solidly grounded empirical findings.

Consumption and Saving

The first chapter in Part Two, "Education and Consumption," by Robert Michael, focuses on how education affects the efficiency with which households are able to obtain a flow of utility from a given flow of money income earned in the market. The basic model used by Michael is a household "production function," in which final outputs (utilities) are produced within the household by combining inputs of goods or services purchased in the market, the time of family members, and the stock of capital owned by the household. Thus the output "dinner" of specified nutritional content and palatability is produced by combining inputs of raw or semifinished materials (food as purchased in the market); the housewife's time in terms of preparation, cooking, etc.; and services of the capital assets represented by kitchen appliances, tables, chairs, etc.

Michael sets forth the hypothesis that education affects the efficiency with which households combine various inputs in order to produce the optimum set of outputs. In this model, education is viewed as affecting productivity largely by way of enhancing the ability to process information, to evaluate new ideas and techniques, to make decisions in the face of imperfect information, to acquire new information in a relatively less costly manner, etc. If this is the way that education operates on the household decision-making process, one would anticipate that, other things being equal, households with more education should be able to get more outputs out of a given quantity of inputs.[20]

The empirical work is based on the view that education should act much like an increase in money income insofar as household decisions are concerned; that is, if education increases household efficiency in the manner described above, households whose members are more highly educated have the equivalent of greater money income and should therefore act in the same way as households that actually possess greater money income. Thus for commodity classes that are relatively responsive to differences in money income, more education ought to be associated with more consumption, money income held constant; but for commodity classes that are relatively unresponsive to differences in money income, the net association between education and consumption ought to be negative. For example, we observe that households with higher incomes are apt to expand purchases of the category "food eaten

---

[20] The hypothesis that a major influence of education is to enhance information processing skills has been argued forcefully by Finis Welch (1970).

away from home" by an amount that is more than proportional to the difference in income. In technical terms, the income elasticity of demand in this category is greater than 1. If higher levels of educational attainment are equivalent to an increase in money income, they ought also to be positively associated with purchases of food eaten away from home, money income held constant.

The empirical results are generally consistent with the efficiency model: In analyzing very broad product categories like "goods" and "services," goods have an income elasticity less than 1, whereas services have an income elasticity greater than 1; the education elasticities are, respectively, negative and positive. Analyzing more refined commodity groups shows a positive association between income elasticity and education elasticity, and the predicted sign of the education elasticities is found in commodity categories representing anywhere from 60 to about 90 percent of total expenditures, depending on the categories included. These quantitative estimates of the impact of educational differences on the enhancement of real income are very rough, ranging from an elasticity of less than one-tenth (e.g., a 1 percent increase in the number of years of schooling raises the household's real income by about one-tenth of 1 percent) to an elasticity estimate of about one-half. The magnitude of the effect cannot be estimated more precisely, given the limitations of the data used for the analysis, although additional refinement is both possible and desirable.

On balance, Michael's chapter suggests an important avenue through which education produces a positive return — in this case, a return totally appropriated by the person being educated. The evidence also suggests that the size of the consumption efficiency return is far from negligible and may represent one of the most important sources of economic gain from investment in formal schooling.

The chapter by Lewis Solmon analyzes the impact of educational differences on propensities to save as well as on the allocation of savings among alternative investment vehicles. In "The Relation between Schooling and Savings Behavior: An Example of the Indirect Effects of Education," Solmon documents the proposition that aggregate saving behavior (especially if one considers the unobservable variable saving plus investment in learning opportunities) is systematically influenced by differences in the educational attainment of the household head; efficiency in portfolio decision making is similarly influenced.

Several possible lines of argument suggest that differences in educational attainment might result in differences in saving behavior. For the most part, the causality tends to run by way of the impact of education on either the level, time path, or variance of income and thence to saving, rather than directly from education to saving. For example, those with higher levels of formal schooling are more apt to be independent proprietors or professionals and are likely to have higher saving propensities because the variance of business and professional earnings tends to be greater than the variance of wage or salary earnings. Other factors that might influence decisions to save are (1) the declining rate of return to investment in formal schooling, which suggests that those with more education are apt to have lower discount rates; (2) the negative association between education and family size, which, as described in a later chapter by Michael, can be attributed to an efficiency phenomenon; (3) the later date of entry into the labor force for those with more education, which should result in a greater tendency to save during the (somewhat shorter) working lifetime;[21] (4) the probable greater efficiency in portfolio management of the more educated, which increases the returns to savings; and (5) the possible effect of educational level on time preference or foresight. The last two factors represent the only influences that run directly from education to saving rather than through the effect of educational differences on income.

In addition, a conceptually more appropriate definition of income and saving suggests that higher educational levels are very likely to be associated with higher "full" saving relative to "full" income. As the Mincer and Rosen chapters in Part One point out, the evidence suggests that there is substantial investment in on-the-job training during the early working years and that such investment is likely to be positively correlated (in dollar amounts) with investment in formal schooling. Hence, observed earnings in the early working years underestimate true earnings by the imputed cost of investment in learning and training on the job (i.e., the difference between observed earnings and what the individual could earn on a job with no learning opportunity). This entire differential can be considered to be invested or saved.

Solmon presents a variety of empirical results using a selected

[21] It was mentioned earlier that working lifetimes are in fact very little different for those in different educational categories, since retirement ages tend to be positively related to educational attainment.

sample of households derived from the membership of Consumers Union of the United States. Estimates are presented including and excluding income and saving in the form of on-the-job training, and separate estimates are given for different educational groups as well as for the entire sample, with interaction terms between educational level and income. On the whole, the results offer strong support for the simple descriptive proposition that those with more formal education tend to save more out of a given income than those with less formal education. This is clearest from regressions estimated separately for families with different levels of formal schooling. Those with less than a high school education have the lowest propensity to save out of income; those with at least one graduate degree have the highest propensity; and other groups fall appropriately in between. Regressions that combine all groups and use income-education interactions do not show significant differences among educational levels when standard definitions of saving are used.

Results using the full-income and full-saving definition are stronger, as one would anticipate, because of the positive association between formal schooling and investment in on-the-job training. Here both the separate regressions for educational groups and the overall regression with interaction terms show significant differences in saving as a function of educational level, with the results uniformly supporting the hypothesis that those who have had more education save more than others.

These results do not necessarily demonstrate a wholly independent influence of differences in educational attainment on saving propensities. It is difficult to construct an unambiguous test of whether educational level affects time preference and foresight. Nonetheless, the results are consistent with the hypothesis.

One additional result is the relation between a subjective estimate of household saving plans and actual saving by educational level. Inclusion of a saving-plan variable reduces the net influence on actual saving of a variable like income, since higher planned saving is found among families with higher income. But the coefficient of saving plans, which represents the degree to which such plans are carried out, is generally higher for households with higher levels of educational attainment, a result consistent with the notion that one of the effects of formal schooling is to expand the time horizon of the household and to increase its awareness of the future relative to the present.

The saving-plan results may turn out to reflect what could be one of the most significant impacts of schooling on behavior — an increased awareness of the future consequences of present actions and a modification of behavior to take better account of those consequences. And the impact of education on present versus future choices might also be one of the most important ways in which additional education results in behavior patterns that provide not only direct benefits to those being educated but also an increased flow of indirect benefits to society as a whole. A society whose citizens are able to strike a better balance between present and future claims on resources is surely one in which all manner of decisions, ranging from personal financial ones to population and fertility ones, are more compatible with improvements in the general welfare.

Solmon's chapter also examines the relation between educational attainment and a collection of attitudes with respect to savings objectives, efficiency in portfolio selection, and risk. Differences in the attitudes of sample members are strongly associated with differences in levels of educational attainment, standardizing for the influence of other variables like income, age, and number of children. The results suggest that families with more education are likely to place much more weight on saving for the purpose of educating children and providing for inheritance, whereas educational level is negatively associated with savings objectives such as building up a business or providing for emergencies.

These relationships can plausibly be interpreted as reflecting both the distinctive characteristics of occupational choice as it relates to educational level and a positive association between educational level and orientation toward the future rather than the present. Highly educated persons have a greater stock of human capital and, on balance, expect both relatively rapid increases in income and less short-term variability in income due to transitory factors like unemployment. Thus providing for emergencies looms as less important for more highly educated heads of families, and such families are apt to have already made sufficient provisions for the future, so that saving to build up capital in the form of owned businesses is also a less-important objective. The concentration of responses by the more educated on saving to provide for children's education and for inheritance seems clearly associated with a longer view of the relevant horizon for family decision making.

Respondent preferences for particular types of assets in a portfolio clearly indicate a perceptible gain in the efficiency with which assets are managed as educational level rises, as well as a markedly lower degree of aversion to risk on the part of highly educated families. Holding income and age constant, respondents with more education were much less likely to prefer asset forms like savings accounts and savings bonds and much more likely to prefer common stock, real estate, or mutual fund investments. Unlike the former, the latter are all variable-price assets with a significant degree of risk as well as a higher expected rate of return under the kind of conditions experienced in the United States over the past several decades. Thus the marked preference for both higher yield as well as riskier assets on the part of the more educated population suggests a difference in efficiency that facilitates a higher return to savings.

Other preference patterns indicate that more educated families are more aware of the capital gains potential in certain forms of investment and of the consequences of inflationary price changes and that they are better able to adjust portfolios to those changes. Such families are much more concerned with expected yields on investments than with safety of principal or current return. All these patterns can be interpreted as reflecting a positive association between rational investment policy and level of educational attainment, as well as a markedly greater ability on the part of the more educated to adapt their portfolio decisions to changing economic circumstances.

Thus in the area of saving behavior and portfolio choice, we find evidence to buttress the findings reported elsewhere in this volume: Differences in educational level have a major impact on the ability of individuals to adjust to changing circumstances, whether the question includes managing their economic affairs in the labor market, managing their own private financial affairs as consumers and investors, or planning the number and spacing of their children. And in a world where information flows are growing exponentially and where optimal decision making requires the efficient processing of increasingly large amounts of new information, the ability to adapt effectively to changes is likely to be of major importance.

The chapter by Gilbert Ghez, "Education, the Price of Time, and Life-Cycle Consumption," is also concerned with the impact of differences in educational attainment on consumption behavior, but its emphasis is on the lifetime profile of consumption rather than its structure or the efficiency with which households make consumption decisions. The model developed by Ghez suggests that the lifetime consumption path is determined by the pattern of life-cycle variation in wage rates. According to Ghez, a change in wage rates will generate four different types of effects on consumption, some of which are offsetting:

1 An increase in wage rates will raise the cost of using time rather than market goods in the production of household output, thus inducing a substitution of goods for time.

2 An increase in wage rates will raise the cost of household activities (outputs) that are relatively time-intensive, thus inducing a substitution toward activities that are relatively goods-intensive.

3 If wage rates are expected to increase, the cost of time-using activities will be higher in the future than at present because the price of time will be higher, thus encouraging a substitution of consumption away from the future toward the present.

4 Unforeseen or imperfectly foreseen increases in wage rates will increase consumption because they result in greater wealth (higher discounted future income) for the household; "windfalls' of this sort tend to increase consumption when they are received.

Assuming that wage rates typically tend to rise over most of the life cycle, the effects of the first and second of these influences should produce an unambiguously positive correlation between wage rates and consumption of goods. The effect of the third factor is an unambiguously negative correlation between consumption and wage rates, whereas the wealth effects depend on whether unforeseen changes in wage rates are positive or negative. Ghez assumes that expectations are unbiased and hence that changes in wage rates have no net wealth effect on consumption.

The empirical tests of this model, conducted on the 1960 BLS survey of consumer expenditures, indicate that consumption is positively related to wage rates for each educational class; thus the first two effects outweigh the third. The wage rate coefficient is a bit higher for the highest education class, but is not consistently or strongly related to education. For example, households with a head having 12 or more years of schooling increase consumption by about six-tenths of 1 percent for every 1 percent change in earnings, whereas families headed by those with eight or fewer years of schooling show a bit less response. One might argue that educational attainment is positively associated with a higher level of certainty about future income, which in turn might mean less reluctance to expand consumption as current earnings rise. The argument is plausible but speculative.

Although the empirical results are consistent with Ghez's model, in which the positive association between wage rates and consumption is explained by the substitution of goods for time (resulting from the higher price of time associated with rising wage rates), that is not the only possible explanation of this result. In the Ghez model, as pointed out earlier, it is assumed that there are no overall wealth effects on consumption because expectations are judged to be unbiased. Ghez argues that the mean difference between expectations about wage rate changes and actual wage rate changes is best regarded as zero for any given group, although there may be positive and negative deviations for individual group members. But the argument supposes that people will act as if they were absolutely certain of receiving the expected wage rate (presumably the observed mean wage for their group) and hence that positive consumption effects for those whose realized income exceeds expectations will be offset by negative consumption effects for those whose income falls short of expectations.

Uncertainty itself, however, may affect the adjustment of consumption to income. People expecting a given increase in income may plan to increase consumption by less than would be the case if their expectations were certain, simply because the cost of being wrong is too high. If I plan consumption on the basis of my best estimate of expected income, I could be in serious financial trouble if things turn out less well than anticipated. If things turn out better than anticipated, nothing much is lost but an opportunity to consume now and to improve the distribution of consumption between present and future. Thus the existence of uncertainty itself is a possible explanation for the positive correlation between wage rates and consumption. The slight but positive association between the wage rate–consumption correlation and educational level seems compatible with that hypothesis—there probably being relatively less variance in the distribution of expected income changes for those with higher levels of education.

The next three chapters examine aspects of human behavior (criminal activity, fertility, and attitudes) that have traditionally been ignored by economists. The chapter by Isaac Ehrlich, "On the Relation between Education and Crime," explores an area in which the indirect effects of education on behavior are of major potential importance. Ehrlich first develops a model to explain individual participation in illegal activities. Unlike many of the implicit models used by criminologists and psychologists, Ehrlich's model specifies that the motivations that underlie decisions to engage in illegal activities are similar to those underlying decisions to engage in legal ones; i.e., criminal activity is viewed as an alternative "occupation" to working at a regular income-producing job.

In this view of the world, the decision to engage in illegal activity is made because the expected income from that occupation is greater than the expected income from more traditional forms of work. The payoff from illegal activity consists of the expected rewards (the loot, in more common parlance), modified by the probability of being apprehended or convicted. The payoffs from normal economic activity are simply the expected values to be derived from earnings from work. Thus individuals are assumed to react to opportunities and costs; some will decide that the opportunities in illegal activities are greater than those in legal activities, and/or that the costs are less, and vice versa for others.

Educational attainment could enter the model in a number of possible ways. First, education may act as an efficiency parameter and may influence efficiency (productivity) equally in both illegal and legal activities. If so, one would not be able to tell a priori whether more education tends to increase or decrease participation in illegal activities. For example, there may be certain kinds of illegal activities in which more education does not pay off because it has no effect on the efficiency with which the activity is carried out, does not lower the probability of apprehension or conviction, and has no influence on anything else. Since higher education always yields some return in legal activities, in this case higher levels of education would be associated with a reduced incentive to engage in criminal activity. Alternatively, educational differences might have the same productivity-enhancing influence on illegal activity for all individuals, but might tend to enhance market productivity more for some than for others and hence result in a differential incidence of criminal activity among different groups.

Finally, differences in educational attainment might have an impact on the supply (law-enforcement) side of an illegal-activities model. In Ehrlich's work the demand for illegal activities is related to the economic incentives of the participant, whereas the probabilities of apprehension and conviction are related to the resources employed in law enforcement. But the effectiveness of law enforcement might be enhanced if either potential victims or law-enforcement officials—or both—had more education.

One interesting insight from the Ehrlich model is the possible explanation of racial and age differences in the incidence of illegal activities. Some studies have produced evidence that suggests a different rate of return to investment in formal schooling for white and nonwhite population groups; especially for males, the data seem to show that the rate of return to schooling is much less for nonwhites than for whites.[22] If the potential returns from participation in illegal activity were equal for both groups, a lower return from legal activities would tend to result in a higher incidence of participation in illegal activities for nonwhite males, other things being equal.

An empirical implication of this relationship is that the distribution by years of schooling of nonwhite males engaged in illegal activities ought to be different from the comparable distribution of white males, relative to the schooling distributions of those engaged in legal activities in both groups. Ehrlich provides some evidence that this in fact is the case. Among inmates of institutions in 1960 aged 25 to 34 the average schooling level of nonwhite males and females was slightly higher than that of white males and females; the corresponding statistics for experienced members of the labor force show exactly the reverse relationship—higher average schooling for white males and females than for nonwhites. However, these data relate only indirectly to arrest and conviction statistics and constitute only a relatively weak verification of the hypothesis.

The evidence on age distribution of offenders is much stronger and entirely consistent with the model. Here, Ehrlich finds that juveniles not enrolled in school show much higher delinquency rates than those enrolled in school. The model suggests that the rewards from (legal) labor force participation are much higher for those in school than for dropouts, since there is a substantial future earnings return from schooling. The relatively high unemployment rate among teenage dropouts tends to work in the same direction, since it lowers expected returns from legal activities but does not change expected returns from illegal ones.

One of the most striking results of the study, which offers strong

---

[22] See Welch (1967), Landes (1968), and Hanoch (1967).

support for the basic theoretical structure of the model, concerns the differential incidence of arrests for specific types of crimes, using states as the unit of observation. The model suggests that expectations of financial gain and forgone earnings from labor force participation ought to be strong determinants of crimes against property like robbery and embezzlement, where direct financial gain is a major consideration. Such factors ought to be of lesser or no importance in explaining differences in the incidence of crimes against persons, such as murder, rape, or aggravated assault. In regressions run across states, the predicted differences show up clearly: The potential gain and potential cost variables were consistently significant in explaining crimes against property, but were unimportant in explaining crimes against persons.

Finally, there is some evidence in the Ehrlich chapter to suggest that more effective law enforcement may be one of the indirect benefits of higher levels of educational attainment. In an empirical analysis of the effectiveness of law enforcement in preventing illegal activities—derived from a simultaneous equations model involving both the demand for illegal activities and the supply of law enforcement—the educational level of the community showed a significant and positive influence on the effectiveness of law enforcement in reducing the rate of criminal activity. This result might come about because higher educational levels lead potential victims to take more effective measures of self-protection, because higher educational levels are associated with greater community cooperation with law-enforcement bodies, or because the educational level of law-enforcement bodies themselves, other things being equal, results in greater effectiveness per dollar spent.

The impact of educational attainment on reducing criminal activities via more effective law enforcement through any of the specified channels and the finding in the next chapter by Michael concerning the greater tendency of more highly educated families to adopt technical innovations earlier and more rapidly than other groups constitute two specific and important instances of the effects of educational attainment which are nonmonetary and which accrue partly to society as a whole rather than only to those being educated.

"Education and Fertility," by Robert Michael, asks whether the educational level of parents has any net influence on the quantity and quality of their children. The model used by Michael specified that children provide a flow of services to parents that varies directly with their number and quality and that parental demand for children is derived from the demand for child services in conjunction with the costs of limiting the quantity of children via contraception. Because having children involves sexual activity, which confers positive benefits on the household, decisions about the desired number of children in the household must take account of the costs of spacing or preventing births through the use of contraceptive devices. Thus the costs of avoiding children are nonnegative, and the observed number of children in completed families would be affected by the existence of any differential in these costs among families.

Economic factors like family income and the price of husband's and wife's time would of course have an impact on the optimum level of child services and thus on family size: most studies show slight but positive correlations between family income and number of children and negative correlations between the implicit price of the wife's time and number of children. Over and above these relatively straightforward but indirect influences of educational level, Michael asserts that the role of formal schooling might have an additional influence via its effect on the efficiency with which families practice contraception, rather than through its impact on income or the price of time. The argument rests on the relation between education and efficiency in processing information. Since a variety of contraceptive devices are available in the market and since innovation and technical changes have been relatively rapid in this area, it ought to be true that different levels of formal schooling result in a differential efficiency factor in "producing" children. [23]

Empirical tests of this model produce results consistent with the efficiency hypothesis. Standardizing for total income, husband's wage rate, and other demographic characteristics of the family, both the educational level of the husband and the relative (to the husband) educational level of the wife have a significant negative association with the number of children.

Additional evidence concerning the influence of the wife's education on the choice of contraceptive techniques and on the level of education expected for children supports the notion that educa-

---

[23] That test may have more power to explain behavior in the past than in the future. The diffusion of technical knowledge about contraceptives has been very rapid, and it is not clear that large differences among groups classified by income or education still exist.

tion may influence fertility through a number of different channels—income, the price of time, contraceptive efficacy, and perhaps the incentive to invest in human capital in children. As Michael stresses, the results reported in his paper are preliminary and do not represent completed research. They serve to indicate the diversity of ways in which education appears to influence this important aspect of behavior.

The final chapter in this volume, "The Influence of Education and Ability on Salary and Attitudes," by Albert Beaton, focuses on the relation between educational attainment, basic ability as measured by IQ, and a variety of economic, social, and political attitudes. The relation between earnings and the attitude variables, and between ability and educational attainment, is also examined. The analysis in Beaton's chapter is based entirely on the NBER-TH sample of Air Crew veterans, which has provided the empirical base for a number of the other chapters in this book.

The strong positive association between ability levels and educational attainment is thoroughly documented, as is the equally strong positive association between educational attainment and earnings (given ability) and between ability and earnings (given educational attainment). Beaton also documents the positive association between business or professional self-employment and earnings for given educational attainment and ability classes.

One of the most interesting sets of results concerns the relation between nonpecuniary aspects of the employment situation and money earnings. Respondents were asked several questions about attitudes toward their jobs: whether they regarded them as interesting, challenging, enjoyable, etc. In general, these are aspects of jobs to which positive monetary equivalents would be attached; one could, for example, use a measure of job interest or challenge to represent nonmonetary consumption benefits from work, a type of benefit conceptually similar to the nonmonetary benefits that people enjoy from leisure-time activities. Theoretically, it would be anticipated that the monetary compensation for any given job is inversely related to the nonmonetary consumption benefits associated with that job: an equivalent position that lacks the nonmonetary benefit would presumably require higher monetary earnings to induce people to take it.

The evidence from the NBER-TH sample indicates that nonmonetary job benefits such as enjoyment, interest, and challenge are strongly and *positively* related to earnings; people who receive relatively high money earnings also find their work situations more enjoyable, etc., and thus have more rather than less consumption benefits than others. The data also indicate that respondents with more education tend to regard their work as more challenging and interesting, and as holding a better chance for advancement, than the job situations of less well educated people, although educational level appears to be negatively associated with expectations about job responsibility. On the whole, the results suggest that the observed inequality of earnings would be increased if account were taken of the nonmonetary benefits of the work environment and that the returns to educational attainment are higher than suggested by analysis of the monetary returns because consumption benefits from work tend to be positively associated with the level of educational attainment. Thus the rate-of-return estimates in the Taubman-Wales chapter, for example, would tend to understate the true return to investments in higher education.

The social and political attitudes of respondents, as reported in self-rating on a liberal-conservative scale and in several attitude variables (whether young people have too much or too little freedom, whether people are overly concerned with financial security, and whether the pace of racial integration is too fast or too slow), tend to be generally conservative in this relatively high-income, heavily entrepreneurial, and almost entirely white sample of respondents. However, there is a consistent tendency for differences in educational attainment to move respondents toward the less-conservative end of the spectrum for most of the attitude questions. That is, respondents with more education were less likely to think that the pace of racial integration is too fast, less likely to think that young people have too much freedom, etc.

Ability measures also turned out to be associated with political attitudes. Here, the higher-ability groups were apt to be somewhat less conservative than others with respect to questions about the appropriate amount of freedom for young people or the appropriate pace of racial integration. Ability measures, on the other hand, tended to be associated with a greater tendency to rank oneself as politically conservative. Finally, the attitudes of the self-employed business proprietors in the sample were clearly much more on the conservative than the liberal side, whereas teachers and self-employed professionals tended to be on the liberal side of the scale. These results concerning the effects of education and ability on attitudes are of particular interest because they represent partial correlations or net effects; that is, the effects of education are measured with the influence of ability and occupational status held constant.

Respondents were also asked a battery of questions about factors associated with success in particular jobs or professions. The results are what might be expected from a high-income sample of entrepreneurially oriented respondents: With virtual unanimity, respondents regarded "one's own performance" and "hard work" as the major factors associated with success, whereas being lucky or unlucky was considered unimportant. And there are some interesting relationships involving the influence of education and ability on the evaluation of factors important for career success. In general, the more able respondents tended to give low rank to the importance of "having the right connections," and they also indicated that ability to get along with people was relatively unimportant. In general, it appears that the most able respondents considered ability itself to be sufficient for occupational success, whereas other respondents considered other factors relatively more important.

The data show a very strong association between average earnings and the respondent's ranking of the relative importance of his own performance and hard work: those who ranked these factors as very important tended to have substantially higher salaries than others. One is tempted to regard these results as essentially ex post rationalization: those who have achieved success attribute it to their own hard work and ability and not to factors unrelated to their own inputs. However, other data indicate that financial success as measured by total earnings is positively associated with hours spent at work, which in turn argues that the findings might well be taken at face value.

The final set of variables measures the attitudes of sample respondents toward education itself. Questions deal with aspects of the educational process that the respondents felt to be relatively important or relatively unimportant. By an overwhelming majority, the sample considered the acquisition of basic skills to be the single most important function of the educational process, with career preparation next, followed by general knowledge. Activities and social awareness were regarded as relatively unimportant functions of schools.

Based on the responses to the schooling-importance variables, there is some indirect evidence in the pattern of average earnings that suggests that general training rather than specific training entails higher economic productivity. Those who ranked general knowledge as more important had consistently higher salaries than those who ranked it as less important, whereas those who regarded career preparation as relatively unimportant tended to have higher average salaries than others. These results presumably reflect, in part, the heavily entrepreneurial nature of the sample, since career preparation would hardly be rated highly by independent entrepreneurs. One might, however, also expect career preparation to be highly rated by lawyers, doctors, and other professionals, who obviously must be trained for their future occupations in school, and this is not the case according to the data. In fact, the association between education in years and evaluation of the relative importance of general knowledge and career preparation is characterized by statistically (highly) significant signs: The higher the level of education, the more importance assigned to the general-knowledge function and the less importance assigned to the career-preparation function. And these are among the strongest relations involving educational attainment and any of the attitude variables.

This last set of results, although based on the subjective evaluation of men who are many years beyond the completion of formal schooling, has clear implications for educational policy. The data show that in a relatively successful, high-ability group of men at the peak of their career earnings profiles, those with more education regard the acquisition of general knowledge as a much more important (productive) function of schools than preparation for specific careers. These results are consistent with the well-documented fact that the majority of people end up in careers that have little direct relevance to their specific training in school.

SUMMARY   Although the chapters in this volume cover a wide-ranging set of issues, a number of unifying themes can be traced out.

First is the firmly documented finding that investments in formal schooling apparently yield a "profit" both to the individual being educated and to society as a whole, after standardizing for the influence of innate ability and family background on earnings. Making no allowance at all for the fact that education provides some direct consumption benefits, or for the fact that there are likely to be substantial social and private returns other than those reflected by direct earnings differentials, the evidence suggests that the lower limit on returns to higher education is in excess of borrowing costs.

A second major finding is that the payoff to formal schooling is not restricted to those with favorable family background factors or high ability. Although there is some evidence that those with very high ability get better-than-average returns from investing in formal schooling, the returns are substantial throughout at least the upper half of the ability distribution. Our best results come from a sample restricted to men with above-average ability, but even the lowest segment of that sample shows a significant return to investment in higher education. Thus it is not the case that education has no payoff except for those at very high ability levels.

A quite different kind of result, which shows up in many of the chapters in this volume, is that higher education apparently tends to enhance decision making generally. The probable explanation is that formal schooling increases information-processing skills. Thus in a world in which technical change is rapid and new situations are continually emerging, formal schooling yields a substantial benefit in enhancing the problem-solving capacity of those being educated. Another way to make the same point is to say that the returns to schooling are apparently greater in a world where change is relatively rapid than in one where change is relatively slow.

Finally, there is considerable evidence scattered throughout these chapters indicating that one of the ways in which education produces benefits is to stretch the time horizon for individual decisions and create a relatively stronger preference for the future as against the present. The evidence here is largely indirect, but it tends to show up consistently.

References

Hanoch, Giora: "An Economic Analysis of Earnings and Schooling," *Journal of Human Resources,* vol. 2, no. 3, pp. 310–324, Summer 1967.

Jencks, Christopher, et al.: *Inequality,* Basic Books, Inc., Publishers, New York, 1972, p. 24.

Landes, William: "Economics of Fair Employment Laws," *Journal of Political Economy,* vol. 76, no. 4, pp. 507–522, July–August 1968.

Malkiel, B., and J. Malkiel: "Male-Female Pay Differentials in Professional Employment," *American Economic Review,* vol. 63, pp. 693–705, September 1973.

Mincer, Jacob: "On the Job Training: Costs, Returns, and Some Implications," *Journal of Political Economy,* vol. 70, part 2, pp. 50–79, Supplement: October 1962.

Welch, Finis: "Labor-Market Discrimination: An Interpretation of Income Differences in the Rural South," *Journal of Political Economy,* vol. 75, no. 3, pp. 225–240, June 1967.

Welch, Finis: "Education in Production," *Journal of Political Economy,* vol. 78, no. 1, pp. 35–49, January–February 1970.

Welch, Finis: "Black-White Differences in the Returns to Schooling," unpublished paper, National Bureau of Economic Research, New York, June 1972.

Part One:

The Impact of Education on Earnings

2. Mental Ability and Higher Educational Attainment in the Twentieth Century

by Paul Taubman and Terence Wales

INTRODUCTION
AND
SUMMARY
OF FINDINGS Many important changes have occurred in higher education in the United States since 1900. At the turn of the century very few people finished high school, but most of those who did attended college. For example, only about 7 percent of the population born around 1880, but 70 percent of all high school graduates, entered college. After World War I there was a big increase in the number of students attending high school but a sharp decrease in the fraction of high school graduates attending college.[1] However, after World War II the fraction of high school graduates attending college increased, until by 1970 about 50 percent of the eligible age group and 60 percent of all high school graduates attended college.[2]

The organization of higher education also changed greatly. For example, many four-year colleges changed their status to universities, numerous two-year colleges were founded, and normal schools became teachers colleges, which in turn expanded into standard four-year colleges. As the number of institutions of higher learning has increased, attempts have been made (for example, in California) to integrate community colleges, four-year colleges, and universities into statewide systems of education.[3] Partly in response to the increased demand for higher education at a reasonable cost, state-operated institutions have expanded to become more important in terms of the number of students and the quality of faculties.

The introduction of new courses and a change in emphasis between general and technical education have also shifted the focus of higher education. In part, these changes reflect the formation of

[1] In part this represented a shift in educational policy toward supplying more education at all levels (Finch, 1946; Folger & Nam, 1967).

[2] These estimates are derived from the methods given in Taubman and Wales (1972*b*, App. B). See also Folger and Nam (1967).

[3] See Jencks and Riesman (1968).

47

new disciplines and the growth in knowledge. However, they also reflect shifts in the composition of the student population. In 1900, a large fraction of college graduates became medical doctors, lawyers, theologians, or engineers. Since 1900, there has been a marked shift in careers toward business and other professions.[4]

There were several basic causes for these changes. First, there was the need for the educational system to adapt to new conditions in society. These new conditions included the increased demand of the wealthy for education as a consumption or status good, a shift in the occupational mix toward scientific skills, and the belief that education was required to obtain a good job. Second, there was the desire to make as much high-quality education as possible available to all those who could benefit from it.

Change comes no more easily to the academic world than elsewhere. Any alteration in graduation requirements or course offerings raises substantial opposition and debate. Expansion in the size of the university has caused controversy paralleling that caused by the expansion of high school education.[5] Much of the debate has concerned the need for quality in education and the question of who would or should benefit from higher education.[6]

One particular argument against the expansion of higher and secondary school education has perhaps been raised more than any other. The basis of the argument is that the courses given at most higher-level institutions of learning are oriented toward training people to use mental facilities and certain learned tools to solve various abstract and practical problems. But to be able to acquire the tools and to learn how to solve problems, a person must have a certain threshold level of mental ability or IQ.[7] Therefore, if many students below this threshold level were admitted to institutions of higher learning, the resources they used would be wasted. In addition, the admission of unqualified students in large

[4] See Wolfle (1954).

[5] See, for example, the statement by the president of Harvard in Finch (1946).

[6] It is generally assumed that benefits from education can be measured by the additional future income attributable to education, by the consumption value, and by any external factors such as the value to society of a better-functioning democracy.

[7] It is sometimes maintained that the threshold level is at least one-half a standard deviation above the population mean.

numbers might interfere with the instruction of those who would benefit from the education.[8]

An argument in favor of expansion points to the "loss in talent" that occurs when many students above the required threshold level cannot enter college and therefore never have the chance to develop their talents. Some proponents of expansion indicate that excessive heterogeneity in ability levels could be avoided if expansion took the form of added variety in the types of educational institutions.

These viewpoints involve contradictory assertions that can be resolved only by reference to empirical evidence. For higher education in the United States, the facts under dispute are: (1) Did the expansion in college enrollment since 1900 lead to a decline in the average mental ability of college students? (2) Did the expansion lead to a reduction in the loss of talent? (3) At what minimum level of mental ability do individuals (or perhaps society) cease to receive any benefits from education? While these questions are important, very little research has been undertaken to answer them.[9]

Our main interest in this chapter is to examine the first two questions by determining the relationship, in various samples spanning the twentieth century, between the percent of high school graduates who enter college and their mental ability at the time of college entrance.[10] The samples used, which are often referred to by name, are drawn from the Project Talent study and the studies done by Barker, Berdie, Berdie and Hood, Benson, Little, O'Brien, Phearman, Proctor, Wolfle and Smith, and Yerkes. Each of these studies presents information on the number of high school graduates entering college by IQ or aptitude test score. To make the tests comparable, we converted the scores to a percentile basis.

The information obtained in answering these two questions can also be used in analyzing other important economic problems. For example, for many purposes in economics it is important to know whether the average ability level of persons with various amounts of education has remained constant over age groups. Thus we may

---

[8] This could occur with a class of a very wide range of abilities if teachers pitched their instructional level too low.

[9] Partial exceptions are Berdie et al. (1962) and Darley (1962).

[10] In a recently completed study addressed to the third question, we found that rates of return to higher education do not vary with ability for those in the top half of the ability distribution, except perhaps for people with graduate education and very high ability. See Taubman and Wales (1972*a*).

wish to determine how income varies over time for people with a given amount of education. If the average ability level of those with a given amount of education has remained constant over time, we can answer this question by studying income differences for various age groups with a given educational level, as available, say, in the 1960 census. But if the average ability level within an education level is not constant over age groups, the income differences in the census occur because of both age and ability differences.

In addition, the coefficient of education in an equation relating education to mental ability plays an important role in determining the economic returns to education. It can be shown that when returns to education are estimated using data that do not include a mental-ability variable (such as the census data), the estimated effect of education on income will be biased upward if ability and education are positively related.[11] Further, if this relationship has changed over time, then the bias will change accordingly.

Subject to some qualifications, as given below, our major conclusions are as follows:

1   As shown in Figure 2-1, the average ability level of high school graduates

---

[11] If the true equation is

$$Y = \alpha A + \beta S + u \qquad (2\text{-}1)$$

where Y is income, A is innate ability, S is educational attainment as measured by highest grade completed, u is a random-error term that is independent of A and S, and α and β are parameters to be estimated, then the estimation (by least squares) of the equation $Y = cS$ will yield a coefficient c, with expected value given by

$$E(c) = \beta + k\alpha \qquad (2\text{-}2)$$

where k is the coefficient from the (least squares) regression

$$A = kS \qquad (2\text{-}3)$$

Thus, as long as ability is positively related to income ($\alpha > 0$) and as long as educational attainment and ability are positively related ($k > 0$), then the estimate of c in Eq. (2-2) exceeds β, which, from Eq. (2-1), represents the true impact of variations in S on Y.

On the other hand, if we have estimates of the ability-education relationship for various time periods and if this relationship has changed for various cohorts, it is possible to obtain separate estimates of the effects of education and ability on income in a single cross section that includes the various cohorts.

Thus, Eq. (2-2) expresses the estimated education coefficient in terms of income differential due to education β, the income differential due to ability α, and the increase in ability associated with educational changes k. Since we can obtain an estimate of k, Eq. (2-2) has only two unknowns. If another estimate of Eq. (2-2) can be obtained in a cohort with a different k, then in principle the two equations can be solved for estimates of both α and β.

who entered college ($\overline{A}_c$) ranges from the 53d to the 63d percentile (measured upward from zero) for the period 1925–1961. Although in the 1930s there was a reduction in the percentage of students entering college, Figure 2-1 indicates that there was an increase in the average quality of college students compared with the 1920s. On the other hand, the postwar boom in higher education resulted in still higher-quality college students than in the 1930s and substantially higher-quality students than in the 1920s. The average quality level has increased because initially only about 60 percent of the most able students went to college, while, as shown below, the growth in the fraction entering college is concentrated in the high-ability groups. There is also evidence in Darley (1962) that existing schools have increased the quality of their students, while new colleges and community colleges have been started to meet the needs of the less able. Thus the more able students may be receiving a better education now.

2   There has been a significant reduction in the loss of talent since 1920. The loss of talent can be measured by the fraction of high school graduates who enter college at various ability levels. The selected values of ability, measured as percentiles (ranging upward from zero), are 25, 50, 75, and 90. At the 90th and 75th percentiles there has been a substantial increase over time in the percent entering college. At the 50th percentile the 1960 values

FIGURE 2-1   *Average ability levels over time, adjusted*

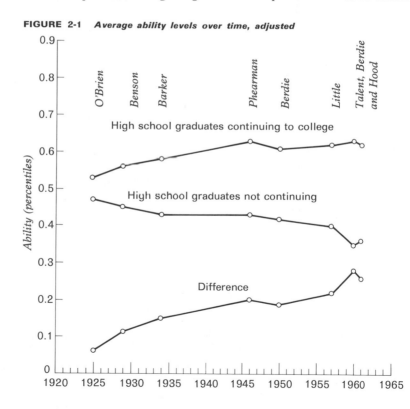

are slightly higher than those for the 1920s, and the values during the 1930s and 1940s are substantially lower. At the 25th percentile the fraction of high school graduates entering college appears to have fallen during the 1930s and 1940s, but by the 1960s was back to the 1920 level. On the basis of this evidence, we conclude that the substantial increase in the fraction of high school graduates entering college since the 1920s occurred primarily at the 75th and 90th ability percentiles.[12]

It should be realized that these results are subject to a number of qualifications, of which the following are among the most important. Many of our samples are statewide rather than nationwide, and some of the states may be atypical. In addition, the samples use different ability tests that had to be converted to a common basis. Our results, which are based on IQ and aptitude tests, reflect only the mental abilities measured by these tests and not all types of mental ability. Finally, we are assuming that the average ability level of high school seniors in the population has remained constant over time. Although there is some evidence in Berdie et al. (1962) that this is true, it has not been completely verified.

We turn now to a consideration of the measures of mental ability and education that we used in the analysis. This is followed by a discussion of the major conceptual and statistical problems inherent in the study, our conclusions, and then a detailed presentation of our estimate of the ability-education relationship for each sample.

MEASURES OF MENTAL ABILITY AND EDUCATIONAL ATTAINMENT

To measure mental ability it is necessary to know what is being measured and to define a set of units to differentiate between people. Following the approach of psychologists, we conceive of mental ability in terms of the capacity to retain ideas and comprehend and solve abstract problems. While there is no perfect empirical counterpart to this theoretical definition, there are several measures on which differential performance is partly determined by the theoretical construct. The more that differences on the measure are determined by mental ability, the more appropriate the measure is as a proxy.

The two most obvious measures which should be related to mental ability are rank in high school class and scores on a standardized set of tests. Although both measures are related to mental ability, one may be a better proxy than the other.

---

[12] The data (for males) prior to World War I, however, yield a picture similar to that of the 1950s and 1960s. Thus the big loss of talent at that time occurred prior to high school graduation.

Standardized tests can be divided into IQ and aptitude (achievement) tests. In principle, aptitude tests measure the amount of knowledge or skill acquired (primarily in school) in particular subjects. IQ tests are thought of as measuring general inborn ability, which does not depend upon previous schooling (or the factors noted above). However, a substantial body of evidence suggests that most IQ tests depend, among other things, on years of schooling, quality of schooling, and cultural background.[13] Thus the difference between IQ and aptitude tests is more a matter of degree than of kind, and we shall intermix information from both types of tests as long as the data can be converted to a common scale.

Consider also the differences between test scores and rank in class. One major difficulty of rank-in-class data is that they are computed on the basis of students in a given grade in a single high school, when in fact different schools in the same city often have students of different quality, and differences in quality generally exist also between urban and rural schools. Therefore, unless information on the quality of the students is available, it may be misleading to equate the ability of individuals who have the same rank in different schools. On the other hand, the same test may be used in all schools in a system, or, at a minimum, test scores can be standardized over a population. In either case students from various schools can be compared.

Another reason why rank in class can be a very poor proxy of mental ability is that rank may be determined much more by such things as docility in class, memorization, and grades in nonacademic courses. These factors may explain the well-known phenomenon that a disproportionately large percentage of girls are in the higher ranks in class in high school.

An individual's rank in class may, on the other hand, be more dependent on such things as drive and motivation, and these characteristics may be crucial for future academic and career success.[14] Thus some studies, such as Berdie and Hood (1963), have found

[13] See, for example, Learned and Wood (1938).

[14] Of course, genetic influences, prenatal and postnatal diet, home and school atmosphere, personal motivation, and drive can all affect an individual's intellectual performance as measured by IQ tests or rank in class. To the extent that all the factors that affect class rank or IQ scores are also relevant in determining income or in determining which are the talented students currently available for college training, our mental-ability index is appropriate in measuring the return to education. Our analysis, of course, is not suitable for determining such magnitudes as the loss of talent that would not have occurred if all children and expectant mothers had had adequate diets.

rank in class slightly more important than IQ or aptitude tests in determining which students enter college. However, contrary evidence exists in Folger and Nam (1967).

Although most studies find that knowledge of both IQ and rank in class significantly improves the prediction of college attendance, we rely on test scores because of the problem of standardization. In order to facilitate a comparison of results from different samples, we converted the ability measures to the same units for all samples. This enables us not only to compare results but also to combine small samples for estimation purposes, as discussed in detail below. The standardization method that we used was to convert the IQ measure for each sample into percentile terms, with the "norm" being the population of high school graduates. Since most of the samples involve statewide tests of graduating seniors (e.g., Minnesota, Kansas, Iowa), standardization consists simply of transforming the raw IQ measure into within-sample percentile terms. This treatment assumes that the distribution by ability of high school graduates is the same in all states. However, even if the sample distribution for a state differs from the national norm, the effect will probably be small, provided ability is used as the dependent variable.[15]

The main advantage of this conversion method is that it avoids the problem of using conversion tables to compare various raw IQ scores. Such tables contain only the major IQ measures and in many cases appear to be based on small samples. Another advantage of our method is that it permits use of results provided by other investigators in which data are presented only in percentile form. For samples that clearly are not representative of the high school graduate population, we converted the data in a more complicated way.

We assume that the different tests and testing procedures yield data that are comparable. This requires that the rankings of individuals be the same if given the same test at different times or different tests at the same time. Various studies have indicated high reliability (of most tests) for individuals. Even greater reliability should be expected when broad groupings are used; hence, there

---

[15] This follows because according to the standard results in errors-in-variable problems, if there is an additive measurement error in the dependent variable that is not correlated with the independent variable, we shall obtain an unbiased estimate of the slope coefficient. Because of the conversion method used, there is no clear reason for not expecting the measurement errors to meet the above conditions.

should be little difficulty in combining the samples. In order to compare and combine samples from different time periods, we make the additional assumption that the average ability level of high school graduates has remained approximately constant over time. Support for this hypothesis is contained in Berdie et al. (1962), which traces the average ability level of high school graduates in Minnesota from 1928 to 1960 and in which there appears to be no trend in the average ability level as measured by the ACE examination. Further supporting evidence is available in Finch (1946).

We are interested primarily in analyzing post-high school educational attainment. For this purpose it is useful to distinguish two stages in the educational process: entrance into college and length of stay in college. Our analysis is concerned with the former aspect, since the necessary data are more readily available. The basic education measure that we use in analyzing the relation between college entrance and ability is the percentage of high school graduates who enter college.

In this study we do not analyze vocational education because there are virtually no data of the form we need. This suggests that the results of our analysis require careful interpretation. For example, in discussing the loss of talent that results when high-ability students do not attend college, it would be important to know how many of these attended vocational school and whether the rate of return to such education was high. Such considerations are particularly relevant in view of the long time period under study and the accompanying changes in emphasis on vocational training. In the 1930s, for example, there was a strong emphasis on this type of education (Anderson & Berning, 1950), although we suspect that in more recent years many equivalent programs have been given by colleges, junior colleges, and community colleges.

CONCEPTUAL AND STATISTICAL PROBLEMS

A question that is of some importance in statistical considerations is the interpretation of the education-ability relationship. That is, does ability "cause" the educational attainment—or vice versa—or does the relationship arise for other reasons?

Causality versus Description

Let us assume that students and their families have a demand function for educational attainment—for both the consumption and investment aspects. Regardless of whether students want either or both of these aspects, plausible arguments can be made that the demand depends upon the student's ability. Indeed, whether one uses students' educational plans or their actual realization of these plans, a substantial body of evidence exists suggesting that the demand for education is a function of ability.[16] This demand will also depend on such other factors as the family's income level, job and scholarship opportunities, and tuition.[17]

On the other hand, educational authorities try to weed out people with low ability levels. What is considered too low may depend upon the physical and budget capacity of the institutions or governments involved. In any event, evidence exists that willingness to promote students to higher grades, to encourage them to stay in school, or to permit them to go to a higher education institution has varied over time.[18] Thus any observed relationship between educational attainment and ability is the outcome of the factors that affect supply and demand. Shifts in these factors can alter the observed relationship without implying any causation; therefore, we conclude that the data on education and ability should not be interpreted in a causal sense. We shall generally use the term *descriptive* to characterize this relationship.

The fact that we interpret the education-ability relation as descriptive provides no guidance for deciding which variable to use as the dependent one in regressions. However, there are two major reasons for using ability as the dependent variable.[19] First, the education-ability relation enables us to correct the bias (of the education coefficient) arising from the omission of ability in income equations. For this purpose we require the education-ability equation to be formulated with education as the independent variable.[20] Second, errors in measuring ability will not bias the coefficient in the regression if ability is used as the dependent variable. There will be a bias if ability is used as the independent variable. On the other hand, there is a rationale for using education as the dependent

---

[16] The plans may be more relevant because one reason students do not fulfill their plans is that the educational authorities exclude those with low ability. That is, the realization in part reflects supply conditions.

[17] The family's income level affects the demand relation because of imperfect capital markets, differences in tastes for present versus future consumption, and the luxury nature of the consumption of education.

[18] See, for example, Folger and Nam (1967) on the trends in the number of students who were not in the normal school grade of their age group. Consider, also, state and federal provision of support for college facilities.

[19] In addition, for samples in which individuals have different amounts of education when tested, it may be possible to correct the bias when ability is the dependent variable.

[20] This is necessary because, as shown in footnote 11, in Eq. (2-2) the estimate of k is obtained from estimating (by least squares) an equation in which education is the independent variable.

variable when dealing with certain nonlinear functional relations. That is, one way to test for nonlinearities is to include the independent variable in squared form. This can be accomplished only if ability is the independent variable.[21]

In general, there appear to be no sound reasons for preferring a particular functional form to relate education to ability.[22] For simplicity, we used the linear form. We have, however, tested for nonlinearities by regressing education on ability and ability squared. Where the nonlinearities are significant, we indicated the extent to which our conclusions are affected. We also experimented with the logarithmic form but have not presented the results, since this form does not fit well in the tails of the distributions, and the estimated coefficients appear to be very sensitive to the scaling of the ability variable—for example, using the midpoints or end points of the decile ranks.

There is one minor statistical point that can be dispensed with now. We have been talking interchangeably of the education variable as representing a situation in which an individual does or does not enter college and representing the fraction of high school graduates entering college. These two concepts can be reconciled as follows. We define a variable D_i as 1 if the ith person enters college and as zero otherwise. Our linear equation for the ith individual is therefore $A_i = h + kD_i$, where A_i is again the ability of the individual. Suppose that we now order the data by ability class and average the observations in each ability group. The education variable then becomes the percentage of people in each ability class who enter college (E_{12}), and the ability variable becomes the average ability level in the class (A).[23]

---

[21] The education variable cannot be included in both unsquared and squared forms as the independent variable because it is obtained by aggregating a zero-one variable, which when squared is still a zero-one dummy variable.

[22] However, for purposes of analyzing the relationship between income, education, and ability, it is necessary that the functional form for the side relation correspond to that of the basic relation. If a dummy variable for college entrance is used in the income analysis, then our linear equation is appropriate. If different dummies are used to represent various educational levels, then our linear equation provides the first step in determining the bias.

[23] Formally, this can be accomplished by multiplying by a grouping matrix G whose elements in the ith row (which corresponds to the ith ability group) are zero for all observations not in that ability group and $1/n_i$ for the n_i observations in the group. This gives $GA_i = hG + kGD_i$. In the ith ability group $GD = n^*_i/n_i$, where n^*_i is the number of people who enter college in that group. Since in the ith group D has n^*_i entries of one and $n_i - n^*_i$ values of zero, its average is n^*_i/n, which is equal to the percentage of people in that ability class who entered college. We denote this percentage as E_{12}.

The linear equation that we estimate for the different samples is therefore $A = h + kE_{12}$. It may be useful at this point to interpret the coefficients h and k. The coefficient h indicates the level of ability at which the fraction of high school graduates entering college is zero. Since in nearly all our samples some students enter college at all ability levels, our estimates of h are generally negative. An alternative interpretation of h may be obtained by solving this equation for E_{12} to give $E_{12} = - h/k + 1/k\ A$. Provided that h is negative, some students will continue to college even at the lowest ability levels. From this equation, $1/k$ can be interpreted as the increase in the fraction of students entering college for each unit increase in A.

Effect of Education on Mental Ability

Our main interest is in determining the relationship between the percentage of high school graduates entering college and their mental ability at the time of college entrance. The ability measures that we use are various IQ and achievement test scores. These are determined in part by the amount of schooling the individual received prior to taking the tests.

The pioneering study of Learned and Wood (1938) clearly demonstrates the extent to which even IQ measures are affected by years of schooling. In this study nearly 28,000 high school seniors were given a 12-hour examination in 1928. One part of the examination was the Otis IQ test. Those students who went on to college were retested in eight-hour examinations in 1930 and 1932. Moreover, exactly the same Otis test was given on the last two occasions. Comparing test scores for those in the sample in 1928 and 1930 and those in the sample in 1930 and 1932, it was found that the average score on this test rose $7\frac{1}{2}$ percent from 1928 to 1930 and 5 percent from 1930 to 1932. In other words, the Otis test (and presumably all other IQ tests) appears to measure educational attainment as well as mental ability.

Consequently, data from samples in which individuals are subjected to tests after having completed their formal education must be treated differently from those in which all individuals are tested as high school seniors. From a statistical viewpoint, the former problem may be analyzed as an error in variables.[24] In nontechnical terms, the problem may be described as follows:

[24] We wish to estimate the (descriptive) relationship between educational attainment S and mental ability A. Let the true relationship be expressed as

$$S = \gamma A + u \tag{2-4}$$

People with more education will score higher on tests because of this additional education. Thus it is difficult to distinguish between the effect of education on test scores and the relationship between the mental ability of students at, say, the end of high school and after additional educational attainment. In this case our regression analysis yields biased estimates of the parameters of the equation relating ability and education. However, as shown in footnote 24 when education is the independent variable, it may be possible to correct the estimate on the basis of a regression of IQ on additional education.

On the other hand, the relation between ability and education is not obscured if it is estimated from a sample in which IQ's are

---

Suppose, however, that instead of observing A, we measure IQ where $IQ = A + z$ and where $E(u,z) = E(A,z) = 0$ but $E(S,z) > 0$. If we use ordinary least squares to estimate the equation $S = gIQ + v$, then

$$\text{plim}\,(\hat{g}) = \text{plim}\,\frac{\sum (S,z) + \gamma\sum A^2}{\sum (A^2 + z^2)} \tag{2-5}$$

Hence $\hat{g}$ from Eq. (2-5) will, in the limit, exceed γ provided that

$$\frac{\sum (S,z)}{\sum z^2} > \gamma \tag{2-6}$$

But the left-hand side of Eq. (2-6) can be interpreted as the least squares estimate of λ in the equation $S = \lambda z + v$. Thus our estimate of $\hat{g}$ exceeds or falls short of γ, as λ exceeds or falls short of γ, and not even the direction of the (asymptotic) bias is determinable without further information. However, studies such as Learned and Wood contain information on the change in z due to a change in education, and hence we can estimate λ using first differences. This permits us to determine the sign but not the extent of the statistical bias, which in general requires knowledge about $\sum A^2/\sum (A^2 + z^2)$.

This ambiguity in the sign of the bias is removed if we postulate the relationship as

$$A = \delta S + w \tag{2-7}$$

Once again, we measure A as IQ and regress $IQ = ds$, which yields

$$\text{plim}\,(\hat{d}) = \delta + \text{plim}\,\frac{\sum (S,z)}{\sum S^2} > \delta \tag{2-8}$$

Thus with S as the independent variable, our estimate of δ will be biased upward and $\hat{d}$ can be used as an upper limit of δ. Of course it will be possible to estimate the extent of bias only if $\sum (S,z)/\sum S^2$ is known. But this term is the least squares estimate of Ψ in $z = \Psi S + v$, and as such it measures the contribution of schooling to knowledge of scores on tests. It may be possible to estimate this relationship from data in Learned and Wood.

measured for individuals with the *same* amounts of education at the time of the test.[25] This condition is satisfied by a follow-up survey, in which the individuals' further educational attainment is determined at a later date. Since all the students will have had the same amount of schooling when they are tested, there can be no differences in the IQ scores that are due to differences in years of schooling.

CONCLUSIONS   As indicated earlier in this chapter, we are interested primarily in answering two questions: Did the expansion in college enrollment since 1900 lead to a decline in the average mental ability of college students? Did it lead to a reduction in the loss of talent? A summary of our results follows.

For the first question, we consider the changes over time in the average ability of students who enter college ($\bar{A}_c$) and in the average ability of those high school graduates who do not enter

[25] That is, in terms of the errors-in-variables analysis, the bias arises because z varies between individuals. If z is constant for all individuals, then $(z - \bar{z})$ will be equal to zero for each person, and all sums involving z's will also be zero.

	Sample	Date	$\bar{A}_c$	$\bar{A}_{nc}$	$\bar{A}_c - \bar{A}_{nc}$
TABLE 2-1 *Average mental-ability level of high school*	O'Brien	1925	.54	.47	.07
			.53	.47	.06
graduates who entered, and did not enter,	Benson	1929	.57	.46	.11
			.56	.45	.11
college, in various samples	Barker	1934	.64	.44	.20
			.58	.43	.15
	Phearman	1946	.68	.44	.24
			.63	.43	.20
	Berdie	1950	.62	.42	.20
			.61	.42	.19
	Little	1957	.68	.43	.25
			.62	.40	.22
	Talent	1960	.65	.37	.28
			.63	.35	.28
	Berdie and Hood	1961	.65	.39	.26
			.62	.36	.26

NOTE: The first line for each entry is the value calculated from the sample; the second line is this value adjusted to the United States population as a whole. A detailed discussion of the adjustment method appears in Taubman and Wales (1972*b*, Appendix C).

college $(\bar{A}_{nc})$.[26] We have calculated $\bar{A}_c$ and $\bar{A}_{nc}$ for most of the samples described below.[27] These results for males and females combined are presented in Table 2-1 in both adjusted and unadjusted form, but only the adjusted values are plotted in Figure 2-1. The adjustments are made to take into account the difference between the percent of students entering college in each sample and in the country as a whole. A detailed description of this adjustment method is presented in Taubman and Wales (1972*b*, Appendix C). In the following discussion we use the adjusted estimates. The $\bar{A}_c$ data suggest a mean IQ of about the 53d to the 63d percentile for those who enter college. The highest $\bar{A}_c$ is .63 in the Phearman and Talent studies; the lowest is .53 in the O'Brien study.

The general pattern of $\bar{A}_c$ is as follows:[28] During the 1920s $\bar{A}_c$ was at its lowest value—approximately 55 percent. During the 1930s it rose to about 58 percent, and it reached a peak of 63 percent in 1946. It remained at approximately this level through 1961, although there may have been a slight dip in the early 1950s. (The dip is more pronounced in the unadjusted data.) While $\bar{A}_c$ was changing, there were also shifts in the fraction of high school graduates entering college. In particular, during the 1930s a smaller fraction of high school graduates attended college than in the 1920s, while during the 1950s and 1960s a larger fraction of graduates entered college than in either of these earlier periods. Thus the reduction in college enrollment in the 1930s resulted in an increase in the average quality of college students. However, the postwar boom in higher education resulted in still higher-quality students than in the 1930s, and in substantially higher-quality students than in the 1920s. This result for the 1950s and 1960s is substantiated in Darley (1962), in which the records of college freshmen in specified colleges have been examined.

[26] We define $\bar{A}_c = \Sigma A_i N_i / \Sigma N_i$ and $\bar{A}_{nc} = \Sigma A_i (N^*_i - N_i) / \Sigma (N^*_i - N_i)$. N_i is the fraction of high school graduates in the ith class who entered college times the *population* of high school graduates in the ith class (N^*_i).

[27] For this question the Proctor study is omitted because of its small size, the Yerkes study is omitted because the results are sensitive to the bias correction procedures, and the Wolfle and Smith data are omitted because of the rate-of-response problem noted below.

[28] One qualification of these results is, as discussed below, that they are drawn from studies involving different states. To the extent that there are differences between states in the college-going behavior of the students, the results may be misleading, although our adjustment method attempts to take this into account.

The data suggest a mean IQ of about the 40th percentile for those not entering college. There is a significant downward trend in $\bar{A}_{nc}$ over the period.[29] The value of $\bar{A}_c - \bar{A}_{nc}$, which describes how much more able the college students were, shows a very pronounced upward trend.

On the basis of these data it is apparent that the quality of college students has not declined. In fact, throughout this period of 40 years, during which a substantially greater percentage of high school graduates entered college, it has even noticeably increased. The basic explanation for this phenomenon is analyzed in the loss-of-talent discussion given below, but it can be summarized as follows: In the 1920s only about 60 percent of the most able high school graduates entered college, whereas by the 1960s the corresponding figure was about 90 percent.

To understand how $\bar{A}_c$ has shifted and to study the loss of talent

[29] $\bar{A}_c$ and $\bar{A}_{nc}$ need not move in opposite directions because of differences in their weights.

TABLE 2-2
Fraction of high school graduates entering college at selected ability levels for various samples

Sample	Year	Percentile (A)			
		.25	.50	.75	.90
O'Brien	1925	.27	.36	.45	.51
		.36	.45	.54	.60
Benson	1929	.25	.36	.48	.54
		.34	.45	.57	.63
Barker	1934	.11	.23	.38	.46
		.26	.38	.53	.61
Phearman	1946	.12	.28	.46	.57
		.23	.39	.57	.68
Berdie*	1950	.24	.37	.54	.66
		.25	.38	.55	.67
Little*	1957	.14	.26	.44	.58
		.33	.45	.63	.76
Talent*	1960	.24	.41	.65	.83
		.31	.48	.72	.90
Berdie and Hood*	1961	.21	.37	.59	.74
		.34	.50	.72	.87

NOTE: The first line for each entry is the value calculated from the regression equation; the second line is this value adjusted to the United States population as a whole. A detailed discussion of the adjustment method appears in Taubman and Wales (1972*b*, Appendix C).

* The nonlinear form of the regression equation was used for these samples; the linear form was used for the others. All equations are presented in the detailed discussion of the samples in Taubman and Wales (1972*b*, Appendix A).

in various time periods, we evaluate the equations presented below to determine the fraction of high school graduates entering college (E_{12}) at selected ability levels (A).[30] The selected values of A are .25, .50, .75, and .90. The last point should certainly include those people who are talented, while .75 lies well above the mean IQ percentile of college entrants. The value of .50 is the median of the distribution, though less than $\overline{A}_c$, while .25 is certainly indicative of the less-able students. In Table 2-2 we present the results for various samples in both adjusted and unadjusted form, but in Figure 2-2 we present only the adjusted estimates [31]

These results suggest the following general pattern: At the 90th

[30] We have estimated both linear and nonlinear equations and have used the latter in our calculations when nonlinearities are significant. However, nearly identical results are obtained from the linear equations. Moreover, for the linear equations the results are almost the same whether education or ability is used as the dependent variable.

[31] This adjustment, as in the case of average ability levels, is intended to take into account differences in the percentage continuing in the sample and in the population.

FIGURE 2-2   *Fraction of high school graduates continuing to college at selected percentiles, adjusted*

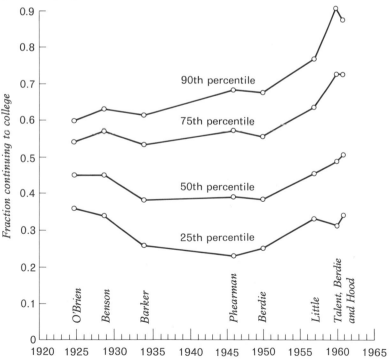

and 75th percentiles, the percentage entering college has increased substantially over time. At the 50th percentile, the 1960 values are slightly higher than those for the 1920s and the values for the 1930s and 1940s are substantially lower. At the 25th percentile, the fraction of high school graduates entering college appears to have fallen during the 1930s and 1940s, but by the 1960s is back to the 1920 level. We do not have exactly comparable data for the pre-World War I era, but the information on men in Yerkes (1921) indicates that the loss in talent (at the various percentiles) for high school graduates was about the same as in the late 1950s. Since less than 10 percent of the population graduated from high school, the loss of talent occurred at earlier educational levels.

As noted above, we estimated both linear and nonlinear equations. In explaining the loss of talent, we find no evidence that the coefficient on the nonlinear term (A^2) is significant in the samples for the period 1920–1940. After the Second World War, however, the coefficient on this variable, which is always positive,

FIGURE 2-3 *Data points from O'Brien sample, 1925*

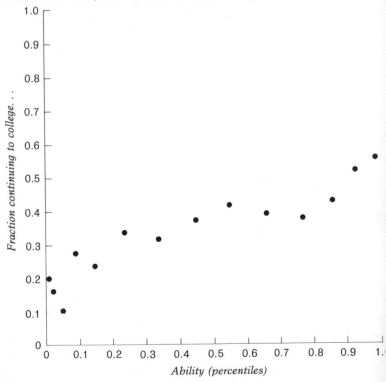

Ability (percentiles)

FIGURE 2-4   *Data points from Project Talent sample, 1960*

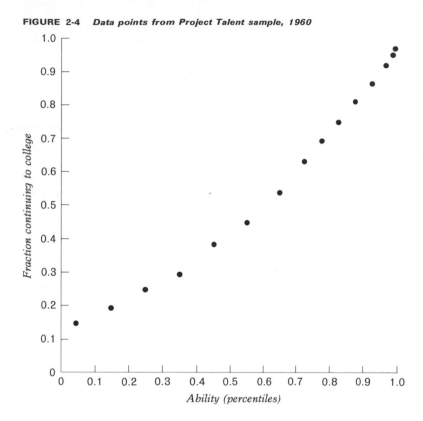

is highly significant. To illustrate the difference between the prewar and postwar periods, we plot in Figures 2-3 and 2-4 (the O'Brien and Talent studies) the actual data points of two representative samples. The nonlinearity in the postwar sample is clearly evident.

On the basis of the percentage who enter college at various IQ levels, it is evident that in the 1950s and 1960s there was less loss of talent than in the 1920s and 1930s. It is interesting to speculate why less talent is lost now than earlier and why the average IQ level of college entrants has risen. To this end we have examined various histories of higher education in the United States, but except for certain comments in Jencks and Riesman (1968), none of these is very explicit on the subject.[32] We suggest that much of the shift occurred because of the changing financial

---

[32] However, the histories indicate that there was a growing trend over time in the amount of undergraduate training required by the traditional professional schools. In addition, many other occupations began to require a formal education as a prerequisite to entrance.

constraints applicable to high school graduates over time. Before World War I very few people completed high school, and very few parents could afford a college education, especially since depressions occurred frequently. In addition, the available data indicate that (for males) college education differed sharply by ability level. The middle to late 1920s was a period of prosperity in which the high school population and the middle and upper classes grew rapidly. Partly because their income permitted it and partly for social reasons, there was a tendency for the children of these groups to attend college.[33] But since the correlation between bright students and wealthy parents was not that high, the distribution of college entrants by IQ was reasonably flat (a low selectivity coefficient). In addition, Jencks and Riesman (1968) argue that in the 1920s colleges as a whole were willing to take any person who applied.

The 1930s generated a whole new set of pressures as income fell, unemployment became rampant, and the high school population continued to expand faster than the population. In the post-World War II era, the percentages of students continuing to college in the upper IQ brackets rose sharply, while those at the bottom rose only slightly. Some possible explanations for this development are that many more middle-class families both could afford to send their above-average children to school and wanted to send them because they believed schooling to be the road for advancement. In addition, the capital markets may have become more perfect with the advent of federal scholarships and loans. Finally, Jencks and Riesman suggest that, starting in the late 1940s, colleges that did not have enough facilities to accommodate the surging demand for space tried to select only the brightest students.[34]

Finally, separate results for males and females are available for some of the samples. The same general pattern over time holds for males and females separately and for the combined sample. The average ability levels of those continuing to college are approximately the same for males and females. As far as the loss of talent is concerned, the fraction of males continuing exceeds that of females at the selected percentiles discussed above, with the

[33] See Goetsch (1940) for a discussion of college-going patterns by parental income.

[34] Jencks and Riesman (1968) argue that the colleges initially assumed the increase in demand to be a temporary phenomenon connected with the GI Bill.

absolute differences becoming larger, the higher the percentile.

For the period prior to the 1930s, we also estimated our equations — with data from Benson (1940) and Yerkes (1921) — for each grade after the sixth. There is a sharp drop in the slope coefficient after the completion of the eighth and twelfth grades. Although average ability increases with educational development, most of the gain occurs from the seventh through the twelfth grades.

References

Abramovitz, M.: A Review Article of E. F. Denison, "Economic Growth in the United States," *American Economic Review*, vol. 52, no. 4, pp. 762–782, September 1962.

Anderson, G. Lester: "What Happens to Minnesota's High School Graduates—Nine Years Later?" *Higher Education in Minnesota*, Minnesota Commission on Higher Education, The University of Minnesota Press, Minneapolis, 1950, pp. 102–115.

Anderson, G. Lester, and T. J. Berning: "What Happens to Minnesota High School Graduates?" *Studies in Higher Education*, University of Minnesota Committee on Educational Research, Biennial Report, 1938–1940, The University of Minnesota Press, Minneapolis, 1941, pp. 15–40.

Astin, Alexander W.: "Undergraduate Achievement and Institutional Excellence," *Science*, vol. 161, pp. 661–667, August 1968.

Barker, Richard W.: "The Educational and Vocational Careers of High School Graduates Immediately following Graduation in Relation to Their Scholastic Abilities," master's thesis, State University of Iowa, Iowa City, 1937.

Becker, Gary S.: *Human Capital: A Theoretical and Empirical Analysis, with Special Reference to Education*, National Bureau of Economic Research, New York, 1964.

Benson, Viola E.: "The Intelligence and Later Scholastic Success of Sixth Grade Pupils," master's thesis, University of Minnesota, Minneapolis, 1940.

Benson, Viola E.: "The Intelligence and Later Scholastic Success of Sixth Grade Pupils," *School and Society*, vol. 55, pp. 163–167, Fall 1942.

Berdie, Ralph F.: *After High School—What?* The University of Minnesota, Minneapolis, 1954.

Berdie, Ralph, et al.: *Who Goes to College? Comparison of Minnesota College Freshmen, 1930–1960*, The University of Minnesota, Minneapolis, 1962.

Berdie, Ralph, and Albert B. Hood: *Trends in Post-High School Plans Over an 11-Year Period,* Cooperative Research Project No. 951, Student Counseling Bureau, University of Minnesota, Minneapolis, 1963.

Bingham, Walter V.: *Aptitudes and Aptitude Testing,* Harper & Row, Publishers, Incorporated, New York, 1937.

Bridgman, Donald S.: "Where the Loss of Talent Occurs and Why," in *The Search for Talent, College Admissions (7),* College Entrance Examination Board, New York, 1960.

Brubacher, John S., and Willis Rudy: *Higher Education in Transition,* Harper & Row, Publishers, Incorporated, New York, 1958.

Corcoran, Mary, and Robert J. Keller: *College Attendance of Minnesota High School Seniors,* A Report Prepared for the Governor's Committee on Higher Education, Minneapolis, January 1957.

Darley, John C.: *Promise and Performance: A Study of Ability and Achievement in Higher Education,* Center for the Study of Higher Education, University of California, Berkeley, 1962.

Denison, Edward F.: *The Sources of Economic Growth in the United States,* Committee for Economic Development, New York, 1961.

Denison, Edward F.: "Measuring the Contribution of Education (and the Residual) to Economic Growth," in *The Residual Factor and Economic Growth,* Organisation for Economic Co-operation and Development, Paris, 1964, pp. 13–55.

DeVane, William C.: *Higher Education in Twentieth-Century America,* Harvard University Press, Cambridge, Mass., 1965

Finch, Frank H.: "Enrollment Increases and Changes in the Mental Level of the High School Population," *Applied Psychology Monograph,* no. 10, 1946.

Folger, John K., and Charles B. Nam: *Education of the American Population,* A 1960 Census Monograph, U.S. Department of Commerce, Washington, 1967.

Fryer, Douglas: "Occupational Intelligence Standards," *School and Society,* vol. 16, pp. 273–277, Sept. 2, 1922.

Goetsch, Helen B.: *Parental Income and College Opportunities,* Contributions to Education No. 795, Bureau of Publications, Teachers College, Columbia University, New York, 1940.

Jencks, Christopher, and David Riesman: *The Academic Revolution,* Doubleday & Company, Inc., Garden City, N.Y., 1968.

Learned, William S., and Ben D. Wood: *The Student and His Knowledge* The Carnegie Foundation for the Advancement of Teaching, Bulletin no. 29, New York, 1938.

Little, James K.: *A State-wide Inquiry into Decisions of Youth about Education beyond High School,* University of Wisconsin, Madison, 1958.

Miller, James C.: *Why the Draft? The Case for a Volunteer Army,* Penguin Books, Inc., Baltimore, 1968.

Morehead, Charles: "What's Happening to Our High School Seniors?" *Journal of Arkansas Education,* vol. 23, April 1950.

Nam, Charles B., and James D. Cowhig: "Factors Related to College Attendance of Farm and Nonfarm High School Graduates: 1960," *Farm Population,* Department of Commerce and Department of Agriculture, Economic Research Service, Census-ERS, series P-27, no. 32, Washington, 1962.

O'Brien, F. P.: "Mental Ability with Reference to Selection and Retention of College Students," *Journal of Educational Research,* vol. 18, no. 2, pp. 136–143, September 1928.

Phearman, L. T.: "Comparisons of High School Graduates Who Go to College with Those Who Do Not Go to College," dissertation, Education Department of the Graduate College of the State University of Iowa, Iowa City, June 1948.

Proctor, William M.: "The Use of Psychological Tests in the Educational and Vocational Guidance of High School Pupils," *Journal of Educational Research Monographs,* no. 1, Public School Publishing Company, Bloomington, Ill., October 1923.

Proctor, William M.: "Intelligence and Length of Schooling in Relation to Occupational Levels," *School and Society,* vol. 42, no. 1093, pp. 783–786, December 1935.

Project Talent: *The American High-School Student,* Cooperative Research Project no. 635, University of Pittsburgh, Pittsburgh, 1964.

Steward, Naomi: "A.G.C.T. Scores of Army Personnel Grouped by Occupation," *Occupations,* vol. 26, pp. 5–41, October 1947.

Taubman, Paul, and Terence Wales: "Education as an Investment and a Screening Device," National Bureau of Economic Research, New York, 1972*a*. (Mimeographed.) To be published as *Higher Education and Earnings,* McGraw-Hill Book Company, New York, 1974.

Taubman, Paul, and Terence Wales: *Mental Ability and Higher Educational Attainment in the 20th Century,* Carnegie Commission on Higher Education, Berkeley, Calif., 1972*b*.

Terman, Lewis M., and Melita H. Oden: *Genetic Studies of Genius,* Stanford University Press, Stanford, Calif., 1947, vol. IV, *The Gifted Child Grows Up.*

Thorndike, Robert L., and E. Hagen: *Ten Thousand Careers,* John Wiley & Sons, Inc., New York, 1959.

Wolfle, Dael: *America's Resources of Specialized Talent,* The Report of the Commission on Human Resources and Advanced Training, Harper & Brothers, New York, 1954.

Wolfle, Dael: "Economies and Educational Values," *The Review of Economics and Statistics,* vol. 42, pp. 178–179, August 1960. (Supplement.)

Wolfle, Dael, and Joseph G. Smith: "The Occupational Value of Education for Superior High-School Graduates," *Journal of Higher Education,* vol. 27, pp. 201–213, April 1956.

Yerkes, R. M. (ed.): "Psychological Examining in the U.S. Army," *Memoirs of the National Academy of Sciences,* Government Printing Office, Washington, 1921.

3. Education, Experience, and the Distribution of Earnings and Employment: An Overview

by Jacob Mincer

by Jacob Mincer

INTRODUCTION This chapter examines the effects of education on particular dimensions of the income derived from labor force (market) activity, where education is viewed as an investment in the stock of human skills or the formation of human "capital." Education can affect earnings rates or earnings per unit period of time worked; it can affect labor force participation, especially at different stages of the life cycle; and it can affect the amounts of time worked as reflected by the frequency and duration of unemployment and part-time employment.

The first part of the chapter is a summary of recently completed research[1] on the relation between the distribution of earnings and the distribution of investments in human capital, including both time and resources used to obtain formal schooling and postschool training on the job. The empirical analysis deals with annual earnings of males, classified by education and age.

In the second part of the chapter, the effects of human capital investment on the distribution of employment are examined. These effects are of some importance for the analysis of annual earnings, since the latter are affected not only by rates of pay per unit of time but also by the amount of time (hours and weeks) worked. The employment effects are viewed as consequences of demand and supply factors, which create individual and group differences in labor force participation and in unemployment.

The third part of the chapter discusses the effects of secular trends in education on the structure and inequality of both individual and family income. The educational trends also contribute to changes in the composition of the labor force that influence the distribution of family income. In general, the first part of the chap-

---

[1] Parts of this chapter draw heavily on the summary chapter of my forthcoming NBER monograph.

ter deals with research that has been completed, whereas the second and third parts report on research still in progress.

A great deal of work on the subject of human capital is devoted to the estimation of profitabilities, volumes, and forms of investment. Empirical calculations are based on comparisons of earnings of workers with differing amounts invested in their human capital. Such calculations follow from the underlying theory that postulates a positive relation between accumulated investments and earnings. The positive and normative importance of the estimated parameters of investment behavior clearly hinges on the degree to which the assumed relation is indeed operative. If the relation between human capital and earnings is a strong one, it should serve as a primary tool for analyzing the structure of earnings and for understanding existing inequalities in labor incomes.

As yet, empirical analyses of income distribution have relied on human capital models only superficially. Direct attempts to relate individual earnings to investments measured in years of schooling show rather weak correlations. The weight attached to human capital analysis cannot rest on such seemingly fragile grounds.[2]

It is important to recognize that schooling is not the only type of investment in human capital, though it is an important early stage in the life cycle of self-investments. Previous estimates (Mincer, 1962) suggest that in terms of costs, the postschool investments of workers who are fully attached to the labor force are not smaller than their schooling investments. Hence the gross relation between schooling and earnings does not adequately represent the human capital earnings function, and this is one reason for the weak empirical correlations.

If we think in life-cycle stages, or contexts in which human capital is built up, the earnings function should include preschool (home) and postschool (job) investments in addition to schooling.[3] In my NBER study (Mincer, 1974) the earnings function was specified to include schooling and postschool investments. Effects of preschool investments were perforce relegated to the unexplained, residual

---

[2] Good scientific practice requires that we not mislabel the ignorance of investigators as "luck" of income recipients.

[3] In reality, the "stages" can and do overlap. The empirical specification of preschool investment requires information on the quantity and quality of the time and other resources parents devote to the upbringing of their children, before or outside formal schooling.

category. To the extent that preschool investments are positively related to schooling and postschool investments, the role of the latter may be exaggerated by the present analysis.

The first task of the study was to derive and estimate the relation between earnings and the accumulated investments in human capital of workers. This human capital earnings function was then applied to answer two questions: (1) How much of the existing inequality in the distribution of labor income can be attributed to individual differences in investment in human capital? (2) Can the intricate yet rather stable patterns of the earnings structure be understood in terms of the behavior of human capital investment?[4]

Though far from precise or complete, the following answers are suggested by the analysis: About 60 percent of the inequality of distribution in the 1959 annual earnings of white urban males can be attributed to the distribution of investments in human capital. Over periods longer than one year, the explanatory power of human capital is likely to be greater. A great deal of the observed structure of earnings is rendered intelligible by the investment analysis, though it is not uniquely predicted by it.[5]

The summary presented below is by no means comprehensive, nor does the exposition follow the sequence or methods of the analysis. The findings are described broadly and somewhat selectively in terms of the three research objectives of the study.

The Earnings Function

If completion of schooling meant completion of investment in human capital, the earnings function would be approximately estimated by a simple regression of earnings (in logs) on years of schooling.[6] As the present study indicates, the observed correlation using this "schooling model" is rather weak. Variation in earnings associated with age is not captured by the schooling model and is, in part, responsible for the low correlation. Though age can be viewed as an inherent depreciation phenomenon in the human capital

---

[4] *Earnings structure* refers to the distribution of aggregate earnings and its partition into schooling and age subgroups. *Patterns* refers to the comparative sets of means and variances and the shapes of the component and aggregate distributions of earnings.

[5] All these findings are derived from the data of the 1/1,000 sample of the 1960 United States census of population. The sample contains individual information for over 30,000 white urban males less than 65 years of age who had some earnings in 1959.

[6] A formal derivation of this result dates back to my unpublished Ph.D. thesis (Mincer, 1957). See also Mincer (1970, Eq. (1a), p. 7).

terminology, the growth of earnings with age is ultimately interpreted in the human capital model as being a consequence of
continued net self-investment activities after the completion of
schooling.

The theory predicts that investments are concentrated at younger
ages, but continue at a diminishing rate throughout much of a person's working life. Because of increasing marginal costs, investments are not incurred all at once in a short period; they are staggered over time and decline continuously—both because benefits
decline as the payoff period shortens and because opportunity costs
are likely to rise with experience. This is true of gross as well as net
investments.

Since earnings are a return on cumulated net investments, they
also rise at a diminishing rate over the working life and decline
when net investment becomes negative, as in old age. The typical

FIGURE 3-1 *Annual earnings of white nonfarm males, 1959*

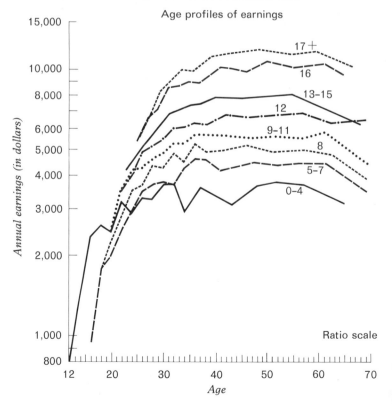

(logarithmic) working-life earnings profile is therefore concave, as illustrated in Figure 3-1. Its rate of growth is a positive function of the amount invested and of the rate of return. Its degree of concavity depends on how rapidly investments decline over time. In effect, the earnings profile is directly proportional to the cumulated investment profile. The magnitude of the cumulated investment is not observable, but is a concave function of experience. Hence, to expand the schooling model into a more complete earnings function, the linear schooling term must be augmented by a nonlinear, concave, years-of-experience term.

This function can be applied in multiple regression analysis to earnings data of individuals who differ in both schooling and age. Although age is not the same as work experience, the latter can be estimated as actual age minus estimated age at completion of schooling (shown in the right panel of Figure 3-1). Clearly, direct

FIGURE 3-1 *(continued)*

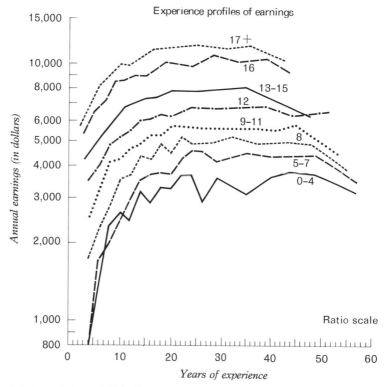

SOURCE: Mincer (1974, Chart 4, p. 68).

information on experience is necessary for specifying earnings functions of individuals whose attachment to the labor force is not continuous.[7]

The form of the earnings function is also of interest. It can be fitted either to dollar earnings or to logs of earnings. In part, this choice depends on whether the focus of interest is on absolute or relative earnings inequalities. However, if dollar values are used, investment variables (schooling and experience) must also be expressed in dollar terms. If they are recorded in units of time—years of schooling and years of experience—the dependent variable, earnings, must be expressed in logs. Given the data restrictions and the focus of interest of this chapter, the logarithmic formulation was used here. Another choice concerns postschool investment as a function of time. Here there is no guidance from theory, except that annual installments of postschool investment—and, *a fortiori,* their "time equivalents"[8]—must decline over the working life. A given form of the investment time profile implies a particular form of the earnings profile. To take the two simplest forms, a linear investment decline implies a parabolic experience function, while an exponential decline of investment ratios gives rise to a type of Gompertz function. The latter yields a somewhat better fit, though such discrimination is rather weak. For the Gompertz curve, a non-declining earnings profile is required—a condition that is satisfied if data are restricted to four decades of working life and to weekly (or hourly) earnings. These conditions are fulfilled in the empirical analyses of annual earnings when weeks worked during the year are used as a standardizing variable.

The two forms of the human capital earnings function used in the analysis are the logarithmic parabola (P) and the Gompertz curve (G):

$$(P)\ lnE_{s,t} = lnE_0 + r_s s + r_p k_0 t - \frac{r_p k_0}{2T} t^2$$

$$(G)\ lnE_{s,t} = lnE_0 + r_s s + \frac{r_p k_0}{\beta} (1 - e^{\beta t})$$

where $E_{s,t}$ is gross annual earnings of a worker with s years of schooling and t years of work experience; r_s and r_p are rates of re-

---

[7] Analysis of female earnings demonstrates dramatically that it is experience rather than age that matters. See Malkiel and Malkiel (1971) and Mincer and Polachek (1973).

[8] The *time equivalent* is the ratio of investment costs to gross earnings. Gross earnings include investment expenditures.

turn on schooling and postschool investments, respectively; k_0 is the investment-income ratio at the start of work experience; β is the annual decline of this ratio; and T is the positive net investment period.

In principle, the earnings function represents a unification of analyses of investment parameters and of income distribution. It provides an analytical expression for the earnings profile as an individual growth curve. Its coefficients are estimates of rates of return and volumes of investment. At the same time, the coefficient of determination of the multiple regression measures the fraction of total earnings inequality (variance of logs) attributable to the measured distribution of investments in human capital.

Note that, in contrast to conventional procedures, the regression procedure for the earnings function makes possible the separation of estimates of rates of return to schooling from the rates on other investment activities. Although in the empirical work, estimates of the rate of return to schooling are produced unambiguously, this is not true of the rate on postschool investments. Rough tests of the difference between these parameters are possible, however, and at the aggregative level of information used here, the null hypothesis of no difference cannot be rejected. Tests can also be performed on the question: Are rates of return different at different schooling levels? The results indicate that rates decline as schooling level rises, although this is not true when hourly or weekly rather than annual earnings are considered.

The earnings function approach also makes it possible to study the relation between schooling and postschool investments. In dollar volumes, the relation is found to be positive. This finding is consistent with a notion of complementarity between the two investment forms, but it does not prove it. The positive correlation may mean simply that in comparing individual lifetime investment programs, the scale of investment varies more than its composition. Logically, individuals should substitute one form of investment for the other, given the comparative advantages of the two forms of investment and a differing relative price structure for each. Yet, because of similar ability and opportunity constraints in schooling and in job training, individuals tend to invest more or less in both. Evidently, scale effects outweigh the substitution effects.

It should be noted that although the more educated put more resources into postschool investments, they do not spend more time at it. The investment-earnings ratio would measure the amount of time (in years) spent in investment (training) activity, provided only expenditures of time were involved. On the average, the correlation between time equivalents (investment-earnings ratios) of school and postschool investments appears to be negligible. The opportunity cost of an hour is, of course, greater at higher levels of schooling; hence the positive correlation between dollar volumes of investment when time volumes are uncorrelated.

The Gompertz curve is a familiar empirical representation of industrial growth. That it fits an individual growth curve is no mere coincidence, since the staggered investment interpretation is suitable in both cases. There is a widespread view that differs with this interpretation of individual earnings growth. According to this view, the individual earnings curve is intrinsically an age phenomenon; it reflects productivity changes due to inherent biological and psychological maturation, leveling off early and declining much later because of declining physical and intellectual vigor.

There is evidence, however, to indicate that this inherent age factor affects earnings only to a minor degree. In data where age and work experience are statistically separable, the earnings curve is found to be mainly a function of experience, not of age, in terms of both its location in the life cycle and the sizes and signs of its growth rates. Earnings profiles differ by occupation, sex, and color in systematic ways not attributable to the phenomena of aging. What is sometimes thought to be an alternative interpretation of experience as learning and of the earnings profiles as "learning curves" is not at all inconsistent with the human capital investment interpretation, provided it is agreed that learning in the labor market is not costless. Even if there exist apparently costless differential opportunities for "learning by doing" among jobs, competition tends to equalize the net returns, thereby imposing opportunity costs on such learning.

Accounting for Income Inequality As noted before, if only years of schooling are used in the earnings function, the correlation between years of schooling and log-earnings of males of working age is less than 10 percent. This does not mean, however, that schooling is unimportant. In part, the correlation is low because direct costs in schooling and related quality aspects of education are not well measured by a mere counting of school years. Moreover, the effects of postschool investments, when not explicitly specified, obscure the effects of schooling on earnings.

If postschool investments are important and differ among individuals, the distribution of earnings will be increasingly affected by returns to accumulating postschool investments as the number of years of experience increases. If postschool investments are not strongly correlated with schooling, the correlation between schooling and earnings will continuously decline with the passage of years of experience. In fact, the correlation between time equivalents (for a definition, see footnote 8) of school and postschool investment is weak, and the correlation between log-earnings and years of schooling declines continuously after reaching an initially strong coefficient of determination of one-third before the first decade of experience is over.

Theoretically, the correlation between earnings and schooling would be highest at the outset of work experience, if postschool investment costs were included as part of income. Although such initial gross earnings are not observable, the distribution of observed net earnings six to nine years later is likely to resemble the distribution of initial gross earnings. Net earnings are less than gross earnings, but both rise as postschool investments cumulate. After some years, therefore, net earnings begin to exceed the level of initial gross earnings. This "overtaking point" is reached after, at most, $1/r$ years of experience, where r is the rate of return to postschool investments. Hence, this point is reached before the first decade of experience is over. This is also the approximate time when we observe the highest correlation between earnings and schooling.

The coefficient of determination (.33) between schooling and earnings within the overtaking subset of the earnings distribution represents an estimate of the fraction of earnings inequality that is attributable to differences in years of schooling, since earnings are then least affected by postschool investments. The inequality of earnings at overtaking is about 75 percent of aggregate inequality, which suggests that the distribution of schooling accounts for 25 percent of the total variance (.33 $\times$ .75). Fifty percent of aggregate inequality, measured by the variance of logs of annual earnings, is attributable to the joint distributions of schooling and postschool investments.[9] The 50 percent figure is an understatement, however, since actual rather than time-equivalent years of schooling were used. The actual count of years fails to reflect either

---

[9] The aggregate log-variance of earnings in 1959 was .68. It was .51 in the overtaking set. The residual variance from the regression of log-earnings on schooling was .34 in the overtaking set. On the assumption of homoscedasticity of residuals from the earnings function, the "explained" variance in the aggregate is (.68 $-$ .34) $=$ .34, which is half of total inequality.

the variation in expenditures of time and money among students attending schools of the same quality or quality differences among schools. An upward correction of the variance of schooling investments to take account of such individual differences raises the explanatory power of schooling to about one-third of the aggregate and raises the joint effects of school and postschool investments to about 60 percent.

These conclusions are based on econometric analyses in which the earnings function was fitted to the microdata of the 1/1,000 sample (Mincer, 1974, Table 10). Even with the use of only two variables—years of schooling and years of experience, where years of schooling are unadjusted for quality and time equivalents of experience are assumed the same for all persons—the explanatory power of the earnings function compares favorably with results of statistical studies of comparable microdata that employ a large number of explanatory variables on a more or less ad hoc basis.[10]

It appears that the substantive conclusions about the quantitative and qualitative importance of human capital investments in the distribution of earnings are not much affected when the population coverage is expanded from white urban males to all males in 1959 or is changed from (male) persons to family units.

The Earnings Structure

Several prominent features of the "skill" (schooling and experience) structure of earnings appear rather stable in temporal and regional comparisons. Aggregative skewness and the growth of inequality with age are the best known. To these we may add patterns of variances and patterns of age profiles of variances within schooling groups which are less familiar and perhaps also less stable.

None of these features is inevitable. Yet—perhaps surprisingly, given the human capital model—they all can be explained by the correlation between the stock of human capital at any stage in the life cycle and the volume of subsequent investment. That this correlation is positive in dollar terms is understandable if individual differences in ability and opportunity affecting investment behavior tend to persist over much of the life cycle. The positive correlation between schooling and postschool investment is an example of such behavior.

Several implications of this positive correlation in dollar terms

[10] See, for example, Jencks et al. (1972).

are observable. Dollar profiles of earnings "fan out" with experience and, *a fortiori,* with age, both across and within school groups. Dollar variances therefore increase with experience and with age. Similarly, because the dispersion of dollar schooling costs increases with the level of schooling, variances of earnings increase with level of schooling. Since mean earnings increase with age and with schooling, there is a positive correlation between means and variances in age and schooling subgroups of the earnings distribution. This correlation contributes to the appearance of positive skewness in the aggregate earnings distribution. This factor is independent of, and in a way more basic than, the shape of the distribution of schooling, which also contributes to the positive skewness of earnings. The change in the distribution of schooling from a positive to a negative skew during the past two decades implies that the distribution of schooling is no longer an important factor in explaining the persistence of positive skewness in the distribution of earnings. Indeed, the 1959 distribution of earnings at the overtaking stage of the life cycle is no longer skewed. The aggregate distribution, however, remains positively skewed.

If we define relative skill differentials in wages by percentage differentials in wage rates among schooling groups at comparable years of experience, we find that these are practically invariant over the working life. Since the logarithmic experience profiles of wages are concave, this finding implies that relative wage differentials among schooling groups increase with age. However, *within* schooling groups, relative wage differentials, measured by variances of logs, show different profiles depending on the level of schooling. As Figure 3-2 shows, the experience profile is clearly U-shaped for the high school group, which is at the center of the schooling distribution. The profile for the group with higher schooling mainly increases, whereas the profile for the lower schooling group decreases and becomes approximately horizontal.

It can be shown (Mincer, 1974, Part II, Ch. 4) that both the intergroup wage differentials and the inequality patterns within the middle levels of schooling reflect a negligible correlation between postschool earning capacity and time-equivalent postschool investment. The same absence of correlation underlies the previously noted invariance of experience profiles of relative wage differentials among schooling groups. The phenomenon arises if experience profiles of postschool investments, in time-equivalent units, are not systematically different among schooling groups. Put another

FIGURE 3-2 *Experience profiles of log-variances of 1959 earnings of males (schooling groups: 8, 12, 16)*

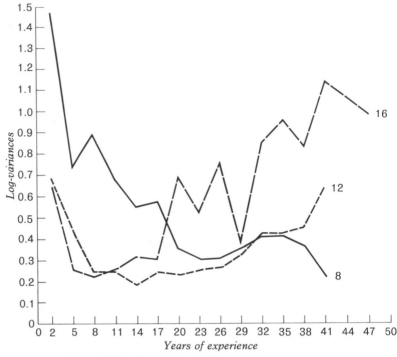

SOURCE: Mincer (1974, Chart 6.2, p. 104).

way, it arises when the elasticity of postschool investments (in dollars) with respect to postschool earning capacity is, on the average, unitary. At the same time, the correlation between postschool investments and earning capacity, and the corresponding elasticity, apparently increases with schooling level.

The central tendency of the elasticities and the systematic positive relation between schooling level and elasticity of investment with respect to earning capacity raise questions for further research. In this connection, it is noteworthy and suggestive that very similar patterns are found in studying the consumption function. The "long-run" elasticity of saving with respect to income is not clearly different from unity, and the "short-run" or cross-sectional elasticity increases with schooling level (see the chapter by Solmon in this volume).

The differential patterns of log-variances by schooling level can also be analyzed by age. The ranking of log-variances of earnings is inverse to schooling level at young ages and positive at older ages. Also, the age-schooling profiles of absolute and relative wage distributions aggregate to the well-known "leptokurtic" shape, with a skewness that is positive in dollars and negative in logarithms. Together with some observation on correlations of earnings of respondents in a 1959 survey of a Consumers Union panel,[11] the distinctive profiles of relative variances constitute strong evidence for the human capital theories and against the purely stochastic theories of income distribution. Systematic rather than chance variation is the dominant component of individual earnings histories and of individual differences in earnings.

HUMAN CAPITAL AND THE DISTRIBUTION OF EMPLOYMENT

The data show that the more educated and experienced workers enjoy larger annual earnings than their less-skilled fellows for two reasons: Their wage rates per hour are higher, and the amount of time they spend in gainful employment during the year is greater. Consequently, inequality in the distribution of annual earnings exceeds the inequality in the distribution of wage rates.

Part of the individual variation in weeks and hours of work during a given year is unrelated to human capital characteristics. Estimates suggest, however, that as much as half of the variation can be attributed to human capital differentials. Since close to one-third of the inequality in annual earnings is attributable to the distribution of time worked, about 15 percent can be ascribed to effects of human capital on the distribution of employment. Though this is a description of average effects in the male labor force, the effects differ systematically by schooling and experience. In particular, the relative importance of employment compared with that of wage rate effects is greater at lower levels of schooling as well as at older ages. At lower levels of schooling the impact of education and job experience is about equally divided between gains in wage rates and gains in employment stability. In contrast, the effects at higher levels of education are accounted for largely by gains in pay rates.[12]

On the average, no more than half of the differences in time spent in employment are due to unemployment. Differentials in labor force participation and in unemployment are therefore of roughly

---

[11] Mincer (1974, Table 14). For a description of the data sources, see Juster (1964, App. C).

[12] The long hours of work reported by some highly trained professionals such as physicians and business executives are the well-known exceptions.

equal importance in understanding the effects of human capital on the distribution of employment.

Theoretically, the employment effects of human capital can originate on both the demand and the supply sides of the labor market. Of course, the demand-supply distinction is not to be equated with the statistical categories of unemployment and of out-of-the-labor-force status. For example, unemployment often originates in layoff, but it also occurs in the course of job quitting and of labor force entry or reentry.

Labor Supply Effects   Effects of education and other training on the amount of time individuals allocate to the labor market derive, in part, from the increase in market earning power resulting from education. Education may also affect the allocation of time by affecting tastes and productivities in nonmarket activities. If education raises market earning power more than it raises productivity in nonmarket activities, the opportunity cost of nonmarket time increases—which tends to increase the time devoted to earning activities. Against this, however, must be balanced the resultant increase in income, which is likely to increase the demand for consumption time or leisure. It may be argued that lifetime income or wealth, rather than current income, is the appropriate income variable in labor supply functions. Wealth does not necessarily increase as a result of education, even if wages increase. If the rate of return to investment in education is equal to a competitive market interest rate, wealth is not augmented by investment, and income effects are nil. If rates of return are higher, wealth is increased, but at a rate lower than the wage rate.[13] As long as rates of return are not exorbitant, substitution effects may well dominate, resulting in more time devoted to the labor market by the more educated and experienced workers.

In part, then, the longer hours per week and greater labor force participation of the more educated may be explained by a possible dominance of the substitution variable in the labor supply function, that is, by their greater market earning power. Note that this is not inconsistent with a "backward-bending" labor supply hypoth-

---

[13] If w_2 is the wage rate of a worker who has s_2 years of schooling and if w_1 is the wage rate of another worker who has s_1 years of schooling, a simple human capital model suggests that $ln\ w_2 - ln\ w_1 = r\ (s_2 - s_1)$, where r is the rate of return to schooling. Let $r = r_0 + \Delta r$, where r_0 is the market rate. Then $ln\ w_2 - ln\ w_1 = r_0\ (s_2 - s_1) + \Delta r\ (s_2 - s_1)$. The percentage increase in wealth is given by the second term on the right. Therefore, the elasticity of wealth with respect to the wage rate is $\Delta r / r < 1$.

esis, according to which hours of work are expected to decline if wealth increases as rapidly as the wage rate. The latter condition and the decline in hours are observed in historical time series, but not in the cross-sectional education-related wage structure.

Essentially the same analysis applies to life-cycle changes in the labor supply of individuals. With a wealth level that, on the average, does not change much during the working life, hours of work and labor force participation grow as the wage rate grows. When depreciation begins to outstrip gross investment in human capital as a consequence of aging and/or obsolescence, the wage rate begins to decline. The decline in hours of work and in labor force participation begins about that time also.[14]

Since the work experience of more educated persons begins some years later than that of persons with less education and since their postschool investments are no smaller, it is not surprising that the more educated retire later in life. Their much higher labor force participation rate in later stages of life, such as in the 60-to-69 age group (Bowen & Finegan, 1969), is to a large extent simply the obverse of their much lower market work rates at ages 15 to 24, when most of them are still in school. In other words, when comparisons are made by years of experience rather than age, the differences in participation rates are small throughout the working life.

In sum, labor supply functions may explain why hours of work and labor force participation increase with education and why the more educated retire later in life but do not have a longer working life in terms of years. The observed positive correlation between education and employment, however, does not prove the dominance of substitution in cross-sectional labor supply functions, even if the attenuation of income effects is true. Other factors which help to account for the observed correlation are health differentials and differences in demand conditions and in job turnover, to mention a few. The empirical sorting out of these factors has barely begun.

A much stronger case for the labor supply hypothesis as an explanation of education-associated differences in employment can be made for the observed differences among women. Their strong substitution responses in the allocation of time between market and home are an accepted explanation of the historical growth of

---

[14] The decline in hours precedes the decline in wage rates. Therefore, annual earnings decline before wage rates do. A detailed analysis of these lags is contained in current NBER research by Becker and Ghez (in press).

the female labor force. The differences in hours and weeks of market work among educational groups are much larger among women than among men, but it does not appear that this is due to greater health, demand, or job turnover differences among women with different educational levels.

As shown in Figure 3-3, the age profiles of female labor force participation rates are a great deal higher for more educated women. In all groups, participation declines when family demand for work at home increases: there are pronounced withdrawals from the labor market in all educational groups when there are young children in the family. The interesting finding is that the more educated women, who otherwise spend more time in the labor market, reduce their market work to take care of their children, particularly their preschoolers, more than do women with less education.[15]

If the quantity and opportunity cost of the mother's time, which was shifted from market to home, represents dimensions of what I

[15] These findings are the focus of current research at NBER by Arleen Leibowitz. See Chap. 7 in this volume.

FIGURE 3-3 *Education and labor force status of women, United States, 1960*

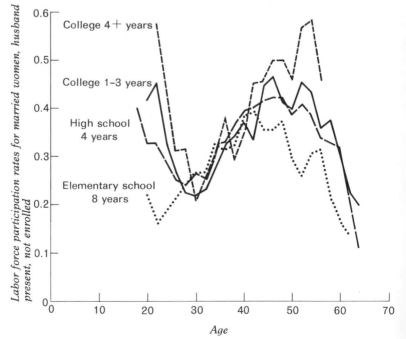

SOURCE: Leibowitz (1972).

call "preschool" investments to human capital of children, these findings may serve as an empirical basis for the expansion of the human capital earnings function. The expanded function may contribute to the explanation of phenomena such as the importance of family background in children's school performance and the positive correlation between the educational attainment of children and that of their parents, particularly the mother. Whether these preschool investments have an independent effect on earnings, beyond affecting school attainment of the child, can be answered only by the expanded human capital earnings function. In any case, the greater earnings—and, presumably, also consumption capacities—of children may be viewed in the family context as a part of the return on the education of mothers. If so, the profitability of educating women may be understated by inferring it from their own earnings alone.

Unemployment Differentials

The time workers supply to the labor market exceeds the actual time they spend in employment by the amount of unemployment they experience. In part, the reduced employment of the less educated is attributable to the greater amount of unemployment they experience.

In studying unemployment differentials, decisions of employers and of workers must be considered. On the supply side, the greater the frequency with which workers enter, reenter, and leave the labor force or change jobs, the greater the frictional unemployment they encounter in the process. Much of the unemployment of married women and of students is attributable to their "dual job holding" with frequent seasonal, and otherwise induced, mobility between nonmarket and market activities. This inter-labor force mobility is clearly a more important explanation of the inverse relation between education and unemployment among women than among men, since education has a stronger effect on labor force attachment of women than of men.

On the demand side, differences in unemployment among education and skill groups occur for several reasons:

1 Industries differ in the degree of skill and education of their work forces. The volatility of demand for labor and the consequent labor turnover and unemployment are, in part, related to the volatility of final consumer demand, which differs by industry. For example, the demand for services is more stable than the demand for durables, construction, and capital

goods. On the whole, though the correlation is weak, the more educated workers are employed in the more stable industries.

This correlation appears to be somewhat stronger for women than for men.

2   A more basic demand factor in creating skill differentials in unemployment results from complementarity and substitution relations between labor and capital in the production process. There is limited evidence, observed in some sectors of the economy, that physical capital is more easily substitutable for unskilled than skilled labor. If short-run fluctuations in output are produced with relatively fixed physical capital, the employment of unskilled labor must fluctuate more than that of skilled labor. Consequently, the less educated in the labor force are observed to have higher layoff rates and unemployment rates in the cross section and greater amplitudes of them during the business cycle.

3   A third factor which operates jointly on the demand and supply side of the labor market is the specificity of training and experience workers acquire on the job. Employers invest resources in hiring, training, and experience of employees to the extent that the resulting increases in productivity are realized in their firms rather than elsewhere. In order to guard against capital losses resulting from quits and layoffs, it is mutually advantageous for employers and workers to share the cost of such investments (Becker, 1964).

Specifically trained workers earn more than they would in alternative employments, but less than their marginal products in the firm. Consequently, such workers are more reluctant to quit, and their employers are less inclined to lay them off. This structure of labor turnover implies reduced frictional and, to some extent, cyclical unemployment. Insofar as specific postschool investments are related to educational attainment, they are a factor in the unemployment differentials observed by education. Worker self-investments appear to increase roughly in proportion to investments in schooling. This positive relation between schooling and postschool investment can be explained by common selective factors of opportunity, ability, and motivation. Employers, in turn, tend to invest more in the more educated workers, either because specificity is more likely in more complex jobs or because they think education confers a greater capacity and motivation for training.

Though geographic mobility increases, quit rates diminish as education increases. Both phenomena are consistent with the specific training hypothesis and cannot be explained by capital complementarities. However, educational differences in layoff rates and in length of job tenure with the same employer are consistent with both hypotheses. It should be noted that unemployment differentials implied by the complementarity hypothesis are directly linked to education. Those resulting from specific training are more properly attributed to specific postschool investments, not to school education.

4   Unemployment is affected not only by the incidence of job separation but also by its duration; duration of unemployment is inversely related to education. The probable reasons are the educated worker's greater efficiency of search time and the employer's greater investment in finding him. The greater efficiency is a result of greater incentives and capacity to acquire information by using financial and other resources rather than one's own time. The greater employer search cost reflects greater specificity of job training at higher levels of schooling, as well as greater concern for individual differences in worker quality.

5   The complementarity hypothesis suggests that in the process of economic growth, defined by growth of physical capital per unit of labor, the demand grows more rapidly for skilled labor than for unskilled labor. If the upgrading of skills does not proceed rapidly enough, above-equilibrium rates of return and greater-than-average unemployment at lower skill levels may persist. Though rates of return to education apparently declined during the first half of this century and remained roughly stable thereafter, there is no clear evidence that education-related unemployment differentials have shown any corresponding changes in the long run. The shortage of good data inhibits strong statements, but these findings tend to cast doubt on the notion of perennial skill shortages.

6   A variety of institutional factors may account for differences in unemployment and labor force participation among educational groups. Minimum wages on the demand side, and income maintenance programs on the supply side, tend to price low-quality labor out of the market. Inexperienced and uneducated workers whose market wage is less than the minimum wage have higher unemployment and reduced labor force participation.

Income maintenance programs such as welfare payments and old-age pensions under Social Security were designed to benefit mainly the low-earning, usually least-educated population. A recognition that these programs contained some disincentives to work led to their liberalization; some additional earnings were allowed without reducing benefits. One consequence of liberalization is an increase in intermittent labor force participation, with attendant frictional unemployment.

Seasonal workers are generally less skilled and educated than the average worker. The unemployment compensation system encourages seasonal work and converts the reported status of some from "out of the labor force" to "unemployed." This does not necessarily affect earnings, but it may do so if it converts employment into unemployment by discouraging seasonal dovetailing.

In conclusion, it is worth noting, particuarly from a policy point of view, that unless the complementarity hypothesis is of some importance, the greater stability of employment of more educated people is not directly attributed to schooling in this analysis, though it is related to human capital investment and education in a broader sense.

SECULAR TRENDS IN EDUCATION AND INCOME INEQUALITY The inequality in the distribution of earnings is affected primarily by the dispersion in the amounts of human capital invested and by the average magnitude and the dispersion in the rates of return.

If skills are measured by time equivalents of investment in human capital, skill differentials in wages change in proportion to the rates of return.[16] If the upgrading of skills persistently lagged behind increasing demands, the rate of return would rise, whereas improved capital markets, public subsidies, and consumption-motivated investment would tend to depress the rates.

The narrowing of income inequality over the first half of this century is consistent with apparent declines in rates of return;[17] with increased income, which permitted financing and increased consumption demands; and with the growth of publicly financed education, primarily at lower levels of schooling. In the past two decades the rate of return and inequality remained roughly stable, even though the trends in income and public financing continued to grow.[18] The suggestion is implicit that there was a countervailing growth of the demand for skills by industry.

Growth of schooling appears to be associated with a decline in the dispersion and in the skewness of the distribution of schooling. The latter is an arithmetic phenomenon due to a finite and often

---

[16] Time-equivalent units are basically not comparable over time unless there is no productivity growth in the creation of human capital. If productivity grows, a unit (say, one year of schooling) today represents a larger increment of skill than in the past.

If Δh is difference in skill and if w_2 and w_1 are the wage rates at higher and lower skill levels, rate of return is

$$r = \frac{\ln w_2 - \ln w_1}{\Delta h}$$

[17] For fragmentary evidence, see Becker (1964, pp. 131–135).

[18] The extension of public financing to higher levels of schooling, however, may widen inequality, as some recent research suggests.

legislated limit on years of schooling. The decreased dispersion in the distribution of schooling may well be a lagged effect of the narrowing inequality of parental income that was observed before 1950. It probably resulted also from governmental subsidies and the spread of compulsory schooling, child labor laws, and minimum wage laws, all of which shortened the lower tail of the schooling distribution. The distribution of earnings within age groups in current data reflects the effects of a mild secular narrowing in the dispersion of schooling and of a stronger reduction in its skewness.

Aside from the change in the shape of the schooling distribution, the continuing growth of education contributes to a reduced inequality of earnings.

The meaning of the upward trends in education is that the level of education is higher in young than in old age groups. This offsets, in part, the age variation in earnings, which is due to the growth of experience with age. Another consequence is that the relative numerical importance of the young and least-educated and the old and most-educated groups becomes smaller, the more rapid the upward educational trends. But these are precisely the groups within which the inequality in earnings is largest. Therefore, the stronger the upward trend in schooling, the smaller the aggregate inequality. It can be shown that if growth in schooling ceased and the distribution of schooling in each age group remained the same as among young earners with less than a decade of work experience, inequality in the cross section as measured by the logarithmic variance would increase by close to 10 percent.

Secular trends in education also affect the distribution of income indirectly via effects on the composition of the labor force and the resulting distribution of employment. The lengthening of schooling and increased enrollment produced a growing intermittent student labor force. The growth of education of women contributed to a growing female labor force whose participation is partial. The resulting cyclical and seasonal sensitivity of the labor force and the updrift in frictional unemployment have been commented upon by labor economists. As far as the distribution of income is concerned, the growing relative importance of the "secondary" labor force widens the dispersion of employment, a factor which tends to widen the inequality of annual earnings.

Although the inequality of *personal* earnings among all earners, including men, women, and teenagers, is of interest, attention to inequality among *family units* is prompted by considerations of economic welfare and of consumption behavior. Effects of the education-induced changes in the labor force are best understood by considering the family context of earning activities. The greater the earning power of a family member, the greater the incentives to participate in the labor force. However, the greater the earnings of other family members and the greater the family nonemployment income, the weaker the tendency to work in the labor market.

The positive correlation between educational attainments of husband and wife is a force in the direction of greater inequality among families than among family heads. However, the "income effect" works in the opposite direction. It dominates particularly in families where the employment of the primary earner is unstable. It appears, on balance, that the existence and growth of a secondary labor force, which is partially induced by the growth of education, contributed not only to the widening of dollar dispersion but also to the narrowing of relative inequality among families.[19]

In conclusion, it is important to note that the secular growth in education, the narrowing of its distribution, and the growth of labor force participation of women have rather small effects on income inequality *insofar as they do not affect rates of return to investments in human capital.* If the secular upgrading of education continues at a steady rate, there are no effects: only acceleration of trends produces changes in inequality. At the same time, unless accompanied by similar reductions in the dispersion of all forms of human capital, even large reductions in the dispersion of schooling produce small changes in inequality. In contrast, changes in rates of return transmitted throughout the economy do affect income inequality almost proportionately.[20]

References

Becker, Gary S.: *Human Capital: A Theoretical and Empirical Analysis with Special Reference to Education,* National Bureau of Economic Research, New York, 1964.

Becker, Gary S., and G. R. Ghez: *The Allocation of Time and Goods over the Life Cycle,* National Bureau of Economic Research, 1974.

Bowen, W., and T. Finegan: *Economics of Labor Force Participation,* Princeton University Press, Princeton, N.J., 1969.

[19] Unrelated individuals are here excluded from the definition of a family.

[20] These conclusions are based on research by Chiswick and myself (Chiswick & Mincer, 1972).

Chiswick, Barry, and J. Mincer: "Time-Series Changes in Personal Income Inequality in the U.S. from 1939, with Projections to 1985," *Journal of Political Economy,* vol. 80, part 2, pp. 534–566, May–June 1972.

Jencks, Christopher, et al.: *Inequality,* Basic Books, Inc., Publishers, New York, 1972.

Juster, F. T.: *Anticipations and Purchases,* National Bureau of Economic Research, New York, 1964.

Leibowitz, A.: "Education and the Allocation of Women's Time," Ph.D. thesis, Columbia University, New York, 1972.

Malkiel, J., and D. Malkiel: "Sex Differentials in Earnings," Princeton University Press, Princeton, N.J., 1971.

Mincer, J.: *A Study of Personal Income Distribution,* unpublished Ph.D. thesis, Columbia University, New York, 1957.

Mincer, J.: "On the Job Training: Costs, Returns, and Some Implications," *Journal of Political Economy,* vol. 70, part 2, pp. 50–79, Supplement: October 1962.

Mincer, J.: "The Distribution of Labor Incomes: A Survey with Special References to the Human Capital Approach," *Journal of Economic Literature,* vol. 8, pp. 1–27, March 1970.

Mincer, J.: *Schooling, Experience, and Earnings,* National Bureau of Economic Research, 1974. Distributed by Columbia University Press, New York.

Mincer, J., and S. Polachek: "Family Investments in Human Capital: Earnings of Women," presented at Population Conference, Chicago, June 1973, *Journal of Political Economy,* April 1974.

4. Education as an Investment and a Screening Device

by Paul Taubman and Terence Wales

INTRODUCTION A cursory examination of studies based on census data reveals that earnings increase with education and that the social rate of return to education is at least equal to the return available to society on other investments (Becker, 1964; H. Miller, 1960). The proposition that education can be treated as an investment in human capital has proved to be powerful and illuminating in its own right and to be a major ingredient in studies of the sources of economic growth and the distribution of income (Becker, 1964; Denison, 1964; H. Miller, 1960; Schultz, 1963). Central to all these studies are two testable hypotheses. First, the (observed or adjusted) differences in earnings by educational level represent the net effect of education, rather than some other personal characteristics that have not been held constant. Second, these differences in earnings represent increases in productivity produced by education.

It has long been recognized that systematic differences in earnings may not be due solely to differences in educational attainment (Becker, 1964; Wolfe & Smith, 1956) and that the omission of a variable positively correlated with education and with a separate and positive influence on earnings biases the education coefficient upward. Many people have hypothesized that, in particular, the omission of mental ability and family background will result in such a bias. Although attempts have been made in a number of studies to standardize for family background and other determi-

NOTE: This study was partially financed through the NBER by a grant from the Carnegie Commission on Higher Education. While we have benefited greatly from discussions with many colleagues at the NBER and our universities, we especially wish to thank F. T. Juster and R. Summers for their long and patient discussions. Also, as the reader will soon realize, this study would not have been possible without the aid of R. Thorndike, to whom we are most grateful.

nants of earnings, no studies of education based on large samples contain the relevant earnings, ability, and education information.[1] Therefore, our first goal was to obtain good estimates of the rate of return to education at various ability and educational levels. Because of data limitations, specific estimates were restricted to returns for higher education, i.e., education beyond the twelfth grade. For the same reasons, only the education of males was considered.

Most studies of the rate of return to education are based on the premise that differences in earnings at different educational levels arise because of the various cognitive and affective skills produced by education. However, this need not be the case. The differentials might arise because the lack of educational credentials is a barrier to entry to high-paying occupations. If this is the case, the social rate of return to education is lower than the private rate, ignoring costs involved in other methods of sorting people.

Although many people have suggested that a primary role of education is to serve as a screening, certification, or licensing device, we are aware of no research in which an attempt has been made to separate the earnings differences due to productivity gains from those due to screening. Our second goal, therefore, was to examine the hypothesis that education adds to income by screening people with low education out of high-paying occupations.

A new and extremely rich data source allowed us to obtain substantially improved estimates of the (private and social) return to higher educational attainment and make crude estimates of the effect of screening on earnings differentials.

In brief, our findings, all of which are subject to qualifications as given in the text, are the following: First, the realized (real) rate of return—ignoring consumption and nonmonetary benefits—to the college dropout or graduate is 7½ to 9 percent and does not

---

[1] Studies for the United States include Ashenfelter and Mooney (1968); Becker (1964); Bridgman (1930); Cutright (1969); Duncan et al. (1968); Griliches and Mason (1972); Hansen, Weisbrod, and Scanlon (1970); Hause (1972); Hunt (1963); Morgan and David (1963); Rogers (1967); Weisbrod and Karpof (1968); and Wolfle and Smith (1956). Except for one segment of the Hause study, each of these studies suffers from one or more of the following serious problems: poor measures of education and ability, small and inadequate sample size, improper statistical technique, or too specialized a sample to permit the formation of generalizations. In addition, only the Rogers study contains enough data to permit estimation of a rate of return, as opposed to simply studying income differentials at a given age. The portion of the Hause study that is based on our sample is discussed below.

vary with the level of mental ability. If we ignore the screening hypothesis, the private and social rates of return are approximately the same. Second, certain types of mental ability and various personal characteristics are as important as education in determining earnings, and omission of these variables biases education coefficients upward by up to 35 percent. Finally, and more tentatively, there is evidence consistent with the hypothesis that education is used as a screening device and that up to one-half of (net) earnings differentials are due to such screening.

Two caveats are in order. First, since this study is based primarily on a population that is much brighter and better educated than average, our results need not apply to the United States population as a whole. Second, because of space limitations, we do not fully document all our assertions here. For more details the interested reader should consult our larger manuscript (Taubman & Wales, forthcoming). Appendix A contains a more complete description of the sample, the follow-up procedures, etc.

Analysis of the NBER-TH Data

In our regressions, we relate earnings in a particular year to a large set of explanatory variables, nearly all of which are zero-one dummy variables. By breaking up the independent variables into discrete categories (for example, eight education classes) we allow for nonlinear effects, and by combining dummies we allow for interactions.[2] As noted earlier, there are scores on 17 ability tests for each person. Factor analysis indicates that four orthogonal factors could be extracted from these scores, two of which quite clearly represent spatial perception and physical coordination and the other two of which we treat as measuring mathematical and verbal ability.[3] We divide the factors into fifths and use a separate dummy for each interval because the effect of ability need not be linear. The main regression equations for both 1955 and 1969—including such measures as t-statistics, R^2, and standard errors—appear in Appendix B. The equations, estimated by ordinary least squares, include measures of education, mathematical ability, personal biography,

---

[2] Thus our functional form incorporates the one advocated by Mincer (1970). However, the use of log earnings could still be justified to eliminate heteroscedasticity.

[3] The factor loadings of the tests are given in Appendix B, whereas the tests themselves are discussed in Thorndike and Hagen (1959). Thorndike believes our mathematical factor is close to IQ while the verbal factor contains too heavy a mechanical skills component to be identified.

health, marital status, father's education, and age; to account for nonpecuniary rewards such as shorter work year, they also include a dummy variable for teachers.[4] Nearly all these variables are significant at the 5 percent level in both years studied, although a few are significant only in one.

The net earnings differentials due to education at two points in the life cycle can be calculated from these equations (see Table 4-1). In 1955, when the average age in the sample was 33, annual earnings of those who attended college were generally 10 to 15 percent higher than at the high school level, although the differential was 70 percent for M.D.'s, 2 percent for Ph.D.'s, and 20 percent for LL.B.'s.[5] In 1969, those with some college received about 17 percent more income than high school graduates, while those with an undergraduate degree, some graduate work, and a master's degree received 25 to 30 percent more.[6] Those with Ph.D.'s, LL.B.'s, and M.D.'s received about 25, 85, and 105 percent more income, respectively, than high school graduates of the same ability level.[7] From 1955 to 1969 the differentials increased at all educational levels, with the greatest percentage increase occurring for the most highly educated. As explained in more detail later, these differentials are independent of ability level except for graduate students. In some versions of the 1969 equations we replaced the college-dropout category with the three categories of those who finished one, two, and three years of college. The coefficient for completing one year of college is essentially equal to that of the some-college variable discussed above, whereas the coefficients for

[4] Father's education is included as a proxy for family background. The personal biography variable is a weighted average of the two indices labeled *pilot biography* and *navigator biography* by Thorndike and Hagen. These indices are in turn weighted averages of information collected in 1943 on hobbies, prior school studies, and family background. The weights used in constructing these indices depend on how well the item predicted success in pilot and in navigator school.

[5] Although not shown here, the returns to B.A. and B.S. holders are the same.

[6] These returns correspond to those of wage rates, since average hours worked are the same at all educational levels except for the combination of Ph.D., LL.B., and M.D., in which hours are 8 percent greater than in the lowest category.

[7] If a dummy variable is included for business owners (but not self-employed professionals), the income differential for non-business owners with a bachelor's degree is raised by 25 percent, whereas the some-college differential is unchanged.

completing the second and third years of college indicate no further increase in income.

Differentials in initial salaries are also worth examining. Mincer (1970) suggests that the more educated also invest more in on-the-job training. As a consequence they may have an income profile that initially lies below that of the less educated, remains below for several years dependent on the reciprocal of the rate of return on training, and rises above thereafter. Our analysis of initial salary by educational level (not presented here) is consistent with part of this explanation since we find that in 1946, 1947, and 1948 the starting salary of high school graduates is nearly the same as that of college graduates, that graduate students receive less than college graduates, and finally that those with some college may earn more than those with a college degree.[8] Since in any year the more educated among the initial job applicants will tend to be older, and since experience adds to income, these results do imply that the earnings profile of the less educated initially lies above that of the more educated. On the other hand, from 1955 to 1969 the growth rates in income of those with a college degree, some graduate work, and a master's degree were essentially the same (although there was still a tendency for faster growth at higher educational levels), which suggests that differences in investment in on-the-job training were not very great at these levels.

The role of mental ability

We have extensively analyzed the role of ability, using the factors mentioned above that represent mathematical ability, coordination, verbal ability, and spatial perception.[9] To allow for nonlinear effects, we divided each factor into fifths, which may be closer to

---

[8] Of course all the people in the sample received some vocational training in the Air Force. If this training is more important for people with no college, the comparisons of starting salary would not be appropriate for the civilian population. However, some of the vocational training would also benefit those who went to college. Most of the high school graduates began work in 1946, but a few were discharged later.

[9] In order of importance in factor, the verbal measure is a weighted average of tests entitled *mechanical principles, reading, general information — pilot, general information — navigator, math B,* and *spatial orientation II.* As described in Thorndike and Hagen (1959), these tests contain such elements as verbal fluency, reasoning, and mathematical skills (see Appendix B). However, knowledge of mechanical principles is contained in the general information — pilot and reading comprehension tests as well as in the first item.

population tenths for the verbal and for the mathematical factors since only those in the top half of the mental-ability distribution were allowed into the test program. We found that of these ability measures, only mathematical ability is a significant determinant of earnings.[10]

In light of some recent literature on the distribution of income (Lydall, 1969), it is interesting to consider the relative importance of the effects of education and ability over time. In Table 4-2 we present estimates of the extent to which earnings of a high school graduate in each of the five ability levels differ from the earnings of the average high school graduate in our sample. In 1955 those in the top fifth earned about 9 percent more than the average, and those in the bottom fifth earned about 8 percent less, whereas in 1969 the corresponding figures were 15 and −10 percent.[11] Thus over time, the income of those in the top fifth has risen faster than the income of those at the low end of the ability scale, and for those in the middle fifths the growth rate has been about the same as that of the average high school graduate in this sample. In 1955 the 17 percent differential between the top- and bottom-ability fifths is greater than the differentials attributable to education, except for the M.D. and LL.B. categories (see Table 4-1). In 1969

[10] The second fifth was not significant, but the other three were (the omitted class was the bottom fifth).

[11] The dollar effect of ability on education is the same at each educational level (except in 1969 for high-ability people who attended graduate school); hence these percentage figures would be lower at higher educational levels.

	Percentage increases over high school graduates in	
Education	1955	1969
Some college	11	17
Undergraduate degree*	12	31
Some graduate*	15	26
M.A.*	10	32
Ph.D.	02†	27
M.D.	72	106
LL.B.	19	84

TABLE 4-1
Extra earnings from education for the average high school graduate in 1955 and 1969

*For those not teaching elementary or high school.

† All table entries are significant at the 5 percent level except for this one. See Appendix B for the underlying equation.

SOURCE: All data in these tables are from NBER-Thorndike sample.

the 25 percent differential is greater than the differential for some college and is quite close to the differentials at all educational levels except LL.B. and M.D. Since our sample was drawn only from the top half of the ability distribution, it is almost certain that for those who are at least high school graduates, ability is a more important determinant of the range of the income distribution than education is.[12]

As far as the interaction between ability and education is concerned, we find practically no evidence of any difference in the effect of ability at the various educational levels in 1955, although there is some evidence that in 1969 those with graduate training in the second-highest (and to some extent highest) ability groups received more income from ability than those at lower educational levels.[13] However, we also find ability to be an important determinant of earnings even for high school graduates.

Finally, in our study of initial salaries, we find that mental ability has no effect on income except for those with graduate training. Together with the Table 4-2 results, this indicates that ability initially has little effect on earnings but that over time the effect grows, and perhaps grows more rapidly for those with graduate training and high ability.[14]

These conclusions on ability and education suggest the following

[12] This comparison assumes that the bias from all omitted variables is affecting the education and ability coefficients in the same proportion. This assumption may be inappropriate for college quality, which is highly correlated with mental ability, as discussed below.

[13] Interaction between ability and education would mean that the joint effects of particular combinations of ability and education subgroups are different from what would have been predicted by simply adding the separate independent effects of the two variables.

For example, if it were shown that those in the top ability fifth averaged $1,000 more income than those in the average ability fifth, *whether or not* they went to high school or college, there would be no interaction between education and ability. If, however, this $1,000 income differential was an average result of a $500 differential for those with a high school education and a $1,500 differential for those with graduate training (as compared with people in the average ability fifth), then interaction between ability and education would exist.

Although there appears to be a significant interaction between graduate education and the top two ability fifths, it is not shown among our measures because of lack of space.

[14] Hause (1972) finds a significant interaction between IQ and education in the NBER-TH sample, and since this finding is at odds with ours, it is appropriate to compare the studies. Hause began his work after we had finished this portion of our study, and in the interval the variable used by Hause and labeled

type of model for the labor market: For most jobs, firms either have little or no idea of what determines success or must engage in so much training and testing that the initial output of all employees without previous experience is similar. In either case firms pay all those in comparable positions the same amount initially and then monitor performances and base promotions and income on accomplishment. Since the highly educated and able perform better and win promotions sooner, the model can be described as one of upward filtration. Such a model is consistent with the human capital concept, but it suggests a somewhat different interpretation of empirical results and somewhat different directions for research. It provides an explanation other than learning by doing for the shape of the age-income profile, whereas a natural extension of the model in which firms try to minimize information costs leads to the screening model discussed below.

A criticism that has been made of many education studies is that the education coefficients are biased upward because relevant abilities and other characteristics have not been held constant. We can obtain an estimate of this bias by observing how the

---

IQ was created; this IQ variable differs from any of our factors. Tests we have conducted with our full sample indicate that if the test scores are entered linearly, the IQ variable yields a higher R^2 in the earnings equation than our first factor does. But if the test scores are entered in the general nonlinear dummy-variable fashion, the reverse is true. Since the test scores are an ordinal index, it is appropriate that an allowance be made for general nonlinear effects. Hause did not allow for such effects, but instead specified a double-logarithmic earnings function. Thus the finding by Hause of an "interaction" between ability and education may be attributable to his selection of a restrictive functional form.

An alternative possibility is that the difference in results is due to the sample truncation procedures used by Hause. He excludes the self-employed from the analysis and also eliminates cases with reported incomes more than three standard deviations from the mean.

TABLE 4-2 Percentage by which earnings of high school graduates of a given ability exceed those of the average high school graduate in the sample

Ability fifth (in ascending order of ability)	Year	
	1955	1969
1	—7.6	—10.0
2	—3.0	— 3.9
3	—1.0	—.4
4	2.4	2.9
5	9.2	15.0

NOTE: See Appendix B for the underlying equations. The average age in the sample is 33 in 1955 and 47 in 1969.

education coefficients change when ability is omitted from our equations.[15] We have calculated the bias in two ways: first, assuming that each factor was the only type of ability that should be excluded, and second, assuming that all abilities should be excluded. In both instances we find that only the omission of mathematical ability leads to a bias of any magnitude. In 1955 the bias on the education coefficients due to omitting mathematical ability was about 25 percent, varying from a low of 15 percent for some college to a high of 31 percent for a master's degree. In 1969 the biases were somewhat smaller, averaging about 15 percent and ranging from 10 percent to 19 percent.[16] The decline in the bias over time occurs because the coefficients on ability did not grow as rapidly between 1955 and 1969 as those on education did.[17] In some studies, rates of return have been calculated using differences in average income between educational groups at various age levels. In this sample such a procedure would overstate the earnings differentials from higher education by 35 and 30 percent in 1955 and 1969, respectively.

Other variables

Several sociodemographic and background variables are statistically significant and important determinants of income. For example, the difference between excellent and poor health in 1969 was worth $7,000 a year, and the 100 individuals who were single earned about $3,000 a year less than others.[18] Those whose fathers had at least a ninth-grade education earned about $1,200 more in 1969 and $300 more in 1955 than those whose fathers had

[15] However, one of our important variables is a mixture of background and ability; thus we can calculate the upper and lower bounds of the bias only by omitting ability. For simplicity in this summary, we use the average of these bounds. The bias is expressed later as the ratio of the difference in the education coefficients (with ability excluded and included) to the education coefficient when ability is excluded.

[16] The 15 percent bias for the some-college category is higher than in other studies and may be due to our use of mathematical ability rather than IQ.

[17] The bias may also be expressed in terms of the coefficient of education in an equation relating ability to education, but since this equation would involve the same people in 1955 and 1969 and since their education changed only slightly, the coefficient would be virtually unchanged in the two years.

[18] In 1969 the people were asked to indicate the state of their health as being poor, fair, good, or excellent. The effects of these categories were statistically significant and approximately linear in 1969—and, interestingly, also in 1955 —although the 1955 t-value is lower.

not entered high school. In Table 4-1's format those whose fathers had a bachelor's degree added $700 and $4,000 in 1955 and 1969, respectively. The other background information is contained in a biography variable constructed by Thorndike and Hagen from data on hobbies, family income, education prior to 1943, and mathematical ability. We find the fourth and fifth (highest) and either the second or third fifths of the biography variable to be significant—of about the same magnitude as mathematical ability —and thus to be as important as educational differences in explaining the range of earnings. In 1955 the age variable was significant and large numerically, while in 1969 its effect was negative and insignificant. This is consistent with the common notion that a rising age-income profile reaches a peak after the age of 40.

Although the results discussed above were obtained from analysis of separate cross sections, it is possible to develop a combined measure of motivation, drive, personality, and whatever other characteristics persist over long periods of time by using the residuals generated in one cross section (denoted by Q) as a variable in the equations in another cross section. In each year the inclusion of Q raised the R^2 from about .10 to .33 and reduced the standard error of estimate by 15 percent, leaving the other coefficients unchanged.[19] Thus we conclude that about two-thirds of the variation in earnings in any year represents either random events, such as luck, or changes in underlying characteristics.

Further examination of the residuals from the regression equations leads to the following conclusions: First, although the equations do not explain well the very high incomes of the most successful, the estimates of extra income arising from education are only slightly altered if the very successful are excluded. Second, when the sample is divided up by education and ability, a test for constancy of the residual variance is rejected at the 5 percent level.[20] However, when the equations are estimated weighting each ob-

---

[19] The relatively low R^2 occurs partly because of the very limited range of education in our sample and of age in each cross section. For example, merging the two data sets but allowing for separate coefficients in each would raise the R^2 to about .30. The other coefficients are the same because Q is necessarily orthogonal to the other independent variables in 1955, and these are essentially the same as the variables used in 1969.

[20] Even when we use the log earnings as our dependent variable or include Q in our equations, we reject the hypotheses of constant variance and of normally distributed errors.

servation by the reciprocal of the standard error of its ability-education cell, the coefficients and conclusions reached above are changed very little.

Quality of schooling

We have explored briefly the effects of including an educational quality variable in the NBER-TH regressions[21] by using the Gourman academic rating, which attempts to measure the quality of undergraduate departments, in the form of fifths of the sample distribution.[22] At the some-college and B.A. levels, only the highest quality fifth affects earnings significantly, whereas for graduate students, earnings are affected by the top two undergraduate school

[21] Since the quality data became available to us at a much later date than the other data, we have not attempted to incorporate the quality implications in the rate-of-return calculations. Of course the direction of the effect is obvious. Lewis Solmon is currently examining the quality question in great detail.

[22] This rating is defined in Gourman (1967).

	Amount ($)	Percentage*
TABLE 4-3 Relation between college quality and earnings: amount by which monthly earnings in 1969 exceed earnings of the average high school graduate in the sample		
Education		
Some college		
Undergraduate quality 1–4	161	14
Undergraduate quality 5†	442	37
Undergraduate degree		
Undergraduate quality 1–4	340	29
Undergraduate quality 5†	457	39
Some graduate‡	166	14
M.A.‡	194	16
Ph.D. and LL.B.‡	633	53
Additional income to graduates as a function of educational quality		
Undergraduate quality 4†	182	15
Undergraduate quality 5†	268	23
Graduate quality 5†	257	22

* Expressed as a percentage of the average income of high school graduates.

† Significantly different from earnings of comparable people who attended schools in the bottom fifths of quality.

‡ For those at an undergraduate school in the bottom three quality fifths and a graduate school in the bottom four. These regression results are based on a sample of 5,000 individuals.

fifths and the top graduate school fifth. The 1969 results, summarized in Table 4-3, indicate that differences in income at a given educational level attributable to college quality effects are very large. For example, the college dropout in the top quality fifth receives more income than anyone not in the top fifth except for those with a three-year graduate degree.[23] Similarly, the three-year graduate degree holder, depending on school quality, earns anywhere from 53 to 98 percent more than the average high school student.

The quality variable may be important for several reasons. First, high-quality schools can impart different or additional income-earning skills as compared with low-quality schools. Second, the quality as well as the quantity of education may be used as a screening device, as we describe later.[24] Finally, one of Gourman's stated objectives in providing the quality ratings is to permit students to match their capabilities, as reflected by S.A.T. ratings, with schools. If individuals' S.A.T. ratings and school quality ratings were perfectly correlated, then the quality rating would be reflecting mental-ability differences rather than differences in the quality of education provided by the school. Evidence in Wolfle and Smith (1956) and Solmon (1969) indicates that school quality and average IQ of those attending are positively correlated, but that within schools there is a wide range of individual abilities. In addition, evidence in Astin (1968) indicates that schools are differentiated by characteristics of their students other than mental ability and that schools have different attitudes toward various forms of social and psychological behavior. Thus the quality variable may reflect individual mental-ability differences not captured in our personal-ability measures; it may reflect other personality differences or quality-of-schooling differences.

THE RATE OF RETURN TO EDUCATION The data for 1955 and 1969, as well as the initial job earnings that have been mentioned briefly, yield information at three points on the age-earnings profile for those in our sample. It is possible to interpolate for the intervening years on the basis of various data collected by the census and to extrapolate beyond 1969 (when the people in the sample averaged 47 years of age) to obtain

---

[23] This group includes Ph.D.'s, lawyers, and M.D.'s.

[24] Some of the schools included in the top undergraduate quality fifth are Berkeley, Brown, Chicago, Columbia, Harvard, Michigan, Minnesota, M.I.T. Princeton, Stanford, Wisconsin, and Yale.

"realized" or ex post age-earnings profiles by educational level.[25] We have constructed such profiles for a person with the characteristics of the average high school graduate in the sample. The differences between these profiles together with information on the costs of education are used to estimate rates of return to education.[26]

Private and social rates of return may differ for a number of reasons, including the fact that earnings are subject to taxes, that costs of education are not necessarily borne by the one who is being educated, and that there are market imperfections based on education (as indicated earlier). If social nonmonetary returns and market imperfections are ignored, differences between our estimates of private and social rates of return occur because the private benefits are calculated after deducting income taxes from earnings and because social costs include the total (per-student) expenditures on higher education rather than just average tuition.[27] However, our estimated social and private rates are very similar because the (before-tax) income streams are the same, and the largest cost component in each instance is forgone earnings.[28] In this discussion, therefore, we concentrate on estimates of the social rates of return calculated after deflation by the CPI from nominal profiles. These rates are presented in Table 4-4 along with nominal private rates.

Compared with the social rate of return to a high school graduate having the same abilities and background, the social rates of return realized in our sample (before deflation) are 14, 10, 7, 8, and 4 per-

[25] For details see Taubman and Wales (forthcoming, App. J).

[26] Earnings provide an inadequate measure of benefits from education if there are nonmonetary returns that vary by educational levels. In our estimates we, in effect, add to the incomes of elementary and high school teachers a large nonpecuniary return. Without this adjustment the rates of return would be smaller at the undergraduate and master's level. No other adjustments are made for nonmonetary returns or for consumption benefits.

[27] The details of construction of the cost estimates can be found in Taubman and Wales (forthcoming, App. L). The foregone earnings are estimated from the sample.

[28] These returns, which are not very sensitive to small changes in the data, are calculated under the following assumptions: First, we do not include GI education benefits as offsets to forgone earnings since we want rate-of-return estimates that are applicable to the population as a whole. Second, we assume that, as in our sample, the average age of people about to undertake higher education in 1946 was 24. However, we also calculate a rate of return for people who are identical to those in the sample but who were 18 in 1946. Since these rates are about the same, we ignore this distinction in our discussion.

	Private	Social	
	Undeflated	*Undeflated*	*Deflated*
Education categories	*by CPI*	*by CPI*	*by CPI*
High school to			
Some college	15	14	11
B.A.	11	10	8
Some graduate	8	7	5
Master's	8	8	6
Ph.D.	4	4	2
LL.B.	12	11	9
Some college to B.A.	7	7	5
B.A. to LL.B.	13	12	10

TABLE 4-4 *Realized rates of return to education, before tax (people entering college in 1946)*

cent for two years of college only, an undergraduate degree, some graduate work, a master's degree, and a Ph.D., respectively.[29] The most striking aspect of these results is the general decrease in the rate of return with increases in education, which holds even though we have adjusted for the large nonpecuniary reward to precollege teachers who are concentrated in the B.A., some-graduate, and master's categories. On the other hand, nonpecuniary returns may be contributing to the low return in the Ph.D. category, which includes college professors. Rates of return calculated without standardizing for ability and background, although not presented here, are generally about 20 percent higher; for example, the some-college return rises from 14 to 18 percent. These rates of return, based on current dollar profiles, differ from those based on constant dollar profiles because inflation increases the absolute differences between the profiles and alters the purchasing power of the investment "costs" and "dividends." Estimates of real rates of return, obtained by deflating by the CPI, are two to three percentage points lower.

A surprising result is that the rate of return to a college dropout exceeds that to a college graduate. This result might in part be attributed to the heavy concentration in the some-college category of self-employed individuals whose earnings probably include a return to financial capital.[30] Including a dummy variable for people who were business owners in 1969, we find that the percentage earnings differential, compared with that of the average high school gradu-

---

[29] The Ph.D. category does not include self-employed professionals.

[30] The questionnaire did not specify whether "earnings" included profits, but it seems reasonable that some owners included some profits in their answers.

ate, is unchanged for college dropouts but is increased by 25 percent for college graduates who are not business owners. Hence, if this 25 percent adjustment is appropriate (and holds at all ages), the rate of return to obtaining a B.A. but not becoming a business owner is about the same as for a college dropout. [31]

Of course, even finding that college dropouts receive as high a rate of return as college graduates is not in accord with findings by others, such as Becker (1964). This difference may be due partly to the fact that in other studies ability is not held constant. The results are therefore influenced by those who drop out of college because they do not have the intelligence, drive, or other attributes to handle the work. But since the college dropouts in our sample were in their mid-twenties in 1946, many probably had a family to support and could not afford (in the short run) a college degree. Thus they may have been "pulled" out of college by attractive alternatives rather than "pushed" out by lack of drive and motivation. For example, a small number of respondents in the sample went on (understandably!) to become airline pilots, a well-paying occupation that does not require a college degree. The results reported here, however, do not depend on this special characteristic of the data.

As explained earlier, except for those with graduate training, there is no evidence of an interaction between ability and education in determining earnings. Further, since the data on initial earnings (although they are "recalled" estimates and hence less accurate) indicate that ability does not affect initial earnings, forgone earnings do not vary by ability level. Therefore, except for those with graduate training, the rates of return discussed above apply to individuals at all ability levels in our sample. For those with graduate training, differences in the rates of return between those in the top two and those in the bottom mathematical ability fifths are approximately two percentage points (centered about the average). [32]

---

[31] However, this dummy-variable procedure understates the true return to some college if obtaining that educational level increases the likelihood that the individual will become a businessman. On the other hand, our sample information about the self-employed obviously does not include data on those who failed earlier in life; thus the dummy-variable coefficient overstates the average return to being self-employed and may overstate the return to education.

[32] In Taubman and Wales (forthcoming) we also calculate rates of return using data from the 1949 census and 1946 data in H. Miller (1960) but with adjustments for the omission of ability and other variables. The rate of return to college graduates in both these cross sections and the some-college rate in the 1946 sample are close to the realized real rates given above. For the some-college group, the 1949 cross section yields a much smaller estimate than the time-series data.

Are investments in education worthwhile? From a social point of view this question involves comparing our social rates of return with alternative returns available to society. Assuming a fixed amount of saving and investment in society, the appropriate alternative rate is that obtainable on physical investment, which is usually thought to be about 13 to 15 percent in real terms (see Phelps, 1962; Taubman & Wales, 1969). Thus when consumption benefits and externalities are ignored, there is overinvestment in the education of males from society's viewpoint, except perhaps for the some-college category and college graduates who are not self-employed. However, if society were to raise the funds through taxation or debt issues without affecting private investment, the risk-free discount rate (probably about 4 percent) would be the appropriate alternative marginal time-preference rate (see Arrow & Lind, 1970). On these grounds, investments in education are worthwhile from society's viewpoint, especially since we have not allowed for either externalities or the consumption value of education. (See the chapters in Part Two of this volume for examination of a number of externalities.)

From a private viewpoint, however, the appropriate alternative return is best represented by an after-tax ex post rate of return on common stocks—say, about 10 percent. Since the private after-tax rates of return differ from the before-tax rates by less than one percentage point, we conclude that (in addition to some college) obtaining a B.A. or LL.B. degree is a profitable investment, although, subject to the qualifications on the college-dropout results mentioned earlier, it would be better to drop out after two years of college. The private return to education is more profitable relative to alternative assets than the social return because of the various subsidies given to higher education.

EDUCATION AS A SCREENING DEVICE The analysis of earnings differentials and rates of return to education has been conducted without considering the ways in which education might increase income. Becker and others have shown that if education produces additions to an individual's cognitive or affective skills, his income will increase. However, a number of people have asserted that a primary role of education is to serve as a credential, particularly in the highly paid managerial and professional occupations.[33]

[33] See, for example, Griliches and Mason (1972), Hansen et al. (1970), and Thurow and Lucas (1972). For lower-paying occupations such as skilled laborer, the required credential may be a high school diploma.

Under what circumstances will such screening result in extra earnings for the more educated, and how will it affect the calculations of the social rate of return to education? Suppose that a person is paid his marginal product in any occupation in which he works and that education, mental ability, and other personal characteristics add to an individual's marginal productivity. As long as these factors affect marginal productivity differently in various occupations, we can speak meaningfully of high- and low-wage occupations. To demonstrate that education is being used to screen people out of high-paying occupations, we must show that some people with less education are not in the occupation in which their marginal product and earnings could be maximized and that, on the other hand, highly educated people are allocated more efficiently.

If education is used to screen people, the extra earnings a person receives from education are due both to the skills produced by schooling and to the income redistribution effect resulting from supply limitations. But since the latter is not a gain to society, the social return will apparently be less than the private return to education. This conclusion, however, overlooks one particularly important component of the problem, which can best be considered by asking why firms use education as a screening device. There are several possible answers, including snobbery and a mistaken belief in the true importance of education. On the other hand, the use of such credentials may be motivated by a desire for profit maximization. Suppose that successful performance (in the managerial or sales occupation, for example) depends upon the individual's possessing a complex set of talents and skills, only some of which can be measured easily by appropriate tests. Clearly, firms could attempt to develop and use tests in recruiting people with the necessary skills for particular occupations. But developing tests, examining recruits, and incurring performance errors can be expensive. Alternatively, suppose that firms either know (from past experience) or believe that a significantly larger percentage of college graduates have the desired complex of skills.[34] They may then, to save on hiring costs and mistakes on the job, decide to use information on educational attainment, available at a near zero cost, as a preliminary screening device.

The implications for the social rate of return are clear: If educational screening was not permitted, firms would have to use addi-

---

[34] Note that the larger percentage could occur either because education produces skills or because the more talented receive the education.

tional resources in order to sort people. Hence any sorting costs saved by using education as a screening device are a benefit to society and must be taken into account when comparing the social and private rates of return. In this chapter we do not attempt to estimate the magnitude of these costs, but we do obtain a rough estimate of the contribution of screening to income differentials.

The case for screening can be summarized as one of market failure, arising from the lack of knowledge or the cost of obtaining it. Some people with whom we have discussed this problem believe that firms could obtain the benefits of screening without paying the costs of hiring college graduates by hiring high school graduates on the basis of a test predicting whether they would succeed in finishing college. Although extra sorting costs would be involved, these would be small compared with the costs of hiring college graduates, given the earnings differentials we attribute below to screening. Since firms that hired only high school graduates would have lower costs and higher profits, other firms would soon stop paying a premium to college graduates, and the screen would be eroded. There are several responses to this argument. First, even if the screening function were to vanish in the long run, its consequences would be observable before then.[35] Second, even when there is a profit to be made by discovering and exploiting available information, the actual discovery may not occur for many years.[36] Thus, the use of education as a screening device is certainly not a proposition which should be rejected out of hand.

To test for the existence of screening, we compare the actual

[35] Analogously, in the long run with perfect competition there are no excess profits or rates of return on capital. But in the short run, while capital is being expanded, excess profits could exist and be measured.

[36] See, for example, the first part of this chapter. The two largest and richest samples for investigating the rate of return to higher education net of the effect of ability and family background are the Wolfle-Smith and the NBER-TH samples, both of which were available in the 1950s. The only prior analysis of the Wolfle-Smith data consists of their original few cross-tabulations for males (1956) with some slight extensions in Denison (1964). The data for people of Minnesota, we have learned, were intact and accessible at the University of Minnesota until 1966, but were permanently or temporarily lost when some operations were moved. The Thorndike-Hagen sample was sitting unused in a basement at Columbia Teachers College for over a decade, despite the fact that it is mentioned in Hunt (1963) and was known at least to Lee Hansen. Both samples would have provided data for a series of very useful and important articles in a highly competitive profession. Why did it take up to 15 years for these data sources to be resurrected?

occupational distribution of individuals at various educational levels with the distribution "expected" under free entry. The basic assumption made in estimating the expected distribution is that each individual selected the (broad) occupational category in which his income was the highest. Of course, an individual works in only one (main) occupation at a time. To estimate earnings in any other occupation, we make use of occupational regressions, examples of which are given in Appendix B. The coefficients on the various ability and education variables can be thought of as the valuations of the extra skills produced by ability and schooling. The socio-economic variables may be proxies for other dimensions of skills, and their coefficients interpretable in the same way, although other explanations are possible. Given the earlier discussion of the specificity of the skills produced by education, it is encouraging to find that education (and ability) has larger coefficients in the managerial, professional, and sales occupations than in the others.

Using the occupation equations, we can estimate the individual's potential income in a particular (mth) occupation as the mean income of people in that occupation who have the same education, ability, and other characteristics that he does. But since we do not have measures of all individual characteristics, the potential earnings for each individual will be distributed about this mean. We assume that the distribution of the residuals in our occupational regressions would also hold for people with any given set of personal characteristics currently in any other occupation. Finally, we assume that for any individual, the earnings distributions about the mean in various occupations are independent. The latter is a conservative assumption that biases our results against accepting the screening hypothesis. That is, if the distributions about the means are positively correlated, people who earn more in one occupation would do so in all others; hence, fewer people would pick the occupation with the lower mean income.

For simplicity, we assume that the distribution of wages in the mth occupation (for individuals with the same characteristics as the ith individual) is normal, with $\hat{Y}_{im}$ and variance σ_m^2. Assuming income maximization, the probability that the ith individual will choose the mth occupation is given by

$$p_m = \int_0^\infty f_m(Z) \prod_{j \neq m} F_j(Z) \, dZ$$

where f_m is distributed as $N(\hat{Y}_{im}, \sigma_m^2)$ and F_j is the cumulative density of f_j.[37] If there is a large number of people at the educational level under consideration, then p_m can be interpreted as the expected fraction of individuals in the mth occupation at that educational level, and we have an estimate of the distribution of people by occupation and education that should occur with free entry and income maximization.

Table 4-5 contains the expected and actual occupational distributions for the high school, some-college, and B.A. categories, together with the means and standard deviations of the corresponding existing income levels for 1969.[38] The most striking result is that for the high school group, where the actual fractions of people in the three lowest-paying occupations are considerably greater than the expected fractions. In the some-college group this result holds but is less pronounced, whereas for the undergraduate degree holders the actual and expected distributions are essentially the same in the lowest-paying occupations.

In general then, under the assumptions of free entry and income maximization, very few people at any educational level included in our sample would choose the blue-collar, white-collar, or service occupations. In practice, however, a substantial fraction (39 percent) of high school graduates, a smaller fraction (17 percent) of the some-college group, and only 4 percent of the B.A. holders enter these occupations. Since the discrepancy between the expected and actual distributions is directly related to education, we conclude that education itself is being used as a screening device to prevent those with low educational attainment from entering the high-paying occupations.[39] Table 4-5 also indicates that at each educational level, the expected fraction exceeds the actual fraction for the technical and sales categories by about 10 and 14 percentage points, respectively. As explained later, such constant differences at each educational level would occur if there were occupation-specific skills or risk preferences uncorrelated with education.

A risk-averse individual may select his occupation on the basis

---

[37] In the calculations ∞ was replaced by the mean plus three standard deviations. If there are only two occupations, the calculations involve the joint probability of receiving a given wage in the mth occupation and a smaller one in the other occupation.

[38] There is almost no one with graduate training in the blue-collar, white-collar, or service occupations.

[39] Although not presented here, the same general pattern of results holds for 1955.

TABLE 4-5 *Expected and actual distribution by education and occupation, 1969*

Occupation and educational level	(1) Number of people	(2) Actual fraction	(3) Expected fraction	(4) Column 3 minus column 1	(5) Mean income (monthly)	(6) Standard error of income
High school						
Professional	11	1.5	9.5	8.0	960	274
Technical	85	11.5	21.0	9.5	1,220	577
Sales	56	7.6	22.0	14.4	1,120	548
Blue-collar	211	28.6	1.3	−26.3	844	165
Service	50	6.8	1.4	−5.4	824	177
White-collar	24	3.3	.5	−2.8	754	127
Managerial	299	40.6	42.4	1.8	1,485	907
Some college						
Professional	49	5.8	14.8	9.0	1,260	501
Technical	82	9.6	19.1	9.5	1,285	579
Sales	80	9.4	21.8	12.4	1,300	614
Blue-collar	87	10.2	.8	−9.4	882	182
Service	32	3.8	1.2	−2.6	840	228
White-collar	21	2.5	.6	−1.9	785	194
Managerial	501	58.8	39.8	−19.0	1,680	884
B.A.						
Professional	257	25.0	17.8	−7.2	1,412	674
Technical	29	2.8	14.1	11.3	1,370	458
Sales	90	8.8	25.5	16.7	1,490	865
Blue-collar	18	1.8	.9	−.9	950	244
Service	11	1.1	.9	−.2	920	244
White-collar	11	1.1	.4	−.7	840	212
Managerial	610	59.4	38.3	−21.1	1,850	911

of the variability of income as well as the mean; thus it might be argued that our estimates of the expected fractions for the low-paying occupations are too small because we have not allowed for the attractiveness of the small standard error of income in these occupations (see Table 4-5, columns 5 and 6). This is a plausible reason for believing that our estimates of the expected fractions may be in error for any particular educational level. But unless high school graduates are more averse to risk, it does not explain the differences between actual and expected fractions that prevail across educational levels, since occupational standard errors do not differ much by education.[40] If there are differences in risk preference, then our previous estimates of the rate of return to education would be biased upward since an income-determining characteristic correlated with education would not have been held constant.

There is, however, an alternative plausible explanation for our results. Since we can observe an individual in only one occupation, we calculate his expected earnings in other occupations from the mean and variance of people with the same set of measured characteristics, e.g., education, ability, and age. Unfortunately, these measured characteristics explain only a small portion of the variance in earnings in the various occupations. Some of the unexplained variance undoubtedly occurs because of luck or other temporary factors, but the rest occurs because some types of skills, talents, and abilities have not been measured. For simplicity, if all these unmeasured skills are represented by a single variable X, then in the implementation of the test for screening we are assuming that the mean and variance of X are the same in each occupation.[41]

If X is more important for performance in one occupation than in others, we would expect the effect of X on earnings to be higher in this occupation, which in turn should induce more people with X to choose employment in it. But unless X is correlated with education, we shall estimate an equal "misallocation" of people at all educational levels. However, if both X and education are highly rewarded in a particular occupation, then it is not appropriate to use the mean earnings of that occupation to estimate the potential earnings in it of people who are outside it (since the average level of X differs). To the extent that this problem is important, we overstate in our calculations the fraction of high school and some-college people in the high-paying occupations and thus obtain an upper bound to the importance of screening.

We have no way of determining the importance of the omitted variables, nor do we know of any studies that would be informative.

---

[40] The chapter by Lewis Solmon in this volume suggests that high school graduates may well be more risk-averse than college graduates.

[41] We actually require the equality of mean and variance of $d_i X_i$, where d_i is the effect of X on earnings in the ith occupation. But the most likely reason for X to have the same distribution over all occupations is that the d_i are equal for all i.

Nevertheless, it is of some interest to study the effect of omitting mental ability since, if the calculations had been performed with census data, this would have been an obvious candidate for the omitted (occupation-specific) variable. Indeed, in our equations we do find that mathematical ability has a bigger effect on earnings in the higher-paying occupations. The omitted-variable argument would lead us to expect that the larger the fraction of people at each educational level in the managerial occupation, the higher the ability level, and to expect high school graduates who are managers to be, on the average, more able than other high school graduates. Analysis of our sample indicates that both these expectations are borne out, but that the effects are not pronounced. For example, the mean ability level of managers is .47 and .62 for high school and college graduates, respectively, while the corresponding means for all high school and college graduates are .43 and .60.[42] Consequently, to the extent that the omission of other occupation-specific skills follows the same pattern as that of mental ability, the problems caused by their omission may not be serious.

We can attempt to estimate what the rates of return to education would have been if there had been no screening.[43] These are of interest because they represent the extent to which the returns presented earlier reflect increases in productivity rather than discrimination in the job market. To calculate returns to education, we weight the income differences due to education in various occupations by the expected distribution of people across occupations. These returns are upper bounds to those which would actually occur, since they do not allow for income levels to adjust as the occupational distributions change. Also, they are unadjusted estimates in that they do not allow for differences in ability, background, age, etc. However, they can be compared with estimates obtained using the actual distributions, and the percentage differences between these two sets of estimates will probably be reasonable approximations to differences in returns adjusted for relevant factors.

We have calculated the percent by which income in the some-college and B.A. categories exceeds high school income for the

[42] Those in the top fifth receive a score of .9, and each successive fifth declines by .2.

[43] As explained above, calculation of the social rate requires information on the sorting costs saved by screening. Since we are assuming these costs to be zero in our calculations, the social (but not the private) rates will be underestimated.

actual and expected distributions for 1955 and 1969. In 1955 the earnings differentials due to education, under the assumption of no entry barriers, were only about one-half to one-third as large as actual returns, whereas in 1969 they were about one-half as large. This suggests that the effect of screening on the returns to education is in fact substantial at these educational levels and that without screening, the returns might be 50 percent below those presented earlier.[44]

To sum up, the screening model implies that the supply of people to the high-paying occupations is artificially reduced, resulting in a redistribution of earnings to the more highly educated. Although this redistribution represents a private gain, a complete analysis of the social gain requires information on any extra sorting costs that would be incurred if education could not be used for that purpose.

CONCLUSIONS   Our results are helpful in determining whether society has over-invested or underinvested in education. Since none of the deflated social rates of return presented in Table 4-4 exceeds 11 percent, and very few exceed even 8 percent, and since the before-tax return on physical capital is generally thought to be about 13 to 15 percent, it appears that society has invested too many resources in education, assuming that the supply of saving is fixed and that externalities are not of major quantitative significance. Further, the rates are lower, the higher the educational level (excluding lawyers and M.D.'s), suggesting that the overinvestment is more severe at the higher levels.[45] However, if the externalities or consumption benefits discussed in Part Two of this volume yield large-enough returns, or if educational investments tend to come out of increased savings, expenditures on education would be economically justified. Further, we find that the rates of return at the some-college and B.A. levels are higher than they would be if there were free entry into the high-paying occupations. That is, since the part of the return to education that reflects the income redistribution due to the credential aspect of education does not benefit society, its effect should be subtracted from actual rates when studying the question of whether or not

---

[44] Moreover, if there were no screening, the forgone earnings of those at the high school level would have been greater.

[45] However, to the extent that lower rates at high educational levels reflect non-pecuniary returns, the overinvestment is diminished somewhat.

there has been overinvestment in education.[46] Since we find screening to be important quantitatively, our conclusion that overinvestment in education has occurred is strengthened.

[46] However, as mentioned above, if screening were not practiced, the costs to firms (and society) of finding suitable employees would increase. These costs are therefore one of the benefits of the existing educational system and should be included when the income redistribution aspects due strictly to screening are excluded.

References

Arrow, K., and R. Lind: "Uncertainty and Evaluation of Public Investment Decisions," *American Economic Review,* vol. 60, pp. 364–379, June 1970.

Ashenfelter, O., and J. D. Mooney: "Graduate Education, Ability, and Earnings," *Review of Economics and Statistics,* vol. 50, no. 1, pp. 78–86, February 1968.

Astin, A: "Undergraduate Achievement and Institutional 'Excellence,'" *Science,* vol. 1, p. 668, Aug. 16, 1968.

Becker, G. S.: *Human Capital: A Theoretical and Empirical Analysis, with Special Reference to Education,* National Bureau of Economic Research, New York, 1964.

Bridgman, D.: "Success in College and Business," *Personnel Journal,* vol. 9, no. 1, pp. 1–19, June 1930.

Cutright, P.: "Achievement, Military Service, and Earnings," Social Security Administration, Washington, May 20, 1969. (Mimeographed.)

Denison, E.: "Measuring the Contribution of Education in the Residual Factor and Economic Growth," OECD, Paris, 1964.

Duncan, O. D., et al.: *Socioeconomic Background and Occupational Achievement: Extensions of a Basic Model,* U.S. Department of Health, Education and Welfare, Office of Education, Bureau of Research, Washington, May 1968.

Folger, J. K., and C. B. Nam: *Education of the American Population,* A 1960 Census Monograph, U.S. Department of Commerce, Bureau of the Census, Washington, 1967.

Gourman, J.: *The Gourman Report,* The Continuing Education Institute, Phoenix, 1967.

Griliches, Z., and W. Mason: "Education, Income and Ability," *Journal of Political Economy,* vol. 80, part 2, pp. S74–S103, May–June 1972.

Hansen, W. L., B. A. Weisbrod, and W. J. Scanlon: "Schooling and Earnings of Low Achievers," *American Economic Review,* vol. 60, pp. 409–418, June 1970.

Hause, J.: "Earnings Profile of Ability and Schooling," *Journal Of Political Economy,* vol. 80, pp. 108–138, May–June 1972.

Hunt, Shane J.: "Income Determinants for the College Graduates and Return to Educational Investment," *Yale Economic Essays,* vol. 3, pp. 305–357, Fall 1963.

Jencks, C., and David Riesman: *The Academic Revolution,* Doubleday & Company, Inc., Garden City, N.Y., 1968.

Lydall, H.: *The Structure of Earnings,* Oxford University Press, New York, 1969.

Miller, H.: "Annual and Lifetime Income in Relation to Education: 1939 to 1959," *American Economic Review,* vol. 5, pp. 962–986, December 1960.

Miller, S. M., and F. Riessman: "The Credentials Trap," in S. M. Miller and Frank Riessman (eds.), *Social Class and Social Policy,* Basic Books, Inc., Publishers, New York, 1968, pp. 69–77.

Mincer, J.: "The Distribution of Labor Incomes: A Survey with Special References to the Human Capital Approach," *Journal of Economic Literature,* vol. 8, pp. 1–27, March 1970.

Morgan, J., and M. David: "Education and Income," *Quarterly Journal of Economics,* vol. 78, pp. 346–347, August 1963.

Phelps, E.: "The New View of Investment: A Neoclassical Analysis," *Quarterly Journal of Economics,* vol. 76, pp. 548–567, November 1962

Rogers, Daniel C.: *Private Rates of Return to Education in the United States: A Case Study,* Yale University Press, New Haven, Conn., 1967

Schultz, T. W.: *The Economic Value of Education,* Columbia University Press, New York, 1963.

Solmon, L.: "The Meaning of Quality of College and Universities," National Bureau of Economic Research, New York, 1969. (Mimeographed.)

Taubman, P., and T. Wales: "The Impact of Investment Subsidies in Neoclassical Theory of Investment Behavior," *Review of Economics an Statistics,* vol. 51, pp. 287–298, August 1969.

Taubman, P., and T. Wales: *Mental Ability and Higher Educational Attainment in the Twentieth Century,* National Bureau of Economic Research and Carnegie Commission on Higher Education, Berkeley Calif., 1972.

Taubman, P., and T. Wales: *Higher Education and Earnings,* McGraw Hill Book Company, New York, forthcoming.

Thorndike, R. L., and E. Hagen: *Ten Thousand Careers,* John Wiley & Sons, Inc., New York, 1959.

Thurow, L., and R. E. B. Lucas: *The American Distribution of Income: A Structural Problem,* Joint Economic Committee, Washington, 1972.

Weisbrod, B., and P. Karpoff: "Monetary Returns to College Education, Student Ability and College Quality," *Review of Economics and Statistics,* vol. 50, pp. 491–497, November 1968.

Wolfle, D., and J. G. Smith: "Occupational Value of Education for Superior High School Graduates," *Journal of Higher Education,* vol. 27, pp. 201–213, 1956.

5. Ability and Schooling as Determinants of Lifetime Earnings, or If You're So Smart, Why Aren't You Rich?

by John C. Hause

INTRODUCTION The way in which ability influences earnings, either directly or by its impact on the productivity of schooling, is currently not well understood. Measurements of specific abilities (e.g., the enviable capacity to succeed consistently in obtaining large grants and comfortable per diems) and general ability (e.g., measured IQ) are the product of genetic, environmental, and experiential factors that are difficult to disentangle. For many important models it is probably unnecessary to break down measured ability into its components. Suppose that the prospective earnings E of an individual can be expressed as a function of measured ability A at time t_o, a set of

NOTE: This chapter has been neither reviewed nor approved by the directors of the National Bureau of Economic Research. The project underlying it has been supported by funds from the U.S. Office of Education channeled through the National Research Council. Research was carried out with the aid of grants from the Carnegie Commission on Higher Education and the National Science Foundation and with the general funds of the National Bureau. Computer time was provided by the University of Minnesota.

This chapter significantly extends (and heavily cannibalizes) an earlier version published in the May 1971 supplement to the *American Economic Review.* The empirical portion of this study would have been impossible without the generous cooperation of those assembling the important primary data. I am indebted to D. C. Rogers for allowing me to use his basic data tape. I am also indebted to Torsten Husén for allowing me to use the remarkable data on Swedish males from Malmö and to Ingemar Fägerlind for coordinating the collection of the Swedish earnings data. The American Institutes of Research prepared the Project Talent data tape. And Robert Thorndike was most cooperative in making available to the NBER his massive collection of data from 1955 on.

Comments by Finis Welch on the original version were perceptive and valuable. Computations were carried out by J. Sanguinetty, M. Sternfeld, and A. L. Norman. Norman also developed a very useful program for estimating missing observations that greatly facilitated the Project Talent calculations. Margareta Forselius and Karlis Goppers provided much assistance with the Swedish data.

other personal characteristics P_o at t_o, additional schooling or other investment to increase future earnings S, and time for $t \geq t_o$:

$$E(t) = F(A_o, P_o, S, t) \qquad (5\text{-}1)$$

A_o and P_o specify the initial state of the person at t_o. Although A_o and P_o may include simple, easily measured factors (e.g., race or sex) as well as complicated functionals of factors operating before t_o, it may be that A_o and P_o adequately summarize the initial state *for the purpose of analyzing how* S *affects the earnings profile* E(t). If this condition is satisfied, so that a complete biography of the individual from conception until t_o is unnecessary, a value-added analysis of the schooling increment S is feasible.

This study takes a slightly less agnostic view of the role that ability plays in determining the earnings stream $E(t)$. The measure of A_o is a test score (or set of test scores). Loose hypotheses can readily be developed on how A_o is related to $E(t)$ for additional schooling after t_o (including $S = O$). The main interest in these hypotheses stems largely from our ignorance of *how* schooling affects the earnings stream. If we reason that many people regard schooling as an important way of increasing their prospective earnings, we expect to find (and, in fact, do find) a significant tendency for earnings to rise with the level of schooling attainment. This discovery throws little light on the "technology" by which schooling augments subsequent earnings. An analysis of the role of ability, however, gives some insights into this black box.

The following section discusses some hypotheses on the roles of ability and schooling as they affect earnings. Later, some of these hypotheses are tested, using several cohorts of individuals for whom data are available on ability, achievement, other personal and background characteristics, and earnings.

SOME HYPOTHESES ON ABILITY AND EARNINGS *Ability* is usually defined as the power to do something. Many of the tests designed to measure ability have been developed in an educational context where the relevant power is the capacity to learn and master cognitive tools. Learning through formal schooling and learning those things which increase a person's economic productivity, however, are not identical, although one would expect an empirically significant positive correlation between the two. There are, in fact, several well-documented empirical relationships that also point to a positive association between earnings and measures ability. An empirically significant positive relationship exists both between level of schooling attainment and earnings after people have been working for a few years (see Tables 5-2, 5-7, and 5-9, for example) and between measured ability and level of schooling attainment (see Tables 5-2, 5-5, 5-7, and 5-9). Our knowledge of the technological relationship between schooling and earnings is meager, but this lack has not impeded the making of sweeping conjectures. Several output components of schooling which may affect earnings have been suggested (or asserted). A casual catalog includes (1) specific skills to perform well-defined tasks, (?) general cognitive skills that enable people to locate and handle information more efficiently, (3) "social skills" that increase the capacity to deal with (or manipulate) others, (4) development of greater rational foresight and self-discipline, and (5) conditioning to certain attitudes (e.g., obeying orders, punctuality) and to the performance of routine tasks that increase personal productivity in modern economic organizations. From this list it seems likely that measured ability is associated primarily with general cognitive skills and with the capacity to acquire some of the more complex specific mental skills. Since these skills (and skill levels) depend upon both schooling and measured ability, one expects a positive interaction of schooling and ability on earnings, unless, of course, these skills have no effect on earnings.[1]

To my knowledge, neither learning theory nor economic theory has been developed to the point where a powerful theory of the earnings profile can emerge. Even so, interpreting ability broadly as "learning power" immediately suggests several simple hypotheses. Consider the earnings profiles of a cohort of people with the same schooling attainment. If people with greater ability learn the same job skills as others, but more quickly, their earnings profiles will rise more rapidly than the profiles of those with less ability as long as their economic productivity is increasing more rapidly.

If full job competence is attainable by people of lower and higher ability, the influence of ability disappears after a period long enough to allow those with lower ability to attain full productivity.

---

[1] It is beyond the scope of this chapter to investigate the other hypotheses on schooling outputs and earnings. Some of them appear to be difficult to evaluate because data for observing marginal changes are not available. For example, children are exposed to substantial experience related to conditioning of certain attitudes before they reach the legal age for leaving school. If further schooling has little effect on this dimension, then it will not be easy to measure directly the impact of schooling on earnings from this source.

On the other hand, differential ability may limit the complexity of skills that people are able to master. In this case, an ability effect on earnings can persist over time as long as more complex skills yield higher earnings. If one considers different schooling levels, it seems plausible that persistent ability differentials in earnings should become more important at higher levels of schooling. At the lowest levels of schooling attainment, jobs consist largely of well-defined tasks that do not require great cognitive ability, and output is easily measured in these jobs. At high levels of education, more jobs have no obvious upper limit, in terms of the degree of skill that is economically productive. Since the efficiency with which people can find and assemble economically relevant information depends significantly on cognitive capacity and skills, there is no reason why the marginal returns to such skills should become negligible in many "high-level" jobs.

Attempts to understand the relative slope of the logarithm of the earnings profile of high- and low-ability people are not carried far by a priori argument (see Appendix C).

Initial earnings of people first entering the labor force could have a positive, zero, or negative simple correlation with ability. A positive correlation could indicate that those with higher ability are immediately more productive and that employers can observe this fact at the time of hiring. In this case, there is no guarantee that the percentage rate at which high-ability people acquire specific job skills exceeds the rate for less-skilled people. A low positive or zero simple correlation between initial earnings and ability could reflect the fact that employers have imprecise information about the current and future productivity of new members of the labor force at the time they are hired. After employees have gained experience, the reassessment of their productivity and the higher speed with which the more able workers acquire specific job skills should combine so that the percentage rate of increase in earnings will be higher for those with more ability (at least initially). A negative simple correlation between initial earnings and ability could arise if ability is a strong complement of on-the-job training which must be paid for by reduced initial earnings. In this case, at some point in time the relative earnings of high-ability people would have to rise more rapidly than those of less-able people to make worthwhile the former's greater investment in training.

In addition to determining the relationship between earnings, schooling, and ability at different points on the earnings profile, i is also useful to consider how these factors are related to lifetime (discounted) earnings. Even if people have identical ability and schooling, the growth of individual productivity over time may differ between jobs. In the absence of nonpecuniary occupational tastes, there would be a tendency for entry rates to different occupations to be governed by the condition that they lead to the same (net) present value of earnings. Thus significant dispersion of earnings at different points along the earnings profile is in principle compatible with relatively little dispersion in the net present values. Since people presumably take into account prospective profiles of earnings over time and not merely the earnings for a single year when they make decisions about schooling and occupation, the attempt to establish statistically the determinants of the present value of earnings (or closely related functions of the earnings profile) plays an important part in understanding these decisions. The preceding remarks on ability and how it may affect the earnings profile also imply that there is likely to be a positive correlation between ability and discounted earnings.

We consider next the relationship between ability and discounted earnings for different levels of schooling. A number of expository and statistical models express earnings (usually for a single year after earnings profiles have flattened out) as a linear function of schooling, ability, and an uncorrelated random variable:[2]

$$Y = \beta_0 + \beta_1 S + \beta_2 A + u \tag{5-2}$$

This relationship does not seem plausible. It implies that schooling and ability are perfect substitutes in determining earnings (because of the linear form). More important, it implies that the marginal product of additional schooling is independent of ability (because of separability). The latter assumption is implausible for two well-known reasons. First, there is the systematic tendency of higher-ability people (as measured by IQ or other tests) to acquire more schooling than others. Second, the opportunity cost of forgone earnings is a large part (more than half) of the cost of obtaining higher levels of schooling for most people (Schultz, 1968). Equation (5-2) implies that the opportunity cost of acquiring additional schooling is greater for more able people; yet this schooling yields

---

[2] See, for example, Hansen, Weisbrod, and Scanlon (1970) or Ashenfelter and Mooney (1968).

the same increment to earnings to everyone, independently of ability. Thus the economic incentive to acquire additional schooling implied by this model is greater for those with less ability, and their expected rate of return would be higher.

An alternative specification that captures the opportunity cost of acquiring schooling in a more plausible way replaces the level of earnings Y by log Y in Eq. (5-2). In this formulation, the level of earnings for people with different ability increases equiproportionally with schooling. Even this specification, however, provides no economic rationale for the strong tendency of people with greater ability to acquire more formal education. Table 5-1 (which may contain some response bias) shows the strength of this relationship for male high school graduates of 1960. Although the sons of high income families are more likely to enter college at all ability levels, the ability–college entrance relationship is very strong within family income classes. Tables 5-5, 5-7, and 5-9 show the same positive association between measured ability and terminal level of schooling.

Consider a simple model in which education is acquired solely to increase earnings and in which perfect foresight and a perfect capital market for funds to support schooling are assumed. For this model, equilibrium is attained when the flows of people of different ability to different terminal levels of schooling lead to relative wages such that net present values of earnings are the same for people with the same ability but different schooling attainment. In such a world, regressions of the logarithm of earnings on ability within each schooling class would result in coefficients of ability that are roughly the same for different schooling levels. However, the very imperfect market for educational loans (and perhaps uncertainty

TABLE 5-1 Percentage of male high school graduate questionnaire respondents **not** entering college within one year of graduation, 1960			*Family's finances*			
	Aptitude percentile	*Extremely wealthy or wealthy*	*Well-to-do*	*Comfortable*	*Have necessities*	*Barely make living*
	90–99.9	3.7	5.1	7.7	14.5	16.?
	75–89.9	13.5	10.4	19.5	27.0	21.?
	50–74.9	25.3	23.0	40.2	41.8	51.?
	25–49.9	39.4	44.2	59.1	70.3	78.?
	0–24.9	83.5	72.5	77.0	81.6	87.?

SOURCE: Project Talent, *The American High-School Student,* Final Report Coop. Project 635, U.S. Office of Education, Washington, 1964, Tables 11–18.

might well result in coefficients of ability that rise with education. The hypotheses of this section are examined empirically below.

TESTING ABILITY AND EARNINGS HYPOTHESES The four samples of cohort data used to study the ability-schooling-earnings relationship are described in detail in Appendix A. The samples differ substantially in size, in the populations from which they are drawn, and in supplementary variables. The small sample of Rogers has been studied more thoroughly than the others, but parallel calculations with the other samples confirm, qualify, and extend these results.

Results from Rogers's Data The calculations from the important sample obtained by Daniel C. Rogers are based on a survey of 343 white males, primarily from Connecticut, who were eighth graders when tested for IQ in 1935. Table 5-2 shows mean values (and standard deviations of background variables) and the logarithm of earnings for different schooling levels at five-year intervals from 1950 through 1965. The five schooling levels are E_1, high school nongraduates; E_2, high school graduates; E_3, college nongraduates; E_4, college graduates with one degree (and perhaps additional study); and E_5, holders of two or more degrees. The intervention of World War II may make the E_3 group atypically heterogeneous since it includes men who started college shortly before the war, entered the military, and did not return to college thereafter. It also includes those college dropouts who initially entered college after completing military service, attracted in part by GI Bill subsidies that made out-of-pocket costs of college attendance relatively low. The motivations causing men to enter college but not graduate are diverse in any period, and they were probably unusually mixed in this sample. Therefore, one should interpret the results for this subgroup with caution.

The background variables used in the analysis of Rogers's data are subpopulation dummy variables for social class ($SCH = 1$ for the highest two social classes, out of five, and $SCL = 1$ for the lowest two), religion ($RC = 1$ for Catholic background and $RJ = 1$ for Jewish background), private school attendance ($PS = 1$ for precollege private schooling), and marital status ($NM = 1$ if not married in 1965). No attempt will be made in this chapter to rationalize the precise role played by these variables in the earnings function. None of them were highly correlated with measured

TABLE 5-2 Means and standard deviations* of log earnings, IQ, and background variables by educational level, Rogers sample	Educational level	Sample size N	LE65	LE60	LE55	LE50	LDE4%	IQ
	E_1	60	8.857 (.326)	8.708 (.281)	8.664 (.279)	8.569 (.335)	11.836 (.221)	95.9 (11.8)
	E_2	117	9.001 (.392)	8.764 (.336)	8.662 (.320)	8.550 (.338)	11.872 (.324)	102.3 (11.1)
	E_3	51	9.262 (.557)	9.057 (.439)	8.900 (.428)	8.668 (.478)	12.070 (.429)	107.8 (9.59)
	E_4	68	9.456 (.539)	9.253 (.479)	9.008 (.432)	8.689 (.535)	12.211 (.519)	115.8 (11.00)
	E_5	47	9.640 (.574)	9.414 (.607)	9.061 (.502)	8.525 (.624)	12.262 (.445)	117.3 (10.0)

*Numbers in parentheses are standard deviations.
SOURCE: Data tape of D. C. Rogers.

ability (IQ). They do, however, help to prevent an exaggeration of the role of ability in the regressions, and they also help to eliminate some sources of differential earnings that make it difficult to estimate an ability effect from the small samples that are available.

In Table 5-2 all the mean earnings estimates increase with schooling except in 1950, when the E_5 group had very little postschool experience. (There is one trivial reversal in 1955.) The standard deviations of the logs of earnings are substantially lower for E_1 and E_2 levels, which suggests, in principle, that weighted regressions should be used if all schooling classes are pooled in one regression. The table shows the positive association of IQ and schooling attainment, which suggests that schooling and IQ have a positive interaction on earnings—a hypothesis proposed above. Marital status is not systematically related to schooling attainment, but is included in the empirical work because of the strong tendency for unmarried men to have substantially lower earnings than married men. The entire set of background variables based on Rogers's data is frequently used in regressions in this chapter and is denoted by X^* in the following discussion and tables.

The size of the schooling subgroups in this sample is small, leading to large standard errors in many of the parameter estimates. Even so, there are some suggestive patterns that broadly conform to some of the hypotheses, although they cannot be confirmed with high statistical significance.

Several theoretical and empirical arguments in the preceding section explain why schooling and ability are unlikely to be perfect substitutes in producing earnings. Table 5-3 provides some

SCH	SCL	RC	RJ	PS	NM
.033	.917	.750	—	.033	.050
.034	.829	.650	.017	.094	.077
.196	.529	.431	.039	.235	.039
.412	.427	.325	.059	.470	.059
.446	.319	.298	.170	.383	.042

evidence for this by showing the linear regressions of 1965 earnings and discounted lifetime earnings (at 4 percent) on IQ and the background variables X^*.

The pattern of IQ coefficients (except in E_3) is broadly consistent with the belief that the coefficient of ability increases with educational level in linear regressions. IQ is only trivially related to earnings for the lowest schooling level, but appears to make a moderate empirical difference in earnings as the schooling level rises. An approximate chi-square test of the statistical hypothesis that the 1965 IQ coefficients are equal across educational classes (excluding the peculiar E_3 class) indicates that the probability of the null hypothesis is less than .05.[3] This result and the array of IQ coefficients in Table 5-3 suggest that there is positive interaction between IQ and educational level and that the linear model is misspecified because it does not allow for interaction when educational levels are pooled in one regression equation.

The low coefficient for the E_3 group (some college) is anomalous. This result may be sample-specific, for historical reasons already mentioned, or there may be some unobservable factor that leads to self-selection by those who terminate their schooling at this level. Still it is unclear why the effect of IQ on earnings should be this weak.

[3] For this test, a weighted mean was constructed from the IQ coefficients of the 1965 regressions in Table 5-2. Let $w_i = (1/\sigma_{\beta_i})/\Sigma_j (1/\sigma_{\beta_j})$, where σ_{β_i} is the estimated standard error of β_i, the IQ coefficient of schooling group E_i. Let the weighted mean $\beta_w = \Sigma w_i \beta_i$. Then $\Sigma[(\beta_i - \beta_w)/\sigma_{\beta_i}]^2$ is approximately chi-square with three degrees of freedom (for the four educational classes). In this case, the chi-square value is 9.5.

TABLE 5-3
Linear regressions of earnings on IQ and background variables (X*), Rogers sample

Educational level	Sample size N	1965 earnings		Discounted lifetime earnings (4%)	
		β_{IQ}	R^2	β_{IQ}	R^2
E_1	60	−3.5 (26.9)	.16	−115 (367)	.19
E_2	117	74.6 (35.8)	.19	756 (592)	.09
E_3	51	−2.2 (127.2)	.34	−589 (1,606)	.23
E_4	68	186.4 (94.7)	.29	1,668 (2,625)	.21
E_5	47	223.0 (154.5)	.19	1,968 (1,754)	.19

NOTE: Numbers in parentheses are standard errors.
SOURCE: Author's computations are from data in Rogers sample.

Table 5-4 contains regressions of the logarithm of earnings on IQ and the background variables X^* and is designed to explore the hypothesis that IQ differentials affect earnings equiproportionally at all educational levels. As before, IQ continues to have a very weak association with earnings of high school nongraduates, and we also get the continued anomaly of a small coefficient for E_3. Nonetheless, the pattern of IQ coefficients across schooling levels for 1965 earnings, and for discounted lifetime earnings, is consistent with the argument that ability should tend to increase earnings at least proportionally for increasing levels of schooling. Indeed, the IQ coefficient on 1965 earnings and discounted earnings appears to jump substantially for the highest educational level, a suggestive result, although the difference in the E_4 and E_5 coefficients in this small sample is not statistically significant.

To facilitate comparisons with other samples in which different tests are used to measure ability, the product of the IQ coefficient and one standard deviation of the test score for each schooling cohort is shown, in brackets, in the 1965 column of Table 5-4. Since the dependent variable is the natural logarithm of earnings and since the standardized IQ coefficient is usually small, the latter can be interpreted as being approximately equal to the relative increase in earnings associated with a change of one standard deviation in the IQ.

In order to study how IQ affects earnings for a given schooling level, regressions can be run using as dependent variables the differences in the logarithm of earnings for distinct years. The co

TABLE 5-4
Coefficients*
on IQ from
regressions
of log earnings,
by year or by
discount rate,
on IQ and
background
variables (X*),
Rogers sample

Educational level	Sample size N	1965	1960	1955	1950	4%
E_1	60	.024 (.35) [.0026]	.14 (.29)	.20 (.29)	−.27 (.36)	−.01 (.24)
E_2	117	.70 (.32) [.078]	.36 (.29)	.32 (.28)	.28 (.30)	.45 (.27)
E_3	51	.36 (.78) [.035]	.17 (.66)	.32 (.62)	.04 (.68)	.00 (.63)
E_4	68	.92 (.63) [.101]	.70 (.55)	.53 (.51)	.74 (.69)	.42 (.61)
E_5	47	1.32 (.90) [.132]	1.01 (.99)	−.18 (.97)	−.17 (1.11)	.78 (.75)
Pooled†	345	.49 (.23)	.46 (.20)	.29 (.20)	.15 (.22)	.35 (.19)

* Numbers in parentheses are standard errors. Coefficients and standard errors are multipled by 100. The bracketed figures are the product of the IQ coefficient and one standard deviation of IQ, from Table 5-1, and were *not* multiplied by 100. The 1965 IQ coefficient for E_5, for example, implies a 1.32% rise in earnings with a one-point rise in IQ, and since the standard deviation of IQ is 10 for E_5, this magnitude of IQ change implies approximately a 13.2% change in earnings.

† The pooled regression includes the background variables and the dummies for educational level.

SOURCE: Author's computations are from data in Rogers sample.

efficient of an independent variable can then be interpreted as the percentage change in earnings over time associated with the variable. The coefficients of IQ that would be obtained from this calculation can be read directly from Table 5-4 by taking the difference in the coefficients for any pair of years. For E_5 (two or more college degrees), IQ appears to have an effect that increases substantially over time. This tendency of ability to become more important as labor force experience increases is pervasive, but is weaker at lower levels of schooling. Although occupational information was unavailable, the larger rise in ability effects over time among the highly educated might be due in part to substantial earnings by high-ability professional men, whose earnings may increase rapidly after their lengthy training is completed. (The initial small negative correlations of IQ with earnings for this group in 1950 and 1955 may also be due partly to the late labor market entry of these professionals.

On the basis of Rogers's sample, what conclusions can be drawn about the important problem of bias in the returns to education when ability is ignored? It seems to be well established that mean IQ increases with schooling level. If IQ is positively correlated with earnings at each schooling level, an earnings differential calculated by taking the difference in mean earnings for each schooling level will exaggerate the potential gain for a person of given ability who acquires more schooling. For the Rogers sample, Table 5-2 indicates that mean IQ is about 13 points higher for college graduates than for high school graduates; the corresponding differential in IQ for college graduates with two degrees over high school graduates is 15 points. The coefficients on IQ for levels E_4 and E_5 in Table 5-4, multiplied by the corresponding IQ differentials, imply that lifetime earnings (discounted at 4 percent) of the average high school graduate would be 6 percent and 8 percent less than the earnings of those who attained the E_4 and E_5 levels, respectively. A similar calculation based on the 1965 earnings-IQ coefficients implies that the average high school graduate (who terminated his education with high school) would earn 13 percent and 18 percent less than the mean E_4 and E_5 individuals, respectively. Thus, this sample indicates the existence of an empirically significant bias in using earnings differentials to calculate the apparent increase in earnings for high school graduates who subsequently take one or more college degrees. Because the IQ-earnings relationship is negligible for high school nongraduates, there is no overstatement of the increased earnings of those who actually completed high school (although there would be an overstatement of the gains to a person whose ability is that of the mean high school nongraduate).

The sample provides a modest but positive rationalization of the strong association between schooling attainment and IQ. The discounted lifetime earnings coefficient for those with two or more degrees is larger in magnitude than the high school coefficient. The product of the difference in the coefficients and the difference in the mean IQ's indicates that lifetime discounted earnings increase 5.4 percent more for a person with IQ 117 than for a person with IQ 102, if both have two degrees.[4]

[4] This magnitude of interaction between IQ and schooling is considerably larger than the 1 percent increase obtained by Rogers (1969, Table 9, p. 115). The difference arises in part because Rogers used an age-in-school variable that is correlated with IQ and because of other differences in formulating a statistical model and handling the data. As explained in App. A., Rogers's sample of 364 was reduced by 21 observations to eliminate individuals with extreme personal

The IQ coefficients for high school graduates and for college graduates with one degree are almost identical for discounted earnings. However, the 1950 IQ coefficient for high school graduates is quite small in comparison with that for college graduates with one degree. The small IQ coefficient for high school graduates suggests that the opportunity cost of earnings while attending college differs little over a wide range of ability, whereas ability makes a larger relative difference early in the earnings career of college graduates. Clearly this provides some incentive for those with higher IQ to attend college.

Results from the Project Talent Data These results are based on a sample of about 8,800 white males who were high school juniors in 1959, when they took ability and achievement tests and provided certain background information, and who in 1966 had full-time employment and responded to a mail questionnaire. Although most of the college graduates have not had more than one year of postcollege work experience, and although later points along the earnings profile are not yet available, it is interesting to compare this large sample with the Rogers evidence. Table 5-5 is analogous to Table 5-1 and provides data on earnings, weeks worked, and background variables by schooling level. The five schooling levels are E_1', high school nongraduates; E_2', high school graduates; E_3', college dropouts (with one to two years of college); E_4', college dropouts (with three to four years of college); and E_5', college graduates. A number of ability and achievement variables are available for this sample. The tests included in the table are C001 (a composite test score which is reported to be highly correlated with IQ), C004 (a quantitative test-composite score), R410 (arithmetic computation), and R430 (clerical checking). The background variables include high and low social class (SCH' and SCL', obtained from a composite socioeconomic status variable, $P*801$, developed by Project Talent), religion ($RC = 1$ for Catholic background, and $RJ = 1$ for Jewish background), nonpublic school attendance ($PARS = 1$ for parochial school attendance in 1959, and $PRVS = 1$ for private school attendance), not

---

characteristics. This procedure could lead to some modification of the IQ coefficients. Rogers measured social class by a four-valued single variable, whereas I trichotomized the sample by dummy variables. Finally, my results are based on coefficients from individual regressions by schooling level to allow for full interactions with the other variables. Rogers pooled his observations in a single regression in which the IQ-schooling interaction was allowed (but no other schooling-level differences).

married in 1966 *(NM)*, and a variable for region of school in 1959 ($S = 1$ for U.S. Office of Education, Region 5—Southeast).[5]

The logarithmic mean earnings for 1966 are irregularly ordered with respect to schooling attainment. The mean for high school nongraduates is slightly larger than the mean for high school graduates. This may reflect a differential response bias favoring nongraduates with high earnings, although direct evidence is not available on this point. The differences in the mean of log-weeks worked are partly responsible for the lower earnings means of the E_4' and E_5' schooling levels. If we assume that earnings per week are unaffected by the number of weeks worked and if we standardize all 1966 earnings to the 3.90 mean of log-weeks worked of the E_1' class, the five log-earnings figures for E_1' through E_5' are 8.54, 8.47, 8.42, 8.38, and 8.56, respectively.[6] This adjustment reduces the differentials between log-earnings of the schooling levels, although only the rank of college graduate earnings is changed. The ranking is probably influenced significantly by the productivity gains that have already been achieved by those in the lower levels of schooling attainment, and behavior of similar samples suggests that the rank-

[5] The Project Talent data bank does not include the 1966 place of residence of respondents. The only geographic information readily available is region of 1959 schooling.

[6] In fact, this adjustment appears to be too large. Within schooling class, the regression coefficients on log-weeks worked are about .7. I shall not burden this footnote with ad hoc conjectures rationalizing this result.

TABLE 5-5
Means and standard deviations* of log earnings, ability, and achievement variables and background variables by educational level, Project Talent sample

Educational level	Sample size N	LE66	LE62†	LNWK (log of weeks worked)	C001 (IQ composite)	C004 (quantitative composite
E_1'	183	8.535 (.404)	7.913 (.555)	3.90 (.14)	139 (50)	72 (31)
E_2'	3,853	8.475 (.454)	7.833 (.580)	3.91 (.13)	166 (44)	95 (36)
E_3'	1,914	8.411 (.514)		3.89 (.20)	192 (42)	121 (42)
E_4'	793	8.302 (.598)		3.81 (.32)	202 (38)	135 (42)
E_5'	2,097	8.271 (.597)		3.61 (.50)	217 (31)	156 (40)

* Numbers in parentheses are standard deviations.

† Sample sizes for these two educational levels are 63 and 1,854.

SOURCE: Data tape on subsample of high school juniors, Project Talent.

ing will be altered in favor of those with more schooling in the future. I intend to test this conjecture in a future study.

The significant tendency of abstract ability (C001 and C004) to rise with level of schooling parallels the Rogers data. The more specific skills (R410 and R430) also tend to rise with schooling, but within schooling level, standard deviations for these variables are relatively much larger than the mean differences between schooling levels. The inverse relation between fraction married and level of schooling in these data is consistent with the young age of this cohort in 1966. The association (or lack of association) between the remaining background variables and schooling is also similar to Rogers's findings.

Regressions are reported for the logarithm of 1966 earnings on *one* of the ability or skill variables and $X'* = (SCH', SCL', RC, RJ, PARS, PRVS, NM, S, LNWK)$.[7] Table 5-6 shows the coeffi-

[7] The variable *LNWK* (log of weeks worked) is included as an independent variable for two reasons. First, including it makes the results more comparable with the 1950 calculations from Rogers's data and the Thorndike sample (both of these give earnings on a full-time equivalent basis). Second, many individuals with E_4' and E_5' schooling attainment were relatively new to the labor force and worked less than a full year (as suggested by the considerably lower mean value of *LNWK* for these two groups). As far as this study is concerned, this source of variation of the log of earnings is largely "noise" at the higher educational levels.

Including *LNWK* reduces the magnitude of the ability and skill coefficients for the three lowest educational levels, but not by enough to greatly change the statistical or empirical significance of the coefficients shown in Table 5-6.

R410 (arithmetic computation)	R430 (clerical checking)	SCL'	SCH'	RC	RJ	NM	S	PARS	PRVS
38 (13)	39 (18)	.399	.279	.328	.016	.284	.137	.022	.011
40 (10)	40 (16)	.314	.283	.331	.015	.398	.165	.061	.012
42 (9)	41 (15)	.169	.465	.315	.041	.462	.159	.099	.026
44 (9)	41 (14)	.107	.603	.282	.062	.484	.160	.106	.039
47 (9)	42 (13)	.113	.621	.266	.078	.502	.157	.102	.044

TABLE 5-6
Coefficients* on ability and skill measures, from regressions of log earnings (1966) on an ability or skill and background variable (X'*), Project Talent sample

Educational level	Sample size N	Ability or skill variable				
		C001	C004	R410	R430	C004†
E'_1	183	.04 (.059) [.012]	.02 (.125) [.006]	−.06 (.222)	.00 (.30)	.06 (.088)
E'_2	3,853	.02 (.013) [.009]	.06 (.018) [.022]	.11 (.073) [.011]	.12 (.044) [.019]	.09 (.019)
E'_3	1,914	−.03 (.025)	.00 (.100)	.16 (.114) [.014]	.30 (.071) [.045]	.02 (.032)
E'_4	793	.04 (.051)	−.03 (.054)	.44 (.200) [.040]	.44 (.126) [.062]	.00 (.090)
E'_5	2,097	−.01 (.030)	.06 (.027) [.024]	.47 (.117) [.041]	.19 (.080) [.025]	.06 (.027)

* Numbers in parentheses are standard errors. Coefficients and standard errors are multiplied by 100. The bracketed figures are the product of the ability or skill coefficient and one standard deviation of the corresponding test by schooling level and are *not* multiplied by 100.

For completeness, the 1961 coefficients for the first two schooling levels and first four columns are as follows: E'_1 ($N = 63$): .17 (.16); .08 (.25); −.83 (.57); and −.25 (.39). For E'_2 ($N = 1854$); −.08 (.033); −.07 (.037); .05 (.13); and .11 (.089)

† In this column, the other independent variables were *LNWK, RC, RJ,* and *NM.* Other variables more highly correlated with C004 are omitted.

SOURCE: Author's computation from Project Talent sample.

cients and standard error of the different ability and skill measures and (selectively) the product of the ability or skill coefficient multiplied by one standard deviation of the corresponding test measure for the appropriate schooling level. The C001 coefficient (general ability composite) is very weak in its effect at all levels and, in fact, is negative (but not significant) both for college dropouts with one or two years of college and for college graduates. The C004 (quantitative composite) is significant and positive for high school and college graduates (and negative, but insignificant, for college dropouts with three or four years of college).

This pattern seems broadly consistent with the 1950 results from Rogers's data. The ability variables have a very weak association with earnings for high school dropouts. Their influence rises for high school graduates, declines for college dropouts, and rises again for college graduates. For all schooling levels, the quantitative effect of ability differentials on earnings seems to be quite small at early points along the earnings profile. These results also suggest that college dropouts differ in some way from high school and college graduates, and the earnings-ability relationship for them cannot be interpolated simply from results for high school and college graduates. Perhaps dropping out reflects differences in motivation, or perhaps the jobs that dropouts take require specific skills that are less complementary with general cognitive ability than the skills required for jobs taken by the high school graduates. This problem is not pursued further in this chapter. The last column in Table 5-6 shows the regression coefficient of C004 when the other independent variables are *LNWK, RC, RJ,* and *NM.* Since other independent variables that have greater correlation with ability have been left out, the figures indicate the maximum effect that C004 could plausibly exert on earnings. The size of the effect remains small at all schooling levels.

Consider next the more specific skills, R410 (arithmetic computation) and R430 (clerical checking). Not surprisingly, at this early point in earnings careers when people have not yet acquired highly job-specific skills from experience, these skill variables have a stronger effect on earnings than the broader-based ability measures and thus are probably better indicators of differences in current productivity than the ability measures. These measured skills probably increase personal productivity in a number of occupations, but not in all. Differences in the distribution of jobs by educational level may explain why the skill coefficients tend to be smaller for the E_1' and E_2' cohorts.

Although these skills appear to be associated with modest earnings differentials, they are not highly correlated with schooling attainment. Omitting them is therefore unlikely to be a significant source of bias in estimating returns from schooling.

Results from the NBER-Thorndike Data

The NBER-Thorndike sample includes white males who took and passed a battery of tests given by the United States Army Air Force to prospective pilots and navigators during World War II. Earnings data and additional information were obtained from questionnaires in 1955 and 1969. The results discussed here eliminate proprietors, teachers, pilots, and farmers and restrict attention to those born in the period 1921–1925 (which overlaps the Rogers sample).

The means and standard deviations of earnings and the test battery score means of the standard background variables are shown in Table 5-7. They follow patterns by schooling level that

TABLE 5-7 *Means and standard deviations* of log earnings, ability, and background variables by educational level, NBER-Thorndike sample*

Educational level	Sample size N†	LE69	LE55	TST43	FEDL (father's education, low)	FEDH (father's education, high)	RC	RJ	NM	S
E_1^+	489	9.128 (.362)	8.645 (.292)	−.62 (1.57)	.760	.035	.309	.022	.045	.121
E_2^+	535	9.301 (.403)	8.743 (.312)	−.31 (1.58)	.600	.077	.230	.034	.047	.151
E_3^+	900	9.517 (.376)	8.849 (.419)	.45 (1.83)	.536	.133	.231	.040	.044	.174
E_4^+	211	9.600 (.436)	8.842 (.337)	.94 (1.91)	.530	.137	.180	.081	.047	.114
E_5^+	128	9.885 (.494)	8.872 (.328)	.38 (1.83)	.515	.250	.266	.094	.047	.227
E_6^+	53	10.061 (.387)	9.094 (.694)	.51 (1.62)	.472	.245	.264	.057	.057	.151

*Numbers in parentheses are standard deviations.

† Sample size is for 1969 earnings. Sample sizes for the original 1955 earnings for the six education classes are 475, 520, 873, 209, 105, and 36.

SOURCE: Author's computations are from NBER-Thorndike data.

resemble the Rogers and Project Talent data. The six schooling classes are E_1^+, high school graduate; E_2^+, some college; E_3^+, college graduate with one degree; E_4^+, college graduate with two or more degrees; E_5^+, lawyer; and E_6^+, doctor. The last three classes are mutually exclusive. Because of the higher investment in professional training required by lawyers and physicians, these two occupations are distinguished for separate analysis. The ability measure TST43 is a composite of 17 Air Force tests taken in 1943. These statistics are from a subsample of people born between 1922 and 1925. Consequently, virtually everyone in this subsample had completed high school when ability was measured, whereas relatively few had higher schooling attainment at that time. This means that measured ability differentials in this sample cannot be attributed to schooling differentials prior to the testing in 1943.

The background variables include father's education ($FEDH =$ 1 if father had at least a college degree, and $FEDL = 1$ if father did not graduate from high school), religion ($RC = 1$ if Catholic, and $RJ = 1$ if Jewish), marital status ($NM = 1$ if not married in 1969), and region ($S = 1$ if from U.S. Office of Education Region 5 − Southeast).

In 1969 the logarithmic mean earnings for E_1^+ through the E_4^+ schooling attainment levels rise consistently and continue to rise for the two professions of law and medicine. One minor reversal of this pattern occurs in the original earnings means in 1955, where those with two or more college degrees (E_4^+) earned about 7 percent less than those with one college degree. This irregularity may well reflect the relatively limited earnings experience in 1955 of those with high levels of formal education. The ability measure TST43 rises significantly with schooling attainment over the first four schooling classes. It does not separate the schooling levels (in terms of the extent to which one standard deviation of the test score overlaps the mean score from adjacent levels) as strongly as the Rogers and Project Talent samples because initial screening had already been imposed before these men were given the battery of Air Force tests. More specifically, this factor means that high school graduates in this sample have atypically high measured ability.

Table 5-8 shows the ability variable coefficients from regressions of the logarithm of earnings on TST43 and background variables $X\dagger^* = (FEDH, FEDL, RC, RJ, NM, S)$. Several patterns in these coefficients are strikingly similar to the results from Rogers's data in Table 5-3. In 1969 the coefficient for the group having some college is less than the coefficient for either high school graduates or college graduates, and it has lower statistical significance. The coefficient increases substantially for those with two or more college degrees over those with a single degree. This increase is much more dramatic in the Thorndike sample and is statistically highly significant. The two professional groups are small samples, which yield coefficients that lie between those for one-degree and two-degree college graduates, but closer to the one-degree level.

The tendency for ability coefficients to increase over time within schooling level is another common characteristic of the Thorndike and Rogers samples. (Compare the 1955-to-1965 increase in Table 5-4 with the 1955-to-1969 change in Table 5-8.) A substantial increase in the ability coefficient of high school graduates is observed in both samples. The substantial increases for lawyers and doctors resemble more closely the Rogers E_5 class (which includes doctors and lawyers) than the Thorndike E_4^+ class (which excludes them). The 1955 coefficient for the Thorndike college graduates with two or more degrees seems surprisingly large. For comparable schooling levels, the Thorndike sample implies in most cases a

TABLE 5-8 Coefficients* on 1943 ability from regressions of log earnings on TST43 and background variables (X^{+*}), NBER-Thorndike sample		Educational level	Sample size N†	Year	
				1969	1955
		E_1^+	489	.0267 (.0102) [.042]	.0061 (.0085)
		E_2^+	535	.0213 (.0110) [.033]	.0206 (.0086)
		E_3^+	900	.0265 (.0067) [.048]	.0274 (.0053)
		E_4^+	211	.0715 (.0144) [.137]	.0600 (.0113)
		E_5^+	128	.0441 (.0242) [.080]	.0252 (.0177)
		E_6^+	53	.0303 (.0336) [.049]	−.064 (.104)

* Numbers in parentheses are standard errors. The bracketed figures are the product of the TST43 coefficient and one standard deviation of the test score by schooling level. The ability variables had a different scaling in the original data, and the coefficients were not multiplied by 100.

† Sample sizes for 1955 earnings regressions are slightly smaller than those for 1969 given in the table because of prior rejection of extreme observations. For these six education classes, they are 475, 520, 873, 209, 102, and 36.

SOURCE: Author's computations are from NBER-Thorndike data.

smaller earnings differential associated with one standard deviation of measured ability (within schooling level) than the Rogers data. However, at the highest schooling level—two or more college degrees—both samples suggest a 13 or 14 percent earnings differential with this much variation in ability.

Taking the sample means of TST43 for E_1^+, E_3^+, and E_4^+ individuals and multiplying them by the ability coefficients for college graduates with one degree and with two or more degrees leads to figures indicating that neglect of ability differences results in overstating the potential earnings gains to (average) terminal high school graduates by 2.8 and 11.1 percent, respectively. This is a substantial understatement of the bias for the population, since the Thorndike high school graduates had unusually high ability because of Air Force prescreening.

FIGURE 5-1 *Structure of the Swedish school system, 1928–1950.*

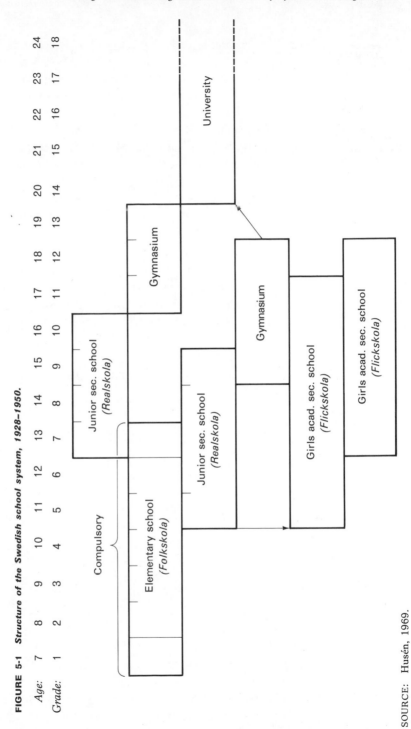

SOURCE: Husén, 1969.

The Husén sample includes some 450 Swedish males who were third graders in Malmö when originally tested in 1938 and who answered a questionnaire in 1964. Earnings data were obtained by searching records of past income tax returns.

Table 5-9 summarizes the available earnings data and background variables by schooling attainment. The seven schooling levels are E_1'', *folkskola* completed (*folkskola* is the Swedish elementary school); E_2'', *folkskola* completed (usually at age 14); E_3'', some *realskola* (secondary school); E_4'', *realexamen* (*realskola* completed usually at age 16 or 17) and technical school graduate; E_5'', *studentexamen* (completion of the gymnasium, roughly junior college, at ages 19 to 21); E_6'', university degree (excluding E_7''; and E_7'', physician or dentist. The ability measure TST38 is the total score from four subtests and is highly similar in content to IQ tests. The background variables include dummy variables for social class ($SCH'' = 1$ for the highest of four classes of a discrete social-class variable and $SCL'' = 1$ for the lowest), private school

TABLE 5-9
Means and standard deviations^a of log earnings, ability, and background variables by educational level, Husén Swedish sample

Educational level	Sample size N^b	LE68	LE64	LE59	LE54	LE49	TST38
E_1''	18	9.494 (.278)	9.249 (.223)	8.833^c (.267)	8.986 (.232)	8.154^d (.458)	34.1 (12.7)
E_2''	235	9.455 (.318)	9.208 (.305)	8.996 (.229)	9.033 (.182)	8.225 (.349)	44.3 (13.5)
E_3''	59	9.515 (.380)	9.328 (.266)	9.058 (.239)	9.035 (.259)	8.234 (.450)	50.9 (13.9)
E_4''	66	9.849 (.393)	9.562 (.322)	9.191 (.283)	9.042 (.245)	8.133 (.393)	56.3 (12.5)
E_5''	51	10.061 (.346)	9.574 (.491)	9.260^e (.376)			59.6 (11.8)
E_6''	26	10.236 (.286)					60.6 (9.2)
E_7''	5	10.529 (.167)					66.8^f (4.6)

^{a} Earnings means are deflated by the Swedish Consumer Price Index (1949 = 100) Numbers in parentheses are standard deviations.
^{b} N is for 1968 earnings and all other nonearnings variables, and was lower in earlie years. Cells with very few observations are indicated.
^{c} Sample size 120.
^{d} Sample size 7.
^{e} Sample size 20.
^{f} Sample size 8.
SOURCE: Author's computations are from data in Husén Swedish sample.

attendance in 1938 ($PS = 1$), never married ($NM = 1$), and serious prolonged illness during the late teens or thereafter ($PHLTH = 1$).

As Table 5-9 indicates, by 1968 (mean age 40) there are large differentials in earnings between some of the educational levels, with the more highly educated obtaining greater earnings. The table includes only those who responded to the 1964 questionnaire, and response bias may be partially responsible for the slightly higher mean of log-earnings for E_1'' over E_2''; another calculation not limited to questionnaire respondents yielded mean log earnings for E_2'' and E_1'' of 9.401 and 9.320, respectively, in 1968. At the time members of this sample were in school, the Swedish educational system was organized strongly in the continental tradition, under which relatively few people obtain high levels of education. Most children terminated their formal study with the completion of the *folkskola* (elementary school) at the age of 14. The attrition rate of those starting the *realskola* was high, and only a little over half

SCH"	SCL"	PS	NM"	PHLTH
	.428		.111	.056
.017	.404		.089	.127
.068	.203	.017	.068	.051
.152	.136	.030	.106	.091
.294	.156	.059	.098	.078
.539	.039	.238	.077	.077

obtained the secondary *realexamen* degree (or equivalent past-*folkskola* degree from more vocationally oriented alternatives). This difference in educational systems probably explains why there is such a modest tendency for the 1938 test score to rise after E_4'' *(realexamen)* is achieved in this sample (except for the small E_7'' group—highly trained physicians and dentists). There is a very strong tendency for the highest socioeconomic class to become an increasingly important source of students attaining schooling beyond E_4''.

Almost all the direct schooling costs at the university level were absorbed by the Swedish government, and university admission was limited almost entirely to people who passed the *studentexamen* (i.e., attained level E_5''). In this sample, slightly over a third of those passing *studentexamen* achieved a university degree (E_6'' and E_7''). These facts indicate that a relatively small proportion of those with middle and low socioeconomic backgrounds found it worthwhile getting a university degree even if they passed the *studentexamen.* In turn, this result suggests that those terminating formal education with the *studentexamen* did not believe that the higher earnings of university graduates were enough to offset the out-of-pocket living costs incurred while studying at the university and the opportunity cost of forgone earnings. Thus it may be that the investment motive for higher earnings played a less-important role in Sweden than in the United States in determining university attendance during this period.

Table 5-10 shows the pattern of the ability (TST38) coefficient by schooling attainment over time. Other independent variables are $X''*$ ($= SCH''$, SCL'', PS, NM'', $PHLTH$). All ability coefficients are positive for 1968, although the statistical significance of the individual coefficients is low. The pattern of coefficients over time and across schooling levels is much less regular than the comparable calculations from Rogers's data. This irregularity may be due partly to the very small size of the samples (especially for E_1'' and E_6'') and to earnings statistics' being based on actual annual earnings instead of the full-time annual equivalent earnings (or controls for weeks worked) available in the other samples. It appears that measured ability plays a more important role for E_4'' and E_5'' than for the lower E_2'' and E_3'' levels. The size of the ability coefficient is surprisingly large for E_5'' in 1964 and 1959, where a change of one standard deviation in the test score is associated with a change in earnings exceeding 13 percent. The

TABLE 5-10 Coefficients* on 1938 ability from regressions of log-earnings on TST38 and background variables (X″*), Husén Swedish sample	Educational level	Sample size N	Year					
			1968	1964	1959	1954	1949	1968†
	E_1''	18	.39 (.61) [.049]	−.23 (.78)	−.86‡ (.68)			
	E_2''	235	.05 (.80)	.13 (.16)	.14 (.14)	.19 (.12)	.12 (.27)	.32 (.19) [.037]
	E_3''	59	.22 (.38) [.001]	.32 (.29)	.11 (.27)	−.54 (.33)	.04 (.71)	.40 (.47) [.050]
	E_4''	66	.43 (.39) [.054]	.46 (.38)	.35 (.36)	.62 (.51)	−.84§ (.81)	.03 (.58) [.105]
	E_5''	51	.58 (.41) [.068]	1.19 (.86)	1.09 (.83)			1.06 (.78) [.106]
	E_6''	26	.22 (.66) [.010]					

* Numbers in parentheses are standard errors. Coefficients and standard errors are multiplied by 100. The bracketed figures are the product of the TST38 coefficient and one standard deviation of TST38 by schooling level, and are *not* multiplied by 100.

† This column gives regression coefficients on IQ measured in 1948, 10 years after the original tests. The scaling is different from that in the 1938 tests, and so the coefficients are not strictly comparable, although the bracketed products are.

‡ Sample size 12.

§ Sample size 22.

SOURCE: Author's computations are from data in Husén Swedish sample.

peculiar apparent drop in this coefficient in 1968 is a small puzzle not yet resolved.

The modal E_2'' class (*folkskola* graduate) deserves serious attention because of the relatively large sample size of 235 (in 1968). Both the empirical magnitude and statistical significance of the ability coefficients are trivial for all years, indicating the small role played by measured cognitive capacity in determining earnings for members of this group. Special vocational schools, trade schools, correspondence courses, and the like are more important in Sweden than in the United States for teaching market-relevant skills. It is conceivable that there is a wide distribution of investment in such training not highly correlated with cognitive ability that tends to mask the ability variable, a hypothesis that will be tested soon with these data. The apparent decline in the ability coefficient in 1968, if genuine and maintained in subsequent years, is compatible with the conjecture that at this modest level of formal schooling, job performance can be mastered with experience to the point where marginal returns to measured ability are negligible. However, the larger positive, though small, effect of IQ as measured in 1948 on 1968 earnings indicates that the influence of ability does persist even at the E_2'' level.

Summary of Empirical Results The data examined in this chapter imply that measures of cognitive ability are associated with an empirically significant, but modest, increase in annual earnings for those with high levels of schooling. In the three samples with earnings data for people with 15 or 20 years of earnings experience, ability coefficients are found at some level of advanced schooling for which one standard deviation of measured ability (within schooling level) is associated with an earnings differential of at least 11 percent. At lower levels of schooling attainment, measures of cognitive ability have a weaker association with earnings, becoming completely negligible for high school nongraduates or, in the Swedish sample, for those who have not obtained some training at the secondary *(realskola)* level.

In the three United States samples there appears to be a distinct tendency for the ability coefficients in earnings regressions to increase with labor force experience. The temporal pattern for the high school coefficients is especially relevant in considering possible bias in the opportunity cost (forgone earnings) of getting a college degree. For early years in the earnings profile, the ability coefficient is very small, and in most cases not statistically significant. This result implies that bias from this source is negligible. For those with 15 or more years of earnings experience, there is a more significant bias if ability differences are disregarded. Taking the product of the differences between the sample means of ability for two schooling levels and the regression coefficient on ability for the higher of the levels yields the bias in predicting the expected increase in earnings from the schooling increment to a person with the mean ability of those terminating schooling at the lower level. This calculation indicates a positive bias of 13 and 18 percent for average high school graduates who obtain one or several college degrees (Rogers's sample); the corresponding biases implied by the Thorndike data are (at least) 2.8 and 11.1 percent.

The modest contribution of measured ability in explaining the differences in earnings, in contrast with the strong association of measured ability and final schooling attainment, is not very sur prising since most of the ability measures considered here are designed to forecast academic potential and achievement. The coefficients of determination of the within-schooling-class regressions are low, and (more important) the standard deviations of the residuals continue to be large, despite the homogeneity imposed by narrow age range, criteria for omitting observations, and the sets of background variables included in the regressions. In no regression of annual log-earnings does the standard deviation fall below .24. The task of identifying the main determinants of this residual variation remains a major challenge to students of the distribution of earnings.

References

Ashenfelter, O., and J. D. Mooney: "Graduate Education, Ability, and Earnings," *Review of Economics and Statistics,* vol. 50, pp. 78–86, February 1968.

Becker, G. S.: *Human Capital and the Personal Distribution of Income,* Woytinsky Lecture no. 1, University of Michigan, Ann Arbor, 1967.

Griliches, Z.: "Notes on the Role of Education in Production Functions and Growth Accounting," in W. L. Hansen (ed.) *Education, Income, and Human Capital,* Studies in Income and Wealth 35, National Bureau of Economic Research, New York, 1970, pp. 71–115.

Hald, A.: *Statistical Theory with Engineering Applications,* John Wiley & Sons, Inc., New York, 1952.

Hansen, W. L., B. A. Weisbrod, and W. J. Scanlon: "Schooling and Earnings of Low Achievers," *American Economic Review,* vol. 60, pp. 409–418, June 1970.

Husén, T.: *Talent, Opportunity, and Career,* Almqvist and Wiksell, Uppsala, 1969.

Project Talent: *The American High-School Student,* Final Report for Coop. Project 635, U.S. Office of Education, Washington, 1964, Tables 11–18.

The Project Talent Data Bank: A Handbook, American Institutes for Research, Palo Alto, Calif., April 1972.

Rogers, D. C.: "Private Rates of Return to Education in the United States: A Case Study," Ph.D. dissertation, Yale University, New Haven, Conn., 1967. A shortened version is given in *Yale Economic Essays,* vol. 9, pp. 88–134, Spring 1969.

Schultz, T. W.: "Resources for Higher Education: An Economist's View," *Journal of Political Economy,* vol. 76, pp. 327–347, May 1968.

Thorndike, R. L., and E. Hagen: *Ten Thousand Careers,* John Wiley & Sons, Inc., New York, 1959.

6. The Returns to Investment in Higher Education: Another View

by Paul Wachtel

by Paul Wachtel

INTRODUCTION Estimates of the rate of return to investments in education frequently omit any reference to differences in costs among schools, largely because the requisite data are not available.[1] For this chapter a sample of individuals and the college each attended was available, and therefore it was possible to calculate the specific costs of each individual's college education. The assumption was that if cost differences among schools are associated with earnings differences among graduates, these differences should be considered in estimating the rate of return. If cost and earnings differentials are perfectly correlated, rates of return will be unaffected; if they are not, rates of return will vary inversely with costs.

Besides providing estimates of the returns to higher education on the basis of both years of schooling and costs per year, the study represents a very preliminary investigation of the importance of school quality: if colleges operate as efficient firms (at the limits of their production-possibilities frontier), then cost differences will reflect quality differences. However, it is not at all clear that colleges have either the necessary incentives or the knowledge to make efficient use of the resources used in the production of education. Thus there may be many other determinants of college quality besides costs. However, if cost differences alone, which are only a partial determinant of quality, prove to play an important

NOTE: This research was supported by National Institute of Education Grant No. OEG2-71-0479B to the National Bureau of Economic Research. I am grateful to Barry Chiswick, F. Thomas Juster, Jacob Mincer, and Lewis Solmon for many helpful comments and to Stanley Liebowitz for able research assistance.

[1] Early studies of returns (e.g., Becker, 1964), use aggregate average estimates of costs and returns. More recently, estimates of returns from a human capital earnings function (Chiswick & Mincer, 1972) use the number of years of schooling as an index of investment costs because of the paucity of data on other differences in investment costs.

role in the determination of earnings, that would demonstrate the importance of college quality in general as a determinant of earnings.[2]

The data examined are from the NBER-TH sample, which is described at length elsewhere in this volume (Chapters 4 and 5). The respondents are in many ways atypical: They fall in the upper half of the population ability distribution; most obtained their college education after completing their military service and were therefore somewhat older than the average college student; and they had had access to large educational subsidies as a consequence of the GI Bill.

The results show that the variation in investment costs among colleges is an important determinant of earnings. In addition, the estimated rates of return to schooling are lower when all costs are considered than when years of schooling are used as a proxy for all direct and indirect investment costs. This finding supports the hypothesis that students with higher earning potential invest more per year of schooling. Finally, rates of returns on the direct (tuition, etc.) and indirect (forgone earnings) components of investment were estimated, and large differences were observed between the rates.

THE MODEL AND THE DATA The basic framework for the analysis is the human capital earnings function developed by Becker and Mincer. The model states that the earnings of the ith person at time t can be written as the sum of an initial earnings endowment[3] E_{i0} and the sum of returns to all previous human capital investments $r_{ij}C_{ij}$:

$$E_{it} = E_{i0} + \sum_{j=0}^{t-1} r_{ij}C_{ij}, \, t \geq 1 \qquad (6\text{-}1)$$

where r_{ij} is the rate of return and C_{ij} is the cost of investments by the ith person in the jth period. The cost of investments can be expressed as a fraction k_{ij} of potential earnings: $C_{ij} = k_{ij}E_{ij}$. Substituting into Eq. (6-1) and expanding yields Eq. (6-2).

$$E_{it} = E_{i0} + r_{i1}k_{i1}E_{i1} + r_{i2}k_{i2}E_{i2} + \ldots + r_{it-1}k_{it-1}E_{it-1} \qquad (6\text{-}2)$$

[2] The issue of school quality is not further taken up in this chapter. However the importance of quality-related differences among schools is discussed in Solmon and Wachtel (1973). Solmon is now undertaking an extensive examination of various measures of college quality and their effect on earnings.

[3] The initial time period is assumed to be the age of high school graduation since this study is devoted to the returns to college education; therefore, $C_{i0} = 0$

The final form of the earnings function is obtained by substituting recursively into Eq. (6-2) as shown in Eq. (6-3):

$$E_{it} = E_{i0} + r_{i1}k_{i1}E_{i0} + r_{i2}k_{i2}(E_{i0} + r_{i1}k_{i1}E_{i0}) + \dots$$
$$= E_{i0} \prod_{j=1}^{t-1}(1 + r_{ij}k_{ij}) \tag{6-3}$$

For estimation purposes, Eq. (6-4) is obtained by taking the natural logs of Eq. (6-3) and using the approximation that $ln\,(1 + x) = x$ when x is small:

$$ln\,E_{it} = ln\,E_{i0} + \sum_{j=1}^{t-1} r_{ij}k_{ij} \tag{6-4}$$

Mincer has pointed out that k is not zero in the postschool years because of investments in on-the-job training. Following Mincer, it is assumed that investments in the form of on-the-job training follow a linearly declining pattern over the life cycle. In addition, the log of weeks worked W is included as a correction for less than full-year employment. The assumption that the returns to college investments are constant for all investments and all individuals yields the estimating equation:

$$ln\,E_{it} = b_0 + b_1 g_{it} + b_2 g_{it}^2 + b_3 ln\,W_{it}$$
$$+ r \sum_{j=1}^{s} k_{ij} + u_{it} \tag{6-5}$$

where u_{it} is a residual, labor force experience g is measured from the year of first full-time job after high school, and s is the number of years of college education.[4] The least squares coefficient on the investment variable Σk_{ij} is the average rate of return on college investments. It should be noted that in this interpretation, all the returns from education are assumed to be in the form of earnings; other possible benefits, such as the consumption value of attending college and the psychic benefits of being educated, are ignored.

Previous estimates of the returns to schooling have been restricted by the availability of data for direct schooling costs that could be matched with individual earnings. The assumption in

---

[4] Data on time spent in the military are not available. It is therefore assumed that no human capital investments took place during military service unless the initial job experience preceded the war, and then military experience is considered part of labor force experience. About 20 percent of the respondents reported an initial job prior to 1945.

most studies is that the only costs of schooling are forgone earnings; that is, k is equal to one for each year in school. This amounts to assuming that direct private costs are equal to the part-time earnings of students and that the earnings are in turn perfectly correlated with interschool variation in costs. This last assumption is not plausible. The effect of interschool cost differences on the return to education has never been examined, nor has the validity of forgone earnings as a proxy for total costs been tested.

In this study direct cost data for each college or university attended by sample respondents are used to make an explicit calculation of k, the ratio of costs to potential earnings. The total cost of schooling are the indirect costs (forgone earnings) and the direct ones. Alternative measures of direct costs are available; here tuition charges are used to measure direct private costs, and total school expenditures per full-time equivalent student are used t measure direct social costs.[5] Using expenditures per student as measure of direct social cost implies that colleges produce a single homogeneous product — student years. Different product mixes research work, graduate and undergraduate training, sports, an intellectual endeavors are therefore ignored.

To estimate ex post returns to schooling, each k should be a measure of costs as a fraction of potential earnings at the time the educational investments took place. However, the available co data postdate most of the investments. If costs (tuition or e penditures) have become relatively greater over time, calculate values of k will need to be adjusted accordingly. On the average expenditures per college student have in fact increased more quickly than earnings in the postwar period. The increase ma reflect improvements in the output of colleges, as well as an i crease in the relative cost of education. Average tuition charg in private institutions have increased almost as much as expen tures and more than earnings, but tuition charges in public stitutions have increased less than earnings.

---

[5] The expenditure data were obtained from unpublished U.S. Office of Edu tion sources and refer to the 1963–64 school year. The data are for gross c rent expenditures; no allowance is made for the capital account of colleg The tuition data are taken from *Higher Education: Basic Student Charg 1962–63*, U.S. Office of Education Circular 711. Most of the responder however, attended college in the immediate postwar years. It is therefore nec sary to assume that cost differences among colleges remained unchanged. Th is some limited evidence in Solmon (1973) that college cost and quality rankir are fairly constant over time.

Opportunity costs for each individual were calculated from the 1960 census.[6] For the undergraduate years, opportunity costs are represented by the median income of white high school graduates in the state where the respondent attended college, adjusted for age of the respondent. For the graduate school years, the data used were average earnings of white college graduates in the state where the respondent attended graduate school, adjusted for age. The census data do not provide the necessary race-age-education earnings breakdown by state, and so the figures were calculated by interpolation from national and regional averages.[7]

The adjustment for age represents an upper limit for opportunity costs. Human capital theory suggests that earnings increase with age because of increased labor force experience. The use of opportunity costs based on average earnings of persons of the age at which the respondents attended college implies that the military experience of the respondents was of the same value as an equivalent amount of time spent in the civilian labor force. If this is not the case, the age adjustment will lead to an overstatement of opportunity costs. The adjustment is significant, as the average age of the respondents at college graduation was 26, and age-earnings profiles are very steep at that age.

It might be argued that respondents have higher opportunity costs than the population average for their age-education group, since they are all drawn from the upper half of the ability distribution. However, in Chapter 4 Taubman and Wales report that the starting salaries of the NBER-TH respondents are not related to ability and amount of education. Their predicted initial salary in 1947 dollars is $4,089 for those with some college, $3,464 for those with an undergraduate degree, and $3,460 for those with

---

[6] The 1960 census is used because the data provided are more detailed than in previous censuses and are almost coincident with the cost data. The tuition and expenditure cost data are adjusted to the census income year (1959) by the consumption expenditures deflator.

[7] Earnings of adult white male high school and college graduates in each state and region were derived from the nonwhite and total data. Regional data for white male earnings, classified by age and education, were used to approximate state medians for 22- to 24-year-old high school graduates and 25- to 29-year-old college graduates. The ratio of all adult white male earnings in each state to the appropriate regional age group for each education class was used to make the adjustment. Finally, national differences in income by age for each education class were used to adjust the estimated state median earnings for 22- to 24-year-old high school graduates and 25- to 29-year-old college graduates to the age of the respondent at the time of his schooling.

graduate education. The average opportunity cost based on 1960 census data is $4,744, or $3,648 in 1947 dollars.

Conventional wisdom has it that many other factors determine earnings in addition to specified human capital investments. Social background, luck, and ability can affect the dispersion in observed rates of return among individuals. However, estimates of the basic earnings function discussed in the following section provide estimates of the expected value of the distribution of rates of return. The effect of ability and social class on the dispersion of rates of return is also examined below.

ESTIMATION OF RATES OF RETURN

Estimates of various specifications of the basic earnings function for 1969 earnings are shown in Table 6-1. In the first set of equations it is assumed that forgone earnings are the only cost of schooling. In the second set, expenditures per full-time equivalent student are used to represent the cost of direct social investment. Finally, in the last pair of equations tuition payments are taken as a measure of direct private investments.[8] The sample sizes for the expenditures and tuition equations differ because direct cost data were not available for all the colleges attended by the respondent.[9]

Each equation allows for different rates of return to the direct and indirect components of investment r_D and r_I. The investment variables can be written as

$$r_I s_i + r_D \sum_{j=1}^{s_i} \frac{D_{ij}}{E_{ij}}$$

This follows from the definition of costs $C_{ij} = D_{ij} + E_{ij}$, where D_{ij} is the direct investment cost—either tuition or expenditures. In addition, in the even-numbered equations of each set, direct and indirect investment variables for graduate and undergraduate training are included separately.

The formulation of the indirect investment component implies

---

[8] For schools with different tuition charges for residents and nonresidents, the resident tuition is used for undergraduates only if a respondent's undergraduate college was located in the same state as his high school; it is used for graduates if a respondent's undergraduate and graduate school were in the same state.

[9] Of the 5,086 respondents, 1,246 never attended college and were excluded from the regressions. Also excluded were respondents with zero earnings in 1969 and all medical doctors and airplane pilots. The name of the college attended or the tuition and cost data were not available for about 600 respondents, leaving about 3,000 observations for the regressions.

TABLE 6-1 Earnings functions for investments in higher education* (figures in parentheses are standard errors of the regression coefficients)

	No direct investment†		Expenditures as direct investment†		Tuition as direct investment‡	
	(1)	(2)	(3)	(4)	(5)	(6)
Constant	.2931	.3018	.4064	.4907	.5796	.6043
g	.0225(.0089)	.0195(.0090)	.0227(.0087)	.0198(.0088)	.0278(.0088)	.0224(.0089)
g^2	−.0004(.0002)	−.0003(.0002)	−.0005(.0002)	−.0004(.0002)	−.0006(.0002)	−.0004(.0002)
$\ln W$	.4761(.0874)	.4700(.0874)	.4405(.0858)	.4121(.0857)	.3907(.0842)	.3790(.0842)
s_U		.0644(.0089)		.0326(.0095)		.0410(.0092)
s_G		.0394(.0076)		−.0273(.0136)		−.0155(.0125)
s	.0504(.0049)		.0124(.0059)		.0164(.0058)	
D_U				.1353(.0150)		.2064(.0246)
D_G				.1745(.0318)		.2973(.0589)
D			.1423(.0129)		.2164(.0205)	
R^2	.0463	.0475	.0834	.0897	.0788	.0825
S.E.	.4867	.4865	.4773	.4758	.4773	.4765

* Dependent variable is natural log of 1969 earnings.
† Sample size is 3,045.
‡ Sample size is 3,004.
NOTE: $g =$ labor force experience; $W =$ weeks worked; $s =$ years of college education; $D =$ direct investment costs; $U =$ undergraduate; $G =$ graduate. See text for further details of definition and description of data used and for form of estimating equations.

that students forgo a full year's income. An alternative assumptic
—that earnings from part-time and summer work during schoolir
are on the average one-fourth of full-time earnings—is used t
adjust the estimated rates of return upward.[10] Most of the respo:
dents obtained part or all of their education after World War]
when they had access to the GI Bill, which paid monthly stipenc
to full-time students and covered tuition payments up to $500.
These stipends are not deducted from the calculated investme1
variables; therefore, the coefficients are lower than the rates
return earned by the respondents. Clearly, private rates of retu:
increase when the GI Bill stipends are deducted from costs.

When direct investment costs are ignored, the estimated rate
return to investments in college is 5.04 percent. In Table 6-1 e
(2) indicates that the rate of return to undergraduates schoolir
(6.44 percent) exceeds the return to graduate schooling (3.94 pe
cent). The coefficients differ significantly when tested at the]
percent level.[12] Clearly, the number of years of graduate and unde
graduate schooling are correlated, as all those with graduate schoc
ing completed four years of undergraduate schooling.[13]

The rate-of-return coefficients are somewhat lower than tho
generally found in studies of returns to college investment. If pai
time work is set at three months per year, the rate of return is i
creased by one-third and would be 6.72 percent. If, in additio
an average stipend of $1,000 per year is deducted from direct cos1
the true value of k is not one but .48, and the private rate of retu
would be 10.6 percent.[14] The adjusted rates of return from eq. (

[10] The fraction one-fourth is suggested by Becker.

[11] The stipend varied with the number of dependents and with several chang
in the law during the postwar period. Solmon estimates the average stipe
during the late 1940s at $100 per month.

[12] The test value for the null hypothesis that the coefficients on s_U and s_G a
equal is $F(1, 3,039) = 3.83$.

[13] The simple correlation of s_U and s_G is .33. The mean number of years of scho
ing is 15.96, with a standard deviation of 2.0. Twenty-nine percent of the
spondents had some graduate training; 37 percent had an undergraduate (
gree; and the rest had between 13 and 15 years of schooling.

[14] The calculation is

$$k = \frac{C}{E} = \frac{3/4\,(3747) - 1,000}{3747} = .48$$

The average opportunity cost for the respondents was $4,744, as calculat
from the 1960 census, or $3,747 in 1948 dollars. The median year of colle
attendance is 1948. The corresponding adjustment for undergraduate retur
is $k = .46$; for graduate returns, $k = .55$, as opportunity costs increase w

are 14.0 percent for undergraduate and 7.1 percent for graduate training. Without the GI Bill, rates of return on private investments in schooling would have been much lower and would probably have discouraged many of the respondents from further educational investments.

The direct investment variable for social investment (expenditures) is added in Table 6-1 eq. (3) and for private investment (tuition) in eq. (5). The proportion of variance explained rises dramatically from less than 5 percent in equations (1) and (2) to about 8 percent in the other two pairs. The coefficient of years of schooling (the indirect investment variable assuring that full annual earnings are forgone) declines to just over .01 from .05; in the expenditure equation it is barely twice its standard error.[15] The coefficients on the direct investment variables are significantly larger than the coefficients on indirect investment in both eqs. (3) and (5). Direct investments are much more important in explaining variation in earnings. For tuition, the beta coefficient on direct investment is 5.6 times that for indirect investment, while for expenditures the ratio is 3.5.

In order to interpret the coefficients as rates of return, the investment variables need to be adjusted for part-time work by students and differential growth trends in investment costs and earnings.[16] At this point, no adjustment is made for stipends received

---

education. The value of k for graduate students may be biased upward because of their increased opportunities for scholarships and part-time work, which reduce costs.

[15] The indirect investment variable (the number of years of college) and the direct investment variable (the ratio of direct costs to forgone earnings summed over the years of college) are clearly correlated. If the ratio of costs to forgone earnings were constant, the correlation would be 1.0. However, forgone earnings increase with education and costs and may be different in graduate and undergraduate school. The correlation of direct and indirect variables is .65 for expenditures (eq. 3) and .55 for tuition (eq. 5).

[16] The direct investment variables $\sum_j D_{ij}/E_{ij}$ utilize wage and cost data that postdate the respondents' schooling. The true value of the variable is $\sum_j \bar{D}_{ij}/\bar{E}_{ij}$, where the bar indicates 1947–48 values. For expenditures, $D = 2.27\ \bar{D}$, and for earnings $E = 1.89\ \bar{E}$. The growth rates are based on national average college expenditures and the average weekly wage in manufacturing. Substituting gives the proportional correction factor for the direct social investment variable. The regression coefficients on the measured variable should then be adjusted by the inverse of the ratio of growth in direct costs to the growth in earnings. The average tuition charge increased by the same percentage as earnings between 1947–48 and 1962–63. The average tuition charge for 1962–63 is based on the 1947–48 distribution of students between private and public institutions, applied to the national average tuition in each type of school.

under the GI Bill. Thus, these are the rates of return that would have been earned by the respondents if they had not received any educational subsidies. The adjusted rates of return from eqs. (3) and (5) of Table 6-1 are shown in Table 6-2. The difference between the rate of return on direct and indirect investments is still large. The return to indirect investments, time spent out of the labor force, is very small. If the return to forgone earnings is as low as indicated here, full-time college attendance must have a large consumption component because the economic incentives for part-time attendance are large.[17]

Unfortunately, the sample does not provide any direct information on full- versus part-time college attendance by the respondents. However, the typical respondent had completed four years of college at a school with an annual tuition charge (in 1959 dollars) of $685 and annual expenditures per student of $1,490.

The results in Table 6-1 imply that if the typical respondent attended college without leaving the labor force, his earnings would be unchanged if he attended a college which spent 26 percent more per student and charged 48 percent more in tuition. That is, part-time attendance can be compensated for by an increase in direct investments of less than two standard deviations. These results are only suggestive of the available trade-offs between direct and indirect investment expenditures due to differences in the rates of return.

The total private and social rates of return to education investments can be calculated by taking weighted averages of the returns

[17] Weiss concludes that there is little economic incentive for full-time as opposed to part-time study. The difference in our findings may be due to the larger role of part-time earnings of graduate students in his study. His study includes estimates of the part-time earnings of graduate students (assistantships, fellowships, etc.), while I assume that the only earnings are the GI Bill stipends. As the earnings of full-time graduate students increase, the incentives for part-time study disappear.

TABLE 6-2 Rates of return on direct and indirect investment, adjusted for part-time work and secular changes in costs (in percentages)	*Social investment (expenditures)*	*Private investment (tuition)*
Return on indirect investment	1.65	2.19
Return on direct investment	16.92	21.64
TOTAL RETURN	5.78	5.57

to direct investments (r_D) and indirect investment (r_I). The weights are the average levels of the investment variables adjusted for part-time work and the secular change in costs. In both cases earnings of the respondent are the only returns considered. The social rate of return is based on the cost of schooling investments to society (forgone earnings plus expenditures by the college), whereas the private rate of return is based on investment costs borne by the individual (forgone earnings plus tuition). The total rate of return to private investment is 5.57 percent,[18] and that to social investment is 5.78 percent.[19] Although direct and indirect returns are about one-fourth larger for private investments than social investments, the total returns are almost identical. The reason is that indirect costs are a larger fraction of private than of social investment costs; therefore, the smaller return is weighted more heavily in calculating the total private return. For the same reason, the total returns are not very sensitive to changes in the adjustment of direct investment for secular changes in costs.

Forgone earnings are a large fraction of total investment costs: 72.5 percent of total social investment and 82.6 percent of total private investment. However, the variance in forgone earnings is a smaller proportion of the varianace in total costs; 50.5 percent for total social investment and 75.4 percent for total private investment. Thus years of schooling is hardly an adequate proxy for total schooling investment. When differences in direct costs are taken into account, the total rates of return to both private and social investment are smaller than the comparable rate of return from eq. (1) Table 6-1. When forgone earnings are used as a proxy for all investments, the return is 6.72 percent (i.e., the coefficient on s, adjusted for part-time work by students).

Alternatively, the total rates of return can be obtained by aggregating the adjusted direct and indirect investment variables into a single total investment variable whose coefficient in the earnings model would be the total rate of return. This approach avoids the multicollinearity between the direct and indirect investment vari-

[18] This is not the private return actually earned by the respondents since stipends under the GI Bill were not subtracted from costs.

[19] The standard errors of the total rates could not be calculated because the program used does not provide a covariance matrix of regression coefficients. However, an estimate of the covariance of r_D and r_I from some preliminary experiments in which constant opportunity costs were assumed for all individuals indicates that the standard error of the total rate is about 0.9 percent.

ables that might make the estimates of the individual rates of return unreliable. However, the Table 6-1 regressions with the disaggregated investment variables explain a significantly larger proportion of the variation in earnings than corresponding regressions with a single total investment variable. This would not be the case if the returns on direct and indirect investments did not differ significantly. The total returns estimated by a regression using the aggregate adjusted investment variables are 6.04 percent for social investments and 6.54 percent for private investments.[20] Thus the private returns are just 0.5 percent higher than the social returns.

For the most part, the respondents attended college after spending several years in the Armed Forces and were therefore about four years older than the average college student. This four-year age difference almost doubles the estimate of their potential earnings as students. Thus the total returns that would have been earned by equivalent but younger students with opportunity costs reduced to one-half of the estimated amounts are 8.0 percent for total private investments and 8.1 percent for total social investments.

As previously noted, many of the respondents benefited from the GI Bill, which had the effect of reducing private costs substantially. Adjusting for part-time work and a $1,000 annual stipend increases the return on indirect private investments from 1.64 to 3.42 percent.[21] Assuming that each respondent also received a tuition stipend (up to a $500 maximum) reduces the average level of direct private investments by 80 percent and increases the estimated return on the average direct, private investment from 21.6 to 121.3 percent. However, in this case, direct investments are only a small fraction of schooling investments; the total private return on investments actually made by the respondents would be 9.91 percent.

In eqs. (4) and (6) of Table 6-1, both the indirect and direct investment variables are disaggregated into undergraduate and graduate school components. The disaggregation adds less than 1 percent to explained variance, but the increase is significant at the 1 percent level.[22] The results indicate that there are large and

---

[20] These are alternative estimates of the total returns shown in the bottom row of Table 6-2. The variables were adjusted for part-time work and secular changes in costs; the standard error of both estimates is 0.5 percent.

[21] Based on eq. (5), Table 6-1. See footnote 14 for the correction factor.

[22] The test value for the expenditure equations is $F(2, 3038) = 10.5$, and for the tuition equations it is $F(2, 2997) = 6.04$.

significant differences in the rates of return earned at the graduate and undergraduate levels. The estimated return on indirect investments is negative for graduate studies. Interestingly enough, the returns to direct social and private investments are larger for graduate than for undergraduate studies.

The increase in returns to direct graduate school investments compared with the increase to undergraduate investments seems to contradict the usual finding that the rate of return declines with the amount of investment in schooling. However, the total rate of return to graduate education is less than the total rate of return to undergraduate education for both the social and private investment equations. Table 6-3 shows the total returns adjusted for part-time work and the secular change in costs, as discussed previously. The private returns are not adjusted for stipends under the GI Bill, and the total returns to undergraduate investments are more than twice the returns to graduate training. This difference is much larger than the difference suggested by the forgone earnings coefficients in eq. (2), Table 6-1. The results confirm the idea that there has tended to be overinvestment in graduate training.[23]

The other coefficients of the model all have the expected signs. The two experience variables do not provide estimates of either the rate of return to postschool investments or the value of k in the first job; the coefficient on experience is the product of the rate of return and k. A coefficient of .02 suggests, therefore, that a return of 10 percent is consistent with an initial k of .2. The span of the postschooling investment period can be derived from the two regression coefficients. The coefficients indicate that the postschool investment period is about 25 years, ending at an average age of 52 for this sample.[24]

Finally, the reader will note the relatively low values for all the coefficients of determination (only between 5 and 10 percent of

[23] This conclusion is also reached by Taubman and Wales (see Chap. 4 of this volume).

[24] These conclusions are based on Mincer's explicit formulation of a linearly declining net investment profile. See Mincer (1970, p. 17).

TABLE 6-3 *Total rates of* *return on* *investment in* *graduate and* *undergraduate* *training adjusted* *for part-time* *work and secular* *changes in costs*	*Social* *investment* *(expenditures),* *percent*	*Private* *investment* *(tuition),* *percent*
Undergraduate	7.67	8.11
Graduate	3.01	3.39

the variance in earnings is explained). This is due to the relatively homogeneous nature of the sample, which has little variance in age, experience, hours and weeks worked, and ability when compared with the population as a whole. All the regression coefficients themselves are highly significant.

The proportion of earnings variance explained can be raised by somewhat less than 2 percent by adding a measure of ability.[25] As would be expected, the addition of an ability measure reduces the rate-of-return estimates. For example, when years of schooling is the only investment variable, its coefficient is reduced from 5 to 4.4 percent with ability included, a reduction of almost 15 percent.[26] The reduction in the direct social investment (expenditure) coefficient is somewhat smaller, about 13 percent. The coefficients on the direct private investment (tuition) variables are reduced by about 10 percent when ability is included in the equation.

THE EFFECT OF ABILITY AND SOCIO-ECONOMIC STATUS ON RETURNS

The estimated rate-of-return coefficients are the mean values of the distribution of average rates of returns received by individuals in the sample. Human capital theory suggests that the amount of, and returns to, educational investments for a particular individual depend on both his supply and demand curves for investments. Becker suggests that supply curves will depend on opportunity factors, and demand curves on ability.

The NBER-TH respondents all had access to GI Bill subsidies which equalized educational opportunities. For this reason a single supply curve for all respondents, as shown in Figure 6-1, is a plausible hypothesis. The supply curve is upward-sloping because opportunity costs increase with age and with the amount of previous schooling. Demand curves for high-ability (D_H) and low ability (D_L) respondents are shown; the curves shift to the right with ability since schooling is more valuable for more able students. Under these assumptions, high-ability respondents will invest more and earn a higher marginal rate of return at every level of investment and therefore have a higher observed average rate of return.

If the assumption of common supply curves is relaxed, as in

---

[25] These results are not shown.

[26] This estimate of the bias from omitting ability is within the range of the Taubman and Wales estimates. Although they use the same sample, their specification differs. In their chapter both ability and schooling are measured categorically (by classes) rather than continuously, as here.

FIGURE 6-1   *Effect of ability differences on the demand for schooling*

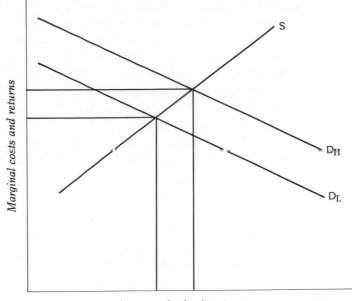

Amount of schooling investment

FIGURE 6-2   *Effect of ability and SES differences on the supply and demand for schooling*

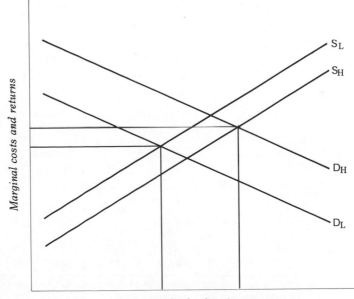

Amount of schooling investment

Figure 6-2, the implications of the model are less conclusive. It could be argued that the supply curve shifts with the socioeconomic status (SES) of the respondent: a higher SES increases educational opportunities and pushes the supply curve to the right. If SES and ability are correlated, high SES respondents may or may not have higher marginal returns, although they will invest more.[27] It is likely that average returns will increase with SES as shown in Figure 6-2, but this result depends on the relative positions of the supply and demand curves.

The effect of ability and opportunity factors on the dispersion of estimated rates of return can be examined by segmenting the sample into ability and SES groups. Ability quartiles were calculated from a constructed IQ measure.[28] An SES variable based on father's

[27] The correlation between SES and ability is very small. The IQ variable is scaled to a mean of 100 and a standard deviation of 10 for the entire NBER-TH sample. The mean IQ of college-attending respondents in the highest SES group is 101.7, and in the lowest it is 100.6.

[28] The IQ variable was constructed from a factor analysis of the Air Force tests taken by the respondents in 1943. The quartiles are based on the test scores of all respondents, including those who did not attend college.

TABLE 6-4
Effect of ability on rates of return*

	Direct investment variable		
	None	*Expenditure*	*Tuition*
Constant	.4410	.5514	.6651
g	.0204(.0088)	.0236(.0087)	.0259(.0088)
g^2	−.0004(.0002)	−.0005(.0002)	−.0005(.0002)
ln W	.4481(.0870)	.4110(.0858)	.3769(.0842)
s_1	.0293(.0066)	−.0011(.0118)	.0115(.0097)
s_2	.0371(.0062)	−.0033(.0109)	.0032(.0092)
s_3	.0535(.0059)	.0103(.0104)	.0128(.0086)
s_4	.0620(.0055)	.0167(.0086)	.0278(.0077)
D_1		.1086(.0339)	.1385(.0506)
D_2		.1392(.0301)	.2226(.0450)
D_3		.1380(.0266)	.2558(.0424)
D_4		.1260(.0175)	.2016(.0315)
R^2	.0593	.0921	.0881
S.E.	.4836	.4754	.4753
N	3045	3045	3004

* Dependent variable is natural log of 1969 earnings. Standard errors of the regression coefficients are in parentheses.

NOTE: Symbols are defined in Table 6-1. Subscripts denote ability quartiles; fo explanation, see footnote 28.

	Direct investment variable		
TABLE 6-5 *Effect of socioeconomic status on rates of return**	*None*	*Expenditure*	*Tuition*
Constant	.3454	.4850	.6232
g	.0222(.0089)	.0251(.0087)	.0273(.0002)
g^2	−.0004(.0002)	−.0005(.0002)	−.0006(.0002)
$ln\ W$	.4637(.0874)	.4211(.0856)	.3803(.0843)
s_L	.0386(.0070)	−.0018(.0131)	.0116(.0113)
s_M	.0486(.0055)	.0104(.0088)	.0171(.0079)
s_H	.0548(.0053)	.0062(.0075)	.0188(.0066)
D_L		.1329(.0347)	.1687(.0607)
D_M		.1245(.0218)	.1977(.0355)
D_H		.1439(.0160)	.2344(.0267)
R^2	.0487	.0869	.0819
S.E.	.4863	.4767	.4768
N	3045	3045	3004

* Dependent variable is natural log of 1969 earnings. Standard errors of the regression coefficients are in parentheses.

NOTE: Symbols are defined in Table 6-1. Subscripts L, M, and H denote low, medium, and high socioeconomic status as defined in footnote 29.

occupation was used as a rough measure of opportunity.[29] The earnings functions were reestimated with college investment variables classified by ability or SES. That is, if X_n is a dummy variable with a value of 1 if the respondent is in the nth group, then the coefficient on $X_n s$ is the indirect rate of return for individuals in the nth group. Only the schooling investment variables are categorized by the ability or status groups. The other variables in the equation have the same coefficient for the whole sample.

In Table 6-4 the investment variables are categorized by ability quartiles, with 1 being the lowest and 4 the highest. In Table 6-5 the investment variables are categorized by the SES groups defined in footnote 29. The categorization by ability or SES adds significantly to the proportion of variance explained.[30]

[29] Three groups were constructed as follows: high—managerial, proprietor, professional, and technical; medium—office worker, salesman, foreman, skilled worker, and others; low—service worker and semiskilled, unskilled, and other blue-collar workers.

The high SES group includes 49.7 percent of the respondents; 13.8 percent are in the low group.

[30] The equations in Tables 6-4 and 6-5 are compared with the corresponding equations in Table 6-1. The increase in R^2 is significant at the 1 percent level for all equations except those which do not include direct investments and those with SES expenditure classification; these are significant at the 5 percent level.

The schooling coefficients indicate that returns tend to increase with both ability and SES. The strongest trends are in the equations without a direct investment variable. These equations suggest that persons in the highest ability quartile earn more than twice the return of those in the lowest quartile and that persons from the high SES groups have a return which is over 40 percent higher than the return to those in the low group.

Total private and social rates of return by ability and status groups are shown in Table 6-6. The regression coefficients are adjusted for part-time work and secular cost changes, as before.[31] Returns increase consistently with both status and ability. The increase in returns with ability is not as large as the increase shown in the equation without a direct investment variable. The return for the high-status group is consistently about 40 percent larger than the return for the low-status group.

If all individuals in the sample have the same opportunities (common supply curve), then persons with higher ability not only should earn a higher return but also will have higher levels of investment. The average number of years of college in the highest ability quartile is 4.4, about 24 percent more than in the lowest ability quartile. However, more able students also make more expensive college investments. Their direct costs (private and social) are about 40 percent greater than the average for the lowest ability quartile.

Differences in the returns to education by ability level in the

[31] Private rates of return understate the returns actually earned by the respondents because stipends under the GI Bill were not subtracted from private costs.

TABLE 6-6 Adjusted total rates of return for ability and status groups	Social investment, percent	Private investment, percent
Ability group		
1 (lowest)	3.3	3.6
2	4.0	4.2
3	5.5	5.8
4 (highest)	6.0	6.7
Socioeconomic status		
Low	4.0	4.1
Medium	5.0	5.4
High	5.5	6.2

NBER-TH sample have been investigated by Taubman and Wales and by Hause. The results in this section suggest that Hause's evidence of a strong interaction between schooling and ability will be mitigated somewhat when costs are fully specified to include cost differences among schools. However, the results do suggest that a strong relationship exists between ability and both the amount of schooling investments and the rate of return.

It is worth noting that the specification of the model in Table 6-4 does not allow for any direct influence of ability on earnings. Ability affects earnings only insofar as it makes schooling more valuable or productive. The results are not a conclusive demonstration of the interaction between schooling and ability because the categorization of the rate-of-return coefficients by ability classes does not add to the explanatory power of the model when IQ is already included as a variable.

The private and social returns to college do increase somewhat with socioeconomic status. However, there is no discernible difference in the average number of years attended. The direct social investment costs are about 14 percent higher for persons from the high socioeconomic group than for persons from the low group.

CONCLUSION The major conclusion to be drawn from this study is that estimates of the rate of return from college that ignore institutional differences in expenditures and tuition are biased upward. This situation results from the tendency of students with higher earnings potential to make more expensive investments. The second conclusion to emerge from this study is that the returns to the direct and indirect components of investments are strikingly different. More research on this issue is clearly needed before we can judge whether part-time college attendance should be encouraged.

The difficulties in arriving at a unique measure of the returns to college that can be applied to future investments are highlighted by these results. Alternative adjustments and assumptions can alter the estimated return. The sample respondents have earned a private return on their schooling investments of almost 10 percent. The social return is about 6 percent, the difference being due to GI Bill subsidies. The adjusted private return is comparable to most estimates, whereas the social return is fairly small. Care should be taken in applying ex post returns from this sample to future investments because the respondents were in many respects atypical and the relative costs of schooling investments have changed. However, the finding of systematic differences in the returns to graduate and undergraduate training, to direct and indirect investment, and to ability and socioeconomic class suggests that these differences are important. They have been previously overlooked mainly because investigation has focused on the size of the rate of return.

References

Becker, Gary S.: *Human Capital: A Theoretical and Empirical Analysis, with Special Reference to Education,* National Bureau of Economic Research, New York, 1964.

Chiswick, Barry, and Jacob Mincer: "Time Series Changes in Personal Income Inequality in the U.S. from 1939," *Journal of Political Economy,* vol. 80, part 2, pp. S34–S66, May–June 1972.

Hause, John: "Ability and Schooling as Determinants of Lifetime Earnings, or If You're So Smart, Why Aren't You Rich?", this volume, Ch. 5.

Mincer, Jacob: "The Distribution of Labor Incomes," *Journal of Economic Literature,* vol. 8, pp. 1–26, March 1970.

Solmon, Lewis: "The Definition and Impact of College Quality," National Bureau of Economic Research Working Paper No. 7, New York, 1973.

Solmon, Lewis, and Paul Wachtel: "The Effects on Income of Type of College Attended," National Bureau of Economic Research Working Paper No. 10, New York, 1973; and *Sociology of Education,* forthcoming.

Taubman, Paul, and Terence Wales: "Education as an Investment and a Screening Device," this volume, Ch. 4.

Weiss, Yoram: "Investment in Graduate Education," *American Economic Review,* vol. 61, pp. 833–852, December 1971.

Welch, Finis: "Measurement of the Quality of Schooling," *American Economic Review,* vol. 56, pp. 379–392, May 1966.

7. Education and the Allocation of Women's Time

by Arleen Leibowitz

by Arleen Leibowitz

INTRODUCTION   Dramatic changes over the last 30 years in the amount of time married women spend in the labor force are well documented. Census data indicate, for example, that whereas only 15 percent of married women were in the labor force in 1940, the comparable figure was 24 percent for 1950, 31 percent for 1960, and 41.5 percent for 1972.[1] These changes in labor force participation have necessarily affected the allocation of time to various activities in the household as well.

The overall increase in labor force participation rates by married women has been accompanied by a change in the age profile of participation. Before World War II, women tended to drop out of the labor force permanently when they married and began to have children. Thus labor force participation rates peaked around age 25 and declined steadily thereafter, as seen in the profiles for 1900 and 1940 in Figure 7-1. During the last 30 years, however, women have reentered the labor force in increasing numbers when family responsibilities lessened, leading to a second peak in the participation profile between ages 45 and 55. Indeed, by 1960, participation rates at 45 to 55 exceeded those at 20 to 24. These changes have caused a pronounced shift in the age and sex composition of the labor force.

In recent years there has been renewed interest in the analysis of labor force participation of married women. Jacob Mincer (1962) took a pioneering step by placing the problem in the household production context: women are seen as choosing not simply between work and leisure, but between work in the home, work in

---

[1] Estimates are for married women, husband present, in March of the year cited. See U.S. Bureau of the Census, *Current Population Reports,* ser. P-50, nos. 22 and 29; see also Bogen (1968), Hayghe (1973), Schiffman (1961), and Waldman (1968).

FIGURE 7-1 *Female labor force participation by age (all women), 1900–1972*

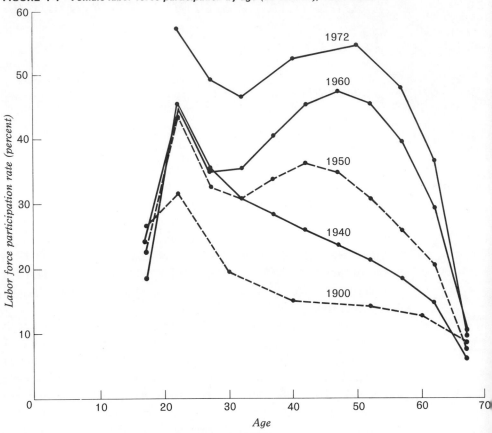

SOURCE: Oppenheimer (1970, p. 8) and Hayghe (1973).

the market, and leisure. Although income affects the total amount of work, the division of work between home and market depends on wage rates, productivity in the home, and the price and availability of substitutes for the wife's labor in the home. Recent studies by Cain (1966) as well as by Bowen and Finegan (1969) have updated Mincer's findings on income and wage effects and have documented the importance of color, schooling, occupation, and the presence of children.

A striking relationship, found consistently by these authors and by other students of female labor force behavior, is that women with more education are more likely to be in the labor force.[2] This

[2] See also, for example, Bancroft (1968); Cohen, Rea, and Lerman (1970); Garfinkle (1967); Lester (1958); Mahoney (1961); Oppenheimer (1970); Perrella (1968); Rosett (1958); and Waldman (1970).

is true in a classification of participation rates by education, and the relationship is even stronger when family income is held constant in the comparison (since women with more education tend to have higher family incomes, which, *ceteris paribus,* reduces labor supply). The most widely accepted explanation for this association is that education raises productivity in the labor market more than productivity in the home, so that the "cost" of not being in the labor market rises and women are induced to seek employment outside the home.

The greater market labor supply of women with more schooling is seen in the labor supply profiles shown in Figures 7-2 and 7-3.[3] These profiles, which have observations for age groups more closely spaced than previously available, show a second effect of education: It varies not only the level but also the lifetime pattern of labor supply.

These profiles reveal that the higher the level of schooling attained by the woman, the greater the supply of labor to the market, except between the ages of 25 and 40, when all women supply nearly the same amount of labor to the market. This seeming paradox may indicate that education does not cause market productivity to exceed productivity in the home equally for all activities and for all ages, since it appears that during the years when young children are in the home, the more educated women are, too.

Since both the shape and level of the labor supply profile of married women differ according to educational attainment, previous regression models that insert education linearly on the assumption that it raises productivity in the market by a greater amount than it raises productivity in the home, and that the relative change in productivity does not change with age, may be misspecified.[4]

Following Mincer, Cain, et al., the difference in the overall level of labor supply by women of different educational attainment may be traced to differences in the productivity of their time. Figures 7-2 and 7-3 seem to indicate, however, that these differences disappear—or at least are not manifest in different labor supplies to

---

[3] These profiles were calculated by the author from the 1/1,000 sample of the 1960 census. Only women who are not enrolled in school, who have been married only once, and who are living with their husbands are included in the calculations.

[4] The manner in which education is treated, for example, in Bowen and Finegan's study (1969) is that education affects the intercept of the labor force participation curve, but not its shape (p. 119).

FIGURE 7-2 *Labor force participation rates by age and education, 1960*

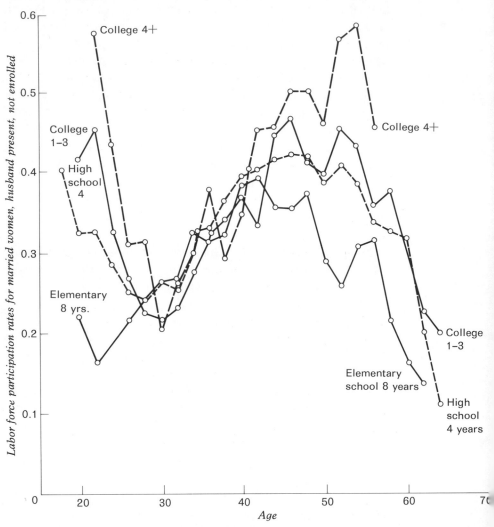

SOURCE: Calculated from 1/1,000 sample of the 1960 census.

the market—during the ages of between 25 and 40. The causes of this change can be traced to the presence of children in the home.

Between the ages of 25 and 40, a woman's life is most often devoted to child rearing. It has recently been estimated that for women born in the 1920s, the median age of the wife at the birth of the last child is 30.5 years (Glick and Parke, 1965, p. 190). Thus most women will have young children in the home until they reach the age of 40.

The importance of the presence of children in altering the labor

FIGURE 7-3 *Weeks worked by married women, husband present, by age and education, 1960*

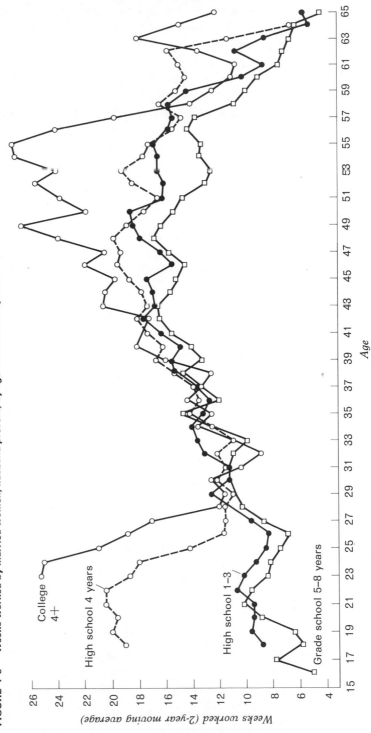

SOURCE: Calculated from 1/1,000 sample of the 1960 census.

supply of the mother can be demonstrated by looking at the "adjusted" labor force profiles calculated by Bowen and Finegan on the assumption that married women of all ages have the same number of children (i.e., that the presence of children is evenly spread over the mother's lifetime, so that each woman has, for example, 0.25 children under six in any year). Under these assumptions, the labor force participation profile would be of the shape shown in Figure 7-4. This profile is in sharp contrast to the actual double-peaked participation profile, which clearly reflects the decline in market productivity relative to home productivity during the childbearing and child-rearing years. The "adjusted" profile, however, has the same shape as the participation profile for males and for single women, but at a lower level.

In this chapter the differences in labor supply by education class will first be documented with data from the 1960 census. Then time-budget data will be employed to show that the higher the educational level of the mother, the greater the time inputs to child care, and that these differences can be used to explain the shape of the labor supply profiles.

EFFECTS OF EDUCATION ON TIME ALLOCATION In the theoretical model of household behavior developed by Becker, utility is derived from the consumption of commodities, and thus the commodities consumed (or produced) are the objects of choice. The general properties of a pure change in income, compensated price changes, and equiproportionate changes in home and market productivity are well known.[5]

Two basic constraints which must be satisfied by any optimizing solution are:

1 The ratio between the marginal productivity of time in home production of any two family members in any two periods of time must be equal to the ratio of the price of their time in these periods.

2 The ratio of the marginal productivity of time and goods in producing any commodity must equal the ratio of the cost of the time and goods inputs.

In this chapter education is postulated to have several effects that influence the choice of commodities and labor force decisions. First, education raises the productivity of time in market work as attested to by the higher wages paid to more educated workers

[5] See Becker (1965).

FIGURE 7-4   *Labor force participation rates, 1960*

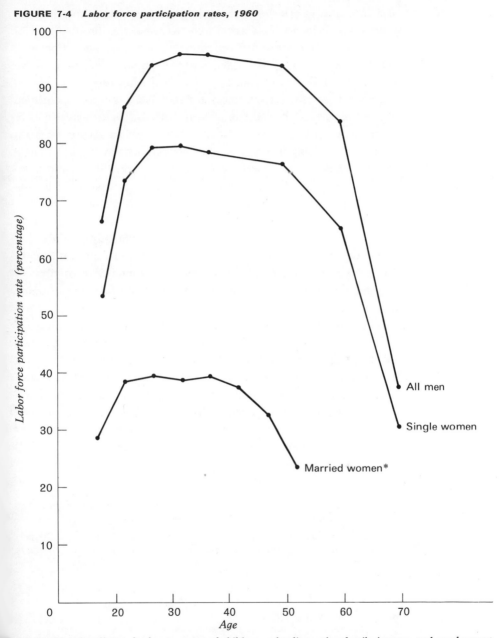

* Adjusted for the effects of color, presence of children, schooling, other family income, and employment status of husband.

SOURCES: U.S. Bureau of the Census (1963, Table 6) and Bowen and Finegan (1969, Table 5-4, p. 109).

which in turn raises the opportunity cost or price of time in home production. Second, education may increase the productivity of time spent in home production: women with more education may get more output for given amounts of time inputs. Because of these two effects, full income will also rise with education.

Given these two effects and the two basic constraints outlined above, we can see that education will work in several ways to alter commodity consumption. First, the more highly educated women have greater family income, because of both their own greater earnings and those of their husbands,[6] and thus they will demand more consumption time. Second, since the opportunity cost of time rises with education, goods will be substituted for time in the production of all commodities, which will tend to increase hours of work. Third, the relative price of time-intensive commodities will rise, which will also tend to cause the demand for consumption time to fall. However, if education increases the productivity of time in the home as well as in the market, the demand for time in home production might increase.

It is proved elsewhere (Leibowitz, 1972) that if education increases the productivity of time in the market more than time in the home, an increase in education will tend to decrease the amount of time used to produce a unit of a given commodity. This decrease in time inputs will be greater (1) the higher the percentage by which the increase in market productivity caused by education exceeds the increase in home productivity, (2) the greater the ease of substituting other factors for time in producing the commodity, and (3) the steeper the rise in home productivity in producing this commodity.[7]

---

[6] The correlation between wife's education and family income other than her earnings is .27 for a random sample of the 1960 census.

[7] Assuming a production function which is homogeneous of degree one, the percentage change in time inputs to producing a unit of a given commodity is shown to be

$$\tilde{t} = S_x \sigma(\tilde{f}_t - \tilde{P}_t) - \frac{t}{\pi}(1 - \frac{1}{\pi})\tilde{f}_t$$

where $\sim$ = percentage change
t = time input per unit of commodity
π = price of a unit = $p_j x_j + t P_t$
$\tilde{P}_t$ = percent change in market price of time
$\tilde{f}_t$ = value of time in home production
S_x = expenditures on goods as a percent of total price, $S_x = \frac{p_j x_j}{\pi}$, and
σ = elasticity of substitution between time and other factors in production of the commodity (Leibowitz, 1972)

The total amount of time spent in producing this commodity[8] will decrease more (1) the smaller the income elasticity for this commodity and (2) the smaller the price elasticity, if the share of time costs in price is below the average for all commodities (i.e., if the relative price of the commodity falls with a change in education) or the greater the price elasticity for commodities with greater-than-average time intensities.

Summing the changes in time inputs over all commodities, one derives the amount of time released for market work as a result of an increase in education. The reduction in total time spent in consumption (or the increase in time supplied to the labor market) is likely to be greater (1) the greater the extent to which commodities with high income elasticities are also characterized by small time costs as a percentage of price (π_i), by greater substitution among factors, and by greater increases in home productivity relative to market productivity and (2) the smaller other family income is, since families with higher income will demand more commodities and therefore more consumption time.

Another way of putting this is to recognize that the marginal utility of goods relative to the marginal utility of time will be lowered by high incomes (since all income must be spent on goods over the course of the lifetime) and that, in order to reestablish the equilibrium conditions described at the beginning of this section, time spent in home production must increase.

ESTIMATION OF LABOR SUPPLY EQUATIONS

Education affects labor supply primarily through changes in wages, home productivity, and elasticity of substitution with other factors of production in the home. In this chapter the market productivity of the wife (or the price of time) at a given point in time was considered to be predetermined by prior investment decisions. Following Mincer (1970), expected wages were estimated as a function of schooling and training investments. These expected wages were then treated as exogenous variables in the labor supply equation.

[8] The total effect on time reduction is described by the following equation:

$$\tilde{t} = \left[(S_x - \bar{S}_x)\varepsilon + S_x\sigma \right] (\tilde{f}_t - \tilde{P}_t) - \frac{t}{\pi}(1 - \frac{1}{\pi})\tilde{f}_t + \eta \tilde{Y}$$

where $\bar{S}_x$ = expenditure on goods as a percent total expenditures for all commodities

$\tilde{Y}$ = percent change in real full income due to a change in education

η = income elasticity of demand for Z_i, and

ε = price elasticity of demand for Z_i (Leibowitz, 1972)

Home productivity is also largely fixed at a given time and is assumed to depend largely on the stock and age structure of children produced in previous periods. The larger the size of the family and the younger the children, the greater the demand for home production by the wife and the greater the marginal productivity of her time in home production. Data on the presence and age of children are used as a gauge of home productivity, although no attempt is made to specify the exact relationship between them in this section.

Since the allocation of time between home and market by one family member is influenced by the relative productivity in home and market of other family members, the difference between the education of the husband and wife is used as a measure of the relative cost of their time in home production.

Family income, other than the wife's earnings, was considered here as an exogenous income variable. Although the income tax is not explicitly considered in this analysis, it should be noted that the earnings of more highly educated women are, on the average, subject to higher marginal tax rates because of the higher incomes of their husbands and the progressive nature of our tax structure. These women could be expected to supply even more time to the labor force relative to less-educated women, if both groups' income were subject to the same tax rate.

The age variable is included to capture the effect of differential rates of depreciation in home and market productivity.[9] If home productivity increases relative to market productivity as women grow older, age will have a negative effect on the supply of labor, assuming an optimum distribution of working time over the life-time. In the life-cycle context, age will also have a negative effect on weeks worked if the rate of interest exceeds the rate of time preference for the present, thereby shifting consumption time to later ages. It may also pick up a cohort effect if the quality of education has changed over time or if older women have less market experience.[10]

Cain (1966) as well as Bowen and Finegan (1969) have shown that black women have higher labor force participation rates than white women. Race was included in the regressions to test whether the greater supply of labor by black women could be "explained"

[9] See Chap. 8 of this volume.
[10] See Becker and Ghez (1972).

by racial differences in economic variables or whether race continued to have a significant net effect on weeks worked.

Weeks worked per year was chosen as the dependent variable because it is a measure of labor supply that covers a long enough period to be unaffected by seasonality (in contrast to hours worked per week), because it has better statistical properties with greater likelihood for homoscedasticity than in the case of labor force participation rates, and because it is a better measure of labor supply than membership in the labor force.[11]

A linear model incorporating these variables can be written:

$$\text{Weeks} = a + (b_1 + b_8 T) W_w + \sum_{i=2}^{4} b_i C_i + b_5 \text{Young} + b_6 A$$
$$+ b_7 \text{Dif} + b_8 (V + TW_h) + b_9 \text{Race} \qquad (7\text{-}1)$$

where $W_w =$ wife's wage, estimated from Eq. II-1 in Leibowitz (1972)

$W_h =$ husband's wage

$C_i =$ number of children in three age ranges

Young $=$ age of the youngest child in years

$A =$ age of the wife, in years

Dif $=$ wife's educational level minus husband's educational level

$V =$ nonwage income; and

Race $=$ dummy variable equal to one for black and zero for white. Other nonwhites were excluded from the sample.

Here "other family income" is composed of husband's full income plus nonwage income. The total effect of wife's wages on weeks worked is comprised of a substitution effect (b_1) and an income effect $(b_8 T)$, since an increase in wages not only increases the value of time but also raises full income. It is expected that b_1 will be positive, since the higher the wage, the more labor will be supplied to the market. Since higher family income will lead the wife to reduce the amount of labor supplied to the market, the sign of b_8 is expected to be negative. Thus the direction of the total effect of wages on weeks worked cannot be predicted a priori, since it is composed of a positive substitution effect and a negative income effect.

---

[11] A fuller discussion of the desirable characteristics of a variable measuring labor supply is found in Leibowitz (1972, pp. 44–49).

It is expected that the greater the number of children in the family, the greater the marginal productivity of the wife's time will be in the home and the less time she will supply to the labor market. The younger the child, the greater the expected impact on weeks worked. The older the youngest child in the family, the lower the marginal productivity of time in the home and the more labor the mother is expected to supply to the market. Thus it is anticipated that b_5 will be positive.

The higher the wife's education is relative to her husband's, the greater her market wages are relative to his and the greater the likelihood of her working outside the home. Thus b_7 is expected to be positive. The household production model does not give unique predictions about the effects of age and race on labor supply, and so we have no prediction about the signs of b_6 and b_9.

The data used to estimate the parameters of this equation are 1,730 observations selected from the 1/1,000 sample of the 1960 census.[12] Women who had completed 9 to 12 years of school were selected by a one-in-forty random sampling of the census tape to form the group called *high school women.* Women who had completed at least one year of college were selected by a one-in-ten random sampling and called *college women.* Women with one to eight years of school completed were selected by a three-in-forty sampling and were labeled *grade school women.* The samplings were unequal in size to assure a larger working sample of the grade school and college women, who are found at a lower frequency in the general population.

Wage and Home Productivity Effects

The results of estimating such a model of labor supply separately on each of three schooling groups and on a pooled sample of the groups are presented in Table 7-1. These equations show an average wage elasticity at the mean of 1.10 for college women, 1.6 for high school women, .334 for grade school women, and .94 for the pooled sample. That is, a 10 percent increase in wages will induce the average college woman to work 11 percent more weeks

[12] The sample is restricted to white and black women (other nonwhites are excluded) over 14. Only women who were married once, living with their husbands, and not currently enrolled in school were included in the sample. In recoding noncontinuous variables, medians were used in most cases, and estimates were made for open-ended intervals. The specifics are available upon request. A description of the sample is contained in U.S. Bureau of the Census, *Description and Technical Documentation; 1/1,000, 1/10,000, Two National Samples of the Population of the United States,* United States Census of Population and Housing, 1960.

	Grade school, 708 observations	High school, 450 observations	College, 572 observations	All, 1,730 observations
TABLE 7-1 **Supply of labor:** **1959—weeks** **worked by** **married women**				
Independent variable				
Weekly wage ($)	.07214 (.806)	.3655 (3.44)	.2297 (3.30)	.2026 (6.10)
Husband's income	−.00208 (−1.00)	−.00754 (−3.24)	−.00594 (−3.97)	−.00505 (−4.89)
Education difference	.0428 (.17)	.5917 (1.91)	.2679 (.99)	.3067 (2.02)
No. of children under 3	−8.084 (−4.66)	−3.494 (−1.96)	−5.940 (−3.32)	−6.037 (−6.01)
No. of children 3–5	−3.457 (−2.14)	−4.670 (−2.77)	−6.529 (−4.44)	−5.273 (−5.84)
No. of children 6–11	.3210 (.29)	−1.286 (−1.19)	1.405 (−1.18)	−.7252 (−1.13)
Age of youngest child	.2901 (2.86)	.5116 (4.48)	.4646 (4.16)	.3975 (6.39)
Race	6.6228 (1.85)	6.757 (1.46)	1.457 (.32)	7.371 (3.84)
Age	−.5119 (−7.70)	−.4049 (−4.85)	−.6954 (−8.09)	−.5718 (−14.04)
Constant	28.425 4.89	7.9858 (1.03)	29.273 (5.31)	24.767 (8.68)
R^2	.1107	.2126	.2419	.1780

NOTE: *t*-values in parentheses.
SOURCE: Calculated from 1/1,000 sample of the 1960 census.

a year, while the average high school woman will increase weeks worked by 16.5 percent, and the average grade school woman will increase weeks worked by 3.3 percent. Income elasticity at the mean is −.38 for high school women, −.32 for college women, and −.09 for grade school women, although in the last case the coefficient is not significantly different from zero. Thus a 10 percent increase in income would cause a reduction in weeks worked of 3.8 percent for the average college woman, 3.2 percent for the average high school woman, and 0.9 percent for the average grade school woman. For each educational level, the results are consistent with Mincer's finding, on the basis of Standard Metropolitan Statistical Area (SMSA) data, that the absolute value of the own wage elasticity exceeds the absolute value of the income elasticity (Mincer, 1962, p. 93).

The home productivity effect comes through quite strongly in the variables representing presence of children. The younger the children, the more market productivity falls relative to home productivity. In the regressions, the negative effect on weeks worked of having children under 5 is stronger than the negative effect of having children 6 to 11. Bowen and Finegan point out that the presence of older children in the family may actually facilitate participation in the labor force by the mother, since older children can look after younger ones.[13] However, this effect cannot account for the greater participation of more highly educated women, since they are more likely to space their children closely.[14] The variable representing the age of the youngest child is also quite significant in all four cases.

The difference in education between husband and wife, which reflects differences in market productivity, is significant in the pooled equation but less so in the separate equations. The fact that college-educated wives have, on the average, 0.961 more years of schooling than their husbands—in contrast to high school-educated wives, whose education exceeds their husbands' by only 0.32 years, and grade school women, who have 0.49 fewer years

---

[13] Bowen and Finegan (1969, p. 99) find that among women with children under 6, the added presence of children aged 14 to 17 raises adjusted participation rates by a statistically significant amount.

[14] See Ross (1972). Her calculations from the 1960 census 1/1,000 sample of the mean interval between first and last child for white women aged 35 to 39, married once, and with husband present are shown below.

	Mean interval between first and last child (in months)
Women with two children	
College graduates	40
High school graduates	52
Elementary school graduates (eight years)	56
Women with three children	
College graduates	74
High school graduates	85
Elementary school graduates (eight years)	88
Women with four children	
College graduates	99
High school graduates	110
Elementary school graduates (eight years)	120

of schooling than their husbands—helps to explain why college-educated wives supply more labor than high school-educated wives. But this variable does not explain much of the difference in participation within education groups.

Other Environmental Variables

Cain (1966) as well as Bowen and Finegan (1969) found race to be very significant in their studies of the labor supply of married women. It was also highly significant in a labor supply equation fitted over all education groups, with wages estimated by the same equation for all groups (Leibowitz, 1972). However, in the regressions for separate education groups, race was not significant. Intrafamily substitution may be an important cause of the greater labor supply of married black women, since black women have more schooling relative to their husbands than white women.[15] Thus the educational difference variable may be absorbing some of the effects attributed to race in previous studies.

An F-test ($F = 1.81$) reveals that the three labor supply equations can be said to differ significantly from one another at the 10 percent level. In order to determine whether a significant difference exists among the variables relating to the presence of children, t-tests are used. In particular, the hypothesis to be tested is that better-educated women are deterred more than less-educated women from supplying labor to the market by the presence of young children.

The effect of children on weeks worked can be obtained from the regression coefficients relating to the presence of children in the labor supply equation. Table 7-2 shows t-tests for two-by-two comparisons of these regression coefficients from equations estimated separately for the three education groups. The coefficients themselves are negative, indicating that the presence of children reduces the number of weeks worked. Applying the appropriate

[15] The difference between wife's and husband's education by level of education and race is shown below.

Schooling level of wife	Black women	All women
College	3.278	0.961
High school	1.175	0.320
Grade school	0.257	−0.489
All women	0.831	0.201

SOURCE: Calculated by the author from the 1/1,000 sample of the 1960 census.

one-tailed test, we note no significant differences between high school and college women. Further, children under 3 seem to be an equally forceful deterrent to the market labor supply of women in all three education classes. Table 7-2 shows, however, that college-educated women supply significantly less time to the labor market than grade school women when children of 3 to 5 and 6 to 11 years are in the home. High school women are significantly more deterred from the labor force by the presence of children 6 to 11 than grade school women are.

These differences arise because of a difference in the rate at which women increase their supply of market labor as their children

TABLE 7-2 The effect of children on weeks worked; comparisons by schooling level of women		*t-values*		
Groups compared		*Children under 3*	*Children 3–5*	*Children 6–1*
I.				
	College–grade school	.016	−2.02*	−1.95*
	High school–grade school	.08	−1.13	−2.01*
	College–high school	−.68	−.77	−.4936
II.				
	College–grade school	−.065	−2.03*	−1.68*
	High school–grade school	.95	−1.19	−1.84*
	College–high school	−1.05	−.73	1.147
		Regression coefficients		
I.				
	College	−9.5506*	−8.6604†	−3.8845†
	High school	−8.0459†	−6.9942†	−3.1747†
	Grade school	−9.9037†	−4.4213†	−1.0774
II.				
	College	−9.8947†	−8.6686†	−3.5655⁻
	High school	−7.5829†	−7.0899†	−3.7207
	Grade school	−9.7470†	−4.3838†	−1.1503

NOTES: I—Regressions where weeks worked was regressed on wage, education difference, race, age, husband's income, urban, children under 3, children 3 to children 6 to 11, constant. II—Equations where weeks worked was regressed education, husband's education, race, age, husband's income, urban, South, children under 3, children 3 to 5, children 6 to 11, constant.

* Significant at 5 percent level.

† Significant at 1 percent level.

SOURCE: Calculated by the author from 1/1,000 sample of the 1960 census.

grow up (since the presence of children under 3 does not have a significantly different effect on the labor supply of women with different schooling levels and since elder children inhibit labor supply less than younger ones for all three groups of women).

For grade school women the coefficient on children 3 to 5 is only half that for children under 3—a difference of 5.5 weeks— but for college women the comparable difference is a mere 0.9 weeks. Although the presence of school-age children has no statistically significant effect on the labor supply of grade school women, it does for college and high school women.

Thus we can conclude that college and high school women supply significantly less labor to the market than women with less schooling when children 3 and over are in the home.

CHILD CARE AND EDUCATION

Since women with more education can generally realize higher wages than those with less education, they spend a greater proportion of their lifetime in the labor market. As a result, they normally spend a smaller proportion of their time in home production, and time inputs to producing most commodities at home can be expected to fall with increasing education. Since women of higher educational attainments have been shown to be more deterred from market work by the presence of children, child care must differ from the kinds of household production carried out throughout the entire lifetime. If home production behavior is consistent with known labor force behavior, the discussion above implies that child care must be characterized by (1) smaller price elasticity and smaller elasticity of substitution between time and goods relative to other household production, given a greater increase in market price of time than in home productivity due to rising education; (2) greater income elasticity; or (3) greater increases in home productivity relative to market productivity, given price and substitution elasticity.

These factors will be investigated on the basis of time-budget data. The latter will also be used to demonstrate that more highly educated women tend to provide relatively smaller time inputs to the kinds of household production carried on throughout the life cycle, but relatively greater time inputs to child care.

The Cornell Sample

Time inputs to various activities were calculated by the author (see Table 7-3) from time budgets collected by Dr. Kathryn Walker of Cornell University.[16] The time budgets were based on time spent in various household activities and other work recorded in 10-minute intervals for two days by 1,296 husband-wife families (all residents of the Syracuse, New York, area) in 1967–68.

Table 7-3 presents average time inputs to various domestic activities by women of differing schooling attainments. The low-education group consisted of women who had not gone beyond

[16] The author is indebted to Dr. Walker and Mrs. Irma Telling for providing these data, collected for the research project *Use of Time for Household Work* in the Department of Consumer Economics and Public Policy, New York State College of Human Ecology, Cornell University.

TABLE 7-3
Time inputs to household activities (minutes over two days)

Activity	High-education group	Low-education group	Total
Meal preparation (wife)	153.41	154.39	153.92
Meal preparation (husband)	12.85	10.53	11.65
Laundry (wife*)	27.26	31.12	29.25
Physical care of children			
By wife	129.51	116.40	122.36
By husband	14.90	12.26	13.46
By others	5.67	4.41	4.98
Other care of children			
By wife	90.96	79.17	85.86
By husband	40.77	31.51	36.77
By others	44.74	36.38	41.1?
Number of children	2.17	2.41	2.2?
Physical care per child			
By wife	59.6	48.3	53.4
By husband	6.9	5.1	5.9
By others	2.6	1.8	2.2
Other care per child			
By wife	41.9	32.9	37.5
By husband	18.8	13.1	16.1
By others	20.6	15.1	18.0

* Minutes in *one* day.

NOTE: Sample sizes for meal-preparation and laundry-time inputs are 627 an? 667 for high- and low-schooling groups, respectively. Since child-care averages a? calculated only for families with children, sample sizes are 493 and 591, respectivel?

SOURCE: Calculated by author from time budgets collected by Dr. Kathryn Walk? of Cornell University.

high school graduation; the high-education group included wom-
en who had at least one year of college or training beyond high
school. Two household activities carried on throughout the lifetime—meal preparation and laundry work—are represented
in this table. Two kinds of child care are distinguished as well:
"Physical care" includes time spent bathing, feeding, and dressing
children and administering first aid or caring for a sick child.
"Other care" is defined by Walker as "all activities related to the
social and educational development of family members, such as:
helping with lessons, reading to children, taking children to social
and educational functions" (K. Walker, 1967). The time accounting allowed both parents' time to be allocated to the same activity
if they were engaged in it simultaneously. It should be noted that
activities were very narrowly defined in the Cornell sample; for
example, driving children to an activity would be included in the
category "chauffeuring" rather than "child care."

Table 7-3 shows that the amount of time spent by the low-education group in meal preparation and laundry work was the same as,
or greater than the amount spent by the high-education group.
This, and the fact that husbands of women with more schooling
spent greater amounts of time in meal preparation, substituting
their own time for their wives', is consistent with the greater price
of time of the more educated women.

In spite of the greater price of their time, however, better-educated mothers spent more time in child care than those in the lower
education group, particularly in the investment activity—"other
care." This is not due solely to a substitution of the mothers' time
for the fathers' or other persons', since husbands of the more highly
educated women also spent more time with their children—most
significantly in the "other care" activity. These mothers also used
more of the time of other adults in providing care for their children.
The bottom panel of Table 7-3 shows time inputs per child and
verifies that the greater time inputs are not the result of better-
educated women having more children: it is simply that children
of the higher schooling group receive more hours of care—both
in total and per child—than children whose mothers had less
schooling.

The Purdue   A study of time use among Indiana families in 1961–62 reveals
Sample   the same pattern of greater time inputs to child care by the more
educated women (Manning, 1968). Families recorded the time

they spent in child care and other household activities during an entire week at four different seasons. Child care was defined in this survey as:

> . . . bathing, dressing, feeding and putting children to bed; helping children with lessons; chauffeuring children; caring for sick children; preparing formulas for babies and special food for small children and the sick. This task excluded reading to and playing with children, supervising them at the same time other activities were being done, and general concern or responsibility for children (p. 30).

Table 7-4 shows child-care time for women of differing schooling levels by family composition. Again, in all families with children, the greater the education of the wife, the more time she spent in child care. Small sample sizes within the groupings of families by age of children preclude any firm conclusions about the way in which time inputs vary by age structure of the family and education of the mother. However, the fact that the differential in time inputs by schooling level appears to be greatest for families with preschool-age children is consistent with the findings from the census data.

TABLE 7-4 *Child-care time by family composition and education of wife (hours per week)*

| | | Years of schooling of wife | | | | | | | |
| | | Less than 12 | | 12 | | 13–15 | | 16+ | |
Age of children	No. of records*	Wife	Help†	Wife	Help†	Wife	Help†	Wife	Hel
11–17 only	90	1.2	0.1	2.1	0.1	0.7		3.3	
6–10 only	16			5.9	‡	4.3			
2–5 only	33	0.4	‡	7.4	0.4	9.5	0.8	10.1	0.
Under 2 only	24			11.2	0.8	13.4	0.8		
11–17 and 6–10	79	1.8		4.5	0.1	4.4	0.6	6.1	
2–5 and under 2	31			16.7	0.3	17.4	2.2	17.5	3
Mixed ages	112	10.7	0.5	7.2	0.7	15.5	1.3	13.0	1
All families with children	385	5.4	0.3	5.9	0.4	7.7	0.7	10.8	1
Number of families in sample		9		45		29		17	

* Families completed four weeks of record keeping, but some had children home during the summer or whereas others moved from one family category to another as children were born or left home.

† Time inputs by persons other than the wife.

‡ Less than 0.05 hours a week.

SOURCE: Manning (1968).

Once again, it is important to note that the more educated wives are not substituting their own time for that of other workers, since both kinds of time inputs are greater in families where the wife has more education. Table 7-5 compares child care to other forms of household production: We see that time inputs to child care rise with education, so that women with college degrees devote more than twice as many hours to child care as women with fewer than 12 years of schooling, 83 percent more time than high school graduates, and 59 percent more time than women with one to three years of college. However, time inputs to other household tasks tend to fall with education (although there is a tendency for time inputs to rise slightly at the highest level).[17]

TABLE 7-5
Time spent on household tasks by women of various schooling levels (hours per week)

	Years of schooling of wife			
	Less than 12	*12*	*13–15*	*16+*
Meal preparation	10.4	9.0	9.0	9.4
Washing	4.3	4.3	3.5	4.0
Physical care of children	4.8	5.3	6.1	9.7
All tasks	49.70	48.10	46.9	54.3
Number of observations	10	47	35	19

SOURCE: Manning (1968).

The French Sample

The finding that more highly educated women devote more time to child care and less to other household tasks is also consistent with the results of a study of 174 Parisian households with working wives (Guilbert, Lowit, & Creusen, 1967). In this study, time budgets were recorded for 15-minute periods on both a working and a nonworking day. The sample was divided among three classes of workers—professional (corresponding to a high-education group), employees (white-collar workers), and workers (blue-collar workers). As seen in Table 7-6, professional women devoted the least amount of time to housework and the most to child care, on both working and nonworking days. This pattern also holds for professional men on Sundays. The fact that this was true for women on Sundays as well as on working days indicates that it

---

[17] The author is grateful to Sarah L. Manning for providing these unpublished results.

TABLE 7-6
*Median hours
per day spent
at each activity
by three kinds
of French
working families*

| | *Wednesday* | | | | | |
| | *Women* | | | *Men* | | |
Activity	*W*	*E*	*P*	*W*	*E*	*P*
Housework	2.80	2.31	1.35	0.14	0.17	0
Total time spent with children	0.95	1.27	1.46	0	0.15	0.04
Total time spent in professional activities, transportation, and domestic duties	13.87	13.06	11.70	10.93	11.18	10.98

NOTE: W = workers; E = employees; P = professional workers.
SOURCE: Guilbert, Lowit, and Creusen (1967).

is not simply the result of the shorter workday for professional women.[18] Although professional women devoted fewer hours to home production (housework and child care) during the week, they spent more time with their children, both absolutely and relatively (to the entire home production time).

Since professional families can be expected to have greater incomes and more schooling than white- or blue-collar families, these data support the hypotheses that child care has greater income elasticity than other household activities and that differential productivity for child care increases with education.

Regression Analysis of Cornell Data   To determine which of the three factors outlined at the beginning of this section on child care and education is primarily accountabl for the greater time inputs to child care on the part of the mor educated women, despite the greater price of their time, furthe analysis of the Cornell data was undertaken. In regressions relatin time inputs to demand factors, prices, and substitutes, the pric of the wife's time (as gauged by hours worked) was found to hav a strong negative relationship to time inputs in all four kinds c home production considered (physical care, other care, meal pr paration, and laundry work). Time inputs to all activities wer found to be positively and significantly related to demand factor

In laundry work, capital goods and others' time proved to be goo substitutes for the wife's own time. In meal preparation, the hu:

---

[18] Professional women spent 8.89 hours in paid work and transportation, wh workers spent 10.12 hours and employees spent 9.48 hours in the same tivities.

			Sunday		
	Women			Men	
W	E	P	W	E	P
5.81	4.81	3.96	0.78	1.20	0.48
0.93	1.87	2.82	0	0.29	0.79
7.12	6.87	6.87	2.18	2.29	3.62

band's time was a good substitute for the wife's. For each 10 minutes her husband spent in meal preparation, the wife reduced her time input by 4 minutes. In both types of child care, however, the husband's time input proved to be a complement to rather than a substitute for the wife's time, since she increased the amount of time she devoted to child care when the husband did.

When the sample was again divided into two schooling groups, the husband's time was found to be more complementary for the high-education group. In addition, time inputs by others were, quite significantly, only a good substitute for the low-education group. Women whose last year of school was not above high school reduced the amount of time spent in other care by 11 minutes for each 100 minutes spent by others, and they reduced the amount of time spent in physical care by 14 minutes for each 100 minutes spent by others.[19] The high-education group did not cut back their time inputs when other workers spent more time with their children. The explanation proposed is that other workers (baby-sitters, grandmothers, other children over six) are more similar in education and ability to the mothers with little schooling and are therefore good substitutes for them. However, if education increases the productivity of time spent in child care, better-educated women would find these other workers relatively unsatisfactory substitutes. In fact, mothers in the high-education group spent the same amount of time in child care whether or not other workers also cared for their children.

[19] None of the families included in the sample had other adults living in the household.

Since better-educated women spend more time in child care, other factors are at work in addition to the smaller possibilities for substitution in other household activities. The quality of child care produced by the less-educated women is surely within the production-possibility frontier of the more educated women (e.g., they could spend as much time in child care as women with less schooling and could employ substitutes to the same extent). The fact that they do not, but spend more of their own time in child care, implies that at least one of the two other factors discussed above is at work: high income elasticity for child care or increased productivity of time spent in child care with increased education. And it is not solely the greater productivity of the more educated women's time spent in child care that leads to their greater time inputs, since that could not account for the greater time inputs to child care by husbands and other adults in families where the wife is highly educated. Increased time inputs by all family members most probably reflect the greater income elasticity for child care.

An alternative explanation of the data involves looking at the demand for time spent in child care rather than at supply factors, as in the above discussion. This alternative hypothesis is that women with more education have a greater time preference for the future (as evidenced by their own investments in human capital) and are thus more willing to make large investments of time in young children and collect the returns in the future.[20]

However, given the result on substitutability of time inputs, the demand hypothesis will not be a satisfactory explanation of the data unless we also postulate that only parents' time, and not that of others, yields returns in the future. This is an extreme form of the productivity argument. Thus, even when demand factors are taken into account, we must still rely on supply factors to explain highly educated women's greater time inputs to child care.

SUMMARY   One inference to be drawn from the greater market labor supply of more educated women than of less-educated women is that the former spend less time in producing commodities at home. We have shown that women with a greater price of time are able to reduce time inputs to household activities, such as meal preparation and laundry work, by the use of capital goods or the substitution

[20] I am indebted to F. T. Juster for pointing this out.

other workers' time for their own. This is not done, however, in child care. In child care, women with more schooling show even lower elasticities of substitution than the average, since available substitutes cannot provide as high-quality care as they themselves can. In addition, the husband's time is a complement to, and not a substitute for, the wife's time, as in the other activities. Probably, high income elasticities for child care as well as a differential productivity effect further induce better-educated women to devote more time to child care.

In summary, the higher price of time of better-educated women leads to their greater labor force participation and their smaller family size. The difference in the shape of labor supply profiles can be accounted for largely by the finding that the elasticity of substitution of time for other factors of production is smaller in child care than in household activities carried on throughout the life cycle. The substitutability of time and goods in the two kinds of activity has been shown empirically to be the most important cause of the differences in the labor supply profiles. However, it has also been argued that differential productivity and high income elasticities are additional factors in explaining why the labor supply of the more educated women does not exceed that of the less-educated women during the 25-to-40 age period.

References

Bancroft, Gertrude: *The American Labor Force: Its Growth and Changing Composition,* John Wiley & Sons, Inc., New York, 1968.

Becker, Gary S.: *Human Capital: A Theoretical and Empirical Analysis, with Special Reference to Education,* National Bureau of Economic Research, New York, 1964.

Becker, Gary S.: "A Theory of the Allocation of Time," *Economic Journal,* vol. 75, pp. 493–517, September 1965.

Becker, Gary S., and Gilbert R. Ghez: *The Allocation of Time and Goods over the Life Cycle,* National Bureau of Economic Research, New York, 1972. (Mimeographed.)

Bogan, Forrest, and Edwin O'Boyle: "Work Experience of the Population in 1967," *Monthly Labor Review,* vol. 91, no. 1, pp. 35–45, January 1968. (Reprinted as Special Labor Force Report no. 107.)

Bowen, William G., and T. A. Finegan: *The Economics of Labor Force Participation,* Princeton University Press, Princeton, N.J., 1969.

Cain, Glen G.: *Married Women in the Labor Force,* The University of Chicago Press, Chicago, 1966.

Cohen, Malcolm S., Samuel A. Rea, and Robert J. Lermań: *A Micro Model of Labor Supply,* BLS Staff Report Paper no. 4, U.S. Bureau of Labor Statistics, Washington, 1970.

Garfinkle, Stuart: "Work Life Expectancy and Training Needs of Women," *Manpower Report No. 12,* U.S. Department of Labor, Manpower Administration, Washington, May 1967.

Glick, Paul C., and Robert Parke, Jr.: "New Approaches to Studying the Life Cycle of the Family," *Demography,* vol. 2, pp. 187–197, March 1965.

Guilbert, M., N. Lowit, and J. Creusen: "Les budgets-temps et l'étude des horaires de la vie quotidienne," *Revue Française de Sociologie,* vol. 8, pp. 169–183, Avril–Juin 1967.

Hayghe, Howard: "Labor Force Activity of Married Women," *Monthly Labor Review,* vol. 96, no. 4, pp. 31–36, April 1973. (Reprinted as Special Labor Force Report no. 153.)

Leibowitz, Arleen: "Women's Allocation of Time to Market and Non-market Activities: Differences by Education," unpublished Ph.D. dissertation Columbia University, New York, 1972.

Lester, C. E. V.: "Trends in Women's Work Participation," *Population Studies,* vol. 12, part 2, November 1958.

Mahoney, Thomas A.: "Factors Determining the Labor Force Participation of Married Women," *Industrial and Labor Relations Review,* vol. 14 pp. 563–577, July 1961.

Manning, Sarah L.: "Time Use in Household Tasks in Indiana Families, *Purdue University Agricultural Experiment Station Research Bulleti No. 837,* Lafayette, Ind., January 1968.

Mincer, Jacob: "Labor Force Participation of Married Women: A Study of Labor Supply," in H. Gregg Lewis (ed.), *Aspects of Labor Economics* Universities–National Bureau Conference Series 14, Princeton University Press, Princeton, N.J., 1962.

Mincer, Jacob: "The Distribution of Labor Incomes: A Survey," *Journal of Economic Literature,* vol. 8, no. 1, pp. 1–26, March 1970.

Oppenheimer, Valerie Kincade: *The Female Labor Force in the United States,* Population Monograph Series, no. 5, University of California Press, Berkeley, Calif., 1970.

Perrella, Vera C.: "Women and the Labor Force," *Monthly Labor Review* vol. 91, no. 2, pp. 1–12, February 1968.

Rosett, Richard: "Working Wives: An Econometric Study," in Thomas F. Dernburg, Richard N. Rosett, and Harold W. Watts (eds.), *Studies In Household Economic Behavior,* Yale University Press, New Haven, Conn., 1958, pp. 51–99.

Ross, Sue G.: *Timing and Spacing of Births,* National Bureau of Economic Research, New York, 1972. (Mimeographed.)

Schiffman, Jacob: "Marital and Family Characteristics of Workers: March 1960," *Monthly Labor Review,* vol. 84, no. 4, pp. 355–364, April 1961. (Reprinted as Special Labor Force Report no. 13.)

Smith, James P.: "The Life Cycle Allocation of Time in a Family Context," Ph.D. dissertation, University of Chicago, Chicago, 1972.

U.S. Bureau of the Census: *Current Population Reports,* ser. P-50, nos. 22 and 29, Washington, D.C., 1950.

U.S. Bureau of the Census: *1960 Census of Population: Subject Report PC(2)-6A Employment Status and Work Experience,* Washington, D.C., 1963.

Waldman, Elizabeth: "Marital and Family Status of Workers: March 1967," *Monthly Labor Review,* vol. 91, no. 4, pp. 14–22, April 1968. (Reprinted as Special Labor Force Report no. 94.)

Waldman, Elizabeth: "Changes in the Labor Force Activity of Women," *Monthly Labor Review,* vol. 93, no. 6, pp. 10–17, June 1970.

Waldman, Elizabeth, and Anne M. Young: "Marital and Family Characteristics of Workers: March 1970," *Monthly Labor Review,* vol. 94, no. 3, pp. 46–50, March 1971. (Reprinted as Special Labor Force Report no. 130.)

Walker, Elizabeth: "Homemaking Still Takes Time," *Journal of Home Economics,* vol. 61, no. 8, pp. 621–624, October 1969.

Walker, Kathryn: *Definition of Household Activities,* Use of Time Research Project, New York State College of Human Ecology, Cornell University, Ithaca, N.Y., 1967.

8. Measuring the Obsolescence of Knowledge

by Sherwin Rosen

by Sherwin Rosen

INTRODUCTION In this chapter a method is outlined for determining rates of obsolescence and depreciation of knowledge and skills, and preliminary estimates are presented of identifiable parameters for white male high school and college graduates in 1959. The conceptual framework of the study rests on the by now well-known view that knowledge embedded in human agents of production can be treated as a kind of capital (Becker, 1964; Bowman et al., 1968). Learning is the embodiment of a portion of existing knowledge in oneself and represents the acquisition of a capital good or investment. Since embodied knowledge is not directly observable, estimation requires some prior economic analysis. Therefore, a model of optimum accumulation of knowledge is developed here, based on the hypothesis that individuals learn from their working experiences.

PRELIMI-NARIES Generally speaking, several dimensions of capital deterioration must be distinguished. First there is the concept of *obsolescence,* defined as negative changes in capital values that are solely a function of chronological time. Obsolescence occurs because stocks of knowledge available to society change from time to time. Different generations of graduates acquire knowledge from schools at various points in time, and obsolescence is obviously related to some concept of "vintage." Knowledge available to be learned systematically changes as research and innovation push out the frontiers of various subjects. Sometimes new knowledge proves

NOTE: I am indebted to Edward Zabel, Richard Rosett, and G. S. Maddala for advice on a number of points. Yoram Barzel and F. Thomas Juster contributed useful comments on an initial draft. Financial support from the Carnegie Commission on Higher Education and the National Institute of Education is gratefully acknowledged, but they do not bear any responsibility for the views presented in this chapter.

received knowledge to be incorrect or at least less general than was supposed at an earlier time. Similarly, production innovations often render useless skills associated with prior methods. In both cases, capital losses are imposed on those embodying the earlier knowledge and skills. However, this need not necessarily be the case. New discoveries can augment previously available knowledge in an essentially orthogonal manner. Moreover, both the process of simplification—which renders existing knowledge more accessible to students—and innovations in teaching methods themselves make standard exposures to learning environments more productive. Such changes increase value added from given resource inputs and reduce private and social costs of learning In these cases no absolute capital losses are involved, but there is a real sense in which patterns of relative capital losses emerge Finally, gross output of educational institutions can change from time to time if there are corresponding changes in "raw material." It is often argued, for instance, that the process of evolution implies increasing ability of successive generations. As will be clear from the discussion below, there are few possibilities for distinguishing among these dimensions in my work, and usually all are combined into a single rate of obsolescence.

The second concept that must be identified is *depreciation,* defined as negative changes in capital values which depend on the age of persons possessing knowledge and skills, and which are more or less independent of chronological time and generational differences. Depreciation arises because the ability of individuals to apply acquired skills and knowledge to income-producing opportunities systematically changes with age. Some have maintained that appreciation characterizes early phases of working life, analogous to the effects of storage on the quality of wine. However depreciation finally occurs as a result of increasing probabilities of death and morbidity as well as general deterioration of mental and physical capacities associated with aging. Further, it will argued below that learning is not wholly confined to schools, but occurs for very long periods after formal schooling ends. Capacity to learn and adapt to new situations may decrease with age.

Two general methods are available for examining questions concerning obsolescence and depreciation of capital goods. Direct observation is one possibility. In the case of physical capital, engineering studies of the useful life of machines and case studies of particular innovations may be valuable. In the case of human skills, there are opportunities to engage in psychological and physiological testing of individuals at different ages. For scientific knowledge, citation studies determining half-lives of publications and related methods are often suggestive (Lovell, 1973). The problem may also be cast into the standard framework of technical change by studying educational production functions, relating learning measures to a variety of educational inputs (Coleman et al., 1966), and computing various productivity measures. An alternative and complementary methodology may be derived from an economist's perspective by recognizing that all problems of obsolescence and depreciation ultimately relate to the theory of capital value. Observations on changes in capital values, rather than on their physical counterparts, provide a great deal of information on deterioration rates (Hall, 1968). Though not widely known, value methods have been applied with great success to certain types of physical capital, such as transportation equipment (Cagan, 1971; Hall, 1971). A similar approach is taken here. It is based on a natural application of the theory of capital and is useful for organizing the measurement problem. Furthermore, valuation methods have some practical advantage in that knowledge or skill as capital, though a useful construct for many problems, is not yet capable of direct measurement. Only the consequences of learning are observable through effects on income and other behavioral variables.

A few more clarifying comments are necessary before turning to specifics. First, in all these problems the major difference between knowledge capital and physical capital is the former's absence of observable market valuation. However, no real difficulty arises on that score, for services of knowledge and skills embodied in people are traded on well-developed rental markets — namely, labor markets — and rental values contain the same information as capital values. The theory of capital is just as well carried out in terms of flow or rental prices as in terms of stock or asset prices as long as the accounting is done correctly. Second, it is necessary to keep in mind that all models of the sort put forth below, whether relating to knowledge or to machines, are no better than the valuation hypothesis applied to them. It will be assumed here that individuals are systematically paid in proportion to the services of their knowledge. Knowledge undoubtedly has many characteristics of a common property resource, since acquisition of a portion of the existing stock by one person in no sense diminishes the quantity available for others to acquire. But learning activities require personal expenditures of resources in terms of outlays of money, time, and effort. Since acquisition of learning is not free, there is no reason to suppose that implicit market rental prices of existing skills do not systematically reflect social as well as private productivity.

If, in addition to embodying existing knowledge in people, learning creates new knowledge available to society at large, private marginal product may differ from social product. That is, private incentives for learning and investment can affect realized patterns of obsolescence. By concentrating on individual behavior, I am justified in ignoring feedbacks between embodied learning and the creation of new knowledge whose values are not captured by their innovators. Thus patterns of obsolescence rates are treated as exogenous; the analysis refers to new knowledge as it has actually evolved, on the basis of previous private incentives for accumulation and not on the basis of how new knowledge *should* have evolved in the presence of appropriate subsidies to inventive activities that would confer external benefits to society as a whole.

The remainder of the chapter is organized as follows. First, the nature of valuation methods is illustrated by means of a simple example, and a basic analytical difficulty is examined: Since individuals can partially avoid the consequences of obsolescence by "retooling" and learning new techniques as part of their working experience, observed market incomes (rentals) reflect both knowledge acquired in school and knowledge acquired in conjunction with work activity. Following this example, a theory of learning by experience is sketched that is based on the principles of capital accumulation. The model is made operational by demonstrating an explicit mechanism in the labor market whereby optimum learning can be achieved and by showing that life-cycle earnings can be approximated by a nonlinear function of age or work experience. Estimated parameters are sufficient to identify depreciation-obsolescence rates, certain "vintage" effects, and some "ability" factors. Finally, preliminary estimates of the model using 1960 census of population data are presented and interpreted, and tentative conclusions are made. Data limitations preclude identification of all parameters at this stage of the investigation, although the feasibility of the method is indicated.

AN EXAMPLE To what extent is it possible to estimate depreciation and obsolescence rates from observations on carnings of individuals po sessing various amounts of education obtained at different points in time? Clearly, some kind of vintage model (Solow, 1960) is required by analogy with technical change and depreciation of physical capital. Let us take automobiles as an example. Ideally, information exists on last year of school completed, major subject ("make" and "model number"), year of graduation (vintage), and age (depreciation) and can be related to annual rentals or income (Griliches, 1967). Consider the following elementary model.

Let X_t denote earnings of persons t years of age in a cross section, all of whom have completed the same level of formal education; h_t denotes an index of knowledge and skill possessed by a person age t, and R is the implicit market rental price per unit of knowledge during the year of observation. Suppose individuals receive their education at age "zero," where t represents years of work experience, and working life is N years in length. Estimation requires further specification.

1   Assume that the conditions for existence of a capital aggregate are fulfilled (Fisher, 1965), meaning that knowledge of various ages and vintages can be (conceptually) measured in "equivalent units." For example, the stock of knowledge acquired from one vintage is a fixed percentage more or less than the stock of another vintage, and similarly for skills possessed by people of different ages. It is clear that assumptions of this sort are necessary for estimation to proceed at all. If knowledge and skill depreciate at rate δ_j in the year of life j, the current stock of skill of a person age t is his initial stock multiplied by a factor $\prod_{j=0}^{t-1} (1 - \delta_j)$. In addition, successive generations enter the labor market with increasingly larger initial stocks of knowledge. Let γ_i represent an annual improvement factor in knowledge obtained from school in calendar year i, taking the origin as N years ago. γ_i is related to the relative rate of obsolescence in year i. It follows that

$$h_t = h_0 \prod_{i=0}^{N-t} (1 + \gamma_i) \prod_{j=0}^{t-1} (1 - \delta_j) \qquad (8\text{-}1)$$

where h_0 is initial knowledge of a person N years of age in the cross section. Then Eq. (8-1) describes the evolution of knowledge over successive generations. Obsolescence and depreciation factors are not separately identified in this formulation, since age and vintage are linearly related. However, this fact has little bearing on the conclusions to be derived from this example.

2   A natural assumption concerning valuation is that earnings are proportional to the services of knowledge rented at each age. That is,

$$X_t = Rh_t \qquad (8\text{-}2)$$

Equation (8-2) is based on the assumption that there is competition in the labor market and that persons possessing greater skills earn correspondingly greater amounts. It is important to note that Eqs. (8-1) and (8-2) constitute a "theory" of income determination for individuals—a quite elementary theory to be sure, but a theory nevertheless. Manipulation of these equations reveals that

$$X_t / X_{t-1} = (1 - \delta_{t-1}) / (1 + \gamma_{N-t+1}) \qquad (8\text{-}3)$$

Comparing earnings of persons one year apart in age (or vintage) provides estimates of combined obsolescence-depreciation factors for each year.

Are such estimates reliable? The provisional answer must be "no." If the δ and γ terms are all positive, Eq. (8-3) implies that age-earnings profiles in the cross section are monotonically decreasing: older persons possess less skill because they received less from their education (acquired at an earlier date) and also because what they did learn has depreciated over a longer period of time. The conclusion is unaltered if some of the initial depreciation terms are negative (indicating "appreciation"), as long as they are not too large in absolute value. In any event, the major prediction of Eqs. (8-1) and (8-2) is clearly rejected by observation. Earnings rise with age for at least 15 years after graduation at every level of schooling (Hanoch, 1967), indicating that the model is at best seriously incomplete.

Evidently, knowledge is not produced only in schools, and learning does not cease after formal schooling ends. Instead, after some period of full-time school activity, knowledge is most efficiently acquired by shifting its source of production to the labor market and allowing people to *learn from their working experiences*. It can be argued that formal schooling equips students to learn new skills more effectively on their own, but whatever the role of formal schooling, it is certain that if individuals learn from work experience, the stock of knowledge at each age consists of several vintages. Individuals have strong incentives to acquire new skills as they become available in order to maintain their capital intact, and these incentives must be incorporated in the model. Owners of used cars seldom undertake expenditures nee essary to make them indistinguishable from new cars, but the same is not true of skills.[1]

The result of this logic suggests that in addition to depreciation and obsolescence effects, net learning or investment terms should be incorporated into the function describing the evolution of embodied knowledge over a person's lifetime. Moreover, current gross accumulation costs must be subtracted from gross rentals (earnings capacity) to arrive at the age-earnings function (Becker, 1964). This, however, causes a serious conceptual difficulty to arise. Knowledge embodied in a person is not directly observable, and it is necessary to estimate capital accumulation (in value terms) at each age as well as obsolescence and depreciation rates. If working life is N years, N observations on income are available, one for each age. Yet it is necessary to estimate more than N variables — gross capital accumulation or learning at each age, as well as terms in γ and δ. Hence the problem cannot be solved without imposing a priori restrictions on some of the unknown variables to reduce their number. The solution adopted here is to posit a particular relationship between working experience and learning, based on a model of optimum learning in the labor market. My restrictions stem from a particular learning model and must stand or fall on the basis of that particular construction. It should be borne in mind that basic observational limitations preclude a straightforward accounting approach to the problem. The example above shows that in principle, rates of obsolescence and depreciation cannot be estimated as a "pure" problem in measurement and in the absence of a model.

The model I constructed is discussed in some detail in the following section. I have tried to make the arguments as accessible as space limitations permit and to spell out all assumptions underlying the estimates that will follow.

THE MODEL First, I shall sketch the general economic framework of the model and then analytically state the problem and its solution, and finally I shall derive age-earnings profiles implicit in the model and suitable for estimation.

---

[1] Skills are more like residential structures than consumer durables in this respect. The entire issue usually is ignored in durable goods studies: Expenditure after initial purchase is treated as "normal maintenance," but so-called maintenance expenditures are really investments and change the economic life of the goods.

Markets for Learning Opportunities

Economists have long recognized that labor market activities involve simultaneous purchases and sales, or tie-in contracts, between workers and their employers, and that approach is pursued here. Learning is a *joint product* of work activity. A learning environment is implicit in every assignment of work routine and each job is associated with a definite amount of learning opportunity and work activity. Suppose that knowledge is completely vested in the person acquiring it and has general market value, not specific to any firm. Workers sell the services of their knowledge, but at the same time they purchase opportunities to learn something, depending on the type of job chosen. By the same token, firms purchase the services of their employees' knowledge and also sell them opportunities to learn, depending on the type of job provided. For a given job and implied work-learning combination, individuals apply their existing knowledge and skill both to produce marketable output for employers and to embody additional knowledge in themselves. In making employment applications, workers are faced with a great variety of choices among various jobs, each offering different opportunities to learn. It is choice among jobs—each associated with a fixed learning potential and work assignment, but with the ratio between the two varying from job to job—that offers a margin of choice and the possibility for constructing operational models of optimum accumulation of knowledge in the labor market.

Markets for learning opportunities are cleared through the market for jobs. Market equilibrium is characterized by a set of implicit prices of learning options revealed to workers and employers in the form of equalizing wage differences between jobs. Ordinarily, jobs yielding larger learning possibilities sell for higher unit prices, and an individual working at one of them earns less income than he could if he worked at a job with a lesser possibility for learning. Earnings forgone is the price paid for learning in the labor market. Workers demand jobs with learning content and are willing to pay that price to increase their future earning prospects. Learning options are supplied because the learning content of work is not fixed once and for all, but can be altered by reallocating resources from production of physical output to teaching. Firms engage in multiple production and in a sense also are in the "education business." Given market prices for learning, employers choose the optimum combination of work-learning activities offered by *designing* jobs in the appropriate manner. The costs of providing greater learning opportunities are the additional physical output lost as a result of devoting greater proportions of input time to teaching and learning rather than to current production. Rising supply price results from increasing marginal rates of transformation between marketable output forgone and learning activity, and a competitive market insures that learning opportunities are supplied at marginal production cost.[2]

As will be seen below, maximization of lifetime wealth by workers implies optimum choices of jobs over the life cycle. A corresponding progression through a sequence of work activities is implied and constitutes a theory of occupational mobility. Moreover, such choices generate observable lifetime earnings patterns.[3] Thus the model yields an age-earnings generating function, whose parameters depend on variables relevant for making the best choices. Age-earnings profiles are determined by obsolescence and depreciation rates, initial stocks of knowledge, and a few other parameters, thus providing a basis for estimation.

Learning by Experience

A complete statement of the problem and its solution requires more precise specification. Attention is focused on one human factor of production, a particular kind of skill and knowledge. Let h_t denote the stock of knowledge embodied in a person at the beginning of period t. z_t represents gross learning between periods t and $t + 1$, defined as the gross change in stock between those dates. Assume that depreciation-obsolescence occurs at a constant geometric rate δ over the time spanned by the data.[4] Then gross learning equals the net change in stock plus depreciation:

$$z_t = (h_{t+1} - h_t) + \delta h_t = h_{t+1} - (1 - \delta)h_t \quad (8\text{-}4)$$

[2] The reader is referred to Rosen (1972) for details and some wider implications of markets for learning options. A related model has been developed by Ben-Porath (1967). The novelty of the present model lies in the joint-product–learning-market construction, in a learning-by-experience context.

[3] The theory can be viewed in terms of supply and demand for *lifetime* incomes, in that workers choose an optimum progression through a hierarchy of work-learning activities. Thus current labor market contracts involve implicit forward contracts for future income. To the extent that work-connected learning is firm-specific and workers share returns, lifetime earnings patterns must be the same as in cases where knowledge has general market value, as long as there is competition in the market for lifetime earnings.

[4] Since there is no possibility of distinguishing between age (depreciation) and work experience (obsolescence) in census data, δ must be treated as a combined deterioration rate. No analytical difficulties arise if δ is not constant over working life, but empirical implementation is more difficult.

Of course, z_t must be nonnegative. Each work activity or job is associated with a given value of an index I, measuring the size of the learning option connected with it. I is an index of gross learning potential on each job and represents the amount of "space" and "time" devoted to learning rather than to current production. For concreteness, the reader might think of this index as the labor market analogue of the teacher-student ratio relevant to formal schooling. For example, the value of I associated with management trainees exceeds that for executive vice-presidents; the value for carpenter's apprentices is greater than that for journeymen carpenters; etc.

As noted above, labor market equilibrium establishes a functional relationship between implicit prices and learning attributes of jobs. Let the function $P(I)$ represent the market equilibrium (shadow) price of jobs offering a learning-potential index of I. $P(I)$ is implicit learning expenditure incurred by the worker on option I. On the assumption of a rising supply price of options, $P'(I)$ and $P''(I)$ are positive: the marginal cost of learning opportunities is positive and increasing. Further $P(0) = 0$, for no expenditures need be undertaken if learning is zero. A person's earnings equal the value of services he has to sell *minus* the cost of the learning option he buys. If R_t is the implicit market rental price on the services of embodied knowledge h in period t and if y_t is observed earnings during that period, then

$$y_t = R_t h_t - P(I_t) \qquad (8\text{-}5)$$

where $R_t h_t$ is earning capacity, or the value of services rented during the period, and $P(I_t)$ is expenditure on the learning option purchased at age t. Thus $P(I)$ is market-determined in such a way to "equalize" wages across work activities with alternative learning values. Given current knowledge, Eq. (8-5) shows that the worker is confronted by a market-determined trade-off between current earnings (y) and learning opportunity (I). Current income is sacrificed if positive I is chosen, but future earnings prospects are enhanced through increased future values of h. The assumptions on $P(I)$ ensure concavity of the transformation function.

Obviously, the next step requires specifying a relationship between learning options and actual learning. Notice my continual use of the terms *option* and *opportunity* in discussing learning possibilities. The reason for this is to allow for differences among individuals in the amounts of real knowledge obtained from the same work activity. Workers differ with respect to ability and other requisites for learning. To account for these facts, it is helpful to postulate a production function relating gross learning to the nature of the job I and to embodied knowledge h. The amount a person knows clearly affects his capacity to learn:

$$z = \alpha f(I, h) \qquad \text{with } z \geq 0 \text{ and } f(0, h) = 0 \qquad (8\text{-}6)$$

where α is a generalized ability parameter that may vary from person to person.[5] Assumed properties of the production are as follows: (1) $f_I > 0$, $f_h > 0$—jobs with greater learning content increase realized gross learning, and additional knowledge increases real learning capacity; (2) f_{II} and f_{hh} are negative—marginal products of knowledge and options in producing learning are diminishing; (3) $c \geq f_{Ih} \geq 0$, where c is a constant—more knowledge can increase the real investment capacity of a marginal option, but only to a limited extent; and (4) $f(I, h)$ is concave—learning in the labor market is not subject to increasing returns.

Wealth (discounted lifetime earnings) at age of entry into the labor force is

$$\sum_{t=0}^{N} y_t / (1 + r)^t \qquad (8\text{-}7)$$

where r is a fixed rate of discount. The problem is to choose a sequence $\{I_t\}$ over working life that maximizes lifetime earnings [Eq. (8-7)], subject to the restrictions (8-4), (8-5), (8-6), and h_0, an initial endowment of knowledge at the time of entry into the market. Optimum values of I_t and starting stock h_0 imply corresponding values for z_t in each period, by Eq. (8-6). Hence the sequence $\{I_t\}$ and h_0 imply a corresponding sequence $\{z_t\}$ describing learning patterns over working life. Moreover, $\{z_t\}$ and h_0, along with Eq. (8-4), describe the evolution of knowledge $\{h_t\}$ over the life cycle. Finally, $\{h_t\}$ and $\{I_t\}$ can be substituted into Eq. (8-5) to generate observable age-earnings patterns.

In this chapter interest is centered on income profiles resulting from optimum accumulation rather than on the occupational mobility function I_t. Therefore, it is convenient to transform the problem by directly substituting the constraints (8-4) and (8-6)

[5] More generally, Eq. (8-6) might include t as an argument to allow for life-cycle changes in learning capacity. That possibility is ignored here.

into the definition of income [Eq. (8-5)] at the outset. Define total cost of realized learning as $F(z,h)$. Then if $I = g(z,h)$ is an inverse function of f, $F(z,h) = P[g(z,h)]$. The assumptions on P and f imply the following: (1) F_z and $F_{zz} > 0$—marginal cost of learning is positive and increasing; (2) $F_h < 0$ and $F_{hh} > 0$—greater knowledge can decrease the total costs of learning, but at a decreasing rate; (3) $F_{zh} \leq 0$, but exceeds some negative amount—greater knowledge can decrease the marginal costs of learning, but only to a limited extent; and (4) $F_{zz}F_{hh} - F_{zh}^2 > 0$—total cost is a strictly convex function of learning and knowledge. Learning is subject to increasing cost because larger options are available only at increasing unit price, and learning is not subject to increasing returns to scale.

The problem can now be stated simply as follows. Maximize

$$\sum_{t=0}^{N} \{R_t h_t - F[h_{t+1} - (1 - \delta)h_t, h_t]\}/(1 + r)^t \qquad (8\text{-}8)$$

with respect to a sequence of values $\{h_t\}$, subject to h_0 and $h_{t+1} \geq (1 - \delta)h_t$. At a given level of skill, the term $[Rh - F(z,h)]$ in Eq. (8-8) defines a trade-off between actual learning and current earnings. It also describes the effects of greater knowledge on these terms of trade and on future trade-offs. Choice of $\{I_t\}$ is suppressed, but is an automatic consequence of choice of $\{h_t\}$, from Eqs. (8-4) and (8-6).

Maximization of Eq. (8-8), subject to the initial endowment and the restriction that gross learning cannot be negative, is a dynamic programming problem. Only the major features of the solution are discussed here, and formal proofs are omitted.[6] The following two properties are essential:

1   Optimum learning patterns consist of two segments. Define a *critical age* T, where T is at most $N - 1$ (age at retirement minus one year). Then optimum gross learning is positive at all ages less than T and is set equal to zero for all ages greater than, or equal to, T: $z_t > 0$ for $t < T$, and $z_t = 0$ for $t > T$. Gross knowledge is accumulated up to the critical age T, after which no investment options are purchased. From time T onward, gross learning is zero, and embodied capital is allowed to deteriorate at the depreciation-obsolescence rate δ. Specialization and nonmarginal behavior

---

[6] The problem is formulated in terms of dynamic programming in Rosen (1971), an early version of this chapter. Derivation and rigorous proof of the optimum policy are also found there.

beyond age T follow from the fact that embodied knowledge has no value after working life ends, but accumulation is always costly. Certainly no investment option is chosen in the last year of working life, since only zero returns can be obtained on it. The critical age T is less than $N-1$ if certain limiting properties of $P(I)$ and $\alpha f(I,h)$ obtain. When $F_z(0,h) > 0$, marginal cost of learning can exceed marginal return at ages less than $N-1$, so that $T < (N-1)$.

2 A necessary condition for optimality during the "investment period" $t < T$ is

$$(1 + r) F_z(z_{t-1}, h_{t-1}) - R_t - F_h(z_t, h_t)$$
$$+ (1 - \delta) F_z(z_t, h_t) \qquad t < T \qquad (8\text{-}9)$$

Using the notation $F_{it} = F_i(z_t, h_t)$ to avoid writing the arguments of the functions each time, Eq. (8-9) can be rearranged to read:

$$F_{zt-1}\left[r + \frac{\delta - (F_{zt} - F_{zt-1})}{F_{zt-1}}\right] = R_t - F_{ht}$$

The meaning is clear. F_z is the marginal cost of learning in terms of current income forgone. The term on the left converts stock costs into periodic flows through amortization by a factor reflecting interest expense, depreciation-obsolescence, and capital revaluation next period. The term on the right is marginal revenue in flow terms, reflecting next period's rental value and the marginal value of knowledge for increasing future learning capacity. An equivalent expression in terms of stocks can be obtained by iteration of Eq. (8-9):

$$F_{zt} = \frac{R_{t+1} - F_{ht+1}}{(1 + r)} + \frac{\left[R_{t+2} - F_{ht+2}\right](1 - \delta)}{(1 + r)^2}$$
$$+ \cdots + \frac{\left[R_{T-1} - F_{hT-1}\right](1 - \delta)^{T-t-1}}{(1 + r)^{T-t}}$$
$$+ \frac{R_T(1 - \delta)^{T-t}}{(1 + r)^{T-t+1}} + \cdots + \frac{R_N(1 - \delta)^{N-t-1}}{(1 + r)^{N-t}}$$

This expression states the familiar criterion that marginal cost equals discounted marginal revenue. Finally, if R_t is sufficiently regular, the assumptions on F_{ij} for ensuring sufficient conditions for a maximum are satisfied, and the solution is unique.

Age-Earnings Profiles Explicit solutions for h and y as functions of t can be found by choosing a functional form for F and applying condition (8-9). A slightly more general procedure is adopted here. Condition (8-9) is linearized by use of Taylor's series approximations in the neighborhood of some point. The technique is exact if $F(z,h)$ is quadratic.

For the time being, consider a case where $R = R_t$ for all values of t. Equation (8-9) is approximated near a value $\bar{h}$, implicitly defined by

$$(r + \delta) F_z(\delta\bar{h}, \bar{h}) = R - F_h(\delta\bar{h}, \bar{h}) \qquad (8\text{-}10)$$

$\bar{h}$ is a stationary point, assumed to exist, at which net learning is zero; $\bar{h}$ is maintained indefinitely. In fact Eq. (8-10) is a condition of optimality that would hold at a stationary state if a person had an indefinitely long lifetime. Define a new variable $\tilde{h}_t = h_t - \bar{h}$. The arguments of Eq. (8-9) are h_t, h_{t+1}, and h_{t+2}, so that linearization yields a second-order linear difference equation in h_t. The homogeneous part is

$$\tilde{h}_{t+1} - B\tilde{h}_t + (1 + r)\tilde{h}_{t-1} = 0 \qquad (8\text{-}11)$$

with

$$B = (1 - \delta) + \frac{(1 + r) F_{zz} + F_{hh} - (1 - \delta) F_{zh}}{(1 - \delta) F_{zz} - F_{zh}} \qquad (8\text{-}12)$$

The derivatives in Eq. (8-12) are understood to be evaluated at $(\delta\bar{h}, \bar{h})$. The general solution of Eq. (8-11) as an explicit function of t is

$$\tilde{h}_t = C_1 \lambda_1{}^t + C_2 \lambda_2{}^t \qquad (8\text{-}13)$$

where λ_1 and λ_2 are the roots of Eq. (8-11) given by

$$\lambda = \frac{B \pm \sqrt{B^2 - 4(1 + r)}}{2}$$

It can be shown that λ_1 and λ_2 are real numbers, precluding certain cycles in the generation of $\tilde{h}_t$. C_1 and C_2 are constants determined by initial and terminal conditions h_0 and $z_T = 0$. Therefore, C_1 and C_2 are functions of h_0 and $\bar{h}$. Finally, it follows from the definition of λ that

$$(\lambda_1)(\lambda_2) = (1 + r)$$
$$\lambda_1 + \lambda_2 = B \tag{8-14}$$

The functional form for lifetime income for which estimates can be made is obtained by substituting the knowledge-generating function (8-13) into the definition of earnings:

$$y_t = R h_t - F(z_t, h_t)$$

Choosing a first-order Taylor's approximation for F yields a double geometric function of age or experience (t):

$$y_t = k_0 + k_1 \lambda_1{}^t + k_2 \lambda_2{}^t \qquad t < T$$

where the k's are constants.[7] Furthermore, it has been established that $z_t = 0$, or $h_t = (1-\delta)h_{t-1}$, for the phase $t \geq T$. It is also true that $y_t = R h_t$ for that phase, since no investment costs are incurred then; i.e., $F(0,h) = 0$. Therefore, the complete earnings-generating function over working life is given by

$$y_t = k_0 + k_1 \lambda_1{}^t + k_2 \lambda_2{}^t \qquad 0 \leq t < T \tag{8-15a}$$

$$y_t = (1 - \delta)y_{t-1} \qquad T \leq t \leq N \tag{8-15b}$$

To establish the claim that the model captures all essential features of observed age-earnings profiles, consider Eq. (8-15a and b) more closely. Suppose that λ_1 is less than unity, that λ_2 is greater than unity—the product of $\lambda_1\lambda_2$ exceeds unity from Eq. (8-14)— and that k_1 and k_2 are negative. Then the first two terms in Eq. (8-15a), $k_0 + k_1\lambda_1{}^t$, plot a rising, concave, geometric curve, whereas the third term, $k_2\lambda_2{}^t$, plots falling and increasingly negative values. If k_2 is sufficiently small, the sum of the two curves results in earnings' rising at early working ages, having a relatively flat middle portion, and falling as the critical age T is approached. At

---

[7] The income-generating function for $t < T$ is equivalent to a second-order linear difference equation $y_t - (\lambda_1 + \lambda_2)y_{t-1} + (\lambda_1\lambda_2)y_{t-2} = \text{constant}$, as can be seen by direct substitution. Also, if a second-order Taylor's approximation for $F(z, h)$ is used, terms in $\lambda_1{}^{2t}$, $\lambda_2{}^{2t}$, and $(\lambda_1\lambda_2)^t$ as well as in $\lambda_1{}^t$ and $\lambda_2{}^t$ are required.

age T, Eq. (8-15b) takes over, and earnings fall at rate $(1-\delta)$ until work life ends. Clearly, Eq. (8-15a) can duplicate observed age-earnings profiles. As will be seen, the assumption of constant R is not crucial to this characterization.

Model (8-15a) contains seven parameters — k_0, k_1, k_2, λ_1, λ_2, δ, and T — and can be estimated by maximum likelihood methods from observed earnings.[8] Once the critical age T is found, δ is estimated from the earnings pattern beyond age T. The k's and λ_1 and λ_2 are estimated nonlinearly from the portion to the left of T and identify $(1+r)$ and B, from Eq. (8-14). Equation (8-12) shows that B is a function of the second derivatives of investment costs F_{ij}. With an additional assumption, the F_{ij} terms can be reduced to one more parameter. Suppose the learning-production function is approximated by $z = a I^{1-\beta} h^{\beta}$, where β is the marginal product of knowledge with respect to the output of learning. Next, approximate the equalizing-difference function by a quadratic, $P(I) = A I^2$. Some algebraic manipulation reveals that

$$F_{zh}/F_{zz} = -[2\beta/(1+\beta)]\delta$$

$$F_{hh}/F_{zz} = \beta\delta^2$$

(8-16)

making use of the fact that $\bar{z} = \delta\bar{h}$ at the point of approximation. Substituting Eq. (8-16) into the definition of B [Eq. (8-12)] yields a relation between r, δ, B, and β, allowing identification of β, since r, δ, and B are estimated independently.

Finally, examination of optimality condition (8-9) brings out the importance of future expectations on learning behavior because current choices depend on anticipated future events. No analytical difficulties arise once an actual expectations mechanism is postulated. However, many alternative specifications are possible. At this stage of the investigation, only one possibility is considered involving an assumption of perfect foresight. Write

$$y_t = (1+\rho)^t[Rh_t - F(z_t, h_t)] \qquad \rho > 0$$

(8-17

---

[8] Of course, other investigators have recognized the wealth of information contained in age-earnings patterns. For example, see Johnson (1970) and Mincer (1970). In those papers the distinction between gross and net investment is not clear. Moreover, the equations actually estimated are not explicitly derived from a formal model, and some of the parameters cannot be interpreted. A rather different approach is taken by Eckaus and El-Safty (1972).

where ρ reflects the secular rise over time of cross-sectional age-earnings patterns. On this specification, both anticipated and realized rentals per unit of skill, as well as total costs of accumulation, rise at rate ρ over the worker's lifetime. All the previous conclusions above are unaltered because the factor $(1+\rho)^t$ multiplies both sides of condition (8-9) and cancels out. The knowledge-generating function (8-13) is still valid, though a few minor alterations are necessary. Now the stationary point of approximation is defined by $(r + \delta - \rho)F_z(\delta \bar{h}, \bar{h}) = R - F_h(\delta \bar{h}, \bar{h})$, where the discount factor has been corrected for real growth in the economy. Thus the discount term $(1+r)$ in Eq. (8-14) must be replaced by the "real" rate of interest $(1+r)/(1+\rho)$. Otherwise, Eq. (8-15a) remains intact. Finally, $(1-\delta)$ in Eq. (8-15b) must be replaced by $(1-\delta)(1+\rho)$, since R is growing at rate ρ, though capital is deteriorating at rate δ. Evidently, observed life-cycle earnings beyond age T do not fall if ρ exceeds δ.

ESTIMATION

A model of lifetime earnings patterns of a single worker has just been derived. Although panel, or time-series, data are most appropriate for estimating income-generating functions such as Eq. (8-15a and b), these data are not available in sufficient detail, and parameters must be estimated from cross sections by age of individuals' earnings in a single year. Here the model is transformed to a cross-sectional basis, and then the data and estimates are presented.

A Vintage Model

An advantage of using cross-sectional data for estimation is that it is reasonable to assume equalization of rental prices per unit of real knowledge among all individuals, regardless of age or vintage. The major problem, common to both cross-sectional and cohort data, is to impute current stocks of knowledge and learning that depend on prior learning patterns and expectations across age groups. The method described below employs an implicit assumption of unbiased expectations. In effect, the procedure corrects cross-sectional observations for two types of exponential growth and allows intergenerational comparisons to be made. If these adjustments are valid, observations on individuals τ years of age are proportional to earnings actually received ξ years ago by individuals currently $(\tau+\xi)$ years old, and imputation of prior learning patterns is possible.

Let v denote an index of vintage or "generation number," with

$v = 0,1, \ldots ,N$. Members of the oldest living generation in the cross section are chosen as the origin of v. If $y_t(v)$ is actual income at age t of members of generation v, Eq. (8-4) becomes

$$y_t(v) = (1 + p)^{t+v}\{R_0 h_t(v) - F[z_t(v), h_t(v)]\} \quad (8\text{-}18)$$

where R_0 was the rental price of knowledge N years ago. Later generations receive capital gains because their earnings are higher at any given (z,h,t) combination; younger persons can look forward to greater real wealth if economic growth raises per capita incomes over time. Now as already noted, p has symmetrical effects on marginal returns and costs of learning for each generation and age. Consequently, the approximation (8-13), describing growth of knowledge during the learning period $0 \leq t < T$, still holds, except for correction of the rate of interest to include real growth. $(1+r)/(1+p)$ in Eq. (8-14). Moreover, on the assumptions previously stated regarding $F(z,h)$, the critical age T can be shown to be identical for all generations: $T(v) = T$. However, the constants in Eq. (8-13) are *not* invariant across generations, for they depend on initial endowments, which differ from generation to generation. In other words, C_1 and C_2 are functions of v. They can be written

$$C_i = a_{i0} + a_{i1} h_0(v) \quad i = 1,2$$

where $h_0(v)$ is initial stock of knowledge at time of entry into the labor force of generation v and the a_{ij}'s are constants, dependent on $\bar{h}, \lambda_1, \lambda_2$, and δ.

Assume

$$h_0(v) = (1 + \gamma)^v h_0(0)$$

Initial knowledge of successive generations grows at rate γ, relative to the oldest living generation. γ is an exogenous vintage effect, capturing secular improvements in knowledge obtained from schools and in "basic ability" of individuals receiving diplomas.

A first-order approximation to Eq. (8-18) and some algebra manipulation yield

$$y_t(v) = [k_{01} + k_{11}\lambda_1^t + k_{12}\lambda_2^t + k_{13}(1 + \gamma)^v \lambda_1^t$$

$$+ k_{14}(1 + \gamma)^v \lambda_2^t](1 + p)^{t+v} \quad t < T \quad (8\text{-}1}$$

where the k's are constants. Let X_t denote observed earnings at age t in the cross section. Then $v = (N - t)$ in the cross section, and $X_t = y_t(N-t)$. Substituting for v in Eq. (8-19), an observable function is

$$X_t = b_0 + b_1\lambda_1{}^t + b_2\lambda_2{}^t + b_3\left[\lambda_1/(1 + \gamma)\right]^t$$

$$+ b_4\left[\lambda_2/(1 + \gamma)\right]^t \quad t < T \quad (8\text{-}20a)$$

where the b's are functions of corresponding k's in Eq. (8-19) and of $(1+\gamma)^N$ and $(1+\rho)^N$.

For the period $T \leq t \leq N$, proceed as follows: First, earnings for those ages are defined by $y_t(v) = (1 + \rho)^{t+v}R_0 h_t(v)$, since $z_t(v) = 0$. Second, there is nothing in all the above to alter a previous conclusion that $h_t(v) = (1 - \delta)h_{t-1}(v)$ for $t > T$ within each generation. Finally, $h_t(v+1) \simeq (1 + \gamma)h_t(v)$, for $t > T$. Then

$$X_t/X_{t-1} = y_t(v)/y_{t-1}(v + 1) \simeq \left[h_t(v)/h_{t-1}(v)\right]$$

$$\left[h_{t-1}(v)/h_{t-1}(v + 1)\right] = \frac{1 - \delta}{1 + \gamma}$$

Therefore,

$$X_t = \left[(1 - \delta)/(1 + \gamma)\right]X_{t-1} =$$

$$X_{T-1}\left[(1 - \delta)/(1 + \gamma)\right]^{t+1-T} \quad t \geq T \quad (8\text{-}20b)$$

With the addition of stochastic terms, the cross-sectional age-earnings-generating function Eq. (8-20a and b) can be estimated by nonlinear maximum likelihood methods, with many degrees of freedom. Estimated parameters are sufficient to identify T, δ,γ, and $(1 + r)/(1 + \rho)$ exactly. On the further assumption of a Cobb-Douglas learning production function and quadratic learning-option cost function, the marginal product of knowledge with respect to learning β is also identified. Note that parameters for depreciation-obsolescence, vintage, critical age, and the real interest rate are estimated independently of precise assumptions regarding $F(\bar{z},\bar{h})$ and $P(\bar{I})$.

Data The data source is the 1960 census of population 1/1,000 sample. Records of males 14 years of age or older and not in the Armed

Forces were drawn from the sample and classified by educational attainment, age, race, and employment status. The number of nonwhites at each age was too small to yield reliable estimates of age-income profiles, especially at the college level, and they were omitted from consideration at this time. Age-earnings profiles (excluding nonemployment income) were estimated for white male high school and college graduates from corresponding means at each age; these are presented in Figure 8-1.

A major difficulty concerns the measurement of an earnings concept appropriate to the problem at hand. Most rate-of-return

FIGURE 8-1 *Age-mean labor income, 1959; white male high school and college graduates*

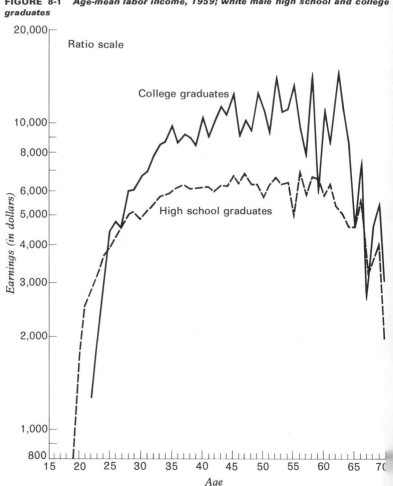

SOURCE: 1960 census of population, 1/1,000 sample.

studies use annual incomes of members of the labor force; in effect, zero values are assigned to leisure time of members of the work force and to individuals out of the labor force. If nonworking time is valued at the hourly wage rate, the computation should refer to hourly wages multiplied by a "standard" number of hours to arrive at an earnings potential. Neither measure seems appropriate to the present problem. A main component of depreciation is inability to work at all, or at least not at maximum efficiency, because of ill health (broadly interpreted). Many individuals retire from the labor force for that reason and also to escape the consequences of obsolescence. Therefore, the value of their "leisure" cannot be evaluated at the wage of those who are still in the labor force. For this reason, the data in Figure 8-1 were computed over *all* individuals, whether or not they were in the labor force. Thus the measure used corresponds to expected yearly earnings of all survivors in 1959, classified by age. Actual earnings of those unemployed and out of the labor force are counted at zero, tantamount to assigning a zero value to their leisure. The earnings measure actually used undoubtedly overstates the case for including nonworking individuals at imputed wages less than those of the employed. No further adjustment has been made for probability of survival up to each age for that reason. Resulting biases are likely to be about the same for high school and college graduates. Thus, between-group comparisons of the estimates should be valid.

The reader will note considerable variability in earnings patterns of Figure 8-1, in contrast to the rather smooth profiles implied by the model. Most of the jaggedness in Figure 8-1 is due to sampling variation.[9] The number of observations on which means are computed falls very sharply with age. For example, there are fewer than 20 college graduates in the sample at each age past 60. Hence sampling variation increases with age. Moreover, the variance of working compared with nonworking individuals in the 1/1,000 sample is extremely high in the older age groups, and the data also exhibit serial correlation with respect to age. This, too, greatly contributes to the variation apparent in Figure 8-1.

The real problem in obtaining a firmer resolution of typical earnings streams is that the sample size (within age groups) is small. Though experimentation with alternative earnings concepts defi-

---

[9] Of course the model admits variations among individuals in h_0, r, and certain parameters in $F(z,h)$, implying corresponding earnings variations. For elaboration, see Rosen (1972).

nitely would be worthwhile, it is clearly unwarranted, given the small samples currently available.[10] Sensitivity of the estimates to alternative earnings measures must await larger samples, soon to be published. Therefore, the estimates presented below are not definitive and are to be taken as an indication of feasibility of the method.

Finally, most studies of rates of return to education smooth age-income data to remove the variability evident in Figure 8-1 and reduce the probability of computing multiple internal rates of return. Though estimates of internal rates of return may not be affected much by smoothing, the same cannot be said of estimated parameters in the present model. Essentially, time-series methods are used to estimate model Eq. (8-20a and b). As is well known, moving averages of random numbers can themselves generate what appears to be systematic cyclical behavior in smoothed series. Thus estimation of Eq. (8-20a and b) on data smoothed in that manner can result in estimates that are simply artifacts of the smoothing scheme and reflect no real underlying parameter of interest. To maintain consistency with the preliminary nature of the empirical investigation at this stage, I have chosen to estimate the model from the raw data of Figure 8-1, with no further adjustment to remove effects of sampling variation.

Estimation   Maximum likelihood estimates of model Eq. (8-20a and b) are obtained by an iterative, least squares procedure. For expository convenience, write Eq. (8-20a) as $X_t = \phi_1(t)$, where $\phi_1(t)$ is the right-hand side of Eq. (8-20a), a nonlinear function of work experience during the period $t < T$. Write Eq. (8-20b) as $X_t = \phi_2(t)$, where $\phi_2(t) = X_{T-1}[(1-\delta)/(1+\gamma)]^{t+1-T}$. Define two variables:

$$\tau = t \quad \text{and} \quad D = 0 \quad \text{for } 0 \leq t \leq T - 1$$

$$\tau = T \quad \text{and} \quad D = 1 \quad \text{for } T \leq t \leq N$$

Therefore, the function to be estimated can be written

---

[10] The sampling base was narrowed by omitting current school enrollees and foreign-born persons. Earnings of the more homogeneous group are larger than those shown in Figure 8-1, but the general patterns remain intact. The high sampling variability seen in Figure 8-1 is also present in data drawn from a narrower sampling base. The real problem is small samples at older ages, and further computation is simply not worthwhile.

$$X_t = \phi_1(\tau) + D\phi_2(t - \tau) + u_t \qquad (8\text{-}21)$$

where u_t is a random variable with the usual properties.[11] For any given value of T, both τ and D are defined, and Eq. (8-21) is estimated by nonlinear least squares. Hence estimates of λ_1, λ_2, δ, and γ in Eq. (8-20a and b) are conditional on the assumed value of T. Unconditional estimates of λ_1, λ_2, δ, γ, and T are obtained by estimating Eq. (8-21) at all possible values of T and choosing the value of T (and associated values of other parameters) that minimizes the sum of squared residuals of X_t.

Obviously, T cannot be estimated with any tolerable degree of accuracy from the data of Figure 8-1, since sampling variation in X_t at older ages is so large. Therefore, Eq. (8-20b) cannot be estimated very well. However, it is clear that some parameters can be estimated with reasonable precision from Eq. (8-20a), the first portion of the earnings pattern. To investigate that possibility, I chose T in the neighborhood of actual age 66 for both groups and fitted the equation

$$X_t = b_0 + b_1\lambda_1{}^t + b_2\lambda_2{}^t + b_3[\lambda_1/(1 + \gamma)]^t +$$

$$b_4[\lambda_2/(1 + \gamma)]^t + u_t \qquad t < T \quad (8\text{-}22)$$

to the right-hand portion of each profile.

It is important to recognize that estimation of Eq. (8-22) does not convey sufficient information to identify δ. However, Eq. (8-22) potentially identifies the real rate of interest, the vintage effect γ, and the parameter B [see Eq. (8-14)] for each education group. Furthermore, B identifies a function relating δ and the second derivatives F_{ij} of F [see Eq. (8-12)]. If $P(\bar{I})$ and $f(\bar{z},\bar{h})$ are approximated by quadratic and log linear functions, respectively, the F_{ij} terms in Eq. (8-12) can be reduced to one additional parameter β. That is, B and the real rate of interest identify a *function* relating δ and the relative marginal product of knowledge β. Estimates of this function for high school and college graduates provide some interesting and informative between-group comparisons. It is important to emphasize that data limitations preclude estimation of the full

---

[11] The slightly unusual treatment of dummy variables in Eq. (8-21) is necessary to make the income-generating function continuous. D and τ are so defined that the two nonlinear segments link up at age T.

model [Eq. (8-20*a* and *b*)] at this time. In principle, all parameters are exactly identified, given a large-enough sample.

The income-generating function Eq. (8-22) has been estimated under two alternative specifications. Each is considered in turn.

First, assume that γ is small enough to be ignored: $\gamma \simeq 0$. Then the estimating Eq. (8-22) becomes

$$X_t = c_0 + c_1 \lambda_1{}^t + c_2 \lambda_2{}^t + u_t \qquad (8\text{-}23)$$

where the c's and λ's are regression coefficients. The systematic portion of Eq. (8-23) can also be written as a second-order linear difference equation:

$$X_t - (\lambda_1 + \lambda_2) X_{t-1} + (\lambda_1 \lambda_2) X_{t-2} = \text{constant}$$

Two methods are available for estimating λ_1 and λ_2 from the data in Figure 8-1: Estimate the linear difference equation equivalent to Eq. (8-23); and estimate Eq. (8-23) directly. The linear functional form is an advantage, but no satisfactory theory is available for estimating nonstationary difference equations. Therefore, I have chosen the second method. The computations are burdensome, but the standard nonlinear regression model applies to Eq. (8-23), and properties of residuals can be tested.

Rather than use packaged nonlinear regression programs, Eq. (8-23) has been estimated by artificially generating variables $\lambda_1{}^t$ and $\lambda_2{}^t$ for various numerical values of λ_1 and λ_2, regressing X on the constructed variables, and choosing the pair of values (λ_1, λ_2) that maximizes the coefficient of determination R^2. This allows examination of the likelihood surface for possible irregularities and problems of convergence to a global maximum. Values of R^2 at various values of λ_1 and λ_2 for high school graduates are shown in Table 8-1, using income data beginning at age 19 and ending at age 65 (i.e., $t =$ actual age minus 19.0, and $T = 47$). Intervals of .05 were chosen on the grid (λ_1, λ_2), and no experimentation was made with finer grids in the neighborhood of the maximum. No attempt was made to compute the information matrix at the maximum, and unconditional standard errors are unavailable. Standard errors, given in the note for the equation at the maximum, are conditional on the maximum likelihood estimate of (λ_1, λ_2). Maximum R^2 occurs at the combination (.85, 1.45) and is close to the maximum likelihood estimate of λ_1 and λ_2. Examination

TABLE 8-1 *Coefficients of determination* (R^2) *for earnings regressions of high school graduates (ages 19 to 65)*

λ_1 \ λ_2	1.20	1.15	1.10	1.05	.95	.90	.85	.80	.75	.70
1.05	.5640	.6174	.6880		.9192	.9298	.9022	.8553	.8026	.7507
1.10	.4240	.4861		.6880	.9065	.9380	.9165	.8669	.8076	.7477
1.15	.3292		.4861	.6174	.8925	.9420	.9274	.8784	.8170	.7539
1.20		.3292	.4240	.5640	.8797	.9435	.9349	.8875	.8257	.7616
1.25	.2265	.2855	.3794	.5238	.8686	.9434	.9398	.8942	.8327	.7683
1.30	.1975	.2539	.3462	.4927	.8590	.9424	.9429	.8988	.8378	.7735
1.35	.1761	.2302	.3206	.4681	.8505	.9408	.9446	.9020	.8415	.7774
1.40	.1595	.2116	.3002	.4479	.8429	.9389	.9455	.9040	.8442	.7803
1.45	.1463	.1966	.2834	.4310	.8360	.9367	.9457	.9053	.8460	.7824
1.50	.1354	.1841	.2693	.4166	.8298	.9345	.9454	.9061	.8472	.7838
1.55	.1263	.1736	.2573	.4041	.8241	.9321	.9449	.9064	.8480	.7849
1.60	.1186	.1646	.2470	.3932	.8188	.9298	.9441	.9064	.8484	.7855
1.65	.1119	.1567	.2378	.3835	.8139	.9275	.9432	.9062	.8486	.7859
1.70	.1060	.1498	.2298	.3749	.8094	.9253	.9423	.9059	.8486	.7861
1.75	.1009	.1437	.2226	.3671	.8052	.9232	.9412	.9054	.8484	.7862
1.80	.0963	.1383	.2162	.3601	.8013	.9211	.9401	.9048	.8482	.7861
1.85					.7977	.9191	.9391	.9042	.8479	.7860
1.90					.7943	.9172	.9380	.9036	.8475	.7858
1.95					.7911	.9154	.9369	.9030	.8471	.7855
2.00					.7882	.9137	.9359	.9023	.8466	.7852

NOTE: For definition of symbols, see text. At the maximum, the equation is

$$X_t = 6311.59 - 6692.94\,(.85)^t - .5305(1.45)^t(10)^{-5}$$
$$\quad\quad\quad\quad (242.47) \quad\quad\quad (.0674)$$

Conditional standard errors are in parentheses. Durbin-Watson statistic $= 2.20$.
SOURCE: Author's computation.

of residuals at (.85, 1.45) did not reveal the presence of serial correlation with respect to age (Durbin-Watson statistic $= 2.20$).

As might be anticipated, Eq. (8-23) was much more difficult to estimate for college graduates because of greater variation in mean earnings. Beginning of work life was chosen to be 23 years of age, and the data were cut off at age 64. Age 65 was not chosen in this case because earnings at that age were unusually small as a result of a large increase in the proportion out of the labor force in the sample data. When the above procedure was straightfor-wardly applied, R^2 statistics did not converge to a maximum, undoubtedly because of ill-behaved residuals. Therefore, a second-order approximation to the income-generating function was tried, adding terms in λ_1^{2t}, λ_2^{2t}, and $(\lambda_1\lambda_2)^t$ to Eq. (8-23). Convergence was achieved, but the Durbin-Watson statistic was estimated at 3.00, revealing the presence of negative serial correlation in the residuals. To account for serially correlated disturbances, X_t and the λ^t terms were transformed by $Q_t^* = Q_t - aQ_{t-1}$, where Q is the original variable and a is an estimate of first-order serial correlation. a was estimated to be -0.5 from the first-stage regres-sion. Finally, transformed data were used to compute Eq. (8-23), and results are shown in Table 8-2. The likelihood surface is smooth, and maximum likelihood estimates of (λ_1,λ_2) are in the neighborhood of (.90, 1.20). The Durbin-Watson statistic indicates no remaining serial correlation.

An attempt was made to estimate Eq. (8-22) without the a priori restriction $\gamma = 0$. The technique is the same as described above, except that computations must be carried out on a three-dimen-sional grid $(\lambda_1,\lambda_2,\gamma)$.

Since true values of γ are undoubtedly small, Eq. (8-22) in its complete form is extremely difficult to estimate. For example, if γ is as large as .05, h_0 $(N-\tau)$ doubles every 15 years—surely an enormous rate of increase. There is another reason for expecting the estimate of γ to be small. It is commonly argued that educational institutions serve as a filtering device for sorting individuals ac-cording to "ability." There is no way of knowing from income data alone whether individuals achieving a specified level of educa-tion in successive generations have been drawn from the same percentile of the ability distribution. The "filter content" of any level of school achievement may be getting coarser over time, and the estimate of γ reflects filter effects as well as improvements in knowledge. In any event, for plausible values of γ, collinearity between variables λ_i^t and $[\lambda_i/(1+\gamma)]^t$ is so high that they can-not be distinguished from one another. For example, examining the grid point (.85, 1.45, .01), zero-order correlation coefficients are .9996 for variables involving λ_1 and .9999 for variables in-volving λ_2! Orthogonalizing the independent variables will not help either. Therefore, the interesting parameter γ is potentially identified, but unfortunately cannot be estimated in this way. No doubt cross sections for several different years would be helpful

TABLE 8-2 *Coefficients of determination (R^2) for earnings regressions of college graduates (transformed data; ages 23 to 64)*

λ_2 \ λ_1	1.20	1.15	1.10	1.05	.95	.90	.85	.80	.75	.70
1.05	.6412	.6819	.7317		.8626	.8622	.8407	.8089	.7746	.7415
1.10	.5255	.5800		.7317	.8569	.8636	.8378	.7960	.7500	.7054
1.15	.4350		.5800	.6819	.8501	.8642*	.8365	.7885	.7351	.6833
1.20		.4350	.5255	.6412	.8434	.8642	.8360	.7844	.7266	.6706
1.25	.3246	.3901	.4844	.6093	.8376	.8639	.8359	.7821	.7217	.6633
1.30	.2922	.3574	.4536	.5845	.8327	.8635	.8358	.7808	.7188	.6587
1.35	.2688	.3332	.4302	.5652	.8286	.8631	.8359	.7800	.7169	.6557
1.40	.2515	.3149	.4122	.5501	.8253	.8627	.8359	.7795	.7156	.6357
1.45	.2385	.3009	.3981	.5380	.8226	.8623	.8359	.7791	.7146	.6522
1.50	.2281	.2899	.3868	.5282	.8204	.8621	.8359	.7788	.7139	.6510
1.55	.2201	.2811	.3778	.5203	.8186	.8618	.8359	.7786	.7133	.6501
1.60	.2137	.2740	.3704	.5137	.8171	.8617	.8360	.7784	.7128	.6493
1.65	.2085	.2682	.3643	.5083	.8159	.8615	.8360	.7783	.7124	.6487
1.70	.2042	.2635	.3592	.5037	.8149	.8614	.8360	.7781	.7121	.6481
1.75	.2007	.2595	.3550	.4998	.8140	.8614	.8361	.7780	.7110	.6476
1.80	.1978	.2561	.3513	.4965	.8133	.8613	.8361	.7779	.7115	.6472
1.85	.1953	.2532	.3482	.4937	.8128	.8613	.8361	.7778	.7113	.6468
1.90	.1932	.2508	.3455	.4912	.8123	.8613	.8362	.7778	.7110	.6464
1.95	.1913	.2487	.3432	.4891	.8119	.8614	.8362	.7777	.7108	.6461

This apparent second maximum is due to rounding.

NOTE For definition of symbols, see text. All variables (i.e., X_t, $\lambda_1{}^t$, $\lambda_2{}^t$) transformed by $Q_t^* = Q_t + .5Q_{t-1}$, where Q_t is the original variable. At the maximum, the equation is

$$X_t = 17209.18 - 11769.50(.90)^t - .4822(1.20)^t(10)^{-3}$$
$$(805.99) \qquad (.3112)$$

Conditional standard errors are in parentheses. Durbin-Watson statistic = 2.02.

SOURCE: Author's computation.

here. Be that as it may, if γ is small, estimates in Tables 8-1 and 8-2 should be reasonable approximations to their specification in the model.

Though the true annual rate of growth γ may be small, power to discern intergenerational differences must increase for generations further apart in age. For example, if γ is .01, the difference in initial stocks of generations 30 years apart is on the order of one-third larger for the younger group. Therefore, as a second-best procedure, specify a step function

$$h_0(v) = \begin{cases} \eta_1 & \text{for } 0 \le v \le m \\ \eta_2 & \text{for } m < v \le N \end{cases}.$$

or, equivalently, $h_0(v) = \eta_2 + (\eta_1 - \eta_2)d$, where d is a dummy variable with value 0 if $v > m$ and value 1 otherwise. Substitution into Eq. (8-20a and b) and (8-22) yields

$$X_t = b_{10} + b_{11}\lambda_1{}^t + b_{12}\lambda_2{}^t + b_{13}(d\lambda_1)^t + b_{14}(d\lambda_2)^t \quad (8\text{-}24)$$

Equation (8-24) has been estimated for high school graduates, with $m = 15$, $d = 1$ for persons having 15 years of experience or less in the cross section, and zero otherwise, distinguishing individuals who received their diplomas after World War II from those who graduated prior to the end of the war. An additional reason for making the break around 1945 is that opportunities for investment in the labor market were substantially different before and after that date. The hypothesis $\eta_1 > \eta_2$ requires estimates of b_{13} and b_{14} to be positive. The estimated equation for high school graduates at maximum R^2 (.85, 1.40) is

$$X_t = 6341.5 - 5655.8\lambda_1{}^t - 2.7358\lambda_2{}^t(10^{-5})$$
$$\quad (2543.9) \quad\quad (.353)$$

$$- 1003.4(d\lambda_1)^t - .4359(d\lambda_2)^t(10^{-5}), \quad R^2 = .9509$$
$$\quad (2466) \quad\quad\quad (.226)$$

(Conditional standard errors are in parentheses.) Since the coefficients b_{13} and b_{14} are negative, the hypothesis of no vintage effects for high school graduates cannot be rejected.

INTERPRETATION OF RESULTS According to condition (8-14), $\lambda_1\lambda_2$ estimates the net rate of discount $(1 + r)/(1 + \rho)$ for each group. Apply the estimates of Tables 8-1 and 8-2 to obtain

$$(1 + r)/(1 + \rho) = (.85)(1.45) = 1.2325 \text{ for high school graduates}$$
$$(1 + r)/(1 + \rho) = (.90)(1.20) = 1.08 \text{ for college graduates}$$

or net discount rates of about 23 percent and 8 percent for high school and college graduates, respectively. Real income per capita rose at an annual rate of about 2 percent from 1920 to 1960. Hence ρ cannot be larger than .02, and real gross discount rates no larger than 26 percent and 10 percent. In either case, the estimates indicate lower real rates of interest for college graduates, as would be expected from the theory of human capital.

The most thorough internal rate-of-return estimates from 1959 earnings data are presented by Hanoch (1967). He reports marginal internal rates of return of about 17 percent for high school graduates and 7 percent for college graduates. It is remarkable that the estimates above, which have been derived by entirely different methods, are so close to his. This surely strengthens confidence in the present approach. Hanoch uses the standard discounted comparison of income streams at two different levels of schooling, including earnings during schooling periods. My estimates are derived only from the shape of lifetime earnings patterns *within* groups, and do not rely on earnings during school. The estimates above are "internal" to each group and avoid all questions of comparability regarding ability differences between graduates at different levels of schooling. At face value, comparison of the two sets of estimates suggests that adjustment of estimated internal rates of return for ability differences is not too important, a conclusion consistent with independent investigations of that question (Becker, 1964). The estimates also suggest that rates of return to formal schooling are not very different from rates of return to learning in the labor market.

λ_1 and λ_2 also identify a parameter B in Eq. (8-14), but further interpretation requires additional assumptions. If the learning function can be approximated by $z = \alpha I^{1-\beta} h^{\beta}$ and if equalizing wage differences are quadratic, condition (8-16) applies, and λ_1 and λ_2 identify a function relating β, the relative marginal product of knowledge, and δ, depreciation and obsolescence.[12] Denote this function by $G(\delta,\beta) = 0$. Then $G(\delta,\beta)$ is the locus of pairs (δ,β) that all result in the same realized age-earnings pattern (for the phase $t < T$). In a sense, $G(\delta,\beta)$ approximates an "isoquant." However, the entire lifetime earnings pattern, rather than an annual flow, is held constant.

β is an index of efficiency of embodied knowledge in creating new knowledge, relative to other requisites for learning. An additional unit of knowledge enables individuals with higher values of β to

---

[12] The general "ability" parameter α is not identified and cannot be estimated from income data alone.

choose smaller and less costly learning opportunities to achieve a given amount of learning. Therefore, β is an index of the extent to which prior knowledge affects present learning capacity. Variations in β across different groups of individuals may be inherent either in the individuals themselves or in the nature of their work activities. In the first case, β represents an index of learning capacity. For example, higher levels of formal education may teach an individual how to use his acquired knowledge to learn new tasks more efficiently. In the second case, higher values of β are not in any sense "superior" to lower values. Production functions differ according to the product produced. If high school and college graduates systematically engage in different types of production activities and if their skills are truly different from one another and constitute different factors of production, there is no reason why their learning production functions should not differ.

Values of $G(\delta,\beta)$ implicit in the estimates of Tables 8-1 and 8-2 are shown in Figure 8-2. The functions are positively inclined larger values of learning capacity must be offset by greater depreciation-obsolescence rates to achieve a constant age-earnings profile. Any personal disadvantage of knowledge deteriorating at a greater rate must be compensated by greater relative learning efficiency of embodied knowledge. Otherwise, earnings profiles could not remain unchanged.

Unfortunately, my inability to estimate the upper tail of the earnings pattern precludes identifying δ. Therefore, it is not possible to state where the true values of δ and β lie within the constraint imposed by Figure 8-2. However, Figure 8-2 suggests lower bound for depreciation-obsolescence rates in the neighborhood of 10 percent for college graduates and 15 percent for high school graduates. I am unaware of comparable estimates in the literature, but these numbers appear rather high, especially when compared with most types of fixed capital. Based on the 10 and 15 percent bounds corresponding half-lives of a "unit" of knowledge are at most 6. and 4.3 years, respectively, and implausibly small, a priori. Of course it is always possible that the quadratic and geometric mean assumptions on which Figure 8-2 is based are not tenable. Inadequacies of data may bias the levels of the curves in Figure 8-2 even if they are tenable. Intuitively, these biases should affect both groups more or less equally. Thus the finding that $G(\delta,\beta)$ is uniformly higher for college graduates than for high school graduates may have greater validity than inferences regarding intercept

FIGURE 8-2 *Implicit functions,* $G(\delta, \beta) = 0$ **(based on estimates in Tables 8-1 and 8-2)**

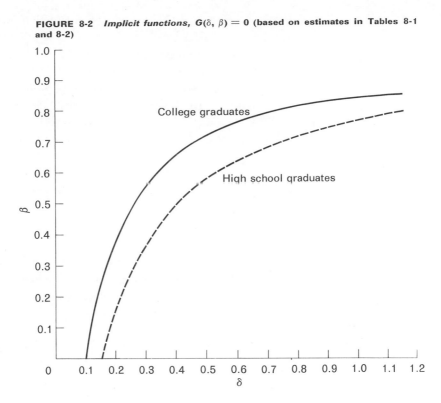

The curves could very well cross in principle, and the fact that they do not is an empirical matter. Therefore, if high school and college graduates are truly subject to the same rate of depreciation-obsolescence, then college graduates are more efficient users of prior knowledge in acquiring more knowledge. If the two groups are of equal learning efficiency, high school graduates are subject to greater rates of depreciation-obsolescence.

CONCLUSION   In this chapter, a very general class of income-generating functions of the form $y = Rh - F(z, h)$ has been analyzed on the basis of the hypothesis that people learn from work experience. Applying the principles of optimum accumulation yields restrictions on the evolution of embodied knowledge and learning over working lifetimes and permits transformation of unobserved knowledge and learning components into specific functions of working experience. A method for estimating depreciation-obsolescence rates and other interesting parameters has been derived from a nonlinear, reduced-form relationship in the model, relating earnings to years of work experience. A portion of the reduced-form function was fitted to 1960 census earnings data. Since limitations of sample size precluded estimating the entire age-earnings function, not all potentially identifiable parameters in the model could be estimated at this time. However, some parameters were estimated, and the results are sufficiently promising to indicate feasibility of the method.

Real rates of interest implicit in income profiles have been estimated for white male high school and college graduates. Estimated values are 23 percent and 8 percent, respectively, and compare well with internal rates of return described in the literature. This comparison and the fact that they are based on an entirely different methodology are strong evidence in favor of the applicability of the model.

Though the form of the model actually estimated is limited, still it is sufficient to identify a vintage effect measuring intergenerational growth of knowledge obtained from schooling. No evidence of positive vintage effects for high school graduates was found but this result cannot be taken as an indication that the quality of secondary schools has not improved over the years. Value added for high school education may very well have increased over time even though gross output did not, because of offsetting changes in the role of high schools as institutes of certification. High school graduates may have been drawn from successively lower percentiles of the ability distribution, high school diplomas exhibiting decreasing "filter-year" content over time. More direct evidence on the point is available in the recent study by Taubman and Wales (1971). The results presented here are consistent with that study though again they are based on different methods.

More tentative conclusions can be derived if learning functions are approximately of the form $z = \alpha I^{1-\beta} h^\beta$, where I is an index of learning opportunities implicit in work activities. In this formulation β measures the relative marginal product of knowledge producing learning, whereas α is a measure of all-around ability. Depreciation-obsolescence rates (δ) have not been identified, since only a portion of age-earnings functions could be estimated. Measures such as β and δ cannot be distinguished on the basis of truncated earnings functions estimated here, since many combinations of these parameters are consistent with observed earnings. Our implicit functions $G(\beta,\delta)$ giving all possible β-δ combinations consistent with observed income patterns for high school and college graduates are identified, and they suggest lower bounds on δ

.10 for college and .15 for high school graduates. It must be stressed that this identification problem is due to a limitation of data and not method. Both parameters are potentially identified from the full model.

For further interpretation, consider the following conceptual experiment. Suppose $G(\beta,\delta)$ were the same for both high school and college graduates. Then any real differences in learning capacity (in the sense of β) between them would be exactly offset by opposite differences in depreciation-obsolescence. If it were possible to "give" typical high school graduates the true (β,δ) combination actually possessed by typical college graduates, truncated income patterns of high school graduates would be practically identical to what is observed. The estimates above indicate larger values of β at *every* possible depreciation-obsolescence rate for college graduates. Therefore, the consequences of depreciation-obsolescence are more severe for high school graduates, for they cannot overcome them as readily. No matter what the true values of β and δ, the result suggests that college graduates are more efficient learners *relative* to their depreciation-obsolescence rates than high school graduates. College graduates' greater learning capacity more than offsets whatever true value of δ they face and it is one factor leading to greater lifetime earnings. Lifetime earnings of college graduates are also larger because they face lower real rates of interest. In addition, it is probable that they enter the market with greater initial knowledge (h_0) and possess greater all-around ability in the sense of α. Needless to say, if this characterization is correct, the model cannot distinguish between the differences in earnings resulting from college education as a selection process and as a real producer of embodied knowledge.

It is apparent that firmer conclusions will require data based on larger samples. The sensitivity of the results to other earnings concepts and other expectations hypotheses also remains to be investigated. Research currently under way will provide some better answers.

References

Becker, G. S.: *Human Capital: A Theoretical and Empirical Analysis, with Special Reference to Education,* National Bureau of Economic Research, New York, 1964.

Ben-Porath, Y.: "The Production of Human Capital and the Life Cycle of Earnings," *Journal of Political Economy,* vol. 75, pp. 352–365, August 1967.

Bowman, M. J., et al.: *Readings in the Economics of Education,* UNESCO, New York, 1968.

Cagan, P.: "Measuring Quality Changes and the Purchasing Power of Money: An Exploratory Study of Automobiles," in Zvi Griliches (ed.), *Price Indexes and Quality Change: Studies in New Methods of Measurement,* Harvard University Press, Cambridge, Mass., 1971, pp. 215–239.

Coleman, J. S., et al.: *Equality of Educational Opportunity,* U.S. Office of Education, Washington, 1966.

Eckaus, R. S., and A. El-Safty: "An Approach to the Estimation of Income-Educational Relations Based on Learning Theory," M.I.T., Department of Economics, 1972. (Mimeographed.)

Fisher, F. M.: "Embodied Technical Change and the Existence of an Aggregate Capital Stock," *Review of Economic Studies,* vol. 32, pp. 263–288, October 1965.

Griliches, Z.: "Hedonic Price Indexes Revisited," *Proceedings of the American Statistical Association Business and Economics Section,* Washington, D.C., 1967

Hall, R.: "Technical Change and Capital from the Point of View of the Dual," *Review of Economic Studies,* vol. 35, pp. 35–46, January 1968

Hall, R.: "The Measurement of Quality Change from Vintage Price Data," in Zvi Griliches (ed.), *Price Indexes and Quality Change,* Harvard University Press, Cambridge, Mass., 1971, pp. 240–271.

Hanoch, G.: "An Economic Analysis of Earnings and Schooling," *Journal of Human Resources,* vol. 2, pp. 310–329, Summer 1967.

Johnson, T.: "Returns from Investment in Human Capital," *American Economic Review,* vol. 60, pp. 546–560, September 1970.

Lovell, M.: "The Production of Economic Knowledge," *Journal of Economic Literature,* vol. 11, pp. 27–55, March 1973.

Mincer, J.: "The Distribution of Labor Incomes: A Survey with Special Reference to the Human Capital Approach," *Journal of Economic Literature,* vol. 8, pp. 1–26, March 1970.

Rosen, S.: "Knowledge, Obsolescence and Income," abstracted in *Econometrica,* vol. 39, pp. 177–178, July 1971.

Rosen, S.: "Learning and Experience in the Labor Market," *Journal of Human Resources,* vol. 7, pp. 326–342, Summer 1972.

Solow, R. M.: "Investment and Technical Progress," in K. Arrow, S. Karlin, and P. Suppes (eds.), *Mathematical Methods in the Social Sciences 1959: Proceedings of the First Stanford Symposium,* Stanford University Press, Stanford, Calif., 1960, pp. 89–104.

Taubman, P., and T. Wales: *Economic Returns to Higher Education,* National Bureau of Economic Research, New York, 1971. (Mimeographed.)

Part Two:
The Impact of Education on Behavior

9. Education and Consumption

by Robert T. Michael

INTRODUCTION It has long been recognized that the influence of education on behavior is pervasive. Even through casual observation, many aspects of the behavior of the individual or of the household are seen to be closely associated with level of schooling. Income, choice of occupation, residential location, geographical mobility, consumption expenditures, leisure-time activities, avocations, characteristics of friends and associates, "lifestyle," and attitudes toward a myriad of personal and social issues all would appear to be relatively strong correlates of education. Governments frequently impose laws regulating the minimum permissible amount of education. This is done in the belief that individuals are better citizens if they are literate and possess basic information about a number of subjects. Moreover, as a result of its influence on behavior, level of schooling is one of the common characteristics by which social scientists categorize people.

Yet, for all the examples of strong correlates of education that one might suggest, very little is known about the causes or the nature of these effects. We may know that more highly educated people earn different incomes or hold different opinions, but we cannot say whether these differences result from specific knowledge acquired as part of education, from a change in the manner in which decisions are reached, or from changes in basic beliefs and values. Although psychologists tell us something of the way

NOTE: This chapter is a nontechnical summary of some of the research reported in my monograph (Michael, 1972). Since this chapter is intended for a wider readership, many technical points are ignored, and the standard economic jargon is modified. I have avoided the use of mathematics entirely. For a more thorough discussion of procedures and of theoretical as well as statistical issues, see the NBER monograph. This chapter was submitted for inclusion in this volume in July 1970, and only very minor subsequent revisions have been made.

one learns, little is known of the process by which learning or newly acquired knowledge affects subsequent behavior.

Leaving aside questions about the causes of the influence of education, even the nature or extent of the effects is not well documented. One of the few factors which have been studied in detail is the relationship between schooling and earning capacity in the labor market. Numerous studies in the past decade have shown that earnings are raised systematically by education and that the purchase of some level of higher education is a wise investment for most people when the return on the investment is measured in enhanced earnings alone. The chapters in Part One of this volume attempt to extend and refine these findings. Other effects of education are less well documented. In part, the purpose of the work on which this chapter reports is to identify and describe the effect of education on another aspect of behavior: consumer expenditure patterns.

In addition to determining the extent to which education affects spending patterns, the chapter also offers an explanation of why consumer behavior might be affected in a specific manner. The explanation is partial at best in that it relates the effect of education on consumer behavior in the home or "nonmarket sector" to the effect of education on earnings in the labor market. Yet, if the same type of influence exists both in the home and in the labor market, then the observed influence of education may operate through its effects on how one uses his or her own time, rather than through its effects on any bargaining power associated with the attainment of a level of education.[1]

WHY EDUCATION MIGHT AFFECT CONSUMER BEHAVIOR In order to analyze why the level of formal schooling might influence consumer behavior, some interpretation of the consumption process itself is needed. The general approach adopted in this stud

[1] One explanation sometimes offered for the observed positive relationship between education and earnings is that schooling is used as a criterion for jobs solely as a means of reducing the competition for those jobs. Schooling helps "zone" people, to use the term suggested by social critic David Hapgood, who says: "The effect of diplomaism is to zone out the person who wants to make his own way to a productive place in society. . . . The degreeless creative odd ball who could perform better than his credentialed competitors is not allowed to compete" (1971). Obviously, however, such an explanation cannot be applied to any directly observed effects of education on productivity in the home since in home production the household is both the supplier and demander of labor services.

follows Becker's formulation of household activities (Becker, 1965; Michael & Becker, 1973). The household is viewed as an organizational unit (comprised of members of the family) which engages in the production of many different things. Within the household the family seeks to achieve as great a level of satisfaction or utility as possible, subject to its resource limitations. The household, then, is a small multiproduct firm which produces many desiderata from which family members derive satisfaction. These desiderata are called *commodities* (for example, good health, physical exercise, nutrition, intercity visits, and children), each of which is produced within the household organization by a production activity (for example, convalescing, bicycling, eating, traveling, and child care).

Each household produces the commodities it desires by combining time and goods (labor and capital) in a productive activity. It is therefore limited in its ability to produce commodities by its available resources of time and goods. This limitation involves essentially a limited amount of available time—24 hours per day per family member—and the particular wage rates at which the household members convert their time into money in the labor market. (Of course, any nonwage income adds to its resources as well.) In this framework, the household uses some of its time directly in producing commodities and some of its time indirectly by first selling the time (or the labor services) in the marketplace and then using the income to purchase goods and market services. These are subsequently combined with the household's nonmarket time in commodity production.

Now, these commodities, in this framework, need not be physical. It is not difficult to name some satisfaction from every activity in which a household member engages. (Thus time and goods used in sleeping produce good health or perhaps a pleasant disposition, whereas time and goods spent in grooming produce a desirable personal appearance, and so forth.) It is possible to translate any activity or expenditure of money or of time into this framework, which is, at this level, simply a language—a way of talking about how households behave. Its usefulness lies in facilitating our analysis of the factors which influence observed behavior.

The study of the effects of education is a good illustration. Given this framework, in which households are viewed as combining purchased market goods with their own time to produce commodities, we can predict that education will affect the household's capacity to convert these goods and time into commodities. That is, education may affect the efficiency with which the commodities are produced. There are, in fact, at least two reasons for predicting that education will raise efficiency.

First, there is the fact—confirmed by both casual empiricism and rigorous statistical analysis—that wage rates rise with education levels (see Part One of this volume). This is consistent with education raising the productivity of labor services in the market. If increases in education raise the productivity of time used in one activity, it seems reasonable to expect education to have an analogous effect on the productivity of time in other activities. Since the household production function framework views consumption as a production activity, it is logical—in light of the observed correlation of education with wages—to expect education to enhance efficiency in consumption.

This expectation depends critically upon the inference that the positive correlation between education and earnings results from an *influence* of education on the value of the marginal product of time in the labor market. There are at least three distinct explanations for this observed correlation: (1) Education may alter the productivity of one's time and thereby affect wage rates;[2] (2) education may screen individuals on the basis of native capacity and thereby operate, in job markets characterized by positive information costs, as certification of some given level of capability; and (3) education may simply operate as a bargaining device which "opens doors" or which "zones" people, thereby establishing non-competing groups.[4]

A positive effect of education on efficiency in nonmarket produc

---

[2] Intuitively, it is clear that this mechanism is at least in part responsible for higher wages. For example, knowledge of anatomy and physiology acquired from schooling enhances the surgeon's skills. Similarly, knowledge of languages, mathematics, literature, history, and so forth, is essential in specific occupations. Although training enhances productivity in specific skills, formal schooling need not be the only way to acquire these skills.

[3] Taubman and Wales (Chap. 4 in this volume) attempt to distinguish direct between these two explanations.

[4] A very different set of distinctions has been suggested by Gintis. He, too, concerned with the mechanisms by which education affects earnings, but distinguishes an effect of education on various dimensions of personal characteristics. In particular he emphasizes the effects of schooling on the "cognitive" (mental) characteristics and the "affective" (psychological) characteristics. Both of these may be viewed as ways in which education alters an individual's productivity, and thus they belong under explanation 1 of the rubric suggested in the text (Gintis, 1971).

tion (holding factor proportions constant) would not be implied by explanation 3 (that education bestows monopoly rents) but would be consistent with either explanation 1 (that education augments productivity) or explanation 2 (that education screens and thereby certifies). Thus, while an observed positive effect in the nonmarket sector cannot help us distinguish between explanations 1 and 2, it can help us select between explanation 3 and explanations 1 and 2. Furthermore, there would be little economic incentive to invest in education as certification for nonmarket production, since in this market the household is both employer and employee.[5]

A second reason for expecting education to increase the efficiency of nonmarket production is the similarity between education and technology. The introduction of additional education into the household's production process is analogous to the introduction of new technology into the firm's production process. When a firm introduces new "technology," it generally is in the form of a new idea (e.g., a new way to organize production) or a new input which embodies some new technique (e.g., a machine with a new capability or a new employee with a skill). Education has similar attributes related to home production. Households composed of more educated individuals have relatively more access to knowledge, concepts, facts, and ideas that may enable the household to arrange nonmarket production more efficiently. Furthermore, since education (or, more precisely, the human capital with which it is associated) is embodied in the individual, it may raise not only the proficiency of the time input used in nonmarket production but also the efficiency of market expenditures, since one use of nonmarket time is the selecting or purchasing of market goods and services.

In other words, in most production activities there are several ways of producing the product, and so the choice of a production technique may be an important determinant of the efficiency with which the production takes place (i.e., the cost of production). One of the expressed purposes of some forms of education is to develop a receptiveness to new ideas. Thus not only may a more

[5] One exception might be the use of education as a screening device in the selection of a spouse. See Jensen (1969).

Another exception might be the psychic satisfaction of simply having succeeded in obtaining certification. (In the terminology of the household production function model, successful certification—or the achievement of some specific level of schooling—might be a direct factor of production in producing the desirable commodity "distinction" or "self-respect.")

educated family have greater access to knowledge and greater facility in assimilating and evaluating new information, but its members may also be more receptive to new ideas and thus be more likely to experiment with, and adopt, improved production techniques. If so, the average level of "technology" employed in household production will be positively related to the education level of the household members.[6]

For both of these reasons—the inferred effect of education on the productivity of time spent in the labor market and the similarities between the role of education in household production and of "technology" in market production—education is expected to enhance the efficiency of nonmarket production and thus affect consumer behavior.

HOW EDUCATION MIGHT AFFECT CONSUMER BEHAVIOR

If education improves the household's capability in converting time and money into commodities, this may affect behavior in two ways. First, since education has a bigger impact on efficiency in some activities than in others, this will alter the relative prices of the commodities. For instance, if education is particularly effective in improving reading efficiency but is ineffective in improving physical exercise efficiency, then, with increases in education, the commodity associated with reading becomes cheaper relative to the other commodity. Economic theory suggests that there will be an incentive to shift consumption toward the relatively cheaper activity.

Second, if education improves the average efficiency of nonmarket production, then households with more educated family members are wealthier in the sense that they can produce more with given amount of time and money. Thus even if their available time and money are held fixed, families with more education will have more real wealth in terms of commodities. Economic theory sug

[6] This attribute of education has previously been suggested as one of the way in which education enhances market productivity. After discussing the importance of the "allocative efficiency of traditional agriculture," T. W. Schul suggests, "In general, where technically superior factors of production are principal source of agricultural growth, schooling counts" (1964, p. 189). a somewhat different context, Nelson and Phelps (1966) suggest that "education enhances one's ability to receive, decode, and understand information An important and clear analysis of the productive value of education has been made, and evidence of the "allocative effect" of education in agricultural production has been adduced by Welch (1970).

gests that this difference in real wealth among households will affect observed behavior systematically.

Turning first to relative price effects, consider the price of some particular commodity, say, a "good diet."[7] Its production uses groceries, cooking equipment, and dishes, as well as shopping, cooking, and eating time. The price of one unit—say, one day's worth—of a good diet would be the sum of the expenditures on the day's groceries, some appropriate fraction of the cost of the durable equipment such as the stove and the dishes, and the value of the household members' time spent preparing and eating the meals per day. If education improved the efficiency in this set of activities, it would mean that the same amount of a good diet could be produced each day in somewhat less time and using somewhat fewer money expenditures.[8] Consequently, the price per unit would be lower. If education affected some commodity prices but not others, some prices would rise and others would fall relative to one another. This would hold true even if all commodity prices fell absolutely but by different proportions.

Suppose, instead, that education had the same effect on the prices of all commodities such that, say, each fell by 5 percent. That would mean (under fairly general conditions) that the previous levels of all commodities could be purchased with 5 percent less time and 5 percent less money. This in effect would raise by 5 percent the time and money the household had at its disposal. Although their actual money income and time resources might be the same, the household with more education could produce more commodities; it would be wealthier in terms of final output without being wealthier in terms of resources. Indeed, this is what it means to be more efficient: a smaller amount of input is required to produce a given quantity of output. Consequently, just as a decrease in the cost of living related to *market* prices increases the household's income in real terms, an increase in education which lowers the cost of living related to *commodity* prices increases the household's income in real terms.

---

[7] The commodity is called a good diet, not a healthy diet, since the desired diet may include more variety and quality than nutritional requirements dictate.

[8] For simplicity, it will be assumed that education affects all the inputs in any activity proportionally, so that if the time used in producing a good diet becomes 5 percent more efficient, the equipment and other purchases used in the production also become 5 percent more efficient.

In this framework, the effect of education is essentially an indirect one. By altering the relative prices of commodities, it induces behavioral shifts toward relatively cheaper items; and by lowering the cost of living in the manner just described, it raises real income and induces behavioral shifts similar to those which accompany any other increase in income. In order to make a prediction about behavior which we can observe and to test the usefulness of our framework, we shall suppose that education has the same proportionate effect on all nonmarket activities in which the household engages. By making this assumption, we eliminate any effect on relative prices of commodities and are left with a very simple prediction: If education *raises* nonmarket efficiency as described, households that have more education but no more money income will shift their expenditures on consumption items in the same manner as households with more money income but no more education. Suppose we compare three households, the first of which has somewhat more income than the other two and the second of which has somewhat more education than the other two (but no more income than the third). We would expect to find the second (more educated) household spending its income on various consumption items in proportions more similar to those of the household with more money income. In short, if education raises real income through nonmarket productivity, it should affect consumer behavior in the same manner as money income affects behavior.[9]

Not only can we infer from observed expenditure patterns the existence and direction of education's effect on nonmarket productivity, but we can also obtain an indication of the magnitude of

[9] It is true that households with more education also tend to have more money income, but this is not the point here. The present argument is that in addition to any effect of education on money income, there is also a nonmarket productivity effect. So in total, education may raise real income both by raising money income and by raising nonmarket productivity. We are interested in determining whether this latter effect is discernible from observed behavior.

Another distinction between the market and nonmarket effects of education relates to the relative commodity prices. It was suggested above that education might affect the relative prices of commodities by a differential effect on the efficiency of their production. Education also may alter relative prices of commodities by its effect on market wage rates and thus on the price of time of family members. The one mechanism (through the nonmarket activities) may be independent of the time intensity of the commodity's production, whereas the other mechanism (through the market wage rate) is closely related to the relative importance of time in the commodity's production. So as available data improve, we should be able to separate these two relative price effects. For now, the latter effect is captured by the observed effect of money income

the effect. By determining the magnitude of the shift in expenditures resulting from, say, a 1 percent increase in the household's money income and the magnitude of the shift resulting from a 1 percent increase in its education level, we can infer the amount of additional income the household with more education acts as if it has. That additional amount is attributed to the nonmarket productivity effect. [10]

Within the conceptual framework employed here, it has been hypothesized that education raises productivity in the nonmarket sector and thereby affects consumer behavior in a specified way. Of course, now the framework is no longer simply a language; instead, it is used in making a substantive prediction about the way education affects behavior. It may be an incorrect prediction, in which case the hypothesis will be rejected. Moreover, even accurate predictions do not prove that the model's description of the process through which education works is correct. At best, we can find that this interpretation of the way education works is useful, since it correctly predicts behavior; other interpretations which give the same accuracy of predictions would be equally good.

THE OBSERVED EFFECT OF EDUCATION The previous section indicated the way in which education might affect consumer behavior; this section reports on some empirical findings related to those predictions. To determine whether expenditure patterns shift in the same way with changes in education as with changes in money income, we must first estimate the two shifts and then see whether the patterns are similar. As the first step, the two separate effects of money and education are estimated. The data were from a survey of over 13,000 households, or consumer units, conducted by the Bureau of Labor Statistics in 1960–61. The data included information on the household's income and expenditure patterns, the education level and age of the head of the household, and the family size.

For statistical reasons, the data were grouped into 157 cells, which were used as the statistical observations. The cells were

---

[10] For example, if 1 percent more money resulted in a shift of, say, 4 percent in the relative expenditure on restaurants, and if a 1 percent increase in education resulted in a rise of 2 percent in the expenditure on that item, we could say that the household acted as if the 1 percent more education was equivalent to a ½ percent increase in money income. If no education effect is observed, then we conclude that education was equivalent to no more money income and that the nonmarket productivity effect is therefore zero.

defined by classes of income, education, and geographic region. For instance, one particular observation was the average value of each piece of information for the 211 households living in the South with incomes between $3,000 and $3,999 per year and with 9 to 12 years of education for the head-of-household. For each observation, the average yearly expenditure on 15 categories of consumption—food for home use, food away from home, clothing, medical care, etc.—was used for the analysis. The definitions of these items are given in Table 9-1.

The presumptions on which this analysis rests are (1) that systematic differences in behavioral patterns across households are related to the magnitudes of the variables used and (2) that behavior of households at, say, different levels of income indicates how any household, on the average, would behave if its income were changed in a similar manner. Thus we observe how income *differences* affect behavior across households, and we presume that this is how income *changes* would affect the behavior of a single household. In some form, this presumption is made in all such statistical analyses. A specific assumption here is that there is a one-to-one relationship between the expenditure categories and the commodities produced. With this and an assumption about the production process, the responsiveness of the household's demand for home-produced commodities to changes in income is the same as the responsiveness of its demand for the market goods. That is, the effect of income on the demand for "food for home use" is the same as the effect on the demand for the commodity "good diet."

TABLE 9-1
Expenditure items

1. Food for home use

2. Food away from home

   Board

   Meals at work and school

   Other meals, beverages, and snacks

   Meals out of home city

3. Tobacco

4. Alcoholic beverages

5. Housing

   Expenditures on rented dwellings by those who rented plus lodging out of home city (adjusted for the percent of renters)

TABLE 9-1
(continued)

6. Utilities

    Fuel, light, refrigeration, water

7. Household operations

    Laundry, cleaning, household paper supplies

    Laundry, cleaning sent out

    Domestic service

    Day-nursery care

    Telephone and other household expenses

8. House furnishings and equipment

    Household textiles, furniture, floor covering

    Major and small appliances, housewares

9. Clothing

    Clothing for family members

    Clothing materials and upkeep

10. Personal care

    Haircuts and hair care

    Personal-care supplies

11. Medical care

    Prepaid care

    Direct expenses: hospitalized illness, physician, dental care, eye care, drugs, medical appliances, etc.

12. Leisure

    Recreation: TV, radio, phonographs, etc.; spectator admissions, hobbies, pets, toys

    Reading

13. Education

    Tuition and fees

    Books, supplies, equipment

    Music and other lessons

14. Automobiles

    Purchase and operation

15. Other travel

    Public transportation in and out of home city

    Car pool

The statistic that indicates the responsiveness of expenditures to changes in income, expressed in percentage terms, is the income elasticity. If the term equals 1.0 for some item, this indicates that expenditures on the item rise proportionately with income. If the term exceeds 1.0, the expenditure on the item rises more than proportionately, and hence as income rises, the percentage of income spent on the item rises. If the income elasticity is less than 1.0, the expenditure on that item rises less than proportionately, or the percentage of income spent on it falls. A similar statistic is used to indicate the responsiveness of expenditures to changes in the level of education. The previous section suggested that if education improves productive efficiency in the home, the effects of income and education will be similar. In particular, if the income elasticity exceeds 1.0, the education elasticity should be positive; if the former is less than 1.0, the education elasticity should be negative.

Notice the asymmetry inherent in the fact that the income elasticity differs from one (1.0), whereas the education elasticity differs from zero. This follows since the latter holds total expenditures fixed, and so the average effect of education on expenditures must be zero—the household cannot spend more on all goods as education rises since it cannot have more income due to the statistical procedure. The most the household can do is to take some money from one item (the theory predicts one of those with income elasticities less than 1.0) and spend that money on other items (those with income elasticities greater than 1.0).

By the statistical procedure of multiple regression, the separate effects of income[11] and education were estimated, and the effects of the age of the head-of-household, the size of the family, and the geographic region were removed. The estimates were made for each of the 15 categories separately and for a broader set of two inclusive categories: *goods* (food for home use, tobacco, alcohol, shelter, utilities, house furnishings and equipment, clothing, reading, and automobiles) and *services* (food away from home, household operations, personal care, medical care, recreation, education, and travel other than automobile). The estimated income and education elasticities for these broad categories are shown in Table 9-2.

---

[11] For statistical reasons, the income variable was the total consumption expenditure, not the measured disposable income. This procedure is commonly used to avoid short-period random fluctuations in income. The variable will be referred to as the income variable, nevertheless.

TABLE 9-2 Elasticity estimates for goods and services		*Income elasticity*	*Education elasticity*
	Goods	0.93	−0.07
	Services	1.12	+0.19

SOURCE: Author's computations.

The income elasticities indicate that the response to a 1 percent increase in income is an increase of slightly less than 1 percent (0.93) in the expenditure for goods and an increase of slightly more than 1 percent (1.12) in the expenditure for services. That is, as incomes rise, households tend to spend proportionately more on services and proportionately less (although absolutely more) on goods. As for the effect of education, the table indicates that a 1 percent increase in the number of years of schooling completed by the head-of-household (say, from 10 years to 10.1 years) lowers the expenditure for goods by a fraction (−0.07) and raises, by about one-fifth of 1 percent (0.19), the expenditure for services. So for these broad categories of expenditures, education does affect the pattern of spending in the same way as income: both shift expenditures toward services.[12]

The results for the 15 separate categories of expenditures are shown in Table 9-3. For each consumption item, the table gives the estimated income elasticity, the estimated education elasticity, and the average yearly expenditure on the item by the households in the survey.[13] According to these estimates, households with higher incomes spend a larger portion of their income on food away from home, alcohol, household operations, clothing, leisure, education, automobiles, and other travel. As income rises, expenditures for food at home, tobacco, housing, utilities, house furnishings, personal care, and medical care rise less than proportionately.

If education raises nonmarket productivity equally in all nonmarket activities, the education elasticities for the first set of items should be positive. In fact, positive effects are observed for food

[12] Given that the average of these elasticities is a constant, knowing the results for either one of these two categories is sufficient for determining the results for the other; i.e., if expenditures shift away from goods, they must shift toward services.

[13] These elasticities were estimated by double-log regressions for most of the items. For a few, income-education and income-age interaction terms were included, and for food at home, tobacco, and utilities, a linear form was used. In these cases, where the elasticities are not constant, the table shows the elasticities at the point of means.

TABLE 9-3
Elasticity
estimates for
15 items

Expenditure item	Income elasticity	Education elasticity	Mean expenditure
Food for home use	0.526	−0.112	$ 989
Food away from home	1.225	0.205	246
Tobacco	0.519	−0.563	91
Alcoholic beverages	1.611	−0.584	78
Housing	0.990	0.372	658
Utilities	0.463	0.052	249
House operations	1.113	0.314	288
House furnishings and equipment	0.981	−0.059	266
Clothing	1.113	0.083	518
Personal care	0.939	−0.125	145
Medical care	0.831	0.030	340
Leisure	1.299	0.147	245
Education	1.594	1.485	53
Automobiles	1.228	−0.347	693
Other travel	1.378	0.097	77
TOTAL			$4,936

SOURCE: Author's computations.

away from home, housing, utilities, household operations, clothing, medical care, leisure, education, and other travel. For alcohol and automobiles, the positive effects are not observed, whereas they are unexpectedly observed for housing, utilities, and medical care. That is, five of the observations are not consistent with the prediction, and the remaining ten are consistent.

Thus, for two-thirds of these 15 items, or about 60 percent of total expenditure, the evidence suggests that education does shift consumption patterns in a direction which is consistent with its raising nonmarket productivity. Notice that this statement takes account only of the sign of the effects and considers a shift associated with education to be either in the same direction or in the opposite direction from the income effect, with no indication of the magnitudes of these effects. If we disregard those items with small relative effects and look only at those with income and education effects different from the averages by, say, 10 percent, then housing, utilities, house furnishings, clothing, medical care, and other travel are eliminated; of the remaining nine items, seven (or 73 percent of the expenditures) are consistent with a positive, uniform education effect. Thus for those items with a sizable effect, the evidence is somewhat stronger.

Where consumer goods are viewed as inputs in nonmarket production, the rate of use of the item, or the flow of services per period, is of most relevance. The yearly expenditure on an item reflects its rate of use, but it does so more adequately for items purchased continually than for durable items where purchases are lumpy. Hence, the empirical results are likely to be more reliable for nondurable items. If the three durable goods (automobiles, housing, and household appliances) are excluded from the comparison, the evidence of a positive education effect is again somewhat stronger. For the remaining 12 items, 9 (or 80 percent of the expenditures) are consistent with a positive education effect.[14] Finally, if both the three durables and those items with small effects are disregarded, the remaining subset includes food for home use, food away from home, tobacco, alcohol, household operations, personal care, leisure, and education. Of these eight items, seven (or 96 percent of the total expenditure) are consistent with a positive effect of education on nonmarket productivity.

These adjustments for durables and items with small effects are perhaps appropriate when the model is being judged on the quantity of items or the fraction of expenditure consistent with a positive productivity effect. Another use of these 15 estimates is to combine them into a single estimate of the magnitude of education's effect on income through nonmarket productivity. In this estimate the sizes as well as the signs of the elasticities are utilized, and to avoid prejudicing the results by selecting items on any particular basis, these qualitative results include all 15 items. One measure of the relationship over all the items is the correlation coefficient, which indicates the joint relationship between the two elasticities across the items. A positive value implies that on the average, an item with an income elasticity above 1.0 has a positive education elasticity (consistent with education raising nonmarket productivity); a negative value implies the opposite relationship (consistent with education adversely affecting nonmarket productivity); a correlation coefficient of zero implies that no relationship exists between the two elasticities (consistent with education having no effect on nonmarket productivity). For the 15 items the

[14] Distinguishing between durable and nondurable goods is somewhat arbitrary. If clothing, medical care, and education are also excluded as durables, seven of the remaining nine (or 86 percent of the total) are consistent.

(weighted) simple correlation was $+.18$, suggesting that, overall, the relationship was a positive one, as described in the first example above.

Another qualitative estimate, and one which indicates the magnitude of the nonmarket effect of education on real income, is a regression coefficient obtained by regressing the observed education elasticity on the observed income elasticity across the 15 items in a particular form.[15] The value of the coefficient, using the estimates in Table 9-3 as observations, is $+.08$. This can be interpreted as indicating that a 10 percent increase in the educational level (e.g., from the mean of 10.0 years to 11.0 years) is *equivalent* to raising the household's level of total expenditure from \$5,000 to \$5,040. So, in addition to an effect of education on income through the wage rate, the results here are consistent with education's also having a small positive effect on real income by favorably affecting the household's efficiency in nonmarket production.[16]

AN EVALUATION The empirical results discussed in this chapter indicate that the level of formal schooling directly influences consumer behavior independently of its effect on money income. Second, the results suggest that the effect of education is not a random or erratic one, but is systematically related to the changes in consumption patterns attributable to differences in levels of income. In addition, the chapter suggests an interpretation of these findings based on the notion of households as nonmarket producers, with education affecting the efficiency of the production process.

[15] The form of the equation used in obtaining the estimate discussed here is $\epsilon_i = \alpha (\eta_i - 1)$, forcing the intercept to be zero, where ϵ_i is the education elasticity of item i and η_i is its income elasticity. For a discussion of the reasons for using this form and for additional estimates of α, see Michael (1972).

[16] Although only this one estimate of the nonmarket efficiency effect will be discussed here, the larger monograph (Michael, 1972) includes numerous others. For example, the regression equation was reestimated including only the nine nondurables: food at home, food away from home, tobacco, alcohol, household operations, personal care, medical care, leisure, and education; and using the constant elasticity form, the value of the coefficient was .50. This suggests that the eleventh year of schooling is equivalent to raising the household's level of total expenditure from \$5,000 to \$5,250. Obviously, these two estimates are considerably different in magnitude and are, at best, rough estimates.

The monograph also considers a more detailed expenditure classification of 50 items and imposes certain constraints on the entire system of demand equations. Overall, the results are qualitatively similar to the result reported here—education appears to have a small but persistent positive effect.

Two reservations must be stressed. First, the magnitude of the overall effect of education was presented as a particular number, but it is simply a rough estimate and should not be treated as more than that. Second, as with any empirical finding, more than one interpretation is consistent with the observation. Although this chapter has focused on an interpretation based on productivity effects, others can be suggested. For example, one interpretation is to attribute the observed effects to changes in tastes or preferences. In this case, the argument would be that tastes change with education in such a way that more educated households desire, and therefore purchase, more of those items with observed positive education effects. This may or may not be true; it can never be rejected as incorrect since the argument is tautological. Other substantive interpretations can be suggested that do predict the same behavior as the interpretation developed here, but they are subject to the same qualification.

To place this work in perspective, one should bear in mind that economists have generally focused their attention on the effects of education related to wage earnings and material well-being in monetary terms. As a result of their success in this direction, an effort is under way to explore other effects of education on well-being. The framework used in this chapter is one way of approaching some of these other effects. It has the attractive characteristic of translating effects into terminology familiar to an economist, thereby enabling him to utilize his analytical tools in studying these other dimensions of behavior. The joys of pure contemplation and the satisfactions of a happy and healthy family are handled in the framework of commodity production, just as is the satisfaction derived from a well-cooked meal. Applied to households' purchases of market goods and services, the approach appears to be a simple, intuitively plausible, and reasonably effective predictor of observed patterns of behavior. Whether it is also useful in dealing with other aspects of human behavior remains to be determined.

Likewise, on the narrower topic of the effect of education on consumption, much work remains to be done. Some of the issues which need exploration are these: Does the effect of education decrease with additional years of training? Do changes in the husband's and wife's education levels have similar effects? Do informal methods of learning—such as on-the-job training, experience, and self-education—have effects similar to those observed for formal schooling? Do all types of formal schooling affect consumer behavior similarly, or does a liberal arts education have a different effect from that of a technical or vocationally oriented education? There also remains the question raised at the outset: Is the effect of education the result of the learning process itself or of the knowledge acquired? The study of education and its effects is far from complete; it is hoped that the work on which this chapter reports is further evidence that this field of study is productive.

References

Becker, Gary S.: "A Theory of the Allocation of Time," *The Economic Journal,* vol. 75, pp. 493–517, September 1965.

Gintis, Herbert: "Education, Technology and the Characteristics of Worker Productivity," *American Economic Review,* vol. 61, pp. 266–279, May 1971.

Hapgood, David: *Diplomaism,* Donald W. Brown, Inc., New York, 1971.

Jensen, Arthur: "How Much Can We Boost I.Q. and Achievement?" *Harvard Educational Review,* vol. 39, pp. 1–123, Winter 1969.

Michael, Robert T.: *The Effect of Education on Efficiency in Consumption,* National Bureau of Economic Research, New York, 1972.

Michael, Robert T., and Gary S. Becker: "On the New Theory of Consumer Behavior," *Swedish Journal of Economics,* vol. 75, no. 4, 1973.

Nelson, R. R., and E. S. Phelps: "Investment in Humans, Technological Diffusion and Economic Growth," *American Economic Review,* vol. 56, pp. 69–75, May 1966.

Schultz, T. W.: *Transforming Traditional Agriculture,* Yale University Press, New Haven, Conn., 1964.

Welch, F.: "Education in Production," *Journal of Political Economy,* vol. 78, pp. 35–39, January–February 1970.

10. The Relation between Schooling and Savings Behavior: An Example of the Indirect Effects of Education

by Lewis C. Solmon

INTRODUC-
TION AND
SUMMARY

Most discussions of the benefits of more, as compared with less, education point out that the lifetime income obtainable by an individual rises with schooling attainment. However, education may have indirect effects on an individual's total utility, either positive or negative, which do not come through increased earnings. These include consumption benefits to the educated individual; for example, schooling may enable people to appreciate the finer things in life or to be more efficient in making consumption decisions.[1] Benefits may also accrue to society at large; e.g., a more educated populace may be more civilized or more tolerant of others.

In the present study we ask whether individuals save more, or save in different forms, as they become more highly educated, thus conferring benefits either on themselves or on society as a whole. Can we identify an additional benefit from schooling due to different savings behavior, over and above the ability to earn more on the job, to enjoy life more fully, to consume more efficiently, to be more civilized, and so on? Savings behavior may, of

[1] See Michael (1972) and "Education and Consumption," Chap. 9, this volume.

NOTE: This work was part of the National Bureau's Project on the Benefits of Higher Education, supported by a grant from the Carnegie Commission on Higher Education. To the project director, F. Thomas Juster, I owe a great debt of gratitude for advice and encouragement at every stage. Many helpful suggestions were made by my friends and colleagues at the Bureau in the last few years: William Landes, Jacob Mincer, Paul Wachtel, Finis Welch, V. K. Chetty, M. Hashimoto, and Michael Lansberger.

The Consumers Union panel data were put in workable form by Carl Jordan at Columbia University, and I benefited from Phillip Cagan's earlier work with the survey.

Excellent research assistance was provided primarily by Teresita Rodriguez and also by Joanne Gallo. My secretary, Catherine Grant, was a great help. Thanks also to Susan Crayne and Antoinette Delak for programming and to Ruth Ridler for editing.

course, affect income, thereby altering an individual's total utility, but this influence does not operate directly on earnings; hence the categorization of the effects of saving as indirect.

The study analyzes the influence of differences in education and other acquired human capital, such as on-the-job training, on the observed savings behavior of individuals who are similar in other important respects, including income and age. Education may influence a person's average savings-income ratio or the extra amount he saves out of a given increment in income. Alternatively, it may affect the uses to which savings are put, i.e., the composition of a savings portfolio of any given size.

The second section examines a number of theories which might be helpful in predicting the relationship between education and savings behavior. The third section discusses the permanent-income hypothesis in more detail and applies this framework to the analysis of the savings-education relationship. The fourth section tests the hypothesized relationships between education and the amount an individual saves. The final section analyzes consumer responses to savings-related questions and suggests some reasons for the observed patterns.

The theory discussed below leads to the prediction that those with more education, *ceteris paribus,* will tend to save more, however savings are defined. This hypothesis is tested by estimating savings functions from a panel of household units. Initially, separate savings functions are estimated for families at each different educational level. Then all families are pooled and a single savings function is estimated, dummy variables being used to identify any difference in marginal propensities to save due to differences in educational attainment.

At the first stage of analysis, savings are defined as the change in financial and nonhousing property assets minus the change in nonhousing debt. Although this definition is close to the customary one used in much economic analysis, savings can take forms other than those mentioned. One objective of this study is to get at the relationship between educational attainment and "full" savings defined so as to take account of types of savings that have traditionally been ignored.

The specific ways of handling additional types of savings are discussed in Appendix D, and I shall note just a few of them here. A dummy variable is used to control for the fact that some famil heads are business proprietors or independent professionals and hence may have incentives to save in the form of business assets. Quantitative estimates of postschool investment in human capital are provided by drawing on previous work of Mincer (1962). These estimates are then included as part of savings. The value of consumer durables purchased is used as an independent variable to explain the traditional financial-savings concept. In general, therefore, a full-savings concept is recognized. Either adjustments have been made to account for an item, or the direction of the bias due to inadequate adjustments is discussed.

For savings functions estimated both with traditionally defined savings and with "full" savings, a pattern evolves in which the marginal and average propensities to save rise with schooling. This relationship appears stronger in the full-savings cases, since on-the-job training (savings in the form of postschool investment in human capital) rises with formal educational attainment (Mincer, 1962). Moreover, we expect the more complete definition of savings to reflect the true relationship more accurately, since savings decisions are likely to be made with an awareness of all possible means of acquiring wealth.

The analysis of consumer attitudes toward saving suggests some reasons why the amount of savings rises with educational attainment. Data are presented on the proportion of each education group selecting particular answers to savings-related questions. Then regression analysis reveals factors associated with the selection of a particular response. In many important cases, educational attainment turns out to be a strong factor in explaining why a particular response was or was not selected.

Apparently, those who were more highly educated had a better understanding of inflation and were better able to protect themselves against it. Better-educated families saved primarily to benefit children (for their education, to help them set up a household, and to leave an inheritance), whereas the less educated saved more to maintain current income (to build a business or to prepare for emergencies). The less educated were more inclined to save in the form of United States savings bonds or savings accounts, whereas the more educated selected riskier assets. The less educated sought safety of principal, whereas the more educated sought capital gains and protection from inflation. Inferences are made concerning the greater efficiency in saving, the greater risk preference, and the longer planning horizons of the more educated families as compared with the less-educated ones.

Both the study of the savings functions and the analysis of attitudes lead to the conclusion that the savings behavior of better-educated families is more beneficial to themselves, and possibly to society at large, than the savings behavior of the less educated. The greater willingness to assume risk is an example of a societal benefit since risky ventures will be able to attract funds.

One reason why the relationship between education and savings has not been studied previously is the difficulty of obtaining data on savings behavior and attitudes of individuals or families, along with other data on demographic, socioeconomic, and educational characteristics. I was fortunate to have data available from a series of questionnaire surveys of members of the Consumers Union taken between 1957 and 1959. The surveys contain detailed information on both current income and the income history of the family, as well as on the amount of its financial-asset holdings at the end of 1958 and at the end of 1959, from which 1959 savings can be calculated. The data include information on the education of the head of the family and on many other socioeconomic characteristics of the family as well as responses to numerous questions on attitudes toward saving-related issues. In addition, there is extensive information on consumer-durable purchases, including housing and automobiles.

The basic sample used over 3,300 families (observations). This number is the remainder of a much larger sample, which was pruned down to eliminate questionable or inaccurate responses. The details of the formulation of the sample appear in Appendix A, which also describes more fully the nature of the sample. In brief, Consumers Union members constitute a select group, well above the national average in income and education. They are also conscientious and planning-minded, as indicated by their willingness to fill out detailed questionnaires and by their membership in the Consumers Union. Thus our survey probably contains more accurate responses, but is also more select in its coverage, than most other samples.

Although unrepresentative of all United States households, the sample certainly does not lack relevance to the economy at large In particular, the relatively high-income, highly educated group in this sample is probably representative of the high-income, highly educated subgroup in the population as a whole. The less well educated and less wealthy segments of the Consumers Union sample are probably somewhat less representative of the corresponding groups in the population.

In general, one would expect sample respondents to be more homogeneous than the United States population with respect to variables that influence savings behavior. Our study asks whether there are systematic differences in savings behavior and attitudes across education groups in the sample. Since the data reveal that differences do exist, we can be reasonably confident that similar differences would also be evident in the larger society, where the same differences in education imply greater heterogeneity in other characteristics.

THE EDUCATION-SAVINGS RELATIONSHIP This section examines some of the possible relationships between education and savings behavior. For this purpose, it will be useful to put aside the problem of a working, quantifiable definition of full savings and merely ask about the relationship between education and willingness to defer present consumption for future consumption. Moreover, it is not important whether postponement is effected by converting current income into financial assets, into physical assets for business, into human capital, or into consumer durables.

There are several reasons why aggregate savings patterns might differ among groups classified according to their educational level:

1 Large amounts of education are associated with high incomes, and the fraction of income saved probably depends upon the level of income. However, the focus in this chapter is on how saving is influenced by education when income is held constant. Savings patterns also depend upon the time path of income. More education effects an initial delay in earning power and, later, a steeper rise in income than is experienced by less-educated people.

In addition, education may change the nature and sources of income and hence may influence savings behavior. Educated people's incomes may differ in regard to variance from period to period, in regard to source (whether from physical or human capital), and in regard to form (in terms of the split between wages and fringe benefits). Differences in variance, source, and form should result in differences in savings behavior.

2 Saving results from particular decisions about the relative value of present and future goods.[2] The subjective rate of transformation over time may well be affected by the amount of education possessed. Since the more educated should expect relatively steeply rising earnings streams, the prospect of increasing comforts might lead them to value future goods less and hence to save less for any level of current income. On the other hand, since the more educated may be better able to realize the worth of future goods, they may save more.

People also prefer present goods because of the shortness and uncertainty of life, which probably vary less with schooling attainment than the other factors!

The actual process of education might affect the tastes and attitudes of students in regard to characteristics influencing savings behavior. According to I. Fisher (1965, p. 62), time preference, or impatience, plays a central role in the theory of interest, where interest expresses a price exacted to exchange future goods for present ones. Time preference is the excess (percentage) of the present marginal desire for one more unit of present goods over the present marginal desire for one more unit of future goods. Thus the rate of time preference for present over future goods of like kind is readily derived from the marginal desirabilities of present and future goods, respectively. The higher a man's time preference, the less likely he is to defer consumption (save), and the higher the price he must be paid to do so.

Fisher has provided a list of personal characteristics that would seemingly influence time preferences and hence savings: foresight, self-control, a habit of thrift, concern over the uncertainty of life, concern for heirs, and concern for fashion and fads. It could be argued that these characteristics are influenced by education. Harold Watts (1958, p. 111) has pointed out that "high education may imply lower consumption, quite apart from the income correla-

[2] Bohm-Bawerk (1891, pp. 253–254) observed that the urgency of present over future goods is "most frankly expressed in children and savages [perhaps the least educated] but still exists in civilized society." Some of the suggested reasons are inadequate powers of representation and abstraction and an unwillingness to devote time to contemplating the future. These factors may differ according to education, so that the more educated better understand the future and are more willing to save for it. As Bohm-Bawerk pointed out: "As a fact the future has a greater place in our economic provision; greater indeed, than people usually think . . . our economical conduct has acutely little reference to the present but is, almost entirely, taken up with the future" (p. 238).

tion, if better educated people are more farsighted and therefore have stronger retirement motives."

On the other hand, a recent survey of the literature on psychological testing to determine the impact of the college experience on students (Feldman & Newcomb, 1969, pp. 33–34) produced the following conclusion: "With a few exceptions, difference-scores between freshmen and seniors show seniors to be more ready to express impulses, more spontaneous, less ready to defer gratification, and less self-controlled or restrained. . . . According to this developmental pattern, college students tend to become somewhat more impulsive and somewhat less self-controlled, orderly and conscientious." This implies that a high level of education would be associated with a high level of consumption, contrary to Watts's conjecture. However, these observations may be the result of the ages of the students, their "growing up" and becoming adults, rather than the result of schooling. Moreover, students probably defer gratification during their years in school and then make up for lost time during the immediate postschool years. To show the net effects of education on attitudes like impulsiveness, changes in attitudes for freshmen and seniors in college should be measured against changes in attitudes for people of comparable age not attending college, one year and four years after graduation from high school.

The argument that education alters tastes, in whatever direction, is relevant only to the extent that these new taste patterns persist in the postcollege years. Feldman and Newcomb (1969, p. 323) summarize recent psychological literature on this subject by saying that "persistence is the general rule."

3 So far, the explanations of observed differences in aggregate savings behavior by education have implied some indirect causation running from education to savings. The impact of education has been through its effect on the incomes or the tastes of individuals. However, there might be another reason for observed patterns which does not imply causation.

Time preference, to repeat, is subjective; it refers to the degree of desirability of present goods over that of future goods, or the preference for comparatively remote or deferred income (I. Fisher, 1965). Hence a person with a high time preference would be less likely to defer current consumption to future periods. Both the decision to remain in school rather than to work and earn income and the decision to save a larger part of income of any size are usually associated with a relatively low time preference.

There are several ways in which students may avoid deferring consumption while attending school. First, they may have access to the capital markets. Traditionally, however, imperfections in lending markets have limited student borrowing if the individuals are unable to provide tangible security for the loan. Second, they can be financed by their families; in this case, decisions affecting school may be made by families as a whole, rather than by students alone. In such instances, families are willing to forgo current consumption (demonstrating low time preference) so that the children can obtain an education. If the children's tastes are influenced by their parents' low time preference, the general argument still holds: Students have low time preference. If, holding socioeconomic background constant, we observe consumption standards of college students and their families to be below those of families which have noncollege offspring of the same age, the inference is that the former are more willing to defer consumption, given the capital-market conditions.

If saving is a function of time preference and if people with low time preference choose to obtain more schooling, then an observation that the more educated groups save more, *ceteris paribus,* need imply nothing about the effect of education on saving. Due to their inherent low time preference, the educated individuals would have been relatively large savers even without education.

To a considerable extent, it may be that the changes which occur during the college period are more a reflection of the cultural and societal forces that impinge upon the colleges and individual students than the effect of deliberate educational policy or program. Even if it were possible to observe changes in attitudes during the college experience, the question arises of whether these changes are due to cultural forces that would have been at work even without the schooling.

4   If better-educated people differ from less well educated people in regard to family size, age, or location, differences in these factors might cause the observed differences in saving among education groups. However, in that event, only a tenuous line of causation could be drawn from education to saving.

5   One factor which should affect the total amount saved is the total rate of return obtainable from this saving. It may be argued that

better-educated people can obtain a higher return because they are able to select a more efficient portfolio. It is generally agreed that one purpose of education is to instill an analytical ability in students. Returns to saving will be high when the saver can estimate and analyze the effects of current and future prices of goods, current and expected returns to various financial assets, the investment alternatives available, and current and future conditions of other aspects of the economy.

It is possible that people with the same income can purchase equally good investment data and advice. However, it would seem that an educated person can do whatever the less analytical person can do and more; perhaps, for example, he can discriminate among advisers more efficiently. Relatively high rates of return to saving should have a positive substitution effect (more income goes into savings). The income effect probably implies more savings as well, although this may be reversible in the sense that as returns rise, consumption may replace some saving. The argument that education increases one's efficiency in saving is analogous to Becker's argument (1967a) that education improves one's efficiency in consumption (see also Michael, 1972).

Becker has argued that as people become more educated, incomes rise. Consequently, the opportunity cost of time rises. In order to produce utility, more goods and less time will be used in the household of a more educated family, other things being equal. In other words, both consumption (C) and income (Y) rise with education. Thus whether C/Y rises with schooling depends upon the relative change in C and Y with education, which in turn depends upon the relative efficiency of the more educated in saving activities, consumption activities, and work activities. Also, since current saving is a way of providing for future consumption, the choice must be made between providing goods in the future (1) by forgoing consumption currently or (2) by working more in the future.

Current saving allows investments to grow for subsequent conversion to consumption goods; it is argued that the more educated person will be able to make his savings grow larger than will the less-educated person. Also, since income paths are steeper for the more educated, any work time in future periods will make possible the purchase of more consumer goods at that time than work by the less educated will. For a more detailed analysis of consumption over time, see Chapter 11 in this volume.

This discussion has yielded some observed relationships between education and savings and several plausible explanations—a not uncommon occurrence. In general, we expect greater amounts of education to be associated with greater saving, and we postulate several reasons for this association.

THE PERMANENT-INCOME HYPOTHESIS One important framework for examining consumption and savings decisions is the permanent-income hypothesis, developed by Friedman (1957, pp. 27–28). In this framework, consumption is determined by relatively long-term considerations, so that any transitory changes in income lead primarily to additions to assets or to the use of previously accumulated balances rather than to corresponding changes in consumption. Hence the change in consumption due to an *observed* change in income (marginal propensity to consume) depends not only upon the fraction of permanent income devoted to consumption (k) but also upon the fraction of an observed change in income which is also a change in permanent income (dY_P/dY).

Since permanent income is not observed, k cannot be estimated directly, but instead we can estimate b, the marginal propensity to consume out of measured income. Two independent explanations of the relationship between k and b at any point in time can be derived. First, $b/k = dY_P/dY$, where dY_P/dY is a function of the discount rate. Also, $b/k = P_r$, where P_r is the ratio of the variance of permanent income to the variance of total income.

The simple specification of a model to explain consumption can suggest routes through which differences in education lead to differences in aggregate savings. We shall be estimating coefficients like b, which may differ with education for two types of reasons. The k's might be similar, but the adjustment coefficients (dY_P/dY and P_r) might vary with education, or the k's themselves might vary with schooling. Hence the question arises of how dY_P/dY and P_r are affected by education. Since dY_P/dY will change as an individual's discount rate r changes or as the coefficient of expectations[3] β changes, we must ask as well how r and β vary with schooling.

To deal with the question of the k's themselves first, we should note that Friedman (1957, p. 54) says that there is no reason why

---

[3] The coefficient of expectations is defined as the change in future-period income expected when current-period income changes. It is assumed that $dY^*_{t-} dY = dY^*_{t+n}/dY$, the asterisk indicating "expected."

the long-run average or marginal propensity to consume must remain constant. He suggests that k is a function of the ratio of wealth to income, the degree of uncertainty contemplated, the rate of interest, and taste factors such as age, family size, and location. It will be argued that the taste factors directly influence the size of k, whereas factors such as the interest rate (related to the discount rate), the ratio of wealth to income, and the degree of uncertainty (related to dY_P/dY and β) influence both k and what we call the *adjustment coefficients* (dY_P/dY and P_r).

The hypothesis that k is larger for larger families might be suggested. Family size depends upon the desire for children and the ability to have the desired number. Probably more educated people practice birth control more efficiently. There is evidence of a persisting inverse relationship between number of children of ever-married women and educational attainment (U.S. Bureau of the Census, 1964).

Age has been said to affect the marginal propensity to consume. As one gets older, he may feel less need to save owing to a shorter expected lifetime. This argument is consistent with a finite horizon which excludes the desire to provide for heirs. On the other hand, a hypothesis more consistent with the empirical results presented below can be suggested. These results are based on a sample including only members of the labor force. It seems reasonable that as people approach retirement, they save more and more in order to have reserves to draw on during the retirement period. That is, people become more aware of retirement needs as that time approaches. The first argument implies a progressively increasing time preference over a lifetime; the second implies a declining time preference over the years immediately preceding retirement.

Watts (1958, p. 109) suggests that the expectations of older spending units tend to be the same as current income, whereas younger spending units are influenced by secular income increases and expectations of rising profiles (particularly in educated households). In the present context, these arguments would imply a larger dY_P/dY, and also a larger β, for younger households. Hence for these younger households, b would be larger, even with the same k. As age increases, changes in observed income would be less likely to be considered permanent or persistent, evoking less reaction in terms of consumption change.

If b's are compared for different groups classified by education and years on the job, those individuals with more schooling and the same experience will be older. Thus even if education has no effect on b, a comparison of education groups with the same experience will reflect an "age effect."[4]

It has been argued that r, the individual's discount rate, affects both k and the adjustment coefficients. It is at the rate r that the individual evaluates expected future returns, thereby obtaining his subjective estimate of permanent income. From studies of education in the United States, it appears that the rate of return to additional schooling declines as more schooling is obtained (Becker 1967, pp. 20–21; Hanoch, 1965). These results are consistent with the hypothesis that more educated people have better access to capital markets. Acceptance of these results leads to the prediction that, other things being equal, b should decline with education, assuming that, in equilibrium, the rate of return equals the discount rate for an individual. However, other things probably are not equal.

Another factor influencing b is β, the consumer unit's coefficient of expectations. According to Friedman (1957, pp. 144–145), the larger the β, the larger the adaptation to any discrepancy between measured and expected income; hence the more rapid the adjustment and the shorter the (retrospective) time span that matters. There is almost no evidence concerning the effect of education on β. It might be hypothesized that since the more educated have less fluctuation in income, any change in Y is considered to be a change in Y_P, and a positive relationship exists between β and education. On the other hand, more educated people might be more cautious and so might react more slowly to any change in current income, not immediately considering it a change in Y_P. Since an increase in β implies an increase in b, there is no way to predict the effect of education on b through the effect of education on β.

Finally, estimates of b should be influenced by what has been called P_r, the ratio of the variance of Y_P to the variance of Y. Among other things, P_r is likely to be a function of the ratio of human to nonhuman wealth and of the nature of a person's employment.

We must now turn to the question of whether education has systematic influence on factors affecting P_r. We shall consider how the nature of employment is affected by schooling and how, in turn, the nature of employment affects saving. The first question

[4] For further discussion of other socioeconomic or taste factors and how they might affect saving, see Watts (1958).

is whether the variance of the transitory component of any income level is higher or lower for a more educated person than for one with less education. If the variance of the transitory component Y_t of measured income Y is high, a larger share of income will be saved as a protection against the "emergencies" which are likely to arise when Y_t is negative. This means that the higher the variance of Y_t, the lower b is, since saving from any change in income will be greater. However, this says nothing about a change in the long-run propensity k.

Income earned by independent businessmen, or entrepreneurial income, is likely to have a relatively large transitory component compared with wage or salary income. A clue to the relationship between the entrepreneurial nature of income and education is found in Table 10-1, which shows the percentage of persons in each age-education group who are self-employed. The percent of self-employed rises with education in each age group. According to the argument in the preceding paragraph, those with more education should save more, since they are more likely to be self-employed and to have a larger transitory component of income. Hence the P_r, as defined above, would be smaller for more educated people, and b would decline with education.

Self-employment can be subdivided into the number of business proprietors (B) and the number of independent professionals (I). Quite likely $\dfrac{I}{(B+I)}$ rises with education. Friedman has observed

TABLE 10-1
Self-employed by age and education (percent)

| Age | *Years of school completed* | | | | | | |
	0–4	*5–8*	*9–11*	*12*	*13–15*	*16 and over*	*Total*
14–24	n.o.*	2.3	1.5	2.1	1.8	2.3	1.9
25–34	2.9	5.4	7.1	7.5	8.3	9.2	7.4
35–44	7.5	10.3	10.3	11.5	16.5	18.0	12.3
45–54	8.8	11.7	14.0	15.5	16.4	26.2	14.9
55–64	15.5	15.6	15.5	16.6	23.8	28.0	17.4
65 and over	25.7	22.9	20.9	30.0	37.5	35.3	26.2
TOTAL	12.0	11.5	9.6	10.2	13.4	17.2	11.6

* No observations.
SOURCE: Leveson (1968, Table III-7).

that the income elasticity of consumption for independent professional families is lower than that for other independent businessmen. One reason for this could be that the independent professionals rely more on human capital for income than on physical capital. The former is less marketable and is not as good security for a loan. Since earnings in this case are more directly tied to the health and energy of the individual, a possible loss of earnings capacity must be counterbalanced by personal saving. Moreover, independent professionals are less likely to be able to participate in group health, accident insurance, and life insurance plans than proprietors of businesses with more employees, and so they must save in lieu of them. This argument would lead to the prediction of a lower long-run k as well as a lower b.

It appears that those who are both highly educated and self-employed are less likely to be in physical-capital-intensive occupations; that is, they rely on human rather than physical capital to a greater extent in earning a living. Saving in the form of investment in one's own business capital should yield a higher return than a portfolio would, if only because it avoids brokerage costs. Whether one has reason to invest in physical capital depends upon whether he is self-employed and also upon the nature of the self-employment (B or I as defined above).

It would seem that as the income level rises, those with less education would be more likely to invest in physical capital for their own businesses, probably enjoying a higher return to saving, defined to include this investment. As education rises, returns to all forms of saving might decline, since there is less likelihood of direct investment compared with portfolio investment. This argument suggests that at higher levels of education, a smaller share of income is saved in all forms. However, estimates of financial saving would probably rise with education. Finally, independent professionals are less likely to have access to various forms of deferred income and pension arrangements provided by corporations; hence they are more likely to save on their own.

Several general points should be made in concluding this section. Regarding a lifetime saving or investment plan, the question arises of whether one who has already deferred consumption by forgoing earnings while in school tries to compensate for this early saving by saving less after entering the full-time labor force. This consideration might lead us to expect less saving from income for people with more education. On the other hand, it could be argued that the habit of thrift, once acquired during the school years, is maintained afterward. The latter possibility suggests a positive relationship between the saving-income ratio and schooling. Similarly, those with enough foresight to stay in school might also have the foresight to defer consumption even after completing their formal education.

Table 10-2 summarizes the influence of the various factors that might be expected to affect the relation between education and savings. This general scanning of existing theory strongly suggests that a positive relationship ought to be observed between education and saving.

EMPIRICAL ESTIMATES OF SAVINGS FUNCTIONS Two types of savings functions have been estimated. First, separate functions were estimated for each of the four education groups; that is, one savings function was estimated for all families whose head had a high school education or less, another was estimated for those with less than four years of college, and so on. The equations to be estimated looked like

TABLE 10-2 *Summary of factors influencing the relationship between education (E) and saving (S) during working life*

Factors affecting saving (X_i)	$\dfrac{dX_i}{dE}$	Reason	$\dfrac{dS}{dX_i}$	$\dfrac{dS}{dE} = \dfrac{dX_i}{dE} \times \dfrac{dS}{dX_i}$
r	—	Declining rate of return to education	—	+
β	—	Caution	—	+
Family size	—	Taste, plus efficiency in birth control	—	+
Age	+	When classified by experience, more educated enter labor force later	+	+
Yt/Y	+	Self-employment	+	+
$I/(I + B)$	+	Independent professionals have more education	+	+
Portfolio return	+	Efficiency in obtaining return	+	+
Human wealth / Nonhuman wealth	+	Definition of education	+	+
Taste for saving (time preference)	+	Foresight	+	+

e relationship hypothesized more largely reflects my predilection than a solid theoretical basis.

$$S_{ij} = a_i + b_i Y_{ij} + U_{ij} \qquad (10\text{-}1)$$

where S_{ij} and Y_{ij} are savings and family incomes, respectively, of families with heads having i educational level and U_{ij} is comprised of other factors in the savings function to be described below. Hence a_i and b_i will be estimates of the intercept and marginal propensity to save for those familes with education i. In these models both the intercepts and slopes can vary among education groups.

The second approach was to combine all families in estimating a single savings function which includes interaction terms between income and educational level. The main interpretive difference is that the latter approach forces all savings functions through the same Y intercept, and we are testing only for differences in slopes (b_i's). The general form of this equation is

$$S_j = a + bY_j + b_1 Y_j D_1 + b_2 Y_j D_2 + b_3 Y_j D_3 + U_j \qquad (10\text{-}2)$$

Here S_j, Y_j, and U_j are data for each family. There are four separate education groups, and the highest (more than four years of college) is not represented by a dummy. D_1 takes on a value of 1 if the education of the head of the household is high school or less, a value of 0 otherwise; D_2 takes on a value of 1 if education is some college and a value of 0 otherwise; and D_3 takes on a value of 1 if education is four years of college and a value of 0 otherwise. b is interpreted as the marginal propensity to save (MPS) of the most highly educated group; $b + b_1$ is the MPS of the group with the least amount of education; $b + b_2$ is the MPS of the next most highly educated group; and $b + b_3$ is the MPS of the second most highly educated group. The t-values on the b_1, b_2, and b_3 tell whether these coefficients are significantly different from zero or whether the MPS of each less well educated group is significantly different from b (the MPS of the most highly educated group).

In general, the regression results tend to confirm the view that the more educated have greater savings, defined as a ratio to income, as an elasticity, or as the marginal propensity to save. However, before the specific results are presented, we must look at the variables besides income and education which may be used to "explain" saving.

The basic income concept chosen in estimating savings function was family income after taxes. This seems to be the best measure of disposable income. However, wife's pretax income was inserted in several of the estimates in order to see whether the composition of family income had effects on saving and whether these composition effects differed across schooling classes. It should be noted that although the coefficient on the family-income variable represents the marginal propensity to consume out of total disposable income, the coefficient on wife's income does not represent the MPS from wife's income. Let

$$S = \alpha_0 + \alpha_1 F + \alpha_2 W \qquad (10\text{-}3a)$$

where F is family income and equals $H + W$ (or husband's income plus wife's income). Equation (10-3a) can be rewritten

$$S = \alpha_0 + \alpha_1 H + (\alpha_1 + \alpha_2) W \qquad (10\text{-}3b)$$

From this simple transformation it can be seen that the MPS from wife's income is equal to the sum of the coefficients on F and W. This implies that if the coefficient on wife's income is positive in an equation which includes family income, the MPS from her income exceeds that from husband's income or from total disposable income. In Friedman's sense, the implication of this result would be that wife's income is considered more transitory than husband's income.

Another group of special independent variables that should be noted are those intended to take account of purchases of consumer durables, an aspect of saving not included in the dependent variable. Three different types of consumer durables are distinguished: housing, automobiles, and others. The value of purchases of small consumer durables and the value of automobiles owned were inserted as independent variables, whereas a dummy was created to indicate whether or not a family had purchased a house within the past year. Also house purchasers were excluded from some regressions, since the behavior of their nonhousing assets is likely to be poorly measured. In explaining savings, we hypothesize negative coefficients on nonhousing consumer-durable variables, since their purchase implies both a substitution effect away from savings (as defined in the dependent variable) to durables and a financing effect (the need to pay for durables by reducing assets or incurring debt).

Some of the regressions include a variable measuring change in the value of holdings of common stocks and mutual funds. This variable reflects *unrealized* capital gains. If all profits were converted into cash and no new purchases or other sales were made, this variable would be zero. The question asked is whether "paper" gains or losses affect savings behavior. The results given below indicate that they do not. The failure of unrealized capital gains to affect saving *might* be due to two offsetting factors. One is that households with unrealized capital gains feel wealthier and hence spend more, giving the expected positive correlation between wealth and consumption. But on the other hand, households with larger capital gains may also expect larger rates of return from savings and tend to substitute savings for consumption, thus imparting a negative correlation between capital gains and consumption.

Some regressions include an occupation dummy. This variable equals 0 if the family head is an independent professional or business proprietor and 1 otherwise; that is, it controls for self-employment. The negative signs on this variable indicate that, other things being equal, savings are higher for those families whose head is self-employed.

The next section will show that average response patterns to attitude questions differed systematically according to the educational level of the group. The significance of these answers to hypothetical questions depends upon whether the respondents act as they say they will. For example, to help explain savings, a variable was inserted which was the answer to the question: What percentage of your income do you aim to save over the next three to five years? The results indicate that respondents with intentions of having relatively large savings did indeed save more. This was a strongly significant variable, even after controlling for many other factors which affect saving.[5]

Introduced with similar objectives was the question: How do you expect the level of prices of consumer goods five years hence

---

[5] When we put in the savings-plan variable, we have to be careful in interpreting the coefficients. In using savings plans, we are talking about financial-asset changes, not about the full-income savings notion. There is a presumption that the effect of putting ex ante savings in the regression will be to reduce the influence of all variables already taken into account by the household in reporting their savings plan. The variables that would clearly be taken into account are all those in the regression, especially factors like income and education. Thus the interpretation of an income coefficient in a regression of savings on income and savings plans ought to be that it reflects the influence on savings of *unanticipated* changes in income—essentially more of a transitory effect than that observed in the other regressions.

to compare with the level of prices at present? There were nine choices, with higher-numbered responses indicating expectations of greater inflation. This variable was introduced to see whether there was a relationship between savings behavior and the extent of inflation expected. No significant relationship was revealed. This might be due to the noncontinuity of the variable or to the fact that different people react differently to the same inflationary expectations.

In certain of the regression estimates, two variables were inserted together—years of full-time labor force experience and earnings in the first year of full-time work. A rather intricate relationship enables us to control for investment in on-the-job training (OJT) when using these two variables for people of the same educational attainment.

Two people with the same education (given equal schooling and equal ability) entering the labor force at the same time can be assumed to be able to obtain the same full income in their first year of employment. Hence it follows that differences in income received are due to differences in opportunity costs (forgone earnings) incurred while obtaining on-the-job training. Those obtaining greater postschool human capital in the form of OJT can expect a steeper income profile; indeed, after some years, income for those with greater OJT will be greater than income for others.

Controlling for education, experience, and current income, we would expect a negative relationship between first-year income and rate of future growth of income (or level of expected future income). To the extent that current consumption depends not only on current income but also on expectations of future income, we would expect a negative relationship between first-year income and consumption or a positive relationship between saving and first-year income. Another way of looking at this point is to postulate that where saving in the form of OJT is (or has been) higher, less saving will take place in other forms.

Tables 10-3 to 10-6 report on savings patterns among the sample of 3,086 families. Families purchasing houses in 1959 and families with extreme incomes (less than $3,000 or over $50,000) have been eliminated. The rationale for these eliminations has several elements. The house buyer's savings in nonhousing forms are seriously altered when purchasing a house. Since our data make it difficult to establish the net amount saved when purchasing a house, it seemed better to exclude these people. The few extreme-

TABLE 10-3 Mean values of financial variables for different education groups, 1959				
			Education class	
	High school or less	*Some college*	*Four years of college*	*More than four years of college*
Number of observations	505	611	855	1,115
Family income after taxes*	7,936	9,025	10,029	10.777
Savings*	627	700	830	960
Savings-income	0.0790	0.0776	0.0828	0.0891
Income*	8,000	9,292	10,682	11,438
Full savings*	1,008	1,419	1,966	2,101
Full savings–income	0.1260	0.1527	0.1840	0.1837
Purchases of selected consumer durables*	295	324	293	272
Purchases of cars*	1,573	1,673	1,604	1,503
Unrealized capital gains*	595	710	936	1,265
Percentage not self-employed	88.51	86.42	89.36	83.77

* Dollars.

SOURCE: All estimates are derived from Consumers Union data collected by the National Bureau of Economic Research. For description of the sample, see Cagan (1965).

income families could potentially have seriously distorted the savings patterns and hence were also dropped.

Table 10-3 reveals only a slight increase in average financial and property saving as a share of disposable income when education increases. However, when on-the-job training and mortgage-principal repayments are added to saving, this "full saving" as a share of full income (earned plus forgone for OJT) clearly rises with schooling level. Of course, some of this strength has been built into the data, since OJT saving was calculated as a function of schooling.[6]

Table 10-4 provides results of regression estimates of savings functions for all observations combined, with the education effect sought through dummies representing interaction between income and education. In the two cases presented where saving was de-

[6] When OJT was recalculated as a function of occupation rather than schooling level, the results were unaffected.

fined as accumulation of financial and property assets only [(1), (3)], the coefficients on the interaction terms did not reveal differences by educational level in the marginal propensities to save. However, when a more complete definition of saving was used [(2), (4)], a strong pattern was revealed: The MPS increased with educational level. The clearest result was that families whose head had had four or more years of college had significantly higher marginal propensities to save than families whose heads had had less than four years of college.

The procedures reported in Table 10-4 forced the savings function of four education groups to have the same Y intercept. This restriction can be eliminated by estimating separate savings func-

TABLE 10-4 Regression coefficients (t-ratios) from equations that pool all observations and use interaction terms between education and income		*Eliminating housebuyers*		*Eliminating house buyers and "extreme" income*	
		(1) Savings	*(2)* Full savings	*(3)* Savings	*(4)* Full savings
Constant		549.6 (2.268)	284.1 (10.81)	446.7 (1.856)	265.3 (10.06)
Family size		−74.38 (−2.887)	−92.16 (−3.340)	−77.97 (−3.072)	−98.76 (−3.622)
Age of head		−4.605 (−1.045)	−51.47 (−10.95)	−7.378 (−1.692)	−52.68 (−11.34)
Family income after taxes		.0838 (11.56)	.1591 (21.72)	.1111 (12.41)	.1875 (20.49)
Value of consumer durables purchases		.0764 (.7990)	.0678 (.6626)	.0233 (.2479)	.0276 (.2726)
Education dummy 1 $\times$ income		−.0169 (−1.439)	−.0437 (−3.509)	−.0112 (−.9645)	−.0417 (−3.371)
Education dummy 2 $\times$ income		−.0176 (−1.900)	−.0306 (−3.175)	−.0120 (−1.275)	−.0265 (−2.688)
Education dummy 3 $\times$ income		−.0092 (−1.253)	.0016 (.2229)	−.0063 (−.8101)	−.0058 (−.7308)
Occupation dummy		−108.5 (−1.021)	−189.3 (−1.661)	−61.80 (−.5828)	−116.2 (−1.018)
Value of cars		−.0436 (−1.495)	−.0708 (−2.270)	−.0968 (−3.283)	−.1176 (−3.714)
Unrealized capital gains		.0043 (1.009)	.0044 (.9530)	.0029 (.6910)	.0030 (.6614)
Income squared					
R^2		.0520	.2019	.0573	.1794

SOURCE: See Table 10-3.

	Panel A: Dependent variable is financial and property saving only			
		Education class		
Independent variables	*High school or less*	*Some college*	*Four years of college*	*More than four years of college*
Number of observations	505	611	855	1,115
Constant	30.08	−45.27	73.47	222.0
	(.0859)	(−.1206)	(.2158)	(.6365)
Family income after taxes	.0564	.0700	.0966	.1169
	(2.978)	(4.187)	(6.523)	(8.552)
Age of head	3.219	2.598	−5.214	−12.63
	(.4531)	(.3139)	(−1.563)	
R^2	.0188	.0297	.0491	.0617
	Panel B: Dependent variable is full savings, including OJT and mortgage payments			
Constant	704.9	1639	2925	2718
	(1.836)	(3.907)	(7.622)	(7.262)
Family income after taxes	.0793	.1178	.1748	.2019
	(3.859)	(6.515)	(11.28)	(15.04)
Age of head	−7.124	−229.91	−69.51	−70.79
	(−.9242)	(−3.324)	(−7.695)	(−8.526)
R^2	.0293	.0752	.1599	.2042

TABLE 10-5 *Regression coefficients (t-ratios) for simple savings function within education classes*

SOURCE: See Table 10-3.

tions for each educational level. Here the results reveal a strong positive relationship between education and saving. Table 10-5 shows that for *either* definition of savings, the marginal propensity to save rises with education. Two other features of these functions should be noted. First, with the change in financial- and property-asset definition of savings, the intercept term does not differ significantly from zero. This is consistent with Friedman's contention that if the factors affecting the relative permanency of income are controlled for (e.g., education), a Friedman-type permanent-income savings function might be capable of estimation, where MPC= APC and is constant. Second, the effect of age on savings is usually negative, always becoming more negative as schooling level rises. At any income level, older people, on the average, save less (dissave more) the higher their educational level. Older people with more education probably feel less compulsion to save, since they have provided for their future earlier in life.

These strong results—particularly the fact that the marginal propensity to save is higher for those with four years of college or more than it is for those with less than four years of college— are revealed again in Table 10-6. This table uses several other factors besides age and income to explain savings. Although signs on these newly added explanatory variables look systematic and are in the directions hypothesized earlier, few are significant. However, in

TABLE 10-6
Regression coefficients (t-ratios) for savings functions that exclude extreme-income observations and home purchasers

Independent variables	*Panel A: Dependent variable is financial and property saving only*			
	Education class			
	High school or less	Some college	Four years of college	More than four years of college
Constant	162.6 (.3357)	−374.8 (−.6939)	−787.2 (−1.453)	164.4 (.3240)
Family income after taxes	.0576 (2.569)	.0543 (2.793)	.0930 (5.617)	.1012 (6.397)
Age of head	−2.025 (−.2464)	5.089 (.5464)	.4330 (.0443)	−13.69 (−1.500)
Wife's income	.0142 (.3966)	.0235 (.6669)	.0423 (1.150)	.0057 (.1752)
Value of consumer durables	−.3316 (.1873)	.2953 (1.712)	−.0604 (−.3636)	−.0355 (−.1831)
Value of cars	−.1689 (−3.268)	−.0662 (−1.195)	−.1694 (−3.208)	−.0049 (−.0817)
Unrealized capital gains	.0129 (.7143)	.0378 (1.969)	−.0002 (−.0459)	−.0010 (−.0937)
Family size	−41.16 (−.7399)	−15.29 (−.2767)	−17.57 (−.3558)	−36.13 (−.7564)
Inflationary anticipation	49.71 (1.133)	−34.35 (−.6290)	87.40 (1.530)	−64.72 (−1.315)
Savings plan	31.06 (3.676)	30.97 (3.397)	53.18 (6.577)	46.62 (5.660)
First income	.0420 (.6393)	.1096 (1.873)	.0463 (.9080)	.0432 (1.162)
R^2	.0806	.0727	.1138	.0938

| | Panel B: Dependent variable is full savings, including OJT and mortgage payments | | | |
| | | Education class | | |
Independent variables	High school or less	Some college	Four years of college	More than four years of college
Constant	942.8 (1.781)	107.4 (1.802)	189.8 (3.183)	268.6 (5.083)
Family income after taxes	.0988 (4.056)	.0973 (4.605)	.1724 (9.907)	.1934 (12.56)
Age of head	−14.27 (−1.593)	−24.47 (−2.404)	−62.01 (−5.875)	−72.62 (−7.775)
Wife's income	.0029 (.0749)	.0023 (.0603)	−.0018 (−.0411)	−.0083 (−.2455)
Value of consumer durables	−.3153 (−1.633)	.3539 (1.859)	−.0733 (−.3992)	−.0467 (−.2325)
Value of cars	−.2235 (−3.967)	.0067 (.1097)	−.1758 (−3.104)	−.0565 (−.9077)
Unrealized capital gains	.0128 (.6476)	.0211 (.9968)	.0026 (.4913)	−.0063 (−.5893)
Family size	−89.31 (−1.472)	−38.10 (−.6258)	−14.71 (−.2701)	−67.83 (−1.371)
Inflationary expectation	102.4 (2.141)	−22.27 (−.3695)	106.1 (1.681)	−45.90 (−.8981)
Savings plan	17.00 (1.845)	23.33 (2.317)	53.90 (6.031)	49.09 (5.736)
First income	.0125 (.1741)	.1791 (2.771)	.0628 (1.111)	.0453 (1.170)
R^2	.0866	.1062	.2081	.2334

TABLE 10-6 *(continued)*

SOURCE: See Table 10-3.

the relationship between savings and income, the strong patterns across education groups persist.

In order to assure that the results would still hold if we included the extreme-income families (under $3,000 and over $50,000) and if we also included home purchasers (controlling for purchase of homes by inserting a dummy), we estimated additional savings functions not reported here. In general, the patterns were much the same though a bit less systematic. Most savings functions still reveal a rising marginal propensity to save and elasticity as education rises. The average savings-income ratio also rises.[7]

In summary, both the average and marginal propensity of a family to save increase with the schooling attainment of the head of the household, after controlling for other important factors. This conclusion holds for several different definitions of saving. Saving represents provision for the future; therefore, greater saving implies greater provision for consumption in old age and for future generations and also greater potential capital formation for production. Hence we may infer that as the educational attainment of our society grows, we shall benefit from the added future wealth, security, and growth made possible by increased propensities to save.

EVIDENCE ON CONSUMER ATTITUDES
The respondents to the Consumers Union survey answered a series of questions dealing with attitudes toward various aspects of saving. When respondents are sorted by their level of education, patterns emerge which suggest relationships between education and such things as time preference, liquidity preference, risk preference, efficiency in making savings decisions, and objectives for saving. Initially, respondents were divided into four education groups: those who completed high school or less, those who completed some college, those who completed four years of college, and those who completed more than four years of college. For each education group, the proportion selecting various answers to these attitude questions was obtained, and systematic patterns by education were revealed. However, since there is a strong correlation between schooling and income or age, it is possible that part of the pattern of responses resulted from differences in income or age rather than from differences in education.

In order to examine the net influence of education on these atti-

[7] An attempt was made to see whether the *level* of income was a factor in the marginal propensity to save. This was done by inserting income squared as an additional explanatory variable. If the savings function is $S = a + bY + cY^2$, then the MPS is $dS/dY = b + 2cY$. If the coefficient c is significantly different from zero, then the level of income does affect the MPS. Although the high t-values on the income-squared coefficients indicated that the level of income does affect the MPS, the insertion of this variable tends to distort the systematic relationship of the MPS by educational level. Neither the coefficients on income nor the MPS (defined as $b + 2cY$) displays any systematic movement with schooling. These results are somewhat disturbing, but may be due to statistical problems arising from correlations among income, income squared, and saving. The strong, systematic relationship between savings and income by education still should be thought of as substantive.

tudes, we estimated regressions with a series of dummy dependent variables that equaled 1 if a particular response was chosen and 0 otherwise. These (1, 0) dummies were regressed on income, family size, age of head of the household, and occupation of the head, as well as on education.[8] Separate regressions were estimated for each of the responses. In almost all cases educational level significantly influenced response in the expected direction, tending to corroborate the patterns shown in simple classification of responses by education group.

It is important to note that if these patterns can be observed in the Consumers Union sample, they would probably be even stronger in the population as a whole. One of the characteristics of the members of the Consumers Union is that those with relatively little formal schooling are probably closer in certain respects to their more highly educated peers than the less-educated members of the general populace are. Those who subscribe to Consumers Union should be more thoughtful, more careful planners, and better informed than others. If there is a discernible difference in behavior between these particular people with low education and the more highly educated, this difference should be magnified when comparing education groups without the special characteristics of Consumers Union members.

The question arises of whether actual behavior parallels the

[8] The use in regression analysis of dependent variables that take on discrete (usually dichotomous) values presents statistical problems, since the assumptions about normality in the error distribution are clearly violated. In general therefore, the regression results presented below must be interpreted with caution.

The statistical problems associated with dichotomous dependent variables are especially severe where the observations tend to cluster about one or the other point, that is, around either a zero or a one response, and they are much less severe when the dependent variable is evenly distributed between the two possible responses.

As a rule of thumb, the reader should be suspicious about regression results when more than 80 percent of the observations are located at one of the two points and fewer than 20 percent at the other; the more extreme the clustering the greater the degree of suspicion.

One of the tables below uses a discrete trichotomous variable ($+1$, 0, -1) and here an additional problem is present. The scaling implied by a $+1$, 0, -1 variable defines the distance between any pair of possible responses. The implied distance is not the same for a scaling of $+3$, 0, -3 as it is for a scaling of $+1$, 0, -1, and these (and other) possible scalings are all arbitrary. Where only two responses are possible, there is no scaling problem, since the statistical properties of the equation do not depend on the numerical value assigned to the two responses.

attitudes and preferences expressed by people responding to hypothetical questions. That is, although certain patterns may emerge from the question studied, only a subsequent study of actual portfolio composition and savings shares can fully confirm the relationships between education or income and factors like time preference or risk aversion. One piece of evidence lends credence to the conclusions presented here. Respondents were asked the percentage of income they planned to save in the upcoming three- to five-year period. The response to this question was inserted as a variable along with income, education, age, and so on, to explain the actual amount of 1959 saving. There was always a strongly significant positive relationship between actual saving and the percentage of income the individual planned to save. Hence, at least in this case, responses to hypothetical questions paralleled actual behavior.

The patterns emerging from the survey of attitudes toward saving can best be analyzed by studying the answers to five separate questions. Tables 10-7 and 10-8 deal with responses to the question: If you expect some inflation during the next few years, what actions do you believe that you and your family can take to protect yourselves against the effects of the inflation? Respondents indicated by their answers whether they understood the meaning of inflation and whether they knew ways to protect themselves against its effects; in other words, the answers reflect one aspect of efficiency in making savings decisions. Replies can generally be classified into three groups: clearly wrong, uninterpretable, and clearly correct.

Table 10-7 shows a marked decline in the percentage answering incorrectly as education increases. Those who answered that the way to protect against inflation is to purchase fixed-dollar assets, to shun debt, or to practice austerity were judged incorrect. Of respondents with a high school education or less, 25.85 percent answered in this manner, and 18.91 percent of those with some college did so, whereas 10.24 percent of those with four years of college and 9.17 percent of those with more than four years of college answered incorrectly. Ignoring the uninterpretable responses, 45.24 percent of those in the lowest education group were incorrect, and this share fell steadily, so that on the same basis, 13.25 percent of those in the highest education class were incorrect. Although income and other relevant factors have not been held constant, these results lead to a tentative conclusion that, at least with respect to inflation, the more educated are more so-

TABLE 10-7
Basic data from
response to the
question:
If you expect
some inflation
during the next
few years, what
actions do you
believe that
you and your
family can take
to protect
yourselves
against the
effects of the
inflation?

	(1) Uninter- pretable*	(2) Wrong way to protect†	(3) Buy business	(4) Common stock	(5) Mutual funds
High school or less					
Number	441	266	3	158	16
Percent	42.86	25.85	2.92	15.35	1.55
Percent of total less uninterpretable		45.24			
Some college					
Number	405	235	14	303	42
Percent	32.59	18.91	1.13	24.38	3.38
Percent of total less uninterpretable		29.38			
Four years of college					
Number	512	165	7	547	56
Percent	31.76	10.24	0.43	33.93	3.47
Percent of total less uninterpretable		15.00			
More than four years of college					
Number	689	205	5	767	92
Percent	30.73	9.17	0.22	34.30	4.11
Percent of total less uninterpretable		13.25			

* Hostile answer, not concerned, do not know, no remedy, abstract formula, other financial assets, other assets, effort, pay price, work harder, save less, other behavior, politics.

† Fixed-dollar assets, shun debt, austerity.

‡ Commodities, old masters, gold, and silver.

SOURCE: All estimates are derived from the Consumers Union data collected by the National Bureau of Economic Research. For a description of the sample, see Cagan (1965).

phisticated (or efficient) investors. Table 10-7 also reveals that the most popular hedges against inflation are common stocks, real estate, and mutual funds, in that order of preference.

In order to deal with the problem of other factors blurring the education-efficiency relationship, a regression model was developed. The dependent variable took on the values -1, 0, and $+1$, according to whether a response was clearly incorrect, uninterpretable, or clearly correct, respectively. The explanatory variables

(6) Real estate	(7) Real assets‡	(8) Education	(9) Go into debt
118	16	5	6
11.47	1.55	0.49	0.58
215	16	5	8
17.30	1.29	0.40	0.64
291	20	4	10
18.05	1.24	0.25	0.62
419	30	6	23
18.74	1.34	0.27	1.03

were family size, age of the head of the household, family income after taxes, and an occupation dummy (zero if independent professional or business proprietor and one if wage or salary employee), along with education (in years of school completed). These results appear in Table 10-8.

From Table 10-8 it appears that education has a strongly positive effect on the likelihood of a respondent's answering the inflation question correctly, even after holding income, age, occupation, and

TABLE 10-8
Factors
affecting
knowledge of
how to
protect
against
inflation*

Independent variable	Coefficient	t-value	R^2
Constant	−.3914	−3.571	
Family size	−.0183	−2.028	
Age of head	−.0026	−1.713	
Family income after taxes	.00002	7.632	
Education	.0494	10.52	
Occupation dummy†	−.1553	−2.020	
			.0560

* Dependent variable has values −1, 0, 1, according to whether the answer was incorrect, unclear, or correct.

† Equals zero if head was independent professional or business proprietor and one if wage or salary employee.

SOURCE: All estimates are derived from the Consumers Union data collected by the National Bureau of Economic Research. For a description of the sample, see Cagan (1965).

TABLE 10-9
Basic data from
response to
the question:
In planning to
save, what
are your goals
in building up
your savings?

	Build own business	Provide for old age	Provide for emergencies	Provide for children's education and help them set up a household
High school or less				
Number	66	361	261	135
Percent	6.72	36.76	26.57	13.74
Average age*	44.5	51.6	44.2	39.6
Some college				
Number	77	345	287	261
Percent	6.44	28.89	24.03	21.85
Average age*	43.2	49.7	42.2	41.9
Four years of college				
Number	94	365	353	408
Percent	6.00	23.31	22.54	26.05
Average age*	39.1	46.4	38.3	40.1
More than four years of college.				
Number	74	497	494	621
Percent	3.41	22.93	22.79	28.65
Average age*	39.8	46.8	38.9	40.0

* Average age of groups: high school or less, 46.4; some college, 43.7; four years of college, 40.2; more than four years of college, 40.9.

SOURCE: All estimates are derived from the Consumers Union data collected by the National Bureau of Economic Research. For a description of the sample, see Cagan (1965).

family size constant. Also, those with higher incomes and those who are self-employed appear significantly more efficient in this sense. From the relationship between education and efficiency in protecting against inflation, we may infer one indirect benefit of schooling: In an economy with a continually changing price level, the more educated are better able to cope with these fluctuations; that is, they are more likely to minimize the costs associated with changes in the price level.

Tables 10-9 and 10-10 refer to the question: In planning to save, what are your goals in building up your savings? Since the age of respondents is a major factor here, the average ages of respondents in each category are provided in Table 10-9. The mean age of all

Provide for inheritance	Buy or build a house	Buy a large item	Increase income	Other
2	40	36	70	11
0.20	4.07	3.66	7.12	1.12
51.5	41.3	47.7	45.3	43.2
2	75	45	85	17
0.16	6.28	3.76	7.11	1.42
51.0	38.9	40.4	43.5	44.8
10	111	59	138	28
0.63	7.08	3.76	8.81	1.78
46.8	36.5	39.2	38.5	39.4
17	160	84	179	41
0.78	7.38	3.87	8.26	1.89
47.5	36.7	39.0	40.9	41.1

respondents with a high school education or less is 46.4 years; for those with more than four years of college it is 40.9 years. In each education class the average age was highest for those whose stated savings goal was to provide for old age or to provide an inheritance for heirs. In the least educated group 36.96 percent had one of these two responses, whereas 29.05 percent of those with some college, 23.94 percent of those with four years of college, and 23.71 percent of those with more than four years of college expressed one of these as the primary goal of saving. In each education class those who selected one of the above goals had a higher mean age than respondents indicating other goals for saving.

In the most educated class the most popular goal was to provide education for children and to help the children set up a household (28.65 percent of respondents). Only 13.74 percent of those in the lowest education class selected this as the primary goal. Here the income effect is probably in evidence as well as the education effect. In all education classes those selecting this savings goal were relatively young.

If we abstract from income, age, and other factors influencing savings goals, some tentative relationships between education and savings goals are suggested by Table 10-9. The less-educated respondents seem to feel that provision for their old age is most urgent and best accomplished through financial markets. As education increases, families tend to be less concerned with retirement but more concerned with the children's education. If one believes that more educated, and hence wealthier, offspring will look after retired parents, perhaps investment in children's schooling is also a provision for old age. However, if depletion of savings in order to educate children becomes necessary before old age, one might postulate that less-educated people have longer-run concerns than more educated people. Of course the greater earning capacity of those with more education implies that they will be better able to accumulate reserves for old age *after* educating their children, whereas the less educated, who earn less, may have to begin saving earlier in life in order to have adequate reserves upon retirement.

These speculations can be brought into clearer focus by looking at Table 10-10, which presents a series of regressions aimed at determining whether—and in what direction—various factors, including education, influence the choice of savings goals. It appears that *after* controlling for family size, age of head of household, family income, and whether the head of household is self-

TABLE 10-10
Regression
analysis of
some data
collected in
response to the
question: In
planning to
save, what are
your goals in
building up
your savings?*

	Provide for old age	Provide for emergen- cies	Provide for children's education and help them set up household
Coefficient on education used alone	−.0166	−.0050	.0194
	(−6.460)	(−2.063)	(7.857)
R^2	.0107	.0011	.0158
Constant	−.3700	.7284	−.0188
	(0.451)	(12.41)	(.0100)
Family size	−.0532	−.0012	.0770
	(−11.25)	(−.2537)	(15.88)
Age of head	.0166	−.0077	−.0014
	(20.74)	(−9.451)	(−1.669)
Family income	.000003	−.000005	−.000001
	(2.898)	(−4.220)	(−1.227)
Education of head	−.0010	−.0083	.0122
	(−.4095)	(−3.295)	(4.863)
Occupation dummy	.0313	.0870	−.0634
	(.7783)	(2.113)	(−1.538)
R^2	.1905	.0358	.0902
Interaction of observations	.264	.219	.238

* The question to be answered is: To what extent can we explain why an answer was or was not chosen? The regressions were run three times with 0, 1 dummies as dependent variables. In each case, 1 was assigned to a particular response, 0 being assigned if the answer was not chosen. The education variable has values of 10, 14, 16, and 18 years. The occupation dummy is 0 if the respondent is a business proprietor or an independent professional and 1 if he is a wage or salary employee. Figures in parentheses are t-values.

SOURCE: All estimates are derived from the Consumers Union data collected by the National Bureau of Economic Research. For a description of the sample, see Cagan (1965).

employed, there is a highly significant negative relationship between education and the likelihood of indicating "provide for emergencies" as the primary savings goal. After controlling for the same variables, there is a highly significant positive relationship between level of schooling and the probability of having as the primary savings goal "to provide for children's education and help them set up a household."

One explanation for the negative relationship between level of schooling and the probability of saving primarily to provide for emergencies may be that more educated people are less concerned

TABLE 10-11
Basic data for responses to the question: If you had some money to invest at this time, how would you invest most of it?

	Savings accounts	U.S. savings bonds	Other U.S. bonds	Common stock and mutual funds
High school or less				
Number	296	94	15	333
Percent	29.71	9.43	1.50	33.43
Some college				
Number	196	55	19	532
Percent	16.30	4.57	1.58	44.25
Four years of college				
Number	208	53	31	838
Percent	13.32	3.39	1.98	53.68
More than four years of college				
Number	359	63	30	1,167
Percent	16.75	2.94	1.39	54.45

SOURCE: All estimates are derived from the Consumers Union data collected by the National Bureau of Economic Research. For a description of the sample, see Cagan (1965).

about risk or are more willing to accept risk, a set of attitudes which could arise from the belief that human capital is more enduring than other kinds of capital. The explanation may also lie in the fact that the more highly educated save more. It is plausible that saving for emergencies is a primary savings goal with a low income elasticity (i.e., one which is satisfied by, say, the first 3 percent of income saved). If so, then the higher a household's saving level, the less likely it is to save *primarily* for emergencies.

The correlation between education and a savings goal concerned with one's children is strongly positive. These results may indicate both that a longer horizon is possessed by the more educated and that educated parents have different tastes (are more eager to see their children educated) even after controlling for other factors such as income and family size.

These relationships between choice of savings goals and education are net of family income after taxes. Hence at any level of income the less educated appear to save in order to maintain income (by building businesses or providing for emergencies), whereas the more highly educated appear to save so that their children

State and local bonds	Other marketable securities	Insurance and annuities	Real estate	Own business
22	9	22	167	65
2.21	0.9	2.21	16.76	6.53
10	15	36	257	82
0.83	1.24	2.99	21.38	6.82
21	21	36	256	97
1.34	1.34	2.31	16.40	6.21
27	24	47	361	65
1.25	1.12	2.19	16.84	3.03

may benefit, eventually providing utility and satisfaction to their parents. It is possible that the savings necessary to replace continuously depreciating physical capital are larger than those required to maintain human capital. One of the attributes of the latter is its greater malleability in the face of advancing technology.

Tables 10-11 and 10-12 analyze responses to the question: If you had some money to invest at this time, how would you invest most of it? In other words, some factors influencing desired portfolio composition are revealed. Table 10-11 indicates that in every education group, the largest percentage of respondents said that they would prefer to buy common stocks or mutual funds with savings. However, less-educated groups were much more prone to prefer savings accounts or United States savings bonds.

There are several possible reasons for these patterns. In the first place, people with a lower level of education probably have lower incomes and consequently have lower total savings in dollars. Considerations relating to the cost of transactions and the acquisition of information suggest that small amounts of funds would more likely be put into savings accounts or savings bonds than into common stock purchases; hence the observed preference by the less educated for savings accounts or savings bonds.[9] The increasing preference for common stocks by educational level may also reflect the tax advantages of capital gains income, with these tax benefits worth more (and better known) to those with more education and more income. On the other hand, one might infer that poorer, less-educated groups are relatively more averse to risk than the more educated and high-income groups.

Table 10-12 enables us to see the partial effects of education and income, holding the other factors constant, on the probability of respondents' selecting particular types of assets as their preferred investments. The relationship between schooling and pref-

[9] Recent refinements in mutual fund plans were not widespread in 1959, when this survey was taken.

TABLE 10-12 *Regression analysis of some data collected in response to the question:* If you had some money to invest at this time, how would you invest most of it?*

	Savings accounts, U.S. savings bonds, other U.S. bonds, state and local bonds	Common stocks and mutual funds	Real estate
Coefficient on education alone	−.0199	.0244	−.0041
	(−8.063)	(8.430)	(−1.906)
Constant	.3009	.2414	.2905
	(4.962)	(3.387)	(5.405)
Family size	−.0077	−.0029	.0015
	(−1.535)	(−.5010)	(.3322)
Age of head	.0049	−.0029	−.0009
	(5.767)	(−2.954)	(−1.175)
Family income	−.000004	.000007	−.000003
	(−3.590)	(5.428)	(−2.688)
Education of head	−.0140	.0195	−.0039
	(−5.411)	(6.387)	(−1.698)
Occupation dummy	−.0127	−.0013	−.0221
	(−.2975)	(−.0268)	(−.5865)
R^2	.0307	.0269	.0038
Percentage who selected this answer	23.8	48.4	16.6

* The dependent variable is 1 for answer selected, 0 being assigned if the answer was not chosen. Figures in parentheses are t-values.

SOURCE: See Table 10-11.

erence for fixed-yield assets (savings accounts, savings bonds and all other government bonds) is strongly negative, whereas the education–common stock–mutual fund relationship is strongly positive (both relationships are net of the effects of income, family size, age, and occupation). The relationship between income level and the decision to buy fixed-yield assets is also strongly negative, whereas the income–common stock relationship is strongly positive, suggesting that the argument concerning economies of scale in investment is plausible.

Are there any implications regarding the indirect or social benefits of schooling to be drawn from the responses to this question? As schooling levels rise, people are more willing to take risks, as evidenced by an increased preference for variable-priced assets with greater education. In our economy, risk preference has historically been associated with higher net yields; hence higher schooling levels are associated with higher private returns. Whether the society as a whole receives any net benefit from the lesser risk aversion of the more educated segments is a more complex question to analyze, although it seems clear enough that at the extreme, a society characterized by complete aversion to risk will be less progressive and dynamic than one characterized by a more even distribution of attitudes toward risk.

Tables 10-13 and 10-14 serve to explicate more directly the motives for saving. Respondents were asked: In selecting among various types of investment, what would be your major considerations? Reponse differentials for education groups may bear on differences in either taste for risk or time preference. Of those families with heads having high school education or less, 60.88 percent indicated safety of principal as the primary consideration. The implication is that risk aversion falls with schooling attainment. A comparison of the percentage of those interested in maximizing current return with the percentage of those desiring capital gains provides clues about time preference.

The current-return choice indicates both an aversion to risk and a short-term outlook. The percentage choosing this as the primary objective fell from 7.38 to 5.39 as education rose from the lowest to the highest class. On the other hand, the percentage who indicated capital gains as their major consideration rose with education from 10.74 to 26.80. Desire for capital gains implies a longer-run view, as well as a greater willingness to accept risk. Moreover, the understanding of, and desire to benefit from, the tax advantages

TABLE 10-13
Basic data for
responses to the
question: In
selecting among
various types
of investment
what would
be your major
considerations?

	Safety of principal	Maximum current return	Capital gains	Ready availability or marketability
High school or less				
Number	618	75	109	51
Percent	60.88	7.38	10.74	5.02
Some college				
Number	567	83	215	56
Percent	46.39	6.79	17.59	4.58
Four years of college				
Number	566	82	396	62
Percent	35.50	5.14	24.84	3.88
More than four years of college				
Number	765	119	591	90
Percent	34.69	5.39	26.80	4.08

SOURCE: All estimates are derived from the Consumers Union data collected by the National Bureau of Economic Research. For a description of the sample, see Cagan (1965).

of capital gains are evident. Another factor could be the greater realization by the better educated that our economy has been inflationary.

Those who saved primarily as a hedge against inflation were more numerous in the more educated classes (14.38 percent in the lowest education class and 27.30 percent in the highest education class). This result may reflect efficiency in the sense of an awareness of the steady rise in prices during the postwar period.

Table 10-14 reveals a strong positive relationship between education and the probability that the major savings objective will be capital gains or a hedge against inflation. These relationships are net of the effects of family income, age, occupation, and family size. The implication is that, *ceteris paribus,* the more educated have a greater awareness of the advantages of capital gains income and the need to protect against inflation.

The savings objective with the strongest negative correlation with education is safety of principal. This is consistent with evidence presented earlier that, all other things being equal, the more educated are less averse to risk.

Finally, there is a negative relationship between education and the probability of indicating the objective of maximum current return. This might indicate either a longer horizon for the more educated or a knowledge of the tax benefits of deferred income from capital gains.

Hedge against inflation	Convenience	Other
146	8	8
14.38	0.78	0.78
288	6	7
23.56	0.49	0.57
459	9	20
28.79	0.56	1.25
602	16	22
27.30	0.73	0.99

TABLE 10-14 *Regression analysis of some basic data collected in response to the question:* In selecting among various types of investment, what would be your major considerations?*

	Safety of principal	Maximum current return	Capital gains	Hedge against inflation
Coefficient on education	−.0330	−.0041	.0205	.0166
	(−11.68)	(−3.202)	(8.548)	(6.636)
R^2	.0342	.0027	.0186	.0113
Constant	.5852	.1670	.0838	.0446
	(8.515)	(5.242)	(1.432)	(.7205)
Family size	−.0254	−.0001	.0072	.0097
	(−4.484)	(−.0524)	(1.498)	(1.890)
Age of head	.0068	−.0009	−.0041	−.0010
	(7.145)	(−2.010)	(−5.072)	(−1.162)
Family income	−.000007	−.0000006	.000009	.0000002
	(−5.372)	(−1.046)	(8.341)	(.1381)
Education of head	−.0229	−.0046	.0133	.0148
	(−7.790)	(−3.341)	(5.313)	(5.578)
Occupation dummy	.0067	−.0083	.0559	−.0512
	(.1388)	(−.3730)	(1.361)	(−1.180)
R^2	.0650	.0043	.0437	.0135
Percent who selected this answer	40.9	5.1	22.0	24.7

The dependent variable is 1 for answer selected, 0 being assigned if the answer was not chosen. Figures in parentheses are t-values.

SOURCE: See Table 10-13.

It is interesting to note that when both income and education are used together, the sign of income is always the same as that of schooling. The responses to this question point out once again that the more educated are willing to assume risks and defer short-run income.

CONCLUSION   This chapter has been an attempt to determine the relationship between education and savings behavior. First, existing savings and consumption-function theories were reviewed with the aim of seeing how education might be a factor in these theories. The general conclusion was an expectation that more education should lead to more saving for individuals who are otherwise similar. Then actual differences in savings behavior across schooling groups were sought. The results indicate that both average and marginal propensities to save tend to rise with the schooling attainment of the family head, other things being equal. It was hypothesized that the growth in savings resulting from higher educational attainment would contribute to the growth of the income and wealth of the society.

Finally, a study of responses to questions concerning attitudes toward saving was made. This revealed systematic differences in response patterns due to education, even after other factors were controlled for. From these results we were able to infer some additional private benefits of schooling in regard to an apparently greater efficiency in portfolio management, and possibly some social benefits as well.

References

Becker, G.: *Human Capital and the Personal Distribution of Income*, The University of Michigan Press, Ann Arbor, 1967*a*.

Becker, G.: *The Allocation of Time and Goods Over Time*, National Bureau of Economic Research, New York, June 1967*b*. (Mimeographed.)

Bohm-Bawerk, E. V.: *The Positive Theory of Capital*, Macmillan & Co. Ltd., London, 1891.

Cagan, P.: *The Effect of Pension Plans on Aggregate Saving: Evidence from a Sample Survey*, National Bureau of Economic Research, New York, 1965.

Feldman, K. A., and T. M. Newcomb: *The Impact of College on Students* Jossey-Bass, San Francisco, 1969.

Fisher, I.: *Theory of Interest*, Augustus M. Kelley, Publishers, Clifton N.J., 1965. (Reprint.)

Fisher, M. R.: "Explorations in Savings Behavior," *Bulletin of the Oxford University Institute of Statistics,* vol. 18, pp. 201–277, August 1956.

Friedman, M.: *A Theory of the Consumption Function,* Princeton University Press for National Bureau of Economic Research, Princeton, N.J., 1957.

Hanoch, G.: "Personal Earnings and Investment in Schooling," doctoral dissertation, University of Chicago, Chicago, 1965.

Juster, F. T.: "The Predictive Value of Consumers Union Spending-Intentions Data," *Quality and Economic Significance of Anticipations Data,* Princeton University Press for National Bureau of Economic Research, Princeton, N.J., 1960.

Juster, F. T.: *Anticipations and Purchases: An Analysis of Consumer Behavior,* Princeton University Press for National Bureau of Economic Research, Princeton, N.J., 1964.

Leveson, I.: *Nonfarm Self Employment in the U.S.,* Columbia University Press, New York, 1968.

Michael, R.: *The Effect of Education on Efficiency in Consumption,* National Bureau of Economic Research, Occasional Paper #116, New York, 1972.

Mincer, J.: "On the Job Training: Costs, Returns, and Some Implications," *Journal of Political Economy,* vol. 70, part 2, pp. 50–79, Supplement, October 1962.

U.S. Bureau of the Census: *U.S. Census of Population 1960, Subject Reports, Women by Number of Children Ever Born,* Final Report PC (2)-3A, table 26, p. 109, Government Printing Office, Washington, 1964.

Watts, H. W.: *Long-Run Income Expectations and Consumer Saving,* Cowles Foundation Paper no. 123, Yale University, New Haven, Conn., 1958.

11. Education, the Price of Time, and Life-Cycle Consumption

by Gilbert R. Ghez

There is now considerable evidence that education has systematic effects on many facets of life. In this chapter I examine generally the effects of education on life-cycle behavior. More specifically, I analyze how education affects the consumption pattern of households over their lifetime. My emphasis is on the timing of efficient consumption and the effect of education on this dimension of household behavior.

As an individual ages, many of his personal conditions change. His economic status; his knowledge about places, people, and techniques; his social environment and marital status; his physical strength; his capacity to recall and absorb new knowledge; his fecundity—all these conditions tend to change with age, thereby resulting in changes in observed behavior. Education is a major determinant of personal conditions. There is ample evidence, some of which is reported in other chapters in this volume, that schooling and even postschool training are received largely at a relatively young age.[1] One would therefore expect education to have distinct effects on observed behavior over the life cycle.

The particular channel analyzed here is the effect of education on consumption behavior through its effect on the wage rate.

Schooling is undertaken largely to raise one's future earnings. While schooling may yield other benefits such as direct consumption value, improvement in the efficiency with which resources are used in the nonmarket sector, and improvement in portfolio management, its most firmly documented contribution lies in raising future market productivity, that is, in raising the future wage rates of the investor.

NOTE: I am grateful to Theodore Schultz for his gracious comments.

[1]See in particular the chapters by J. Mincer and S. Rosen in this volume.

Why does the wage rate—i.e., the price of time—influence consumption decisions? I take the approach that time is important
in consumption, just as labor is important to firms. This view ha●
been put to test in a variety of studies. The application of thes●
ideas to consumption versus savings decisions constitutes the cor●
of this chapter.[2] Put differently, the permanent-income hypothesi●
of consumption behavior is reformulated here to include the cos●
of time. I explore the direction and magnitude of response of consumption to the wage rate—a factor that is greatly influenced b●
schooling.

**THE NEW
VIEW OF
CONSUMPTION**
The new theory of consumption has three basic ingredients. Firs●
households are regarded as producers in the nonmarket secto●
They strive to achieve their goals using their own resources. The●
goals may include prestige, security of one's environment, healt●
children, and a good game of squash. The goals, in turn, enter th●
household's preference function or utility function; for instanc●
an individual may be willing to give up some security if he is con-
pensated by a sufficient amount of additional fame.[3]

The second ingredient of the theory is that at least some, an●
probably most, goals require the use of time, combined with ma●
ket goods and services. Housecleaning, for instance, requires tim●
and effort as well as some equipment. Health is produced with
doctor's advice and drugs as well as patient time, not the lea●
part of which is spent waiting for the doctor's services. Summ●
vacations are produced with transportation services, hotel accom-
modations, and one's own time.

The third ingredient of the theory is the fact that people are concerned with their future and therefore have an incentive to obta●
accurate estimates of their future income and lifetime prospec●
An extreme form of this assumption would be that individuals ha●
perfect foresight. With a lifetime horizon, individuals are fac●
with a lifetime budget constraint, and their basic decision is ho●
to allocate scarce resources over their lifetimes.

In this model the demand for goods is a derived demand, deriv●
in part from the demand for the outputs or goals to which the●
goods contribute. Similarly, the demand for home time (and the●

---

[2] For a more extensive discussion, see Ghez and Becker (forthcoming).

[3] This framework was first developed by Becker (1965) and Lancaster (196●

fore the supply of labor) is a derived demand for a factor of production.

How does the demand for goods vary over the lifetime? One important determinant is the price of time, i.e., the wage rate the individual commands in the market. The theory of investment in human capital predicts, and observed lifetime profiles reveal, that an individual's efficiency at work increases initially and then tapers off later in life. When the wage rate is rising, four effects are set in motion:

1 The cost of using time rather than market goods in the production of each activity is raised, thereby inducing substitution toward goods. For instance, a greater cost of one's time may result in more TV dinners and less elaborate meals. I shall call this effect the *factor-substitution effect.*

2 A rise in the wage rate also raises the cost of time-intensive activities relative to those activities which are less time-intensive. To give an example, a rise in the price of time would raise the relative cost of raising children, an activity for the mother that is relatively time-intensive. As a result, one expects households to substitute toward relatively goods-intensive activities, thereby raising the overall demand for market goods. I shall call this effect the *point-in-time goal-substitution effect.*

3 Moreover, if the wage rate is rising, the cost of all future activities or goals will be greater than the current cost of these goals. Consequently, the household has an incentive to substitute away from future time-intensive activities toward present ones. For instance, the cost of going to a movie is greater for the 45-year-old executive than for the 20-year-old college student. One expects movie-attendance rates to be lower for prime-age executives than for college students. I shall call this the *intertemporal-substitution effect.* The outcome of this sort of substitution is to discourage the consumption of goods when the price of time, and therefore the implicit price of achieving goals, is relatively high.

4 Finally, an unanticipated rise in wage rates will increase the discounted value of the future income stream, hence increasing an individual's wealth: the value of his resources is higher than expected. This increment in real income is consumed, at least in part,

during the period of time that the windfall or human capital gain is received. Thus an unexpectedly high wage rate, via its effect on wealth, causes the individual to raise his consumption. Similarly, an unexpectedly low wage rate will cause him to reduce consumption. The wealth effect is smaller, the more accurately individuals have predicted their future circumstances, and it is nonexistent if the future is perfectly foreseen.

The first two effects of a rising wage rate work toward raising the demand for goods over time. Both the factor-substitution effect and the point-in-time goal-substitution effect make for higher levels of consumption of goods when the wage rate is high than when it is low. The third effect—namely, intertemporal substitution—works in the opposite direction: It tends to reduce the demand for goods when the wage rate is high. The wealth effect, in principle, could work either way: To the extent that people were excessively pessimistic and were always surprised with better wage realizations than they anticipated, the effect would be to make for a rising consumption of goods as long as the wage rate was rising. The converse would hold true if people tended to be optimists and were always disappointed. Since it is unlikely that individuals are systematically pessimists or optimists, given their incentive to make accurate forecasts, I shall assume as a first approximation that their forecasts are correct and that there is no wealth effect.

On balance, therefore, if we neglect the wealth effect, the consumption of goods would be positively related to the wage rate over the life cycle if substitution in production, including both factor substitution and substitution toward goods-intensive activities, dominated the effect of intertemporal substitution.

Over and above the wage rate, an additional variable to be reckoned with is the rate of interest, i.e., the rate at which income can be transferred over time. The higher rate of interest, the greater the incentive to save and to postpone consumption; i.e., the higher future consumption would be relative to present consumption. What this means is that if the price of time did not vary with age, consumption would be steady if the rate of interest was zero, and it would rise as long as the rate of interest was positive.[4]

More formally, one shows that the timing of consumption is described by

---

[4] I am assuming no time preference. Preference for the present would reduce the incentive to postpone consumption.

$$\frac{d \log X(t)}{dt} = b_1 \frac{d \log w(t)}{dt} + b_2 \qquad (11\text{-}1)$$

where $X(t)$ is the rate of consumption of goods at age t; $w(t)$ is the real wage rate at age t; b_1 is the effect on consumption of a 1 percent rise in the wage rate (b_1 is positive or negative according to whether the substitution-in-production effect, including both the substitution between factors in each activity and the substitution toward relatively goods-intensive activities, exceeds or is dominated by the intertemporal-substitution effect); and b_2 is the effect on consumption of the rate of interest; b_2 would be positive if the rate of interest (net of time preference for the present) was positive. To see this, suppose that the wage rate were stationary; Eq. (11-1) tells us that the demand for goods would be rising if b_2 was positive.

Assuming that the parameters b_1 and b_2 are constant, Eq. (11-1) can be integrated to yield the logarithmic consumption function

$$\log X(t) = b_0 + b_1 \log w(t) + b_2 t \qquad (11\text{-}2)$$

The constant of integration b_0 in the consumption function (11-2) is an index of the real wealth of the individual. The higher real income is, the larger is b_0. To the extent that price and income expectations are fulfilled, real wealth is fixed over the life cycle, and so b_0 is independent of age.

EDUCATION AND THE PRICE OF TIME

Until now, I have described variations in consumption with age as if all prices were beyond the individual's control. In this section I show how the price-of-time sequence may be generated by introducing investment in human capital into the model. Considerable evidence has been accumulated on the effects of schooling and on-the-job training on earnings. In the formulation of earlier models, investment in human capital, on the one hand, and consumption behavior, on the other, have been analyzed separately. In other words, consumption decisions and accumulation of human capital decisions have been considered essentially separate. By implication, the supply of time to market activites has been left unexplained. I shall give a brief description of optimum investment, with special emphasis on the price of time.

Assume that, in any period, time may be spent in three different sectors. It may be allocated to consumption activities, to working activites (i.e., to the production of current income), or to the production of human capital (i.e., to increasing future earnings capacity). The latter two allocations combined may be called *market activities.* The current wage rate depends on the individual's accumulated stock of human capital, which can be augmented through net investment. Time spent in training is combined with goods (such as books, instructor's time, and the use of educational facilities) to produce a gross output of human capital. Over the life cycle, one's stock of human capital depreciates, in part through the decay caused by imperfect memory, especially at older ages; in addition, as new techniques are introduced, one's human capital becomes obsolete. Gross output is used to increase future earnings potential and to replace depreciated or obsolete human capital.

There is a strong incentive to invest in human capital at an early age. At young ages, the returns to investment are relatively large since returns are collected over a long period of time—namely, over the whole remaining period of labor force participation. Moreover the cost of early investments is relatively low, since the cost of time is still relatively low. These two mechanisms provide an incentive to concentrate investments in human capital in one's early years.

In the very early stages, the incentive to invest may be so great that the individual spends all his market time in education. During this stage the current wage rate is smaller than the true shadow price of time, measured by the discounted value of marginal return from an extra hour spent in training.

Since no returns can accrue to the individual if he is not at work it follows that during this first phase of life, the shadow wage rate cannot be falling. It will be rising if the rate of interest and the rate of depreciation of human capital are positive; indeed, both positive rate of interest and a positive rate of depreciation reduce the advantage of investment at young ages.

During the first phase, the potential wage rate is also rising. Eventually, it will equal the shadow price of time, at which point the individual enters the labor market.

During the second stage, the individual is at work. Hence the price of time is measured by his current wage rate, whether or not he is investing in human capital. The time pattern of the wage rate depends on the individual's investment decisions. It will rise as long as net investment is positive and will even rise beyond that point if growth in real wages is occurring in the economy. Since investments tend to fall with age, the individual's potential wage rate rises at a declining rate. Eventually the wage rate will tend to fall, when depreciation on human capital—due mainly to faltering health—becomes large.

In the third stage of life, the individual stops working altogether because the value of his time in consumption exceeds the value of his time in the market. After the individual has retired, variations in his market efficiency have no effect on his consumption decisions.

The investment in the human capital decision and the consumption decision are very much interrelated. First, the size of the returns to investment in education depends on the amount of time spent in market activities. Thus if we compare two individuals who differ in their level of real income—because let us say, the first one received an inheritance from his great-aunt—the first individual will take this increased wealth in part in the form of reduced hours of work, thereby reducing the incentive to invest in schooling and postschool training.[5] Second, if we compare two individuals who differ in their amount of schooling, the one who has engaged in more schooling and training will have a steeper wage profile, and therefore his consumption profile will likewise be steeper. The peak wage of the larger investor will occur later in life; therefore, the peak consumption age of the larger investor will also tend to occur later in life. This effect is mitigated insofar as differences in the amount of training result from differences in the cost of funds. To the extent that larger investors are ones for whom the rate of interest is low, the later peak in the wage rate raises the peak consumption age, while the lower rate of interest lowers the peak consumption age.

Formally, these effects may be seen through Eq. (11-1). If we differentiate Eq. (11-1) with respect to schooling S, we get

$$\frac{\partial}{\partial S}\left(\frac{d \log X(t)}{dt}\right) = b_1 \frac{\partial}{\partial S}\left(\frac{d \log w(t)}{dt}\right) + \frac{\partial b_2}{\partial S} \qquad (11\text{-}3)$$

The first derivative on the right-hand side of Eq. (11-3) is presumably positive. It measures the steeper wage profile of those having more schooling. The second derivative on the right-hand side of Eq. (11-3) measures the correlation between schooling and the rate of interest; it may well be negative. The responsiveness of consump-

---

[5] This effect would be mitigated if human capital were also a consumption good, in which case part of the increased wealth would be spent on schooling.

tion to wage-rate changes may also depend on the level of school-ing—i.e., b_1 may depend on S—but there seems to be no compel-ling reason why this should be so. The coefficient b_1 depends basically on substitution parameters of the household, and there appears to be no important reason why these parameters should differ by level of education. This is an empirical question that will be explored further on.

Individuals with more schooling would have greater real wealth if they had more facility at learning or if they had easier access to funds to finance their investments. If this were so, the overall con-sumption profile would be positively related to the level of school-ing. Moreover, the higher wage rate associated with more school-ing induces substitution toward goods, both because it becomes more efficient to use less time relative to goods in the realization of household goals and because time-intensive activities become relatively more costly. These combined income and substitution effects may be looked at through the consumption function (11-2). Taking the derivative of Eq. (11-2) with respect to schooling S, we get

$$\frac{\partial}{\partial S} \log X(t) = \frac{\partial b_0}{\partial S} + b_1 \frac{\partial}{\partial S} \log w(t) + t \frac{\partial b_2}{\partial S} \qquad (11\text{-}4)$$

where $\dfrac{\partial b_0}{\partial S}$ measures the correlation, presumably positive, between schooling and real wealth. While b_1 can, in principle, be negative, the sum of the effects of schooling on consumption through the price of time is almost certainly positive; i.e.,

$$\frac{\partial b_0}{\partial S} + b_1 \frac{\partial}{\partial S} \log w(t) > 0$$

To sum up, consumption and human capital investments are interrelated. One important connection is through the cost of time. The empirical research report which follows provides some mea-sures of this association.

EMPIRICAL IMPLEMEN-TATION The purpose of the empirical work is to estimate the effect of changes in the price of time on consumption behavior over the life cycle.

Before proceeding, it is necessary to put the model in a family context. Up until now I have maintained the assumption that the household is of unit size. Changes in family size and composition may exert some direct influence on the consumption of households. At a given level of income, an increase in family size raises the demand for goods. The number of children in the family is not exogenous, and as several recent studies have shown, it responds to economic variables.[6] Although the determinants of completed family size have been extensively investigated, much less is known about the timing and spacing of children. One factor seems clear, however: Since the raising of children requires time, especially that of the mother, the spacing of children depends on changes in the cost of her time. All other things being equal, the more rapid the rise in her price of time, the greater her incentive to bunch her production of children at the outset of marriage. On the other hand, the timing of children is related largely to the timing of marriage, which itself may depend on expected variations in the cost of time as well as on the success of one's search for a mate. While recognizing that family size is endogenous and should therefore be part of a simultaneous system of equations and decisions, I maintain that *changes* in family size are largely independent of *current* changes in the price of time. Consequently, treating changes in family size as exogenous may not lead to very serious biases.

Moreover, once we put the model in a full-family context, variations in the price of time of each earner will affect consumption as long as he or she engages in market activities. Thus if husband and wife are in the labor force during a certain interval of time, the time rate of change in the consumption of goods during that interval will depend on variations in both their wage rates.

Let us reconsider the expectation model. We have seen above that if individuals possessed perfect knowledge of all relevant future variables, their real wealth would not change over their lifetime. Given conditions of foresight, real wealth is independent of age. Variations in consumption with age would be due exclusively to substitution effects. Perfect foresight is presumably a less-than-perfect assumption, although as I pointed out earlier, there is a strong incentive for individuals to reduce their uncertainty about the future. It seems reasonable to suppose that although some individuals overestimate their future incomes and prices, other individuals underestimate their prospects, so that cohort income and price expectations are unbiased. This unbiased-expectations

---

[6] For instance, see Schultz (1973, 1974).

hypothesis is not in itself innocuous, but it seems sensible enough. It suggests that if we consider a homogeneous group of house- holds—homogeneous with respect to such permanent character- istics as schooling—the observed average wage of this group at any age is a good indicator of what the average household in the group had anticipated.

Reinterview data are not available for testing the model. Instead, I have used cross-sectional data of the United States population, namely, the Bureau of Labor Statistics (BLS) Survey of Consumer Expenditures for 1960–61. Households were cross-classified by:

1 Age of head: single years of age from 22 through 65
2 Education of head: educational level 1: 0 to 8 years of schooling; educational level 2: 9 to 12 years of schooling; educational level 3: more than 12 years of schooling.

Much care was exercised in the choice of the range of ages to be included in the sample. Indeed, as I have already pointed out: (1) at an early age, when all market time is spent in school, the wage rate understates the true price of time, and (2) at a late age, when individuals are retired, variations in the wage rate have no bearing on consumption behavior.

Households were classified by education in order to verify whether life-cycle consumption patterns differ across households differing in their level of schooling. In principle, the level of school- ing of the wife is to be reckoned with, as well as that of the head of the household, presumably the husband. The BLS survey, how- ever, does not report on the schooling level of wives.

Within each age-education cell, I constructed the arithmetic mean of family consumption, earnings, and family size. Consumption was defined as purchases of nondurable goods, plus the imputed value of housing services, plus gifts. In principle, it would be desirable to have estimates of the imputed value of all durable goods. Al- though such an estimate can be constructed for housing, given in- formation on the rent paid by renters, no imputation for other durable goods seems practical in working with this consumption survey.

Earnings E are family earnings before tax. A proper specification would require wage rates of each family earner; these variables are not available in the BLS survey. However, a definite implication of our model is that family earnings and wage rates will be positively correlated over the life cycle because hours of work and wage rates are positively related.

The life-cycle patterns of mean earnings and mean consumption are displayed in Figures 11-1 to 11-3. As predicted by the theory, earnings tend to rise initially, reaching a peak in the mid-forties or late forties and then declining. The rise and subsequent decline in earnings are presumably due not only to the rise and fall in wage rates but also to variations in hours worked. Consumption also shows a distinct rise initially and a decline later in life. Peak consumption occurs at approximately the same age as peak earnings. The consumption profile lies essentially below the earnings profile. The reason for this is that I have plotted earnings and consumption, rather than earnings and expenditures.

Households with a higher level of education have higher earn-

FIGURE 11-1 *Family consumption and earnings by age of head: all education levels combined*

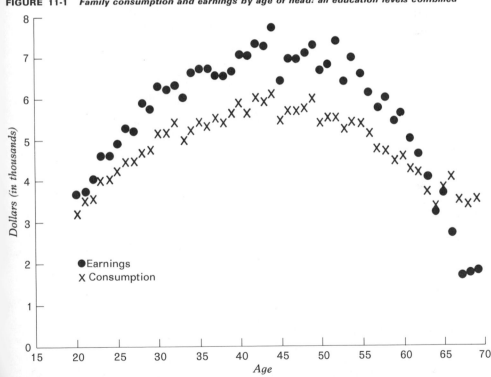

SOURCE: U.S. Bureau of Labor Statistics, *General Purpose Tapes of the Survey of Consumer Expenditures, 1960–61.*

FIGURE 11-2 *Family earnings by age and education of head*

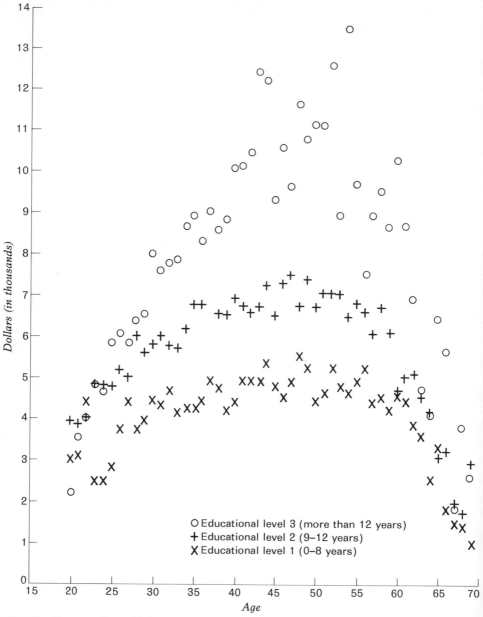

FIGURE 11-3 *Family consumption by age and education of head*

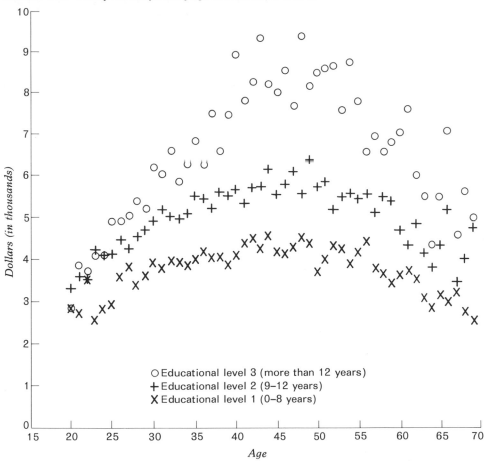

SOURCE: Same as Figure 11-1.

ings profiles, as depicted in Figure 11-2. Their earnings tend to rise more rapidly and for a longer period of time. This is precisely what one would expect if on-the-job training is positively related to schooling. The corresponding consumption profiles are given in Figure 11-3. These show that the higher the level of education, the higher the consumption stream.

To be sure, these are not longitudinal cohort earnings and consumption profiles, since they plot variations at a point in time. They differ from cohort profiles as long as trends in earning power or in nonmarket productivity are present.

Rather than adjusting the data for the existence of trends, presumably in a somewhat arbitrary way, I have used the cross-sectional data directly for empirical estimation. A positive trend in the earnings of households means that older households in the cross section have lower real wealth than younger households. This implies that the observed rise in consumption with age would be smaller than over the life cycle, while the peaking of consumption occurs sooner than for a given cohort. Essentially, a trend in real wages introduces a trend in consumption.[7]

The model of the earlier sections is now adapted to apply to cross sections. In particular, Eq. (11-2) can be applied to averages of consumption and earnings by age of the head of the household. With observations ordered by age, I ran within each education class linear regressions of the logarithm of mean consumption on the logarithm of mean earnings, the logarithm of mean family size and age of head. Let X_t denote mean consumption at age t, E_t denote mean earnings at age t, and Z_t denote mean family size at age t. The estimating equation now reads:

$$\log X_t = b_0 + b_e \log E_t + b_z \log Z_t + b_t t \qquad (11\text{-}5)$$

Results are presented in Table 11-1. Changes in the price of time exert a positive effect on changes in consumption with age. The

[7] This rise in the production of human capital means that improvements in technology in the production of goods are biased toward human capital, or that physical capital is more complementary to skilled labor than it is to unskilled labor.

TABLE 11-1 *Estimates of the life-cycle consumption function: level equations*

Dependent variable: log X							
Data (ages 22–65)	Intercept	Independent variables			Multiple correlation coefficient	Adjusted R^2	Durbin-Watson d
		log E	log Z	Age			
Education All levels	3.4835	.5253 (16.3477)*	.2593 (7.7945)	.0035 (7.2497)	.9904	.9794	1.7386
0–8 years	3.6870	.4859 (13.2405)	.2586 (5.9641)	.0038 (3.7202)	.9717	.9401	2.3476
9–12 years	4.2127	.4219 (7.7016)	.2932 (5.5886)	.0071 (7.1918)	.9577	.9109	2.0118
> 12 years	2.9662	.6001 (9.8524)	.1746 (2.9582)	.0051 (3.8379)	.9659	.9279	2.2035

*Figures in parentheses are t-values.
NOTE: $X =$ consumption; $E =$ earnings; $Z =$ family size.
SOURCE: U.S. Bureau of Labor Statistics, *General Purpose Tapes of the Survey of Consumer Expenditures, 1960–61.*

estimate of b_e for the group "all educational levels combined" is .53. The estimate is significant at the 1 percent level. A 10 percent rise in earnings raises consumption by approximately 5 percent, when family size is held constant. I interpret this result to mean that substitution in production, including both the change in time intensity in each activity and the propensity to engage in more goods-intensive activities as the wage rate rises, exceeds the inter-temporal-substitution effect.

The same positive effect of variations in the price of time on consumption behavior appears within each schooling group. The responsiveness appears to be somewhat larger at the highest level of education and least at the high school level, but all estimates fall within the range of .42 to .60.

These estimates provide a strong test arguing against the Modigliani-Brumberg life-cycle hypothesis of consumption.[8] Indeed, that well-known model asserts that consumption depends on real income and that variations in the price of time will have no effect on variations in consumption with age. In other words, it predicts that $b_e = 0$. This alternative hypothesis seems to be contradicted by the data at all levels of education.[9]

The coefficient of age is supposed to pick up the interest rate effect net of time preference and the effects of trends. For the group "all education," the coefficient is .0035. What this means is that in the absence of changes in earnings with age, consumption would grow at a rate of one-third of 1 percent per annum. One can show

[8] See, in particular, Modigliani and Brumberg (1954).

[9] While the Modigliani-Brumberg model is inconsistent with the BLS data ordered by age, a simple current-income hypothesis fits the data quite well. Indeed, under that hypothesis, variations in consumption depend on variations in total current income, regardless of its source. In a regression of consumption by age on total income, nonwage income, and family size by age (all variables in log form), the coefficient of nonwage income was near zero and statistically insignificant, as the current-income hypothesis would predict. On the other hand, under our derived-demand hypothesis with a lifetime horizon, one would expect the coefficients of total income and nonwage income to be of opposite sign and the ratio of the consumption elasticities with respect to total income and nonwage income to be equal to the ratio of earnings to nonwage income at the mean.

The weakness of the current-income hypothesis has been documented in the vast literature on the consumption function. In particular, it fails to reconcile the long-run stability of the savings ratio with the declining propensity to consume as a function of income observed in cross sections.

What remains puzzling is why the derived-demand hypothesis developed in this chapter does not meet the sorting-by-source-of-income test referred to here.

that correcting for trends in real wages, the pure interest rate net of time-preference effect is no greater than 1 percent.

The positive effect of age appears at all levels of education. The highest effect appears for the high school group. The estimates fall in the range of .004 to .007. Since trends in real wages are not systematically different by level of schooling, the difference in the effect of age in the cross section across schooling groups basically reflects differences in interest rate (net of time preference) effects across these groups. These differences are not very large, nor are the differences systematic by level of schooling.

The level of consumption of those households with more schooling is higher. As shown in Figure 11-3, the whole consumption profile is shifted up at higher levels of education. This effect would be borne out by differences in the intercept of the regression equation if this estimate were unbiased. The intercept estimate, however, is a biased estimator of its true value, and no meaningful statements can be made about it.

The level equations of Table 11-1 display little or no evidence of first-order serial correlation of the residuals, as measured by the Durbin-Watson d statistic. As a further check on the model, however, I have run the same regressions in first-difference form;

TABLE 11-2 *Estimates of the life-cycle consumption function: first-difference equations*

Dependent variable: $\triangle$ log X		Independent variables		Multiple correlation coefficient	Adjusted R^2	Durbin-Watson d
Data (ages 22–65)	Intercept	$\triangle$ log E	$\triangle$ log Z			
Education						
All levels	.0045	.5377 (9.4550)*	.2675 (3.1582)	.8882	.7783	3.0556
0–8 years	.0026	.4642 (8.6485)	.1815 (2.3061)	.8406	.6919	2.8512
9–12 years	.0098	.4041 (4.2662)	.3464 (2.7413)	.6771	.4314	2.5312
> 12 years	.0074	.5495 (6.7195)	−.1262 (−1.1860)	.7308	.5108	2.9477

* Figures in parentheses are t-values.

NOTE: $\triangle$ = first-difference operator for one year differences in age; X = consumption; E = earnings; Z = family size.

SOURCE: Same as Table 11-1.

TABLE 11-3 *Estimates of the elasticity of substitution in production*

Dependent variable: log (X/L_m) Data (ages 22–65)	Intercept	Independent variables		Multiple correlation coefficient	Adjusted R^2	Durbin-Watson d
		log w_m	log Z			
Education						
All levels	−1.0148	.7657 (7.4226)*	.5911 (8.6526)	.8663	.7382	.8195
0–8 years	−.9026	.7518 (3.7126)	.4176 (5.4791)	.6766	.4314	1.2669
9–12 years	−.8148	.8603 (8.5616)	.3004 (5.4808)	.8164	.6486	.8766
> 12 years	−.8777	.8223 (12.7152)	.5058 (5.5780)	.9118	.8231	1.1579

* Figures in parentheses are t-values.
NOTE: X = consumption; L_m = adjusted nonworking time of males; w_m = male wage rate; Z = family size.
SOURCE: L_m, w_m, and Z were constructed from the 1/1,000 sample of the United States population, 1960. The source for X is the same as in Table 11-1.

these results are presented in Table 11-2. Our estimates seem thoroughly confirmed. The life-cycle wage effect is in the order of .5, and the differences by schooling group are not very large.

I also present some estimates of the elasticity of substitution in household production between goods and husband's time. For this purpose, I have used data processed by Gary Becker for a companion project on hours of work over the life cycle.[10] These data are taken from the 1/1,000 sample of the United States population, 1960, and pertain to males. They permit construction of a wage rate variable for males. Consumption time is estimated as total time available, other than that employed for rest and personal care, net of hours of work. The data were partitioned in a manner conformable with the cross-classification used in the BLS survey. Mean consumption time of males L_m, mean wage rate of males w_m, and mean family size Z were computed for each cell. The coefficient of log w_m, in a regression of log consumption relative to L_m on log w_m, is designed to measure the elasticity of substitution in production. Results, presented in Table 11-3, show that it is equal to .77 for the

[10] See Ghez and Becker (forthcoming). Contrary to Becker's treatment of the data, I did not take moving averages of series.

group "all education" and that this estimate is relatively stable across education groups.

To recapitulate, the model summarized in this chapter seems to stand up fairly well in relation to the data. Variations in the price of time over the life cycle, which are basically the result of investments in human capital, influence consumption behavior in a very systematic way. A rise in the price of time raises the consumption of goods and also the amount of goods used relative to time spent at home. On the other hand, there are no important differences in the responsiveness of consumption to the wage rate by level of schooling. What this means is that a relatively stable function exists and therefore that inferences about the effects of education on consumption can be made through its effect on the price of time, since education does not seem to alter the basic response of consumer behavior to the price of time.

References

Becker, G.: "A Theory of the Allocation of Time," *Economic Journal,* vo 73, no. 5, pp. 493–517, September 1965.

Ghez, G., and G. Becker: *The Allocation of Time and Goods over the Li Cycle,* National Bureau of Economic Research, New York, forthcomin.

Lancaster, K.: "A New Approach to Consumer Theory," *Journal of Politic Economy,* vol. 74, no. 2, pp. 132–157, April 1966.

Mincer, J.: "Education, Experience, and the Distribution of Earnings ar Employment: An Overview," Chap. 3, this volume.

Modigliani, F., and R. Brumberg: "Utility Analysis and the Consumpti Function: An Interpretation of Cross-Section Data," in K. Kurihara (ed *Post Keynesian Economics,* Rutgers University Press, New Brunswic N.J., 1954, pp. 388–436.

Rosen, S.: "Measuring the Obsolescence of Knowledge," Chap. 8, t volume.

Schultz, Theodore (ed.): "New Economic Approaches to Fertility," *Jour of Political Economy,* vol. 81, part 2, pp. S1–S299, March–April 19 .

Schultz, Theodore (ed.): "Marriage, Human Capital, and Fertility," *Jour of Political Economy,* vol. 82, part 2, March–April 1974.

U.S. Bureau of Labor Statistics: *General Purpose Tapes of the Survey Consumer Expenditures, 1960–61.*

12. On the Relation between Education and Crime

by Isaac Ehrlich

INTRODUCTION Theoretical attempts to explain participation in illegitimate activities often have been guided by the preconception that since crime is deviant behavior, its causes must be sought in deviant factors and circumstances determing behavior. Criminal behavior has traditionally been linked to an offender's allegedly unique motivation, which in turn has been ascribed to a unique "inner structure" (e.g., deviations from physiological and mental health, spiritual degeneration), to the impact of exceptional social or family circumstances (e.g., political and social anomalies, war conditions, the disruption of family life), or to both. The relation between education and crime has also been generally treated within this framework, for the issues raised have frequently centered upon the role of education in determining or affecting the motivation and propensities of juvenile delinquents.[1]

A reliance on a motivation unique to the offender as the major explanation of crime does not, in general, lead to the formulation of predictions regarding the outcome of objective circumstances. I also am unaware of any persuasive empirical evidence in support of a systematic relation between crime and traditional sociological variables.[2] An alternative and not necessarily incompatible point

NOTE: This paper, a derivative of my doctoral dissertation, was completed in May 1971. Financial support for this work was granted by the Carnegie Commission on Higher Education. I am grateful to E. Moskowitz and Randall Mark for valuable editorial comments.

[1] For an overview of the significance of education and the school in the area of juvenile delinquency, see Eichorn (1965).

[2] For example, Cohen (1964) reports low correlation between homicide rates and such social phenomena as illiteracy, industrialization, farm tenancy, density of rural population, and church membership.

of reference is that even if those who violate specific laws differ significantly in various respects from those who abide by the same laws, the former, not unlike the latter, do respond to *incentives:* costs and gains available to them in legitimate and illegitimate pursuits. Rather than resort to hypotheses concerning unique personal characteristics and social conditions affecting "respect for the law," penchant for violence, preference for risk, or, in general, preferences for crime, one may distinguish preferences from objective opportunities and examine the extent to which illegal behavior can be explained by the effect of opportunities, given preferences. This approach, due largely to initial efforts by Fleisher (1966) and Smigel-Leibowitz (1965) and a significant contribution by Becker (1968), has been used in my work on crime (Ehrlich, 1970, 1973) to develop an economic model of participation in illegitimate activities. The model emphasizes behavioral implications that may be tested against available empirical evidence. It has been applied to, and found largely consistent with, data on crime variations across states and over time in the United States.

This chapter discusses the possible effects of education upon various opportunities available to offenders. Because data required for systematic study of these effects are insufficient, this chapter emphasizes analytical issues. I start with a general exposition of the model of participation in illegitimate activities and derive a few propositions concerning the relation between education and crime. I then examine some empirical evidence bearing upon this relation from arrest, prison, and crime statistics.

THE OFFENDER'S CHOICES

In spite of the diversity of activities defined as illegal, all such activities share some common properties. Any violation of the law may be thought of as potentially raising the offender's money or property income, the money equivalent of his psychic income, or both. In committing a violation, one also risks a reduction in income, however, for conviction entails "paying" a penalty, acquiring a criminal record, and other disadvantages. As an alternative to violating the law, a person may behave legally and earn an alternative legal income, which may also be subject to risks. In general, therefore, the net gain in both activities is subject to uncertainty.

A simple model of choice between legal and illegal activities can be formulated within the framework of the usual economic theory of behavior under uncertainty. A central hypothesis of this theory is that if the two activities were mutually exclusive, one would choose to commit the violation (income prospect I), to take an alternative legitimate action (income prospect L), or to be indifferent between the two as his expected utility from the violation exceeded, fell short of, or was equal to that from the legal alternative—or, in symbols:

$$U*(I) \gtreqless U* (L) \tag{12-1}$$

where U^* denotes an expected utility operator.[3]

The "gain" associated with illegitimate behavior is a function of gross returns and various costs. The term *gross returns* denotes the value of the "output" of an offender's activity, the direct monetary and psychic income he reaps from accomplishing offenses of a specific crime category i. Particularly in the case of crimes involving material gains, gross returns are a function of the offender's skill and ability to commit offenses e_i and the level of various inputs K_i, including his own time, accomplices' services, tools, means of transportation, and other resources used for gathering information, planning and committing offenses, and disposing of stolen goods. In addition, payoffs on most crimes against property and on some crimes against the person depend in large measure on the amount of transferable assets and other human and nonhuman wealth available to potential victims of crime A_i, as well as on the latter's expenditure and efficiency at "self-protection" against victimization c_i. Thus, in general, illegitimate income Y_i can be thought of as a function of the productivity of both the offender and others:

$$Y_i = f_i(K_i, e_i, A_i; c_i) \tag{12-2}$$

For analytical convenience, this income is defined net of direct

---

[3] Note that by this hypothesis crime always "pays" if the variety of monetary and psychic costs and returns that offenders derive from crime, including their "pleasure" from risk, are taken into account. If an offender is free to choose, and always acts to maximize his utility given his opportunities, then his actual engagement in crime indicates that utility is thus maximized. Such a "positive" approach constitutes perhaps the main difference between this analysis and some traditional theories in criminology.

costs of purchased inputs, since those costs could be deducted with certainty from the gross returns.[4]

The monetary and psychic costs associated with illegitimate behavior generally include both immediate and delayed cost elements. Again for analytical convenience, the opportunity costs of the offender's time, which are represented by his returns from the alternative (legitimate) activity, are excluded. Only the costs incurred by the perpetrator if he is apprehended and convicted of the crime (including the prospect of losing the loot) are considered. One such cost element is the penalty that society imposes on convicted offenders in the form of a monetary fine, a prison term, probation, or a combination of these. Unlike a monetary fine, which is a unique quantity, the cost incurred in the case of, say, imprisonment is indirect and specific to the individual. It can be measured as the properly discounted value of his opportunity costs of time spent in prison and his psychic cost of detention, net of any benefits obtained during the period of incarceration. An additional cost possibly incurred by the offender if he is imprisoned, probationed, or even just arrested is a reduction in his future stream of income in legitimate activities as a result of the effect of a "criminal record" on job opportunities (including legal restrictions). This effect would leave a person with less freedom in choosing an optimum occupational mix throughout his working career. The discounted value in terms of income at time t of the future costs of fines, imprisonment, and other possible losses is denoted by F_i.

Since only apprehended and convicted offenders are subject to the loss of F, the final gain is uncertain. If the offender is assumed to have a subjective probability of being caught and punished p_i,

[4] Private self-protection against crime via watchdogs, guards, locks, and other safety devices increases the offender's direct costs of achieving any given gross payoff and reduces the probability that the crime can be carried out successfully. In addition, private self-insurance through the maintenance of valuables in safe-deposit boxes, the marking of personal property to reduce its marketability in stolen-goods markets, and refraining from specific consumption activities reduces the potential loss to the victim and the gain to the offender in case a crime is committed. Private defense against crime thus generates a probability distribution of net outcomes from crime rather than a sure return. Of course, even if the extent of private self-protection against crime were fully known, the gross return from criminal activity would still be subject to random variations. However, Y_i is treated here as having a unique magnitude in order to emphasize analytically the uncertainty associated with punishment and other potential costs of apprehension and conviction.

then according to the usual economic analysis, his expected utility from engaging in illegitimate activity is

$$U^*(I) = (1 - p_i) U(W + Y_i) + p_i U(W + Y_i - F_i) \quad (12\text{-}3)$$

where W denotes income from other sources which, for simplicity, is assumed to be known with certainty.[5]

The alternative legal gain that an individual can achieve by allocating his time and other purchased inputs to a legitimate activity l rather than to i is denoted by Y_l. Generally speaking, a legitimate activity can be regarded as safer than an illegitimate one since the latter includes the prospect of apprehension and punishment in addition to many conventional occupational hazards. Also, losses in legitimate activity may be partly offset by market insurance, whereas no such insurance is provided against punishment for crime. However, there is no full insurance against, say, unemployment — a hazard which is presumably more characteristic of legitimate activity — and legitimate returns in such a case may be reduced to $Y_l - D$, where $D > 0$. Given a probability of unemployment of μ, Eq. (12-1) can now be specified as

$$(1 - p_i) U(W + Y_i) + p U(W + Y_i - F_i)$$
$$\gtreqless (1 - \mu) U(W + Y_l) + \mu U(W + Y_l - D) \quad (12\text{-}4)$$

Equation (12-4) identifies the basic set of opportunities affecting the decision to participate in illegitimate activities: an individual's legitimate and illegitimate earning opportunities, the probability and severity of punishment, and the probability of (and losses from) unemployment in legitimate activity.

The preceding analysis of the offender's choice assumes that legal and illegal behavior are mutually exclusive. The decision to engage in illegal activity is not inherently an either/or choice, however, and in practice, offenders may combine a number of legitimate

---

[5] The expected utility in Eq. (12-3) is derived for simplicity on the basis of two contingencies only: getting away with the crime and being apprehended and punished. In practice, the criminal prospect includes more contingencies, depending upon the form and extent of the punishment imposed and the reward obtained. However, the analysis can easily be generalized to cover any finite number of states.

and illegitimate activities or switch occasionally from one to another during any given period throughout their lifetime. In addition, neither the probability of being apprehended and convicted nor the punishment if convicted is determined by society's actions alone, but may be modified by deliberate actions of offenders. For example, an offender can reduce his chances of being caught or of being charged with a crime by spending resources on covering his illegal activity, "fixing" policemen and witnesses, employing legal counsel, or, in general, by providing "self-protection." The relevant object of choice to an offender might be defined more appropriately as an optimum occupational mix: the optimum allocation of his time and other resources to competing legal and illegal activities.

An attempt to attack this more comprehensive decision problem via a one-period uncertainty model is formally presented in my studies of participation in illegitimate activities (Ehrlich, 1970, 1973), which contain detailed analyses and discussion of the issue. One result derived from that model is that the same set of variables identified in Eq. (12-4) as underlying an offender's decision to enter an illegitimate activity i, when defined in terms of marginal rather than total quantities, also determines the extent of participation in i. In particular, if earnings in both i and l are not subject to strong time dependencies such as those resulting from specific training or learning by doing, many offenders—especially those who are risk avoiders—have an incentive to participate in both activities, partly as self-insurance against the relatively greater risk involved in the full-time pursuit of a risky activity. In that case, entry into i, and the extent of participation in a given period, would be related positively to the absolute difference between current "wage rates" in i and l, $w_i - w_l$, and generally also to the probability of unemployment in l. They would be negatively related to both the probability of apprehension and punishment for crime p_i and the discounted value of the penalty per offense f_i. The analysis also implies that the greater the extent of participation in i and the greater the efficiency of self-protection, the greater the offender's incentive to provide such protection, and vice versa. "Professional" offenders are therefore likely to be underrepresented in arrest statistics, and the converse is true for occasional and less-skilled offenders (see Ehrlich, 1970, pp. 114–119). More importantly, the analysis shows why many offenders tend to repeat their crimes even after being apprehended and punished for previous offenses. Even if there were no systematic variations in preferences for crime and attitudes toward risk from one period to another (these may, in fact, intensify), an offender is likely to make the same choice of an optimum participation in crime if the opportunities available to him remain unchanged. Indeed, it is plausible to assume that legitimate opportunities become much poorer relative to illegitimate opportunities in periods following conviction for crime because of the effect of having a criminal record on legitimate employment opportunities. Recidivism is thus not necessarily the result of an offender's myopia, erratic behavior, or lack of self-control, but rather may be the result of choice dictated by opportunities.

EDUCATION AND CRIME

Is education likely to have a systematic effect on the incentive to participate in illegitimate activity?[6] If the main effect of education on occupational choices were through its role in directing the individual's motivation and propensities toward socially acceptable goals, one might expect to find a negative correlation across persons between education and all criminal activities. The model suggests that the relation between education and crime may be more intricate, however, since it depends in large measure on the way education affects the relative opportunities available to offenders in different illegitimate activities. Broadly speaking, "education" — by which here is meant schooling, legitimate training, and other indicators of human capital[7] — can be regarded as an efficiency parameter in the production of legitimate as well as illegitimate market and nonmarket returns. In addition, education may increase an offender's productivity at self-protection against apprehension and punishment for crime, as well as against various legitimate occupational hazards. Since education generally enhances the pecuniary part of both legitimate and illegitimate "wages," and thus

---

[6] Another interesting source of interaction between education and crime is the possible effect a person's education may have on the likelihood that he will become a *victim* rather than a *perpetrator* of crime, as a result of the systematic relation between education and efficiency at self-protection. The theoretical arguments and specific behavioral implications have been developed by Ehrlich and Becker (1972). Neil Komesar, of the University of Chicago, has been investigating this relation empirically in his doctoral research.

[7] Note that empirical measures of education are all wedded to legitimate activities and are not likely to reflect training specific to illegitimate activities.

the pecuniary opportunity cost of imprisonment and other losses,[8] and may reduce the probability of many hazards, its overall effect on participation in crime cannot be determined a priori and would depend on the extent of its relative effect on the productivities of inputs used to produce legitimate and illegitimate returns and to reduce the relevant risks.

Consider the following cases for illustration. If education were completely general in the sense that it enhanced by the same proportion legitimate and illegitimate wages, the discounted value of punishment per offense, and the marginal productivity of time spent in nonmarket activities without affecting the probability of unemployment or the probability of apprehension and punishment for crime or the relative preference for illegal activities,[9] then the individual's optimum allocation of time to competing activities would not necessarily be affected (see Ehrlich, 1970, p. 30). Higher education in this case would not deter participation in illegitimate activity. In contrast, if education were completely specific to, say, legitimate activity in the sense that it enhanced the legitimate wage w_l and the discounted value of the opportunity cost of imprisonment and other losses per offense f without affecting the opportunities available in illegitimate activity, then it would be likely to reduce the incentive to participate in crime. Moreover, since specific training introduces time dependencies because of its effect on future earnings, persons with such training have an incentive to specialize in one legitimate occupation at least as long as a large fraction of their working time is devoted to on-the-job training. Although no single pair of alternative legitimate and illegitimate activities may provide a perfect empirical counterpart for these extreme cases, the classification of illegal activities according to the degree of their complementarity with empirical measures of education may be analytically useful.

Suppose that pecuniary payoffs on index crimes against property

[8] Future losses resulting from a criminal record may be particularly harmful for individuals who have specific legitimate training and whose earnings are disproportionately high in specific legitimate occupations. The discounted value of the opportunity cost of imprisonment may also be disproportionately large for more educated people if their rate of borrowing against future earnings is relatively low.

[9] Alternatively, it may be assumed that both probabilities decline with education, but the relative reductions do not affect the incentive to participate in either i or l.

(robbery, burglary, larceny, and auto theft) were largely dependent on the level of transferable assets in the community—i.e., opportunities provided by potential victims of crime—and to a much lesser extent on education and training. Also assume that the relative preferences for legitimate and illegitimate activities were either proportionately related to or largely independent of the relative pecuniary returns from these activities. Several propositions concerning offenders' characteristics would follow in this case. Given the probability of apprehension and punishment and the length of time served in prison:

1 Those with a lower level of schooling and training, i.e., those with potential legal income well below the average, would have a relatively large wage differential in crimes against property and a relatively low opportunity cost of imprisonment and thus a relatively strong incentive to "enter" crimes against property. Moreover, according to this theory, they would also tend to spend more time at, or to "specialize" in, illegitimate activities relative to other offenders. In contrast, those with higher education—in particular, those with specific legitimate training—would have less incentive to participate in such crimes.[10]

2 Offenders committing crimes against property would tend to enter criminal activity at a relatively young age, essentially because lack of schooling and legitimate training are not important obstacles to such activities and because legitimate earnings opportunities available to young age groups may generally fall short of their potential illegitimate payoffs. Moreover, since entry of the very young into the legitimate labor force is restricted by child labor laws, compulsory schooling, and federal minimum wage provisions, their entry into criminal activity may frequently precede entry into legitimate activity.

---

[10] A lower level of education that generally results in lower legitimate earnings may also be related positively to index crimes against the person (murder, rape, and assault), although the relation here is less clear than in the case of crimes against property. On the one hand, a lower opportunity cost of time reduces the cost of engaging in time-intensive activities, and these crimes may well fit into this category because of the prospect of long imprisonment terms associated with them. On the other hand, little can be said about the interaction between education and malevolence or other interpersonal frictions leading to crimes against the person. Empirical evidence shows that crimes against the person prevail among groups known to exercise close and frequent social contact (see Ehrlich, 1970, pp. 8–11).

3   Those in school would have less incentive to participate in crime relative to those not enrolled since many of them specialize voluntarily in acquiring education and therefore would view their opportunity cost of time not in terms of their potential current earnings but in relation to the expected future returns on their investment in human capital. In addition, effective school attendance (enrollment net of truancy) poses a constraint on students' participation in crime because it leaves them with less time for the pursuit of all market activities — legitimate as well as illegitimate. Proposition 2 therefore applies, in particular, to youths not enrolled in school.

In contrast to index crimes against property, payoffs on crimes such as fraud, forgery, embezzlement, trade in illegal merchandise, and illegal commercial practices may depend on education and legitimate training in much the same way that legitimate earnings do.[11] Consequently:

4   The average educational attainment of offenders engaged in this class of crimes can be expected to be higher than that of offenders engaged in property crimes.

5   The typical age of entry into such crimes would be higher because entry would follow a longer period of specialization in schooling. In fact, because more highly skilled occupations may involve intensive on-the-job training during the initial period of the working career, entry into related illegitimate activities may occur later than entry into the labor market.

6   A general implication of this analysis concerns the educational attainments of offenders belonging to different racial groups. To the extent that occupational and wage discrimination against non-white workers is greater in legitimate than in illegitimate activities, the critical pecuniary wage differential $(w_i - w_l)^*$, which is the amount sufficient to induce all workers of equal preferences to enter an illegitimate activity i, would be associated with relatively high educational attainment of the worker in the case of nonwhites. Consequently, one may expect the average educational attainments of nonwhite offenders to exceed those of whites in many illegitimate activities.

---

[11] This dependence may be due partly to the fact that engaging in specific legitimate activities is a prerequisite for the commission of specific offenses, for example, embezzlement.

In spite of the general interest in the relation between education and crime, very little detailed evidence on educational attainments of offenders by type of crime has been reported systematically in official crime statistics. Some direct information on the educational attainment of all prisoners in the United States is available on an aggregate level, cross-classified by age and sex.

A generally recognized problem with arrest and prison data is that they relate to offenders who have been apprehended and convicted of crime and who do not make up a representative sample of all offenders. The biases introduced via this selective sampling may be particularly severe where educational attainments of offenders are concerned, for education is likely to be negatively related to the probability of apprehension and conviction. Arrest and prison data are thus likely to understate the average educational attainments of all offenders. Nevertheless, some inferences might still be drawn from these data concerning the comparative educational attainment of offenders involved in different crimes, since the biases inherent in the data may apply uniformly to all crime categories. Another problem with the aggregate arrest and prison data is that, at best, they render possible inferences about only the simple (zero-order) correlation between measures of education and crime, whereas our propositions generally concern the partial cor-

TABLE 12-1
*Median
number of
school years
completed by
prisoners and
labor force
participants
in the United
States, by age,
1960*

Age	Males in prisons, reformatories, and jails			Males 14 yrs. old and over in civilian labor force		
	State	*Federal*	*Jails and workhouses*	*Total*	*Laborers (excl. mine and farm)*	*Operatives and kindred workers*
Total, 25 and over	8.5	9.0	8.9	11.0	8.3	9.1
25–29				12.3	9.8	11.0
30–34	8.9	9.4	9.5	12.1	8.9	10.1
35–44	8.4	9.0	9.2	12.0	8.5	9.8
45–54				10.1	8.0	8.7
55–64	7.9	8.3	8.5	8.7	7.0	8.2
65–74				8.5	6.4	8.0
75 and older	6.4	n.a.*	7.2	8.5	6.6	7.9

* n.a. = not available.

SOURCES: 1960 Census of the Population—Final Report PC(2)—8A (Table 25), U.S. Bureau of the Census, 1963*a*; and 1960 Census of the Population—Final Report PC(2)—5B (Table 8); U.S. Bureau of the Census, 1963*b*.

relation between these variables given the probability and severity of punishment.

Table 12-1 compares Bureau of the Census data on the median school years completed by all offenders in state, federal, and local jails and workhouses with schooling of all males in the civilian labor force and in two specific legitimate occupations. On the whole, male prisoners in all correctional institutions appear to have had less schooling than all male workers in the experienced civilian labor force, and the same holds for females (U.S. Bureau of the Census, 1963a, Table 25; 1963b, Table 8). The reported age-specific schooling attainments become more similar, however, when male prisoners are compared with male laborers (except mine and farm workers) and with operatives and kindred workers—two occupations most frequently stated to be the prisoners' major legitimate occupations (see Table 12-2). Federal prisoners appear

TABLE 12-2
Stated legitimate occupation of male prisoners in the United States, 1960

	State prisons	Federal prisons	Local jails and workhouse
All prisoners, 1960 (number)	193,568	24,162	111,544
Never worked (percentage)	7.37	5.53	2.56
Worked in 1950 or later (percentage)	61.42	74.95	80.29
Last major occupation (percentage of those who worked in 1950 or later) Professional, technical, and kindred workers	1.63	3.58	1.64
Farmers and farm managers	1.04	1.54	0.78
Managers, officials, and props. (excl. farm)	2.14	5.49	2.34
Clerical and kindred workers	2.73	4.75	2.96
Sales workers	2.32	4.84	2.88
Craftsmen, foremen, and kindred workers	12.88	18.73	14.70
Operatives and kindred workers	19.29	22.37	20.80
Private household workers	0.12	0.12	0.22
Service workers (excl. household)	8.20	9.36	10.13
Farm laborers, unpaid family workers	5.48	4.64	6.96
Laborers (excl. farm and mine)	20.01·	12.67	20.14
Occupation not reported	24.15	11.91	16.45

SOURCE: U.S. Bureau of the Census (1963a, Table 25).

to be better schooled than state prisoners in all specific age groups, and this systematic difference may reflect the involvement of federal prisoners in a somewhat different set of offenses—more illegal commercial activities and fewer crimes against the person—from those in which state prisoners are involved.[12] The age-specific schooling attainments of prisoners in local jails and workhouses also appear higher than those of state prisoners, but since the census does not report the distribution of these prisoners by type of crime committed, it is difficult to draw inferences from this evidence alone. It is interesting to note that the median schooling attainments across these three correctional institutions are negatively correlated with the apparent degree of offender "specialization" in illegitimate activity: offenders in local jails and workhouses, who are "best schooled" among prisoners of all age groups, include the lowest proportion of those who never worked and the highest proportion of those who worked in 1950 or later (see Table 12-2). Since offenders convicted for crimes against property constitute the majority of offenders in all correctional institutions, this finding is consistent with the theoretical expectation that for this set of crimes, both the incentive to enter illegal activity and the extent of participation (specialization) should be negatively correlated with schooling and legitimate training.

A comparison of the age distribution of males in two legitimate occupations and in city arrests for various felonies in 1960 is given in Table 12-3. These statistics show that people in younger age groups constitute a greater proportion, and people in older age groups a smaller proportion, of total city arrests relative to the proportion they constitute of, say, construction workers and industrial laborers. There exist, however, significant differences in the age distribution of arrests across specific crime categories. In particular, total arrests for embezzlement, fraud, forgery, and counterfeiting include a much smaller proportion of juveniles and a greater proportion of persons 45 years old and over relative to

[12] In 1960, 54 percent of all state prisoners were convicted of index crimes against property (robbery, burglary, larceny, and auto theft), 24.7 percent for crimes against the person (homicide, assault, and sex offenses), and 10 percent for embezzlement, fraud, and forgery (see *Characteristics of State Prisoners, 1960, National Prisoner Statistics,* 1960, p. 10). In contrast, in 1965, 25 percent of all federal prisoners were convicted for interstate transportation of motor vehicles, 8.3 percent for forgery, 17.9 percent for violations of drug laws, and 29.7 percent for "other federal offenses" (see U.S. Bureau of Prisons, 1965, Table A9).

TABLE 12-3 Comparison of the age distribution of males in two legitimate occupations and males arrested for felonious activities in the United States, 1960; percent of total number in each employment or crime category	Employment or crime category	Age group			
		15–19	*20–24*	*25–44*	*45 and ov*
	Construction workers	7.96*	11.76	44.63	32.65
	Industrial laborers	7.13*	13.21	47.00	32.66
	Total city arrests	14.05	12.21	42.96	24.91
	Robbery	30.95	20.30	30.30	2.90
	Burglary	36.43	15.60	19.50	2.69
	Larceny	31.48	11.63	22.12	7.83
	Auto theft	58.91	12.29	11.62	1.21
	Murder and manslaughter	13.60	17.38	49.17	18.78
	Assault	12.66	16.64	53.31	13.90
	Gambling	3.11	10.14	53.40	33.13
	Embezzlement and fraud	5.02	15.31	63.30	15.65
	Forgery and counterfeiting	13.33	20.78	46.69	18.09
	Buying and receiving property	25.43	17.50	35.37	10.02

*For age group 14 to 19.

SOURCES: U.S. Bureau of the Census (1963c, Table 1); Federal Bureau of Inves
gation (1961, p. 92).

index crimes against property.[13] These findings are generally con
sistent with the proposition, noted earlier, that crimes again:
property are typically committed by the relatively young becaus
they have less investment in legitimate occupations.

Strong empirical support for the proposition that school enrol
ment and participation in criminal activity are negatively correlate
is provided in Simpson and Van Arsdol's 1967 study of juveni
referrals to the Los Angeles County probation department. The
found that the delinquency rate among juveniles 14 to 17 year
old who were not enrolled in school was about 2.5 times high
than the rate for those who were enrolled, but that no large diffe
ence existed in the rate of delinquency for enrollees with educ
tional attainment above or below the modal educational achiev
ment. On this basis, they conclude that ". . . school enrollmei
per se, regardless of relative achievement, presents a deterrent
delinquency" (Simpson & Van Arsdol, 1967, p. 39).

[13] In all arrest statistics, the representation of older age groups is relatively sma
This is due partly to the fact that older and more experienced offenders a
more efficient at self-protection than younger offenders and are thus bett
able to avoid arrest.

The official census publications do not contain direct information on the educational attainment of convicted offenders by race. Census data on schooling attainments of all inmates of institutions in the United States in 1960 indicate, however, that the median number of years of school completed by nonwhite males in the age group 25 to 34 was 8.9, compared with 8.7 for whites (U.S. Bureau of the Census, 1963*a*, Table 22). The respective data for nonwhite and white females were 9.0 and 8.2. In contrast, the ranking of the schooling attainments of white and nonwhite males and females in the experienced civilian labor force was reversed: 12.2 for white males and 12.0 for white females, as against 10.1 for nonwhite males and 11.3 for nonwhite females (U.S. Bureau of the Census, 1963*a*, Table 8). Moreover, the rankings of the schooling attainments of white and nonwhite inmates of older ages were also reversed from those in the age group 25 to 34 and conformed to their respective rankings in the civilian labor force. A possible explanation for these conflicting rankings may have to do with the varying proportions of different categories of offenders in different age groups among inmates of closed institutions. Although the overall proportion of prisoners to inmates of all closed institutions is about one-third (the other two-thirds being in homes for the aged or for neglected children and in various closed hospitals), the proportion of prisoners in the age group 25 to 34 should be much greater, since the latter group is the mean and modal age group of all prisoners. The greater median school attainment of nonwhite inmates in this age group is consistent with the proposition that discrimination in legitimate occupations might result in a higher level of educational attainment for nonwhite offenders.

EVIDENCE FROM CRIME STATISTICS Since crime statistics are based on complaints of victims and statements of witnesses to crime and are collected independently of an offender's arrest or conviction, they are free of much of the selective sampling biases inherent in arrest and prison data. However, they do not provide direct information on offenders' characteristics, and such information must be inferred indirectly. In work on participation in illegitimate activities (Ehrlich, 1970, 1973), information on the rate of specific offenses across states in the United States from three decennial censuses has been used to test the basic propositions of the model via a cross-state regression analysis employing ordinary least squares and simultaneous equation estimation techniques. A major advantage of such analysis is that it permits statistical control of variations across states in measures of average probability and severity of punishment for specific crimes, unemployment and income characteristics, and various demographic variables. Thus partial correlations can be estimated between the rate of specific offenses and each of their explanatory variables. Part of the empirical analysis was consequently devoted to the econometric specification and actual testing of proposition 1, presented earlier.

According to the theoretical analysis, given the probability and severity of punishment for crime, and assuming that pecuniary returns from legitimate and illegitimate activities were either proportionately related to or statistically independent of nonpecuniary returns from these activities, the crime rate in each state is expected to be a positive function of the mean (pecuniary) differential returns from crime ($\overline{w}_i - \overline{w}_l$). Information concerning monetary returns from specific crimes $\overline{w}_i$ is presently unavailable on a state-by-state basis, and so the relevant legitimate earning opportunities $\overline{w}_l$ cannot be estimated directly. It is postulated that the average illegal payoffs of crimes against property depend primarily on the level of transferable assets in the community—that is, on opportunities provided by potential victims of crime—and, to a much lesser extent, on the offender's education and legitimate training. The relative variation in the average potential illegal payoff $\overline{w}_i$ may be approximated by the variation in, say, the median value of transferable assets per family or family income across states W.[14] The preceding postulate and the previous discussion under Education and Crime also imply that those in a state with legitimate returns well below the median have greater differential returns from property crimes and hence have more incentive to participate in such crimes than those in states with incomes well above the median.

---

[14] More precisely, the assumption is that given the relative distribution of family income in a state, variations in average potential payoffs on property crime can be approximated by the variation in the level of the *entire* distribution. the income distribution is of the log normal variety, it can be shown that the variation in its level would be reflected by an equal proportional variation its median value. The relative variation in *potential* payoffs on property crime may be an unbiased estimator of the relative variation in *actual* payoffs if (private) self-protection of property by potential victims were proportionately related to their wealth. See Ehrlich and Becker (1972) for an elaborate discussion the relation between the two.

[15] This argument appears to be consistent with one made by Adam Smith who noted that "the affluence of the rich excites the indignation of the poor, who

The variation in the mean legitimate opportunities available to potential offenders across states $\overline{w}_l$ may therefore be approximated by the variation of the mean income level of those below the state's median. Partly because of statistical considerations, the latter was computed somewhat indirectly, by the percentage of families below one-half of the median income in a state, denoted X ("income inequality").[16] Since X is a measure of the *relative* distance between legitimate and illegitimate opportunities available to potential offenders $\overline{w}_i/\overline{w}_l$, changes in W, X held constant, would amount to equal percentage changes in the absolute wage differential $\overline{w}_i$ — $\overline{w}_l$. Given the full cost of punishment per offense f_i and the probability of apprehension and conviction p_i, an increase in W might then have a positive effect on the incidence of crimes against property, similar to the effect of an increase in income inequality X.

In this empirical implementation the extent of punishment is measured by the length of the effective incarceration period of convicted offenders. If punishment for crime were solely by imprisonment, an increase in the median income W, X held constant, would cause an equal proportional increase in the pecuniary "wage differential" from crime as well as in the opportunity cost of imprisonment to all offenders, and its net effect on crime rates might then be null if changes in the level of pecuniary income did not affect the relative preference for legal and illegal activities (see the discussion above under Education and Crime). In contrast, an increase in income inequality, W held constant, would imply a decrease in both legitimate earnings opportunities and the opportunity cost of

---

are often both driven by want and prompted by envy, to invade his possessions" (Smith, 1937, p. 670). By our reasoning, since potential gains from crimes against property are assumed to be largely independent of education and legitimate training, those with legitimate earning opportunities well below the average would have a greater incentive to commit such crimes regardless of possible envy or hate they may feel toward the more affluent members of society.

[16] An increase in X, with median (and mean) family income held constant, implies a decrease in the mean income of relatively poor families $\overline{w}_p$ and an increase in the mean income of the relatively rich $\overline{w}_r$. Since the latter have an incentive to specialize in legitimate market activities, the increase in $\overline{w}_r$ may have very little negative impact on the total amount of property crimes committed in the community, but the decrease in $\overline{w}_p$ is certainly expected to increase it. This argument regarding the effect of changes in X on crimes against property does not apply equally to crimes against the person because there is no a priori reason to assume that the majority of families with income above the median level do not participate at all in such crimes. The statistical advantage of using X in lieu of $\overline{w}_p$ in the regression analysis is that the correlation of $\overline{w}_p$ with W is high, whereas the correlation of X with W is much weaker.

imprisonment to offenders. In practice, however, a major proportion of offenders convicted for property crimes are punished by means other than imprisonment.[17] Consequently, both income inequality and the median income level are expected to be positively related to the incidence of property crimes in the cross-state regressions.[18]

Table 12-4 shows estimates of the partial elasticities of rates of specific crimes against property to changes in income inequality X and in the median family income W across states. These elasticities were derived from the following regression equation:[19]

$$ln\left(\frac{Q}{N}\right)_i = a_i + b_{1i}lnP_i + b_{2i}lnT_i + c_{1i}lnX + c_{2i}lnW$$

$$+ e_1 lnNW + \mu_i \quad (12\text{-}5$$

where $\left(\dfrac{Q}{N}\right)_i$ = rate of the ith crime category: the number of offense known per state population in year t

P_i = ratio of number of commitments to state and federa prisons to number of offenses known to have oc curred in the same state ("probability of imprison ment") in year t

T_i = average time served in state prisons by offender first released in year t

---

[17] According to rough estimates, 53 percent of those convicted of robbery, 7 percent of those convicted of burglary and larceny, and 82 percent of those con victed of auto theft are punished by means other than imprisonment in stat and federal prisons; see Ehrlich (1970, Table R-1).

[18] By the preceding argument, the estimated regression coefficients associate with X might still be biased upward, and those associated with W downward relative to what their values would have been with the full cost of imprisonmen held constant. Opposite biases on the value of these two coefficients can als be expected, however, as a result of "spillover effects" unaccounted for in th cross-state regression analysis; offenders may migrate from one state to anothe in response to the different opportunities available in different states. It ca be shown that such spillover effects on the incidence of crime would overstat the estimated partial effect of W and understate that of X.

[19] Measures of age composition of the population and of unemployment and labo force participation rates were also introduced into the regression analysis, bu were excluded in the final regressions because the signs of their coefficient were found to be unstable across most of the specific regressions, and the ratio of the estimated coefficients to their standard errors were found to be relativel small. The exclusion of these variables had virtually no effect on the estimate of c_1 and c_2 reported in Table 12-4.

$W =$ median family income in year t

$X =$ percentage of families whose income is less than one-half of W

$NW =$ percentage of nonwhites in the population in year t

$\mu_i =$ a disturbance term

$ln =$ natural logarithm

A discussion of the econometric specification of the model, the estimating techniques employed, and the many problems in the construction of specific variables used to measure the pertinent theoretical variables, which is avoided here for lack of space, may be found in Ehrlich (1970, 1973). It should be noted, however, that to obtain efficient estimates of the regression coefficients, the regression equation (12-5) was weighted by the square root of the population in each state, since an analysis of residuals in unweighted regressions indicated the presence of heteroscedasticity, which was negatively related to population size. (Such heteroscedasticity is consistent with the hypothesis that the stochastic variable μ is homoscedastic at the individual level.)

Despite the shortcomings of the data and the crude estimates for some of the desired statistics, the results of the regression analysis appear to be highly consistent with the proposition that those with lower schooling levels and training, and hence lower potential legal income, have a relatively greater tendency to engage in crimes against property. The rates of robbery, burglary, larceny, and auto theft are found to vary positively with the measures of income inequality and median family income across states in all specific regressions and census years investigated. In Table 12-4 the regression coefficients c_{1i} and c_{2i}, which are estimates of the elasticities of $(Q/N)_i$ with respect to X and W, are generally greater than unity, and virtually all exceed twice their standard errors.[20] Moreover,

---

[20] The coefficients c_{2i} may reflect, in part, the effect of urbanization on the rate of specific crimes (by greater accessibility to criminal opportunities in metropolitan areas) because W is highly correlated with the level of urbanization across states. This may be one reason why the absolute values of c_{1i} in regressions using 1940 and 1950 data are lower than those in the 1960 regressions: the dependent variables in 1940 and 1950 are "urban crime rates," whereas those in 1960 are state rates. Also note that X and W in the 1940 regressions were calculated on the basis of data on wage and salary earnings of workers rather than family income data (unavailable in 1940), and therefore the estimates of c_{1i} and c_{2i} in that year are not exactly comparable with those of the other years.

TABLE 12-4
Weighted regression estimates of the partial elasticities of rates of crimes against property with respect to measures of income inequality (X) and median family income (W) across states in the United States in 1940, 1950, and 1960

Crime category		1940 OLS*		1950 OLS	
		X	W	X	W
Robbery	β	.7222	1.6608	.4798	1.7278
	β/S.E.§	.9294)	(4.2214)	(.7008)	(3.2329)
Burglary	β	1.6939	.8327	1.8697	1.1891
	β/S.E.	(2.8321)	(.8003)	(3.5361)	(2.0207)
Larceny	β	3.7371	.6186	3.3134	1.9784
	β/S.E.	(6.5307)	(2.2095)	(6.1904)	(4.8461)
Auto theft	β				
	β/S.E.				
All crimes against property	β			2.2598	1.5836
	β/S.E.			(4.8419)	(4.5210)

* OLS = ordinary least squares estimates.

† 2SLS = estimates derived by a two-stage least squares procedure.

‡ SUR = seemingly unrelated regression estimates derived by applying Aitken's generalized least squares to the system of all four property crimes following a method devised by Zellner (1962).

§ β = elasticity estimate; S.E. = standard error of β.

SOURCE: Ehrlich (1970, Tables 3 and 5).

point estimates obtained from several 1960 regressions employing different estimation techniques are highly consistent. In contrast, X and W were found to have a lower effect on the incidence of murder, rape, and aggravated assault, and the regression coefficients (c's) associated with X and W in regressions for these crimes were generally less than twice their standard errors (see Ehrlich, 1970, Tables 2 & 6; 1973). The finding that variations in X and W have a relatively larger and more significant effect on the incidence of crimes against property than on the incidence of crimes against the person lends credibility to proposition 1 and to the choice of these income variables as indicators of relative "earnings" opportunities in property crimes.

In addition to testing proposition 1, I also attempted to test directly the partial effect of mean educational attainments on the rate of specific crimes across states. This was done by expanding the regression model [Eq. (12-5)] to include the percentage of males in the age group 15 to 25, census estimates of the unemployment rate for urban males, and the mean number of school years completed by the population over 25 years of age (hereafter designated by symbol Ed). Given the economic and demographic characteris-

| 1960 | | 1960 | | | |
| OLS | | 2SLS† | | SUR‡ | |
X	W	X	W	X	W
1.8409	2.9086	1.279	1.689	1.409	2.120
(2.8247)	(4.2628)	(1.660)	(1.969)	(1.853)	(2.548)
2.0452	1.7973	2.000	1.384	2.032	1.581
(5.0209)	(4.0414)	(4.689)	(2.839)	(4.776)	(3.313)
1.6207	2.6893	1.792	2.229	1.785	2.241
(3.1092)	(5.1392)	(2.992)	(3.465)	(2.985)	(3.502)
1.8981	2.8931	2.057	2.608	2.054	2.590
(4.2550)	(0.3527)	(4.060)	(5.101)	(4.283)	(5.253)
2.0547	2.3345	2.132	1.883		
(5.8090)	(6.1923)	(5.356)	(4.246)		

tics of the population, one might expect a negative correlation between *Ed* and all specific crimes, assuming that education does play some role in directing individual motivation and propensities along socially desirable avenues. The results with respect to the partial effect of *Ed* were disappointing, however, for they showed a positive and significant association between *Ed* and (particularly) crimes against property across states in 1960 (see Ehrlich, 1970, App. R, Tables R-7 & R-14). One possible explanation for these results is that *Ed* works as a surrogate for the average permanent income in the population: Given the distribution of *current* family income (approximated by *X* and *W*), the average schooling attainments may be an efficient indication of the long-run level of income and thus of the true level of transferable assets in a state. Since the latter are expected to be positively correlated with illegitimate opportunities (as is *W*), the positive partial regression coefficient associated with *Ed* in the regression for property crimes may not, then, be so surprising. Another possible explanation is that given *X* and *W*, *Ed* may be negatively related to the level of unreported crimes, which is particularly high for crimes against property (see Ehrlich, 1970, pp. 54–55, and Table R-1, p. 132). Since education may increase the efficiency of law-enforcement agencies and the general public in reporting crime, it might, *ceteris paribus,* be positively related to all the reported crime rates, particularly to rates of crime against property.

In contrast to the disappointing results obtained in testing the partial effect of *Ed* on specific crime rates, interesting and plausible results were obtained for the partial effect of education on the effectiveness of law-enforcement activity across states. In the context of testing the interaction between crime and law enforcement through a simultaneous equation model, an attempt was made to estimate an aggregate production function of law-enforcement activity: estimates of the probabilities of apprehension and imprisonment for crime *P* were regressed on total expenditures for police activity and other variables. Given the level of expenditure on police, the crime level itself, the size and density of the population, and income inequality, it was found that the partial effect of *Ed* on *P* was positive and statistically significant; the estimated elasticity is 2.4 (see Ehrlich, 1973). Since higher educational attainments among the state population would presumably also be reflected in higher educational attainments among all law-enforcement agents, this result may be interpreted as evidence for the role of education of both the potential victims and law-enforcement agents as an efficiency parameter in the production of law-enforcement activity.

CONCLUSION The approach one takes in analyzing the relation between education and crime is not independent of the approach one takes in analyzing the determinants of crime itself. An economic approach to criminality, as developed here and elsewhere, emphasizes the role that objective market opportunities play in determining entry into, and the extent of participation in, illegitimate activities. In this chapter I have attempted to analyze the relation between education and crime by concentrating on the role education may have in determining such opportunities. The analysis suggests that education does not have a uniform effect on illegitimate and legitimate opportunities, but has an effect which varies according to the complementarity of schooling and legitimate training with inputs employed in producing legitimate and illegitimate returns. I have postulated, however, that given the probability of punishment and the length of imprisonment, education would bias relative opportunities away from crimes against property, which constitute the bulk of all felonies in the United States, and increase the cost of crimes against the person. This postulate, and other related ones, are found to be not inconsistent with empirical evidence from arrest and prison data, as well as from crime statistics.

Perhaps the most important finding reported in this chapter is the positive and statistically significant association between the extent of income inequality, measured as the relative density of the lower tail of the family-income distribution, and the rate of all specific crimes against property across states in three census years.[21] There also exists some evidence of a positive association between inequality in earnings and the dispersion in schooling across regions in the United States (see, for example, Chiswick, 1967), as well as a growing body of empirical evidence confirming the importance of education and on-the-job training in determining the distribution of labor and personal income (see Mincer, 1969). A logical inference from these findings is, then, that the extent of specific crimes against property is directly related to inequalities in schooling and on-the-job training. Moreover, it is essentially the inequalities in the distribution of schooling and training, not their mean levels, that appear to be strongly related to the incidence of many crimes. This indicates a social incentive for equalizing schooling and training opportunities which is independent of ethical considerations or a specific social welfare function, provided, of course, that equalizing educational opportunities would also lead to a greater equality in the distribution of actual educational attainments and legitimate earnings. Answers to the question of whether it would pay society to spend more resources in order to promote equality in educational opportunities as a deterrent to crime and to the question of what the optimal expenditure for that purpose should be would depend not only on the effect of such expenditure on the actual distribution of earnings opportunities but also on the extent to which alternative methods of combating crime "pay."[22]

A general implication of this analysis concerns rehabilitation

[21] This finding is consistent with a similar one by Fleisher (1966), who reported a positive association between aggregate arrest rates and the difference between the incomes of the highest and second-to-lowest quartiles of families, based on a regression analysis using intercity and intracity data. His analysis and method of estimation are, however, different from those here, and some of the results are statistically insignificant.

[22] Tentative results obtained in my study of the effectiveness of law-enforcement activity through police and courts indicate that in 1960, for example, law enforcement "paid" (indeed, "overpaid") in the sense that the marginal revenue from apprehending and convicting offenders, measured in terms of the resulting lower social cost of crime, exceeded the marginal cost of such activity.

programs for offenders. If criminal behavior were primarily the result of a unique motivation of offenders, rehabilitative efforts would need to emphasize psychological and other related treatment of convicted offenders. This analysis and the empirical findings indicate, however, that criminal behavior is to a large extent also the result of the relative earnings opportunities of offenders in legitimate and illegitimate activities, and these may shift toward the latter following apprehension and conviction for crime. This suggests that rehabilitation efforts intended as an effective deterrent against recidivism must emphasize specific training of offenders for legitimate activities (perhaps along with other treatments) prior to their release from prison. Much more research is needed, however, in order to confirm the effectiveness of such rehabilitation efforts and of programs for equalizing schooling and training opportunities in deterring participation in specific crimes.

References

Becker, Gary S.: "Crime and Punishment: An Economic Approach," *Journal of Political Economy*, vol. 76, no. 2, pp. 169–217, March 1968.

Chiswick, Barry R.: "Human Capital and Personal Income Distribution by Region," unpublished Ph.D. dissertation, Columbia University, New York, 1967.

Cohen, Joseph: "The Geography of Crime," in David Dressler (ed.), *Readings in Criminology and Penology*, 2d ed., Columbia University Press, New York, 1964, pp. 301–311.

Ehrlich, Isaac: "Participation in Illegitimate Activities: An Economic Analysis," unpublished Ph.D. dissertation, Columbia University, New York, 1970.

Ehrlich, Isaac: "Participation in Illegitimate Activities: A Theoretical and Empirical Investigation." *Journal of Political Economy*, vol. 81, pp. 521–565, May–June 1973.

Ehrlich, Isaac, and Gary S. Becker: "Market Insurance, Self-Insurance and Self-Protection," *Journal of Political Economy*, vol. 80, pp. 623–648, July–August 1972.

Eichorn, John R.: "Delinquency and the Educational Systems," in Herbert C. Quay (ed.), *Juvenile Delinquency: Research and Theory*, D. Van Nostrand Company, Inc., Princeton, N.J., 1965, pp. 25–40.

Federal Bureau of Investigation: *Uniform Crime Reports in the U.S., 1960*, Government Printing Office, Washington, 1961.

Fleisher, Belton M.: *The Economics of Delinquency*, Quadrangle Books, Inc., Chicago, 1966.

Mincer, Jacob: *The Distribution of Labor Incomes: A Survey,* National Bureau of Economic Research, New York, 1969, (Mimeographed.)

Simpson, Jon E., and Maurice D. Van Arsdol, Jr.: "Residential History and Educational Status of Delinquents and Non-Delinquents," *Social Problems,* vol. 15, no. 7, pp. 25–40, Summer 1967.

Smigel-Leibowitz, Arleen: "Does Crime Pay? An Economic Analysis," unpublished M.A. thesis, Columbia University, New York, 1965.

Smith, Adam: *The Wealth of Nations,* Modern Library, Inc., New York, 1937.

U.S. Bureau of Prisons: *Characteristics of State Prisoners, 1960, National Prisoner Statistics,* Government Printing Office, Washington, 1960.

U.S. Bureau of Prisons: *Federal Bureau of Prisons, Statistical Tables, Fiscal Year 1965,* Government Printing Office, Washington, 1965.

U.S. Bureau of the Census: *1960 Census of the Population, Special Reports, Inmates of Institutions,* Government Printing Office, Washington, 1963*a*.

U.S. Bureau of the Census: *Special Reports, Educational Attainments,* Government Printing Office, Washington, 1963*b*.

U.S. Bureau of the Census: *Special Reports, Occupations by Industry,* Government Printing Office, Washington, 1963*c*.

Zellner, Arnold: "An Efficient Method of Estimating Seemingly Unrelated Regressions and Tests for a Regression Bias," *Journal of the American Statistical Association,* vol. 57, pp. 348–368, June 1962.

13. Education and Fertility

by Robert T. Michael

by Robert T. Michael

INTRODUCTION Both casual observation and more systematic empirical findings suggest that couples with more education have fewer children. This chapter is a progress report on a research project which offers analytical explanations for the negative relationship between education and fertility and which attempts to determine empirically the effects of education on fertility behavior when certain economic and demographic factors are held constant.

The analysis focuses on the role of education in household production[1] and its influence on effective use of contraception and on the couple's choices between number of children and child "quality." The empirical results to which the chapter refers were obtained from recent United States cross-sectional data sets. No attempt has been made to summarize the recent and rapidly growing literature pertaining to the economic analysis of fertility.

THE FRAMEWORK The analytical framework used in considering the effects of education on fertility is built upon the notion that households may be viewed as small firms. A firm purchases raw materials, equipment, and manpower and uses them to produce its product. In much the same way, the household purchases consumer-durable and con-

NOTE: This chapter was written as a progress report on a research project supported by the Carnegie Commission through NBER and was submitted for inclusion in this volume in January 1971. I have published two subsequent research papers (Michael, 1971, 1973). The present chapter has been only slightly revised.

I received useful suggestions on earlier drafts from Armen A. Alchian, Gary S. Becker, Barry R. Chiswick, F. Thomas Juster, John R. Meyer, Jacob Mincer, T. Paul Schultz, T. W. Schultz, and Robert J. Willis. Bonnie Birnbaum provided skillful research assistance.

[1] See Chap. 9 in this volume or Michael (1972).

sumer-nondurable goods and services and uses them, along with some of its own "manpower" or available time, to produce items which give it satisfaction. This approach emphasizes that the usefulness of most purchased consumer goods is related to how frequently and intensively they are used. Typically, the household produces a large number of products, and it is assumed that the choices among products and the decisions regarding the productive processes are made jointly by husband and wife.[2]

Suppose that one of the products from which the couple derives satisfaction is "child services," defined as quality-adjusted hours of their offspring. A child yields a flow of services to the household that depends, in part, upon the amount of time and goods the couple chooses to devote to that child.[3] The larger the flow of services per child, the higher the child's "quality."[4] In any period of time, the amount of child services available to the couple depends upon the number and quality of their children. The household can achieve a larger flow of services by raising either the number or the quality of its children and will choose that combination of the two which produces the desired level of services at the lowest cost. Since children remain in the household for a considerable length of time, they are typically described as durable goods, and in one form or another this basic framework of children as consumer durables is the standard one used in contemporary economic analyses of human fertility.

[2] The general approach used here was developed by Becker (1965). My other chapter in this volume discusses this model in greater detail. This "household production function" framework is also utilized in varying degrees in chapters in this volume by Ghez, Leibowitz, Mincer, and Solmon. It is a framework used with increasing frequency in studies of human fertility behavior.

[3] In a more precise formulation, one might argue that there is a distinction between time and goods used to affect the "quality" of the child and time and goods used to achieve satisfaction from a given level of quality (e.g., instructing the child in piano playing versus listening to the child perform at the piano). This distinction will not be made here.

One might also argue that child quality itself is an argument in the household's utility function. See Willis (1973).

[4] Just as a firm might use a certain raw material with larger quantities of capital equipment and more man hours to produce a higher-quality product, the household can raise the quality of its children by devoting relatively more of the couple's own time and more market goods to each child. The economist's use of the term *quality* is not intended to connote a normative judgment. The higher quality unit typically represents a larger amount of the good per unit or a different combination of characteristics per unit and is generally obtainable at a higher cost per unit.

[5] The interested reader is referred to the fertility conference supplement to the *Journal of Political Economy* (see Schultz, 1973), which includes two article

One aspect of treating children as consumer durables which is not frequently stressed and which distinguishes children from other durable goods is that the household must frequently expend resources to avoid having an additional child. The probability of conception is not independent of the household's level of production of another product from which it derives satisfaction—sexual gratification.[6] Since sexual activity is desired in its own right and not simply as a means of having children, its effect on the probability of conception is a by-product, which may be desirable or undesirable, depending upon whether the household wants a child at that time. By comparing the costs of lowering the probability through contraception to the costs (through the risk of conception) of not lowering it, the couple determines its optimum expenditure on contraception and thereby selects its probability of conception.

The net value of a conception may be defined as the expected value of the difference between the monetary equivalent of the satisfaction from the prospective child and the net expenditure of time and money on the child (all properly discounted to convert into common units those benefits and costs which occur over time).[7] If this "net value of a conception" is negative, the household benefits by lowering the probability of conception. The cost of reducing this probability by contraception includes such considerations as the direct expenditure of time and money and the indirect or psychic cost of forgone sexual gratification, impaired health, and conflict with religious beliefs. The couple lowers its probability of conception to the point at which the benefits from a further reduction in the probability are offset by the costs incurred in lowering it.

Two implications flow from this argument. First, since the costs of contraception and the negative benefits of risking additional pregnancies are attributable to the production of sexual gratifica-

---

dealing explicitly with the substitution between quantity and quality of children, as well as several other articles which also employ the theoretical framework used in the present chapter.

[6] There is evidence that the probability is higher the greater the frequency of coition. In a comparison of husbands aged 25 to 29, using no contraception, the percentage of couples with conception occurring in less than six months rose from 32 percent to 71 percent as coital frequency rose from less than twice a week to four or more times a week. See MacLeod and Gold (1953). For additional evidence, see Potter, Sagi, and Westoff (1962).

Of course, the determination of these expenditures and benefits is not a simple matter, and to render this formulation of the problem operative analytically, some simplifying assumptions must be made.

tion, the higher these costs, the lower the level of sexual activity.[8] Historically, one common form of contraception was abstinence, often effected by postponement of marriage. In the terminology of this chapter, the cost of risking an additional conception was sufficiently high to induce couples to forgo some sexual gratification.

Second, since it is costly to avoid having additional children, households will tend to have more than they would "desire" to have. Just as households consume less of a consumer good than they would if its price were zero, they consume more of an "unwanted" item than they would if the price of avoiding it were zero. Thus in light of the costs of avoiding unwanted children—costs in terms of contraceptive expenditures or forgone sexual gratification—the number of children the household effectively "demands" may exceed the number it "desires."[9]

Graphic Interpretation

This second implication can be depicted graphically in a number of ways. Consider a household choosing its optimal probability of conception for, say, the following year. It must decide the extent of its contraceptive activity in light of the costs. Figure 13-1 represents this circumstance. The net benefit of a conception is indicated by the value B, which is negative in the figure.[10] Thus, the expected value of the "benefit" at each probability of a conception is given by $0B$. The curve CC represents the cost of achieving each level of the probability through contraception, assuming that the

[8] This is one application of the phenomenon of joint production in the household sector. For an analytical statement of the price effects of such production, see Grossman (1971).

[9] Some recent surveys have asked couples about the ideal and desired number of children, but unless the assumptions about costs and economic circumstances are specified precisely, the responses are very difficult to interpret. For example, ideally (in a utopian sense), one's children will cost nothing to support, and so the ideal number may be quite large. Similarly, the number of children one wants may exceed the number one has, or expects to have, if he cannot afford all he wants. The point is that unless the assumed circumstances are fully specified, the responses to such questions will differ as respondents make different assumptions.

[10] If B is positive, the couple will not employ contraception, but instead may expend resources to raise the probability of a birth. This paper focuses on the case of a negative value for B.

In order to determine (even in principle) the stream of benefits and costs which go into the term B, it is assumed that the household acts as if all subsequent additional conceptions can be prevented with certainty.

FIGURE 13-1 *The optimal probability of birth P**

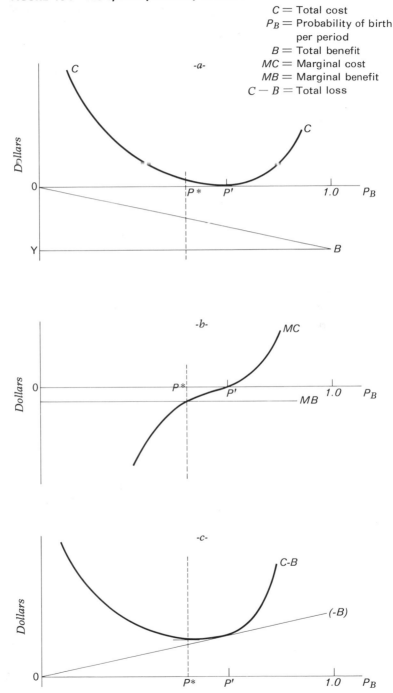

C = Total cost
P_B = Probability of birth per period
B = Total benefit
MC = Marginal cost
MB = Marginal benefit
$C - B$ = Total loss

couple's level of sexual activity in the period would, in the absence of any contraceptive expenditure, imply a probability P' (Figure 13-1a).

Here, the optimal level of the probability is indicated by the intersection of the marginal cost and marginal benefit curves (Figure 13-1b), which is equivalent to the minimum point on the total loss function (Figure 13-1c). As long as the net benefit of a conception is negative, and as long as it is sufficiently more costly to reduce the probability further (i.e., as long as $Y < 0$ and CC is sufficiently convex below P'), the optimal probability $P*$ will lie between zero and P'. Since the net benefit of an additional child is negative, the "desired" probability of conception for the period is zero; but in light of the cost of achieving that probability, the optimal probability (the level "demanded," given the costs) is positive. If the conditions reflected in Figure 13-1 persist for several years, the household can expect to have some number of children from whom the net benefit is negative; thus, a total number of children greater than would be "desired."

Another way of formulating this problem is to consider the household's decision regarding its total number of children without regard to the sequential nature of the process.[11] Figure 13-2 illustrates this case. The total net benefit curve $0B$ depicts the benefits, net of all costs except those related to contraception, of having any number of children from none to N' (where N' is the number produced if the couple does nothing to prevent conception).[12] As it is drawn, the total benefits from children are greatest at the level $\hat{N}$, which might be considered the "desired" number for this household. The curve CC in Figure 13-2a represents the total contraceptive cost of having N children. This cost is zero at N' by definition and presumably is higher the more births are prevented. From these two functions, one can determine the optimal number of children, or the number "demanded," which is indicated in Figure 13-2b as $N*$, the intersection of the marginal benefit and marginal

---

[11] I want to acknowledge suggestions made by Robert Willis on this formulation.

[12] In a more general framework, the household can also influence N' by its decisions about the timing of marriage and the frequency of coitus and, more indirectly, by decisions regarding the couple's own health. Throughout this chapter, the effects of infant and child mortality are ignored, although they could be incorporated.

FIGURE 13-2 *The optimal number of children N**

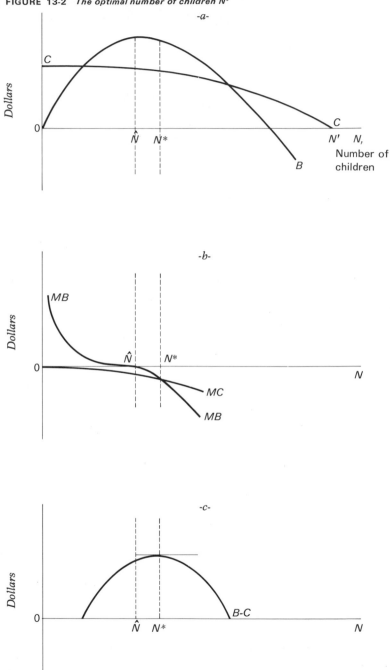

cost curves. (This is equivalent to the highest point on the curve *B-C* in Figure 13-2c.[13])

Since it is costly to prevent conception, households will choose a somewhat larger number of children than they would otherwise want. What, then, are the economic factors that affect the number of children households want? The standard economic analysis of fertility emphasizes the role of income and the price of time.

It has generally been argued that since the demand for most consumer goods rises with income, households with higher levels of income will choose to have more children. The theory does not suggest that the relationship between income and number of children across households must be positive, but only that it is quite likely to be.[14] One of the important implications of Becker's more recent analysis of household production functions is the assertion that the source of the household's income affects its influence on behavior. For fertility analysis, this suggests that the relationship between income and family size is considerably more complicated than has previously been thought.[15] It has also been suggested that as income rises, the price of quality of children falls relative to the price of quantity of children, regardless of the source of the income.[16] This phenomenon would further complicate the relationship between income and number of children in the household. So although income is expected to affect fertility, the direction and magnitude of the effect depend crucially upon whether or not shadow prices in household production (as distinct from market

[13] Again, the determination of the shape of benefit and cost functions is not considered here. The substantive conclusion that $N^* > \hat{N}$ follows as long as CC is negatively sloped throughout and $0B$ is a smooth, continuous function rising monotonically to a peak somewhere between zero and N' and falling monotonically thereafter.

[14] For a more thorough discussion of this argument and the original statement of the analysis of children as a consumer durable, see Becker (1960). On the basis of evidence for other durables, Becker argues that the responsiveness in the demand for quality of children to differences in income will probably be greater than the responsiveness in the demand for the number of children and that the latter may be quite small.

[15] For a thorough discussion of this point, see Willis (1973) and Sanderson and Willis (1971).

[16] See Michael (1973) for a discussion based on joint production in the home. If the "luxuries" consumed by wealthier households are complementary with expenditures on the quality of children, then the relative price of quality is negatively related to the proportion of total expenditure spent on luxuries.

prices of purchased goods and services) are being held constant. One would not expect—and does not observe—much similarity in the estimates of the effect of income on fertility in various cross-sectional studies which "hold constant" quite different sets of variables.

A second important economic factor influencing the demand for children is the price of the wife's time. Since raising children requires a relatively large amount of her time, the cost of a child is relatively high for households in which the wife's time value is relatively high. This suggests that the partial effect of the value of the wife's time on the demand for children will be negative. Empirical research on economic determinants of fertility in the United States tends to support this hypothesis. [17]

An additional economic factor which is generally not included in the analysis of family size is the price of the husband's time. If the husband's time, as well as the wife's, is used in achieving quality in children, the greater the value of his time, the higher the cost of high-quality children. This, too, may reduce the household's demand for child services, but in addition may induce substituting quantity for quality in the production of child services, other things held constant. [18]

In light of the well-documented positive effects of education on wage rates and earnings (see Part One of this volume), probably the most important effects of formal education on household fertility are the indirect effects issuing from the household's level of income and the value of the husband's and wife's time. It has often been observed empirically that the simple relationship between education and family size is negative, and this observation most likely reflects the higher value of time of couples with more education. But in addition, the husband's and wife's levels of education may influence their fertility behavior through several other channels. For example, schooling may alter the couple's preferences for children or their attitude toward their desired family size, or education may affect the way in which household production takes place in such a way that it alters the price of children relative to

---

[17] Several of the articles in the *Journal of Political Economy* supplement bear on this question (see Schultz, 1973). See also Chap. 7 in this volume for a related discussion; that chapter, however, does not focus on a fertility demand equation.

[18] The asymmetry in the predicted direction of effects of the value of the husband's and wife's time follows from the assumption that child quantity is relatively time-intensive for the wife.

the price of other things. If so, couples with different levels of education would face different relative prices of children, and this would affect their fertility behavior.

Although we cannot rule out an education effect on preferences for children, neither can we rely on this explanation to yield hypotheses about observed behavior, since social scientists have no viable theory about the way in which preferences are formed or altered. After the fact, any observed behavior can be ascribed to a change in household preferences. But without a theory about the formation of preferences, one cannot analyze and predict ex ante how a factor such as education might affect behavior by altering preferences. Thus an explanation of observed behavior which is based on changes in preferences is usually tautological. We shall consider, instead, two channels through which education may alter the relative price of children and thereby affect observed behavior. These two channels do not result from changes in the price of time of the parents but, rather, from the assumed effect of education on different household production functions.

Education's Effect on Contraceptive Efficiency It was emphasized above that the household produces its optimal level of the probability of conception by using some market purchases (such as contraceptive appliances or medical advice) and some of its own time. More educated couples may be more efficient in this production—they may be able to lower the probability of conception more cheaply than less-educated couples. If education increases one's awareness of new consumer products and reduces the costs associated with acquiring and evaluating information about their characteristics and availability, more educated couples can be expected to use more effective processes of production and to adopt effective new techniques relatively rapidly.[19] Since many contraceptive techniques of varying effectiveness are available at any given time and since relative effectiveness varies over time as new techniques become available, the selection of techniques seems a likely application of this alleged attribute of education.

If education increases one's receptivity to new ideas or increases one's willingness to reevaluate previously held points of view, the more educated can be expected to be less reluctant to engage in

---

[19] This argument is made in the context of an economic growth model by Nelson and Phelps, who suggest that "education enhances one's ability to receive, decode, and understand information"—or, in short, that "educated people make good innovators" (1966). It is developed extensively by Welch (1970) as the "allocative effect" of education.

contraception, in general, and less reluctant to adopt certain contraceptive techniques, in particular. In the economists' terminology, the psychic costs of using contraceptive devices—costs in terms of conflicts with beliefs or exposure to embarrassment—may be lowered by education.[20]

Another important aspect of production is the manner in which factors of production are utilized. If education increases one's ability to organize production effectively, the more educated not only would choose better techniques of production but also would use the chosen technique more proficiently. The effectiveness of many contraceptive techniques is notoriously sensitive to the care and regularity with which they are used. Education may therefore have a relatively large influence on the proficiency with which couples engage in fertility control.

Fortunately, over the past two decades demographers have collected a large amount of evidence shedding light on some aspects of education's influence on contraceptive use. Table 13-1 summarizes briefly some of this evidence from two independent surveys conducted in the United States in 1955 and 1960, each dealing with about 3,000 married women. The table indicates that the use of contraception is considerably greater among the more educated and that a smaller proportion of the more educated do not expect to use any contraception.[21] Among Protestants, the attitude toward contraceptive use was appreciably more favorable at higher levels of education. Among Catholics, the attitude toward contraception was less favorable at higher levels of education, although the rate of contraceptive use was higher.

The table also suggests that the more educated adopt contraception at an earlier stage in their marriage, and other evidence supports this observed tendency. Demographic evidence from less-developed countries further supports the findings of a higher rate of use and an earlier adoption of contraceptives among the more educated. Furthermore, for countries in which the average level of

[20] This is an instance in which an influence of education on tastes or preferences can be translated into an effect on relative prices.

[21] A couple was classified as expecting not to use contraception if the wife replied "no" to the question: Do you expect to use a method sometime later on to keep from getting pregnant? and *also* replied that she would not use contraception in response to these questions: If you never do anything later on to keep from getting pregnant, aren't you liable to have a child every two or three years until you are forty-five? Is this all right with you, or do you think you might do something later on to prevent pregnancy? See Whelpton et al. (1966, pp. 186-187).

TABLE 13-1 *Percentage of couples of a given educational level with specified characteristics*

Date of survey and source	Characteristic	Education of wife			
		Grade school	High school 1–3	High school 4	College
	Use of contraception				
(1955, p. 128)	Users (wife aged 18–29)	48	66	74	85
(1955, p. 128)	Users (wife aged 30–39)	49	67	73	84
(1955, p. 109)	Users (Protestants)	53	70	80	90
(1955, p. 109)	Users (Catholics)	41	59	61	62
(1960, p. 217)	Having used contraception	66	78	83	88
(1960, p. 189)	Expecting *not* to use contraception (total)	28	15	10	7
(1960, p. 189)	Expecting *not* to use contraception (fecund couples)	7	4	2	2
	Attitude toward use				
(1955, p. 166)	Unqualified approval (Protestants)	50	71	76	85
(1955, p. 166)	Disapproval (Protestants)	26	13	6	2
(1955, p. 167)	Unqualified approval (Catholics)	31	41	32	25
(1955, p. 167)	Disapproval (Catholics)	49	41	49	55
	Adoption of contraceptive (for couples with three pregnancies total)				
(1960, p. 194)	Using prior to first pregnancy	18	23	42	55
(1960, p. 194)	Using prior to fourth pregnancy	76	79	92	92

SOURCES: For 1955, Freedman, Whelpton, and Campbell (1959); and for 1960, Whelpton, Campbell, and Patterson (1966).

education is quite low, there is also evidence that a larger percentage of the more educated women have some knowledge of contraception and are aware of more contraceptive methods.[22]

Additional evidence from the 1955 and 1960 United States surveys suggests that among Protestants, more educated users tend to employ more effective contraceptive methods.[23] The earlier

[22] For example, in a 1964 study of about 1,500 women of childbearing age in Barbados, the percentage of women with any knowledge of contraception rose from 46 percent of those with zero to three years of schooling to 82 percent of those with eight or more years. The average number of methods known, per woman who knew at least one method, rose from 2.5 methods to 3.9 methods for the same two education categories. See Roberts et al. (1967).

[23] Studies of the use-effectiveness of methods in use in the 1950s suggest that the rate of conception per 100 years of exposure was about 14 for the appli-

study indicated that the rate of use of appliance methods doubled from the grade school group (42 percent) to the college-educated group (84 percent), and a stronger relationship existed for a single method, the diaphragm, which was used by 17 percent of the grade school group and by 57 percent of the college-educated women. Similarly, in the 1960 survey, among contraceptive users the rate of use of the diaphragm more than doubled from the lowest education group to the highest. For Catholics, on the other hand, although the rate of use of contraception rose with education, the more educated tended to use the rhythm method more extensively, with only a slight increase in the rate of use of the diaphragm and a strong decrease in the rate of use of the condom.[24] Therefore, the more educated Protestants tend to use more effective methods of contraception, whereas among Catholics this does not appear to be the case.[25]

Finally, a recent study, using a 1965 national survey of some

---

ance methods (condom or diaphragm) and approximately 40 for the less-effective rhythm or douche methods. See Tietze (1962).

[24] See Whelpton et al. (1966, p. 281).

[25] It should be stressed that most contraceptives are quite effective in a physiological sense and that the care with which they are used greatly affects their observed use-effectiveness. In light of the finding from another United States survey in 1960 that 32 percent of families using the rhythm method exclusively were classified as having incorrect knowledge of the ovulatory cycle, this method may be particularly sensitive to the precision with which it is used. See Westoff, Potter, and Sagi (1963, p. 52). Consequently, it is not possible to infer from the evidence cited that more educated Catholics are less-effective users of contraceptives; one can conclude only that they tend to use a method which, on the average, is less effective than other methods. This is particularly true since there is evidence that a larger proportion of Catholics than Protestants have correct knowledge of the ovulatory cycle when standardized by socioeconomic class (white-collar, blue-collar). See Potter et al. (1962, Table 2).

Nor can one conclude that education has no consistent effect on "efficiency" for Catholics. If conformity with religious principles is an objective, the more educated Catholic may be expected to be more aware of, and consequently to behave more consistently with, the Catholic Church's position on contraception. That is, the observed shifts toward the rhythm method and away from the condom for more educated Catholics is what one might expect with a broader definition of "efficiency," which includes for Catholics the nonmonetary costs of appliance methods of contraception. Given the debate among Catholic moralists on the oral contraceptive, the evidence of its relatively widespread use among more educated Catholics (see the text) is not inconsistent with this argument. (Jumping ahead, this point is further supported by the observation in Table 13-2 that in terms of fertility outcomes, more educated Catholics as well as more educated Protestants appear more successful in achieving their desired fertility.)

4,800 women in the United States, indicates that as of that time, the rate of use of the oral contraceptive was more than twice as high among college women than among those with eight or fewer years of schooling. This result held for Catholics and non-Catholics alike and persisted when standardized for age. Similarly, by 1965, the percentage of women who had ever used the oral contraceptive was more than three times as high among the highest education group as it was among the lowest education group. In addition, the report indicated that 14 percent of the grade school group and only 2 percent of those who had at least some high school training had never heard of the oral contraceptive.[26]

Although there are admittedly other factors for which one should standardize in considering the effect of education on contraceptive behavior, this very brief summary of some of the relevant demographic literature clearly suggests that education has an appreciable influence on contraceptive use. The more educated non-Catholics are more receptive to the use of contraception (measured by their attitude toward its use), use contraception more extensively (measured by the percentage of users), adopt contraception at an earlier birth interval, tend to choose more effective methods, and appear to have adopted the new oral contraceptive more readily. The more educated Catholics use contraception more extensively and have adopted the oral contraceptive more widely (13 percent of Catholics with a grade school education, compared with 33 percent of college-graduate Catholics, had ever used the pill). But for Catholics, education appears to have been negatively related to the use of the condom and to a procontraception attitude during the 1950's. Evidence further suggests that at lower levels of schooling, general knowledge about contraception is also positively related to education. In short, the evidence is consistent with the argument that education lowers the psychic and/or transaction costs related to contraception. The more educated behave as if they are more aware of, more receptive to, and more effective in their selection of contraceptive techniques.[27]

---

[26] See Ryder and Westoff (1971).

[27] The recently published report (Ryder & Westoff, 1971) on the 1965 National Fertility Survey, the sequel to the 1955 and 1960 GAF surveys utilized in Tables 13-1 and 13-2, offers additional supporting evidence. The report indicates that more educated Protestants and Catholics have a more favorable attitude toward fertility control (p. 101); more educated couples have a more approving attitude toward abortion (p. 274); and on an age-adjusted basis, more educated couples

Another interpretation of many of these findings, however, is that more educated couples simply want fewer children and, accordingly, have a greater incentive to engage in effective fertility control. In my 1973 article the choice of a contraceptive technique is considered in the context of an elementary stock-adjustment model for children. The 1965 National Fertility Survey data are used to study the relationship between the couple's level of education and the choice of a contraceptive technique, while holding constant the couple's current number of children (i.e., "parity") and the number of children the couple ultimately wants to have. *Within* parity-, race-, and age-specific groups, holding the wanted number of children constant, more educated couples quite systematically selected relatively effective contraceptive techniques. That is, holding constant a measure of the incentive to engage in fertility control, more educated couples used more effective contraceptive techniques.[28]

In the context of Figure 13-1, if education lowers the cost of preventing conception, *ceteris paribus,* the discrepancy between the desired number of children and the quantity of children effectively "demanded" will be reduced. A reduction in the cost of preventing births should be reflected in a reduction in the number of unwanted pregnancies, or in the amount of "excess fertility."

The demographic literature is again useful in indicating the effect of education on these factors. The evidence in Table 13-2 pertains to the extent of completely planned fertility (the proportion of couples that, if the woman was ever pregnant, conceived only when contraception was stopped for that purpose) and to the extent of excess fertility (the proportion of couples that reported that before the last

---

have used contraception more extensively (pp. 110-112, 120, 249) and, in particular, have adopted the oral contraceptive more widely (pp. 146-150). Consequently, a larger portion of more educated couples have "completely planned" their fertility and have avoided "excess fertility" (e.g., pp.240-242).

This study also reports a revealing statistic that indicates an important difference by education in knowledge about the timing of the fertile period in the ovulatory cycle: The percentage of women "correctly informed" about the timing was was 27 percent of respondents with less than four years of high school and 58 percent of respondents with four years of high school or more. These percentages differed by at least 100 percent for color- and religion-specific education groups as well (p. 130).

[28] One qualification should be emphasized. It is observed that more educated couples systematically use more effective contraceptive techniques. The results themselves cannot indicate whether these techniques are inherently more effective or whether they are observed to be more effective as a result of being used efficiently by more educated couples.

TABLE 13-2   *Percentage of couples of a given educational level with specified characteristics*

Date of survey and source	Characteristic	Education of wife			
		Grade school	High school 1–3	High school 4	College
	Fertility-planning status				
(1955, p. 130)	Completely planned (wife aged 18–29)	5	12	28	37
(1955, p. 130)	Completely planned (wife aged 30–39)	4	10	17	29
(1955, p. 130)	With excess fertility (wife aged 18–29)	19	12	6	4
(1955, p. 130)	With excess fertility (wife aged 30–39)	27	18	13	11
(1960, p. 247)	Completely planned (total)	6	13	24	35
(1960, p. 247)	Excess fertility (total)	32	21	14	11
	Desired and expected children				
(1960, p. 100)	Expecting the number wanted	35	46	52	55
(1960, p. 100)	Expecting *more* than the number wanted (total)	38	27	19	15
(1960, p. 100)	Expecting *more* than the number wanted (Protestants)	41	28	19	15
(1960, p. 100)	Expecting *more* than the number wanted (Catholics)	34	26	18	18
	Unwanted pregnancies				
(1960, p. 248)	Last pregnancy unwanted and occurring before any contraception used	15	5	2	0
(1960, p. 248)	Last pregnancy unwanted and resulting from irregular use of contraception	10	9	6	5
(1965, p. 1179)	Births between 1960 and 1965 which were "unwanted" (white)	21*		14	11
(1965, p. 1179)	Births between 1960 and 1965 which were "unwanted" (black)	42*		28	25

* These numbers represent a combination of the "grade school" and "high school 1–3" columns.

SOURCES: For 1955, Freedman et al. (1959); for 1960, Whelpton et al. (1966); and for 1965, Bumpus and Westoff, (1970).

conception occurred, the wife or husband "had not really wanted another child at any time in the future"). The observed increase across education groups in the proportion of couples who "completely planned" their fertility can be interpreted as reflecting a lower average probability of conception among more educated practitioners of contraception. Similarly, the decrease across education groups in the proportion of couples with excess fertility can be interpreted as reflecting the higher probability of conception among less-educated couples who desire no more children.

The figures in Table 13-2 pertaining to discrepancies between the number of children desired and the number expected can likewise be interpreted as reflecting the more educated couple's relative advantage in effectively preventing unwanted births. The table further indicates that unwanted pregnancies associated with both lack of use and irregular use of contraception differ by educational level. Such evidence emphasizes that the care with which contraceptive techniques are used greatly influences their effectiveness. Finally, the last two rows of Table 13-2 indicate the extensiveness of ineffective fertility control, measured by the percentage of births between 1960 and 1965 which were unwanted at the time of each pregnancy.

The empirical evidence summarized here is interpreted as offering support for the hypothesis that education favorably affects the proficiency with which couples control their fertility. The demographic evidence is weakened by the lack of more complete standardization for other relevant factors and by the vagueness of some of the concepts used. Yet the effects indicated in Tables 13-1 and 13-2 are quite strong in most cases. In nearly all cases they are stronger for one-way classifications by education than for similar one-way classifications by other variables. Furthermore, the education effects remain strong whenever a cross-classification by age and income is made.[29] The standardizations made in the within-cell multiple regressions discussed above appear to strengthen the evidence in support of this hypothesis.

Education and the "Quality" of Children

Although the discussion has focused on education's effect on family size through contraception behavior, this is not the only channel

---

[29] For example, the fertility-planning status for the 1955 survey is cross-classified by husband's income and wife's age and education, and although income shows no significant relationship, the education effect remains quite strong. See Freedman et al. (1959, Table 4-20, p. 130).

through which education may influence the number of children. In addition to affecting the costs of preventing unwanted children, education may alter the number of children desired. In the framework outlined above, the household produces both the number and quality of its children and selects the combination that minimizes the cost of achieving its desired level of child services. Economists do not, as yet, have an adequate definition of "quality" (see the discussion above), but one operational definition equates quality with human capital embodied in the child. If education has a relatively large effect on the proficiency with which one produces additional human capital in oneself, it may also have a disproportionately strong effect on the proficiency with which one produces human capital in one's children. That is, more educated parents may find it relatively inexpensive to produce any given level of child services with fewer, higher-quality children. If this shift toward higher quality is quantitatively more important than the related increase in the demand for child services, more educated couples will desire fewer children.

Considerable research has recently been begun on the determinants and consequences of preschool investments in children. Rather than summarizing some of these results here, I refer the reader to Leibowitz's chapter in this volume. One empirical measure of child quality may be the level of schooling the parents expect their children to complete. In my 1971 article I looked briefly at the relationship between the parents' level of schooling and the level of schooling expected to be completed by the oldest child in the household. The data used were from the NBER–Census Bureau's Consumer Anticipation Survey (CAS), a survey of some 4,500 households living in suburban Boston, Minneapolis, and San Jose conducted in May 1968.[30] The subsample consisted of households

TABLE 13-3 Regressions on the number of years of schooling expected to be completed by the oldest child (includes only households with one or more children; wife aged 35 to 39; 583 observations)

Means and standard deviation) of dependent variable		Education of husband	Education of wife	Income of husband (00)*	Standard error of estimate
15.7 (1.79)	(1)	.151 (.034)	.033 (.038)		(1.75)
	(2)	.127 (.036)	.031 (.038)	.003 (.001)	(1.74)

* Measured in $100 units.

[30] For a discussion of the CAS data, see Juster et al. (1969, pp. 216-227).

in which the husband and wife were both present, with the husband not self-employed, but working at a full-time job for 50 to 52 weeks in 1967, and with the wife under age 40. The latter criterion was necessary to avoid excluding older children, since the survey obtained information on the number (up to six), age, and schooling of children under the age of 22. Such a sample is clearly not a typical cross section of American families, since it is restricted to relatively young, suburban families in which the husband is employed full time, with average yearly earnings in 1967 of about $13,000 and an average educational level in excess of 15 years.[31]

The regressions in Table 13-3 control for wife's age (all women included were between 35 and 39) and include only households with at least one child. The expected level of schooling for the oldest child is quite high (nearly 16 years), and the variation across households is rather small (the standard deviation is less than two years). The evidence here suggests that for this subsample, the higher the schooling level of the husband and the wife, the higher the expected level of schooling of the child. This effect persists when a measure of the households' money income is held constant. Since these regressions do not hold constant the number of children in the household, the results reflect the net effect of the husband's and wife's educational levels on the expected schooling level of the child (its quality) through substitutions in production (between quantity and quality) and through substitution in consumption (between child services and other commodities). It is possible to interpret the empirical results in this table in the context of these various substitution parameters,[32] but far too little is known, as yet, to place

---

[31] About 11 percent of the households had earnings of $8,000 or below, with only 2½ percent having less than 12 years of schooling. The educational level of the wives averaged nearly 14 years, with about 3½ percent having attained less than 12 years of schooling.

By way of comparison, the Census Bureau reports that the median educational level of men aged 25 or above in 1968 was 12.1 years and that the mean income (not earnings) of men aged 25 or above in 1967 was $7,418 (U.S. Bureau of the Census, 1970, *Consumer Income,* Tables A and B).

[32] If education is technologically biased toward the production of quality in children, *ceteris paribus,* this would induce substitution toward quality with an increase in the educational level of either parent. If the wife's time is used relatively more and the husband's time is used relatively less in the production of children than in the production of other commodities, then the increase in the price of her time induces substitution away from child services, which can explain the observed difference in the relative strengths of the two education effects. Other explanations of these results can be offered, even in the same context of treating expected years of schooling as a measure of quality and assuming all children in a single household to be of equal quality.

much confidence in either the statistics themselves or any particular interpretation of them.

In the context of an economic framework of household fertility behavior, there are several reasons why the education levels of the parents may affect the quality of the children. The scant empirical evidence adduced to date suggests that the relationship between child quality and parents' schooling is positive; this evidence can be interpreted consistently in the context of that economic framework.

Education and the Quantity of Children

The remaining empirical research discussed here focuses on the relationship between the couple's education and the observed number of children in the household. The above discussion emphasized that· the negative relationship observed between education and fertility probably reflects the indirect effect of education through the economic factors of income and value of couple's time. Beginning with this simple relationship, we can attempt to separate out the effects of income and the value of time to determine the direction and magnitude of any remaining effect of education on completed fertility. Both the hypothesis that education improves contraceptive proficiency (and thereby reduces the number of unwanted births) and the hypothesis that education increases the proficiency with which households produce quality in children (and thereby tends to reduce the number of desired births) imply a negative partial effect of education on the number of children. If the observed effect is in fact negative, additional information would be needed to distinguish between these two production effects—both suggest that the *relative* price of quantity of children rises with education, either through a reduction in the cost of preventing births or through a reduction in the cost of quality.

The observed effect of education on completed fertility depends upon what related factors are being held constant. By the restrictive definition of the CAS sample, the data used here have already been standardized for urbanization and for much of the effects of income, work history, and so forth. Likewise, by the nature of the sample the observed effects of education tend to reflect the influence of higher education. For the subsample of 513 households with completed fertility[33] and wife aged 35 to 39, the means, standard devia-

---

[33] "Completed fertility" in this instance is defined by a "no" response to the question: Do you think you are likely to have one or more (additional) children at some time in the future?

tions, and a simple correlation matrix of several variables are shown in the following table.

Variable	Mean	Standard deviation
Education of husband (years)	15.2	2.5
Education of wife (years)	13.7	2.2
Wage of husband (dollars per hour)	6.30	2.28
Income of husband (dollars)	15,885	6,355
Number of children	2.94	1.20

	Simple correlations			
	Education of wife	*Wage of husband*	*Income of husband*	*Number of children*
Education of husband	.512	.360	.370	−.051
Education of wife		.170	.214	−.106
Wage of husband			.847	.053
Income of husband				.052

Table 13-4 indicates results for three regressions on the number of children in the household. In the first regression, the wife's education level is negatively related to fertility. A negative relationship between wife's education and fertility is frequently observed; this negative association persists at the relatively high levels of education found in this sample. The husband's education level has no statistically significant effect on fertility. However, an increase in the husband's education level, holding the wife's education level constant, implies a decrease in her potential market wage rate relative to his potential wage rate, and so the positive slope coefficient may reflect substitution induced by this relative-price effect.[34]

[34] Suppose the appropriate variables for the regression were the wife's relative wage rate (a measure of her relative value of time) and the husband's education level. Since human capital theory suggests that the log of earnings is linearly related to the level of schooling, given certain assumptions, the wife's relative full-time earnings are proportionate to the absolute difference in the couple's educational levels:

$$ln(Y_w / Y_h) = r(E_w - E_h)$$

where Y is income, E is number of years of education, r is the rate of return to education, and the subscripts denote wife and husband. Then, using the difference in their education levels to represent the relative value of the wife's time, the estimating equation would be:

$$N_i = a + b_1(E_{w_i} - E_{h_i}) + c_1(E_{h_i}) + e_i$$

TABLE 13-4
Regressions on the number of children in the household (wife aged 35 to 39; completed fertility; 513 observations)

	Education of husband	Education of wife	Wage of husband*	Income of husband (00)†	Standard error of estimate
(1)	.002 (.024)	−.060 (.028)			(1.191)
(2)	−.012 (.026)	−.062 (.028)		.002 (.001)	(1.189)
(3)	−.014 (.026)	−.061 (.028)	.018 (.044)	.001 (.002)	(1.190)

* Current hourly rate.
† Measured in $100 units.

To control for the effects of income on fertility, the husband's full time age-adjusted income[35] is included in regression 2 of Table 13 4. The implied income elasticity at the point of means is +.09.[36] The wife's education variable is again negative and statistically significant; the husband's education variable remains statistically insignificant.[37]

To attempt to adjust for the husband's price of time and thereby determine its separate effect on fertility (distinguishing it from the effects of income and education), the husband's current hourly wage

---

where N is the number of children in the household. In a manner analogous to Mincer's discussion (1962) of estimating a labor supply function for married women, b_1 and c_1 can be estimated from

$$N_i = a + b_2 E_{w_i} + c_2 E_{h_i} + e_i$$

as $b_1 = b_2$ and $c_1 = b_2 + c_2$. So from regression 1 in Table 13-4, the coefficient for the husband's education level is −.058 (.026), a statistically significant negative effect. To put it verbally, as the husband's education rises in regression 1, the relative labor market value of the wife's time falls. The positive slope in the regression may reflect this substitution effect.

[35] The procedure used to estimate the age-adjusted income was to predict the husband's income at age 40 from his observed current income, basing the projected growth on information from United States age-income profiles for men with his educational level.

[36] Curiously, +.09 is also the income elasticity that Becker reported for couples who planned the number of their children, from the 1941 Indianapolis survey and also for college graduates in the 1958 Consumers Union sample. See Becker (1960).

[37] By the interpretation suggested for the previous regression, regression 2 implies $c_2 = -.074$ (.028), again statistically significant.

rate was included in regression 3.[38] The estimated income elasticity at the point of means in regression 3 is $+.06$, although the coefficient is now not statistically different from zero. There is no appreciable effect on the negative coefficient for the wife's education variable. The direction of effect of the husband's education level is negative, and the estimated coefficient for an equal increase in both education levels (i.e., holding the wife's relative value of time fixed) is $-.074$ (with a standard error of .028). The husband's wage rate has a statistically insignificant positive effect on fertility.[39]

These regressions suggest that for this sample of relatively wealthy, highly educated suburban families, the wife's education is negatively related to completed fertility. Controlling for the age of the wife, the negative effect persists when variables measuring the husband's education, wage rate, and age-adjusted income are held constant. It is not suggested that these regressions represent a well-specified, completed fertility demand equation, but rather that they indicate, with yet another data set, the persistent negative effect of education on fertility.[40] If such information were accessible, one

[38] The reader may question why the wife's wage rate is not similarly used. On practical grounds it is observable only for women who work; moreover, even if it were measurable, the potential wage of nonworking women would not accurately reflect their true value of time. The current wage rate of working women is not independent of their previous work experience or of their hours worked, both of which are influenced by the woman's fertility. So instead of calculating or predicting the woman's wage rate, the procedure here uses her relative education as a measure of the wife's relative value of time. The husband's wage rate (which is not subject to the same complications) is the link between the price of time and the price of goods in the cross section, where the price of goods is presumed constant.

[39] When entered without the husband's income variable, the coefficient for the husband's wage rate was $+.042$, with a standard error of .025. Consider the effect of the wage variable on the interpretation of previous estimates of a positive income elasticity of fertility. Even if it is presumed that the husband's time is not used in producing children, his value of time will affect the relative price of children. As his value of time rises, the cost of products which do use his time will rise relative to the price of children. This will induce an increase in the quantity of children demanded, implying a positive correlation between his value of time and the number of children in the household. In the absence of a "husband's value of time" variable, this effect is likely to be captured by the income variable, biasing its coefficient upward. Thus in cross-sectional studies which do observe a positive coefficient for the income variable, it is not clear that this reflects an income effect rather than a price-of-time effect.

[40] Similarly, these regressions in Table 13-4 would not serve well as estimating equations for predicting household fertility. Only a small percentage (about 2

would want to look at the influence of the couple's educational level on their fertility, holding constant the household's income and the relevant price-of-time measures for both the husband and the wife. Regression 3 in Table 13-4 includes measures of the husband's income and wage rate; thus the wife's education variable presumably captures the effect of the price of her time, whereas the husband's education variable might be interpreted as capturing other effects of education on fertility. Although the latter variable has a negative sign, the coefficient is not nearly statistically significant. There are several statistical explanations for this, but it will suffice to conclude, at this time, that the empirical analysis is unable to distinguish between these several, closely related effects.

Of course, the observed insignificant effect of the husband's education in regression 3 is consistent with education's having no effect on fertility independent of its effect through income and the price of time. However, other evidence—such as the results discussed earlier pertaining to the relation between education and contraceptive choice and to one aspect of child quality—seems to suggest that education does influence several other dimensions of fertility behavior.[41] These, in turn, would be expected to affect completed fertility. Clearly, these factors are not thoroughly sorted out as yet. As I said initially, this chapter constitutes a progress report on an ongoing research project, and it has dealt with relatively early results.

---

percent) of the observed variation is explained, although these sets of variables are statistically significant at about a 95 percent level of confidence. To predict fertility more effectively, additional variables could be added to the equations, but this was not done here. It is also well known that grouping the observations into homogeneous cells and estimating the equations on cell means would greatly raise the equations' "explanatory power," if that were of particular concern.

Another qualification which should be noted is that in these early regressions the effects of these variables are presumed to be independent and linear. Willis's study (1973) emphasizes one important interdependence between measured income and value of time. Several studies have observed nonlinearities, for example, in the relationship between wife's years of schooling and the number of children—the negative relationship appears to be stronger at lower levels of schooling.

[41] Although this chapter has not discussed the timing and spacing of childbearing, these dimensions of fertility behavior are also likely to be significantly influenced by the couple's level of education. As an example, it appears from these CAS data that more educated women begin childbearing at a later age and space their children somewhat more closely together. There is, furthermore, an indication from these data that more educated women space their children more evenly (i.e., at more regular intervals). (See Michael, 1971.)

References

Becker, Gary S.: "An Economic Analysis of Fertility," *Demographic and Economic Change in Developed Countries,* National Bureau of Economic Research, New York, 1960.

Becker, Gary S.: "A Theory of the Allocation of Time," *Economic Journal,* vol. 75, pp. 493–517, September 1965.

Bumpus, L., and C. F. Westoff: "The 'Perfect Contraceptive' Population," *Science,* Sept. 18, 1970.

Freedman, Ronald, Pascal K. Whelpton, and Arthur A. Campbell: *Family Planning, Sterility, and Population Growth,* McGraw-Hill Book Company, New York, 1959.

Grossman, Michael: *The Economics of Joint Production in the Household,* Center for Mathematical Studies in Business and Economics, Report no. 7145, The University of Chicago, Chicago, September 1971.

Juster, F. Thomas, et al.: "Ex-ante Household Savings Data: Some Preliminary Results," *ASA 1969 Proceedings,* American Statistical Association, Philadelphia, 1969.

MacLeod, John, and Ruth Z. Gold: "The Male Factor in Fertility and Infertility," *Fertility and Sterility,* vol. 4, pp. 10–33, January–February 1953.

Michael, Robert T.: "Dimensions of Household Fertility: An Economic Analysis," *Proceedings of Social Statistics Section,* American Statistical Association, Philadelphia, 1971.

Michael, Robert T.: *The Effect of Education on Efficiency in Consumption,* National Bureau of Economic Research, New York, 1972.

Michael, Robert T.: "Education and the Derived Demand for Children," *Journal of Political Economy,* vol. 81, pp. S128-S164, March–April 1973.

Mincer, Jacob: "Labor Force Participation of Married Women," *Aspects of Labor Economics,* National Bureau of Economic Research, New York, 1962.

Nelson, R. R., and E. S. Phelps: "Investment in Humans, Technological Diffusion and Economic Growth," *American Economic Review,* vol. 56, pp. 69–75, May 1966.

Potter, Robert G., Philip C. Sagi, and Charles F. Westoff: "Knowledge of the Ovulatory Cycle and Coital Frequency as Factors Affecting Conception and Contraception," *Milbank Memorial Fund Quarterly,* vol. 40, pp. 46–58, January 1962.

Roberts, G. W., et al.: "Knowledge and Use of Birth Control in Barbados," *Demography,* vol. 4, pp. 576–600, 1967.

Ryder, Norman B., and Charles F. Westoff: *Reproduction in the United States, 1965,* Princeton University Press, Princeton, N.J., 1971.

Sanderson, Warren, and Robert J. Willis: "Economic Models of Fertility: Some Examples and Implications," *Annual Report,* National Bureau of Economic Research. 1971.

Schultz, T. W. (ed.): "New Economic Approaches to Fertility," *Journal of Political Economy,* vol. 81, no. 2, part 2, pp. S1–S299, March–April 1973.

Tietze, Christopher: "The Use-Effectiveness of Contraceptive Methods," in Clyde V. Kiser (ed.), *Research in Family Planning,* Princeton University Press, Princeton, N.J., 1962, pp. 357–369.

U.S. Bureau of the Census: *Current Population Reports: Consumer Income,* ser. P-60, no. 74, Oct. 30, 1970.

Welch, F.: "Education in Production," *Journal of Political Economy,* vol. 78, pp. 35–59, January 1970.

Westoff, Charles F., Robert G. Potter, and Philip C. Sagi: *The Third Child,* Princeton University Press, Princeton, N.J., 1963.

Whelpton, Pascal K., Arthur A. Campbell, and John E. Patterson: *Fertility and Family Planning in the United States,* Princeton University Press, Princeton, N.J., 1966.

Willis, Robert: "A New Approach to the Theory of Fertility Behavior," *Journal of Political Economy,* vol. 81, part 2, pp. S14–S64, March–April, 1973.

14. The Influence of Education and Ability on Salary and Attitudes

by Albert E. Beaton

by Albert E. Beaton

INTRODUCTION Formal education has long been considered an integral part of the life of young Americans. Since the "Old Deluder" act of 1647, free public schools have been available to the American citizenry. Though most groups of citizens agree on the importance of education, the aims of education and the processes by which it achieves its purpose have always been a matter of debate. Some educators think that the aim of education is to train the mind to orderly thought; others argue that education is a practical method for transmitting important facts and skills; still others feel that the main purpose of education is to establish credentials and personal contacts useful in later life. There is furthermore the latent possibility that formal education is in fact irrelevant and that able young people will achieve the ends of education regardless of their schooling. If this is the case, the apparent effects of education result solely from the fact that the able students tend to receive more education.

Although there is no general agreement about all the objectives of formal schooling, some are commonly expected. Most persons, especially those in less-privileged groups, see education as a key to better jobs, higher salaries, and advancement in socioeconomic status — in short, as the route to wealth, position, and the accumulation of more and superior goods. A closely related expectation is that education provides the key to occupational and social advancement and thus to more productive, challenging, and responsible positions in society. It also seems to be widely hypothesized that those with more education tend to be happier and more satisfied in their careers.

However, many expect much more from schooling than the simple accumulation of knowledge and salable skills; they expect the educational process to affect values, ways of perceiving problems, use of leisure time, and general attitudes toward life and work. Some consider these intangibles to be of paramount importance. It is much more difficult to analyze and document the effect of formal schooling in these areas than in the areas of salable skills, partly because in the former there is no consensus on performance standards. It is not clearly "better" to be liberal than conservative, introverted than extroverted, and so forth, whereas there is general consensus about the proposition that it is better to be rich than poor.

We plan to examine some of the effects of education in this chapter, although the process by which education brings about these effects is beyond the scope of the study. The focus is on the following questions, a few of which have been more intensively analyzed in the chapters in Part One of this volume:

1 Do the more able persons receive more education?

2 Do those persons with more education make more money than those of equal ability and less education?

3 Are those with more education more satisfied in their work?

4 Do those with more education have different attitudes toward life in general?

5 Do those with more education have different views of the factors important to success?

6 Do those with more education have different views about the importance of various aspects of their schooling?

An examination of the effects of education is complicated by the selective distribution of education itself. It can be shown that on the average, those who receive more education have higher aptitude scores, come from families with higher socioeconomic status, and have had more family pressure for educational attainment. If these correlated factors influence attitudes or income, disentangling the effects of education from aptitudes, background, and so on, will tend to be difficult or impossible. A true experiment, in which children of varied abilities, social status, and family pressure are allocated randomly to parents with more or less education, seems neither socially desirable nor feasible. To examine the effects of education, then, we must control as best we can for extraneous influences and keep in mind that other factors may be plausible explanations for particular apparent effects of education.

BASIC DATA To detect the long-run effects of education, the sample must be restricted to older persons. As indicated in Chapter 3 in this volume, the effects of education on people in their twenties and early thirties are complicated by the late arrival on the labor market of those with more formal schooling; for example, medical students may not begin earning professional salaries until they reach their thirties. One might approach the problem by collecting a sample of mature men today, and then looking into their past to find out how they performed in their youth. However, the data one is likely to find from a random sample of this age group are likely to be so irregular and so difficult to collect as to be of little practical value. The alternative is to find a uniform data base collected years ago and try to collect uniform data on the current performance of sample members. Unfortunately, this procedure is biased by the difficulty—in some cases, the impossibility—of locating people. However, the analysis in this chapter is based on a sample collected in this latter way, which appears to be the more feasible method. This section is intended to give the reader a very brief overview of the basic sample and of the major explanatory variables.

The Sample The sample used in this study, designated the NBER-TH sample, consists of mature males (45 to 50 years old) presumably near the height of their careers and at the peak of their earning power. Most have long since finished their formal schooling, and the effects of education have thus been stabilized. This sample (described in Appendix A) was chosen because ability information collected when respondents were in their late teens and early twenties can be analyzed in conjunction with earnings, attitudes, and educational-attainment data collected at later points in time. In general, sample members have higher scholastic-aptitude test scores than the population as a whole and are more entrepreneurially minded. About one-quarter of the sample are in each of the educational categories: high school graduates, some college training, college graduates, and some postcollege training.

The men in the sample were all applicants for aviation cadet training in the Army Air Force in 1943. To qualify, a man had to be single, between the ages of eighteen and twenty-six, of at least average mental ability, and in sound physical health. It is important to note that all were volunteers for flight training. Because of segregation policies at that time, the sample is probably entirely white. Seventeen thousand men were in the original sample in

1943. Thorndike and Hagen followed up these men in 1955 and were able to locate approximately 10,000 for their study (Thorndike & Hagen, 1959). The National Bureau of Economic Research received information from about 5,000 of these men in the 1969–1970 follow-up.

We can speculate that the 1970 sample is a somewhat biased subsample from the original group tested in 1943. They are, perhaps, somewhat less mobile and more successful than those who could not be located or who did not respond. The 1970 respondents had slightly higher test scores on the average than those who were located in 1955.

The Variables After passing the Aviation Cadet Qualifying Test, these men were subjected to a battery of 20 tests, some of which were of a general academic type (reading comprehension, mathematics, etc.) and some of more specific orientation (two-hand coordination, finger dexterity, etc.). The scores on these tests are available for the 10,000 respondents in the Thorndike and Hagen sample. These 1943 test scores and the responses to the NBER questionnaire were used to create the variables described below.

Ability

The study of the effects of education is not tenable without a control for the effects of ability. Perfect control of basic ability is impossible, since no direct measures are available. We have no direct measures of native endowment, nor do we know what portion, if any, of the scores on intelligence tests is genetically or environmentally determined. In any case, most psychologists consider basic ability or intelligence to be a function of more than one set of variables. The school IQ test is widely used as a proxy for basic ability. Strictly speaking, this is a general achievement test that indirectly probes scholastic aptitude. IQ tests are useful in predicting school performance, since it seems reasonable to presume that those persons who have learned more—because of either high basic ability or advantages in lifestyle—will continue to know more and learn more. The relationship of IQ tests and nonscholastic activities is not strongly established. However, imperfect though it may be, scholastic aptitude, or IQ, is the most generally accepted measure of ability available.

This study uses two measures of ability constructed from the tests administered in 1943. It must be stressed that these are proxies not for innate ability but for ability in the late teens or early twenties. Although we may refer to these measures as ability, they are a summary of test scores that represent accumulated learning, skill in the manipulation of symbols, and, in this unusual test battery, visual acuity and some motor skills. The tests are described in Thorndike and Hagen (1959). There is no reason to believe that these measures are not affected by previous environmental conditions (see Appendix E).

The first general-aptitude measure was constructed through a principal-components analysis. The factor score closest to what is usually meant by scholastic aptitude, or IQ, is called *aptitude*. The aptitude scale has been transformed into a scale similar to that used in IQ tests; that is, the population mean is 100, and the standard deviation is 16. Presuming that the minimum IQ of this sample is 100, the scores have been converted so that the minimum possible score is 100 and the mean of this sample is about 112. The scores were divided by 10 for presentation in the correlation and regression analyses.

For tabular purposes, the individuals in the sample were classified into one of five ability groupings according to the tests taken in 1943.[1] We should note that this sample is limited to the upper half of the nation's male students, and thus measurement of the effects of ability probably will be limited. The lowest group in this aptitude classification is about the average of the male population in general.

The education and occupation (EDOCC) scale
Education is not a simple variable either. We can classify individuals into groups such as "high school" and "college," but this classification does not take into account the variation in the quality of education, which can be large. For example, it is possible for

---

[1] For this purpose, the three tests most closely related to a conventional IQ test were used: Reading Comprehension, Numerical Operations, and Mathematics. The highest ability group (5) is defined as those with scores on at least two of these tests in the upper quintile and no lowest-quintile mark; the next highest group (4) is defined as those with at least one highest-quintile score and no lowest-quintile mark; the lowest and next lowest groups (1 and 2) are defined comparably with lowest- and highest-quintile criteria reversed; the middle group is everybody else.

students at some high schools to receive training in calculus, whereas some college graduates never study this branch of mathematics. Simple classification by years of education also fails to take into account the type of education, such as engineering, liberal arts, or teacher training. Classification into education groups based on years is therefore a highly imperfect measure of the amount, quality, and intensity of education received. Nonetheless, at this stage of our knowledge we have no other realistic alternative.

Education is still more complex to analyze because of self-selection. In the post-World War II era the GI Bill made higher education possible for many who otherwise would not have attained this type of schooling; on the other hand, the loss of working years created incentives to seek immediate employment for some who might otherwise have gone to college. Thus the "education" variable reflects a desire for advanced education as well as simply increased educational input.

In this study, individuals were sorted into four education groups for tabular purposes: 12 or fewer years, 13 to 15 years, 16 years, and 17 or more years. All sample members were presumed to have the equivalent of a high school education; most had graduated from high school before applying for aviation cadet training. Those who had some post-high school education, such as a vocational training school, a junior college, or incomplete college education, were placed in the 13-to-15 year group. College graduates without further training were classified as having 16 years of education. Those who graduated from college and attended at least some graduate school were placed in the 17-or-more-year group.

An immediate result arising from preliminary analyses of these data was that this simple educational classification did not take into account one very important factor—occupational status—that could easily obscure the effects of education. One needs to make distinctions among respondents who are salaried, self-employed business proprietors, teachers, and self-employed professionals. We therefore extended the educational scale to eight mutually exclusive categories: self-employed with less than a college degree, self-employed with a college degree or more, self-employed professionals, and teachers. We refer to this scale as the EDOCC scale.

In the regression analyses, education and occupation are separated into one variable representing years of education and three dummy variables: one for self-employed businessmen, another for self-employed professionals, and a third for teachers. Each dummy variable is coded unity for respondents in that group and zero otherwise.

Dependent variables

The other variables used in this chapter have been taken from the 1969–1970 NBER questionnaire. These variables may be organized into sets which are covered in later sections: 1968 (deflated) salary, attitudes toward work, attitudes toward life, attitudes toward determinants of job success, and views on education. These variables will be discussed in some detail in their respective sections. The descriptive statistics—including means, standard deviations, correlation coefficients, the distribution of responses to individual items, and the average salaries of those who responded in a certain way—are shown in the tables.

ANALYSIS Since regression analysis is critical to further discussion, the basic regression equations are summarized here in Table 14-1. The first two columns contain multiple correlation coefficients showing the association between all 25 dependent variables and the major explanatory variables (column 1) and those variables plus all the interactions involving education and ability (column 2). The next five pairs of columns represent the regression coefficients and associated t-statistics for the five major explanatory variables: aptitude, education in years, self-employment in business, self-employment in professions, and teaching. The following 14 columns represent interaction terms in the same format. The results are discussed under the respective headings, which analyze a particular set of dependent variables.

Regression Estimates All the regression equations are statistically significant at the .01 level using only the five major explanatory variables except for extracurricular activities, which is significant when all 12 variables are used, and basic skills, which is not significant in either case. The equations in which the seven interaction variables add significantly to the equations with only the five major variables are noted with one asterisk if the addition is significant at the .05 level and with two asterisks if the addition is significant at the .01 level.

The t-statistics indicate the strength of linear relationships of each individual regression coefficient. We shall tend to view t-

TABLE 14-1
*Regression
equations of 25
variables on
aptitude,
education, and
occupation*

	Dependent[a] variables		Independent variables[b]			
	R_1	R_2	Aptitude	t	Education in years	t
1968 Deflated Salary	.376	.380*	1.007	5	0.812	9
Log (salary)	.430	.432	0.031	8	0.027	14
Attitudes toward work						
Enjoy work	.102	.111	—0.012	0	0.015	2
Challenge	.173	.179	0.014	0	0.042	5
Interesting	.144	.149	0.009	0	0.029	3
Compensation	.114	.136**	0.043	2	—0.001	0
Judgment	.172	.181*	—0.018	1	—0.007	0
Responsibility	.179	.190*	—0.031	1	—0.026	3
Advancement	.193	.205**	0.040	1	0.067	6
Attitudes toward life						
Voting	.063	.080	0.008	0	—0.011	1
Politics	.101	.116*	—0.004	0	0.019	2
Freedom	.124	.133	—0.007	0	—0.026	5
Financial security	.098	.110	—0.011	0	0.016	2
Integration	.216	.225*	—0.041	3	—0.056	8
Determinants of job success						
Own performance	.197	.207*	0.031	2	0.016	2
Right connections	.085	.100	—0.114	4	0.034	2
Congeniality	.092	.101	—0.040	2	0.029	3
Luck	.113	.126	0.009	0	0.051	4
College degree	.485	.488*	—0.044	1	0.217	18
Hard work	.229	.233	—0.013	0	0.026	3
Views on education						
Basic skills	.037	.059	—0.012	0	—0.015	2
General knowledge	.175	.185*	—0.021	1	0.064	7
Career preparation	.200	.203	—0.035	1	—0.090	9
Extracurricular activities	.043	.081**	—0.011	0	0.006	0
Social awareness	.089	.096	—0.043	2	—0.008	0

Self-employed business		Self-employed professional	t	Teacher	t
6.203	13	2.387	2	−5.752	3
0.134	13	0.046	1	−0.175	5
0.112	2	0.083	0	−0.033	0
0.209	6	0.164	1	0.055	0
0.163	3	0.175	1	0.066	0
0.156	3	0.058	0	−0.508	3
0.366	8	0.334	2	−0.565	3
0.326	7	0.282	2	−0.490	3
0.435	7	0.336	2	−0.712	3
−0.054	1	0.062	0	−0.196	1
−0.121	2	0.059	0	−0.206	1
0.003	0	−0.035	0	−0.014	0
0.012	0	0.354	3	0.131	1
0.098	2	0.079	0	−0.065	0
0.314	8	0.247	2	−0.471	3
0.103	1	−0.085	0	−0.108	0
0.074	1	0.309	2	0.126	0
0.277	4	0.165	1	−0.180	0
−0.510	8	0.670	4	0.904	4
0.465	10	0.404	3	−0.295	1
−0.010	0	0.149	1	−0.015	0
−0.035	0	−0.035	0	−0.495	3
0.005	0	0.101	0	0.170	1
0.067	1	0.215	1	0.257	1
−0.039	0	0.192	1	0.237	1

TABLE 14-1 *(Continued)*

	Independent interaction variables[c]				
	Education/ aptitude	*t*	*Education/ business*	*t*	*Education/ profession*
1968 Deflated Salary	−0.001	0	0.490	2	0.764
Log (salary)	−0.001	0	0.008	1	0.010
Attitudes toward work					
Enjoy work	−0.005	0	0.001	0	0.040
Challenge	−0.014	2	−0.014	0	0.028
Interesting	−0.006	0	−0.017	0	0.025
Compensation	−0.008	1	0.011	0	0.094
Judgment	−0.008	1	0.013	0	0.013
Responsibility	−0.011	1	0.010	0	0.054
Advancement	−0.027	3	0.010	0	0.012
Attitudes toward life					
Voting	0.001	0	−0.025	1	−0.007
Politics	0.003	0	−0.028	1	−0.015
Freedom	0.001	0	0.006	0	0.035
Financial security	0.007	1	0.030	1	−0.041
Integration	0.003	0	0.035	2	0.017
Determinants of job success					
Own performance	−0.010	1	−0.020	1	0.009
Right connections	−0.007	0	0.015	0	−0.060
Congeniality	−0.003	0	−0.017	0	−0.051
Luck	−0.001	0	0.033	1	−0.094
College degree	0.009	0	0.054	2	−0.103
Hard work	−0.004	0	−0.030	1	−0.032
Views on education					
Basic skills	0.012	2	0.014	0	−0.011
General knowledge	0.002	0	0.013	0	−0.019
Career preparation	−0.002	0	0.021	1	−0.049
Extracurricular activities	0.013	1	0.059	2	−0.071
Social awareness	0.000	0	0.010	0	−0.029

[a] The dependent variables are discussed in the text.

[b] Some linear independent variables — self-employed business, self-employed profession, and teacher — are coded unity if a respondent is a member of the group and zero otherwise.

[c] The independent interaction variables are the products of the corresponding linear independent variables.

Education/ teacher	t	Aptitude/ business	t	Aptitude/ professional	t	Aptitude/ teacher	t
0.346	0	0.440	1	0.098	0	−0.444	0
0.016	1	−0.007	0	0.000	0	−0.015	1
0.056	1	0.009	0	−0.050	1	−0.012	0
0.040	0	−0.041	1	−0.011	0	−0.013	0
0.047	1	−0.031	0	−0.036	0	−0.025	0
0.159	3	0.058	1	−0.016	0	0.035	0
0.141	3	0.016	0	−0.039	0	0.085	1
0.135	2	0.011	0	−0.042	0	0.063	0
0.145	2	−0.061	1	−0.061	0	0.093	1
0.038	1	0.019	0	−0.091	2	−0.020	0
0.138	3	0.038	1	0.039	0	−0.011	0
−0.008	0	−0.035	1	−0.056	1	−0.024	0
−0.008	0	0.016	0	−0.069	1	−0.059	1
−0.031	0	0.026	0	−0.134	3	0.024	0
0.126	3	0.034	1	0.043	0	0.075	1
0.018	0	0.059	1	0.202	2	0.010	0
−0.047	1	0.051	1	−0.009	0	0.049	0
−0.016	0	−0.070	1	0.064	0	0.045	0
−0.089	1	−0.012	0	−0.074	0	−0.038	0
0.068	1	0.056	1	0.066	1	0.067	0
0.008	0	0.022	0	−0.011	0	0.028	0
0.130	2	0.033	0	0.096	1	0.093	1
0.035	0	−0.042	1	0.035	0	−0.090	1
0.051	1	−0.059	1	−0.034	0	−0.054	0
0.039	0	−0.067	1	0.043	0	−0.093	1

statistics greater than 2 as significant for main effects, but to ignore interaction effects unless the entirety of the interaction variables contribute significantly.[2]

Do the More Able Receive More Education?

Before proceeding to examine the effects of education, we must answer two questions previously raised: Is education, in fact, correlated with ability, and does ability provide a possible alternative explanation for education effects found for other variables? The basic data are shown in Table 14-2, which is based on the first 4,353 respondents to the questionnaire. The bottom line of the table gives the number of persons in each EDOCC classification; the last column is the number in each aptitude classification. The individual cells of the table represent the joint distribution of the EDOCC and aptitude scales. The first line is the actual number of persons in each cross-classification; the second line is the number expected if persons were allocated proportionally to the row and column totals; and the third line contrasts the observed and expected cell frequencies by dividing the difference of the observed and expected by the square root of expected frequencies.

Observing first the employed persons, we note that the observed frequency is much larger than we would have expected in the upper left-hand corner, indicating that those in the lower aptitude categories were much more highly represented in the no-college or some-college category. On the other hand, the observed frequencies in the two highest aptitude categories are much higher than expected in the categories of college graduate and some graduate school. A similar pattern is observed for self-employed business proprietors, although the deviations are less marked than those for the salaried group. The professional self-employed group is drawn much more from the higher aptitude group than would be expected if aptitude made no difference. Teachers show no systematic pattern except for being underrepresented at both aptitude group extremes. The chi-square statistic for this table is 204.4 (n.d.f. $=$ 28), which indicates a very small probability that this sample was randomly selected from a population in which there was no relationship between aptitude and EDOCC.

We conclude, not surprisingly, that there is a relationship be-

---

[2] Statistical significance is not a strictly appropriate concept here since neither random sampling nor other statistical assumptions are met. However, we shall use the measures of significance, t-statistics and F-statistics, as measures of strength of association and hence as indicators of relationships worth pursuing.

TABLE 14-2 *Joint occurrence of ability, education, and occupation*

	Salaried employees				Self-employed				Total N
	≤12 yr	13–15 yr	16 yr	17+ yr	≤16 yr ed.	16+ yr. ed.	Prof.	Teachers	
Ability 1									
O	172	151	107	42	97	25	30	20	644
E	117.5	115.5	136.4	74.1	81.1	42.3	42.3	34.8	
Δ	5.0	3.3	−2.5	−3.7	1.8	−2.7	−1.9	−2.5	
Ability 2									
O	208	198	206	92	154	72	51	66	1,047
E	191.0	187.8	221.8	120.5	131.8	68.8	68.8	56.5	
Δ	1.2	0.7	−1.1	−2.6	1.9	0.4	−2.1	1.3	
Ability 3									
O	279	271	331	191	196	110	115	96	1,589
E	289.8	285.1	336.6	182.9	200.0	104.4	104.4	85.8	
Δ	−0.6	−0.8	−0.3	0.6	−0.3	0.5	1.0	1.1	
Ability 4									
O	99	126	179	97	75	55	59	38	728
E	132.8	130.6	154.2	83.8	91.6	47.8	47.8	39.3	
Δ	−2.9	−0.4	2.0	1.4	−1.7	1.0	1.6	−0.2	
Ability 5									
O	36	35	99	79	26	24	31	15	345
E	62.9	61.9	73.1	39.7	43.4	22.7	22.7	18.6	
Δ	−3.4	−3.4	3.0	6.2	−2.6	0.3	1.8	−0.8	
Total N	794	781	922	501	548	286	286	235	4,353

NOTE: The line labeled O represents observed counts, E represents expected counts, and $\Delta = \frac{O - E}{\sqrt{E}}$ is a measure of discrepancy.

tween aptitude and EDOCC in this sample and that, on the whole, those in the higher aptitude categories were more likely to attend college than those in the lower aptitude categories. We note also that a sizable number of persons in the lowest group (of average ability in the population) do graduate from college and go on to graduate school and the professions.

Do the More Educated Receive Higher Salaries?[3] A man's salary is an extremely complex function of many things, including his occupation, the region of the country in which he resides, the opportunities available to him at change points in his work career, and a host of other factors. The relationship between education and salary is further complicated by personal decisions such as the selection of less remunerative but preferred occupations or factors such as the existence of property income, which may reduce or eliminate the need for a salary. Any relationship between education and salary may be influenced by the differential aptitude of those in different educational categories. Thus we ask the more specific question: Do persons with more education receive larger salaries than those of equal ability but with less education?

Table 14-1 contains two regression equations that measure the relationship between salary and the logarithm of salary with the explanatory variables. Interaction terms are included to detect differential slopes of some explanators at different levels of others.

Salary is measured in thousands of dollars. Statistically, both the multiple correlation of salary and the log of salary are highly significant. Salary does not, of course, have a Gaussian distribution; thus the logarithmic transformation tends to deemphasize the occasional very large salary. Salaries have already been trimmed, in the sense that those greater than $100,000 were set at $99,999, while the deflation to 1955 dollars further reduced the maximum possible salary to about $85,000. In both cases, the multiple correlations indicate substantial predictability from these few variables.

The t-statistics associated with the regression coefficients may be used as a rough measure of the importance of the individual regression coefficients. Almost all the major variables in these regression equations have t-values greater than 2, and in some cases they are very much greater. The largest t-statistic in the salary

---

[3] This analysis is essentially descriptive. For an economic analysis, see Chaps. 2 to 5 in this volume.

equation is associated with the business proprietors' regression coefficient, which indicates that self-employed businessmen had average earnings of $6,203 more than salaried employees after adjustment for education and ability. The significant positive interaction of education and business proprietorship indicates that the gap between self-employed and other employed is larger for the more educated. The same type of relationship also holds, but to a lesser degree, for self-employed professionals. The effects of self-employment must be interpreted with self-selection in mind. It seems reasonable that this group represents mostly *successful* self-employed, since those who failed in business would probably have taken a salaried position by this age. The effect may not, therefore, be considered an estimate of the gain in salary that would occur if the salaried employees randomly switched to self-employment.

Education has the next highest effect. Under the assumptions of the linear model, the regression coefficients of .812 indicate that persons with more education have higher salaries; over the range of this sample (from 12 to 20 years of education) those with an additional year of education averaged over $800 more than those with a year less, making the difference over the eight-year span more than $6,000. Since these are partial regression coefficients, this effect is additive to that of ability.

Ability also has an important effect independent of education. Assuming that the ability measure is roughly equivalent to an IQ scale, we can say that those persons with IQ's 10 points higher averaged around $1,000 more in salary. Since there is no interaction of education and ability, this difference is apparently not related to levels of education.[4]

The teachers in the sample are at a special disadvantage. Teachers earn almost $6,000 less than others of equivalent ability and education.

The regression of the log of salary on these same variables indicates roughly the same important factors, except that the logarithmic scale manages to cancel out the interaction effects.

The effects of ability, education, and employment status on salary can be seen more graphically in Table 14-3. Panel A contains a table of effects for average salary. Notice that both the weighted means and the effects of ability increase monotonically with in-

---

[4] The model estimated in Chapter 5 finds evidence of interaction between education and ability, and Taubman and Wales find limited interaction.

TABLE 14-3
*Relation
between current
salary
(1968 deflated)
and education,
ability, and
occupational
status*

		Panel A: Analysis of mean values			
		Education of salaried employees			
		≤ 12 yr	13–15 yr	16 yr	17+ yr
Ability 1		(137) 0.948	(120) 2.338	(89) −0.046	(36) −0.842
Ability 2		(177) 0.526	(166) −0.119	(179) 0.414	(84) 0.310
Ability 3		(241) 0.663	(236) −0.607	(291) 0.830	(159) 0.719
Ability 4		(84) −0.334	(105) −1.488	(163) −0.781	(88) 1.759
Ability 5		(31) −1.803	(27) −0.123	(88) −0.418	(74) −1.945
	TOTAL N	(670)	(654)	(810)	(441)
Effect		−5.785	−3.146	−0.847	−0.412
Weighted mean		10.491	12.678	15.635	16.424

		Panel B: Analysis of median values			
		Education of salaried employees			
		≤ 12 yr	13–15 yr	16 yr	17+ yr
Ability 1		(172) 0.98	(151) 1.22	(107) −0.46	(42) −0.46
Ability 2		(208) 0.29	(198) 0.55	(206) 0.19	(92) 0.24
Ability 3		(279) −0.01	(271) −0.41	(331) 0.05	(191) −0.37
Ability 4		(99) −0.38	(126) −1.23	(179) 0.06	(97) 0.91
Ability 5		(36) −0.99	(35) −0.22	(99) 0.05	(79) −0.43
	TOTAL N	(794)	(781)	(922)	(501)
Effect		−4.58	−2.36	−0.34	0.69
Weighted median		9.12	11.01	13.41	14.65

creases in ability. There seem to be larger differences between salaries at the extremes of the ability scale. Salary also increases monotonically with education for both employed and self-employed. The big difference here seems to be between the college-educated and the non-college educated. The most unusual group in the table are the highest-ability noncollege-graduate self-employed business-

Education of self-employed businessman		Self-employed professional	Teachers	Total N	Ability effect	Weighted mean
12–15 yr	16+ yr					
(70) −2.663	(17) 0.542	(19) −0.851	(20) 0.574	(508)	−2.199	12.919
(105) −2.109	(55) 2.421	(31) −2.061	(55) 0.619	(852)	−0.766	14.505
(130) −1.736	(82) −1.122	(80) 1.083	(73) 0.170	(1,292)	−0.580	14.942
(54) −1.110	(30) 0.025	(41) 2.428	(32) −0.499	(605)	0.547	15.985
(21) 7.617	(22) −1.866	(23) −0.599	(14) −0.863	(300)	2.997	18.632
(380)	(214)	(194)	(194)	(3,557)		
3.841	6.366	4.558	−4.575		16.484	
18.350	22.709	21.412	11.707			15.037

Self-employed businessman		Self-employed professional	Teachers	Total N	Ability effect	Weighted median
12–15 yr	16+ yr					
(97) 0.55	(25) 0.88	(30) −2.96	(20) .23	(644)	−1.56	10.66
(154) −0.09	(72) 0.02	(51) −1.85	(66) 0.70	(1,047)	−0.70	12.06
(196) −0.78	(110) 1.14	(115) 0.09	(96) −0.60	(1,589)	−0.07	12.67
(75) −1.07	(55) 1.09	(59) 1.72	(39) −1.15	(728)	0.65	13.27
(26) 1.31	(24) −3.23	(31) 2.85	(15) 0.70	(345)	1.80	15.18
(548)	(286)	(286)	(235)	(4,353)		
−0.05	3.99	5.41	−2.44			13.94
13.18	18.50	19.00	11.03			12.62

men, whose average salary is far above that of any other group in the table.

Panel B shows median effects. A median analysis tends to de-emphasize extremely large salaries, and so the medians are in general lower than the equivalent means. The relationships, how-ever, are the same as in the table of means, with the exception of the

TABLE 14-4
Questionnaire items for attitudes toward job

In this section we want to find out how people feel about their work. Just circle the number that best describes your own evaluation. The numbers constitute a scale ranging from 5 (highest, best, etc.) to 1 (lowest, worst, etc.).

	High				*Low*	
Do you enjoy your work?	⑤	4	3	2	1	18
Does your work provide a challenge?	⑤	4	3	2	1	19
Is your work interesting?	⑤	4	3	2	1	20

For the items listed below, how does your total work experience to date compare with what you expected when you first started? (3 = about as expected)

Financial compensation	5	4	③	2	1	21
Requirement for independent judgment	⑤	4	3	2	1	22
Responsibility	⑤	4	3	2	1	23
Prospects for advancement	5	4	③	2	1	24

NOTE: The most common response is circled.

high-ability noncollege-graduate self-employed businessmen, who are now no longer the highest-salaried group.

Our conclusions, then, are that education and ability both contribute to salary in later life. There are indicators that the more able a man is, the more salary he has, regardless of education, and that the more education a man has, the more salary he receives, regardless of ability. Those who are successfully self-employed follow the same general relationship, but at a much higher level of remuneration. The teachers generally receive substantially less salary.

Are the More Educated More Satisfied at Work?

To test whether persons with more education are happier and feel more challenged by their work, seven questions were asked. These are shown in Table 14-4.

The regression of these items on the explanatory variables is presented in Table 14-1. The magnitudes of the multiple correlations are much smaller than those for salary. One reason for this is the homogeneity of response of the sample. Table 14-5 shows the number of persons responding in each category. Of the total sample, 59 percent responded in the highest possible category for the enjoyment of work, and about 88 percent responded in one of the top two categories. Thus almost all persons respond that they enjoy their work, and there can be little difference between the more or less educated or between the more or less able. The distribution of responses is similar for all items except those dealing with financial

	Number	Percent distribution	Mean salary
TABLE 14-5 **Responses to** **questionnaire** **items on** **attitudes toward** **job**			
Enjoy work?			
1	50	1.0	11.2263
2	65	1.3	12.8007
3	496	10.0	12.3209
4	1,437	28.9	14.0508
5	2,929	58.9	16.4036
Work challenging?			
1	93	1.9	10.3173
2	127	2.6	10.3957
3	525	10.6	12.2776
4	1,136	23.0	13.4381
5	3,078	62.1	16.7440
Work interesting?			
1	60	1.2	11.1242
2	95	2.0	11.4588
3	567	11.4	12.7870
4	1,335	27.0	13.3989
5	2,900	58.5	16.7372
Financial compensation			
1	109	2.2	9.6190
2	449	9.1	11.0635
3	1,712	34.5	12.2969
4	1,501	30.3	14.8627
5	1,185	23.9	21.9786
Independent judgment			
1	54	1.1	11.0483
2	204	4.1	11.0904
3	1,356	27.5	13.6093
4	1,505	30.5	13.9745
5	1,810	36.7	18.1240
Responsibility			
1	39	0.8	12.7826
2	190	3.8	11.9103
3	1,189	24.1	13.7002
4	1,365	27.6	13.5217
5	2,160	43.7	17.4811

TABLE 14-5
(continued)

	Number	Percent distribution	Mean salary
Advancement			
1	368	7.5	11.2538
2	556	11.4	11.3509
3	1,741	35.6	13.5897
4	1,088	22.3	15.3702
5	1,131	23.2	20.4778

compensation and prospects for advancement. We are therefore trying to find differences due to education, ability, and employment status on items on which almost all respondents agreed.

The most interesting factor in the regression analysis is the set of large t-values associated with the dummy variable for self-employed businessmen. Self-employed businessmen, when compared with salaried employees, claim to enjoy their work more, find their work more challenging and interesting, and find the financial rewards, requirements for independent judgment, responsibility, and prospects for advancement all better than they expected. The self-employment factor is, then, quite important in determining attitudes toward work. The self-employed professionals tended to respond higher than the salaried subjects on the requirements for independent judgment, responsibility, and prospects for advancement.

Those with more years of education tended to find their work more enjoyable, more challenging, and more interesting than those with less education and to feel that their chances for advancement were better, although the former group tended to feel that they had less responsibility than they expected when they started. Teachers responded about the same as the salaried as far as enjoying work and finding work challenging and interesting were concerned, but had negative coefficients on the other four items. They felt that the financial compensations were less, that the requirements for independent judgment were less, and that the responsibility and prospects for advancement were less than when they started. We should note that the teachers in this sample are not typical of teachers in general, since they are all males, whereas most teachers are female. Also, perhaps the teachers are men who are disappointed at not being school administrators at their present age.

The interaction between education and teaching indicates that these negative views are less strongly held by the teachers with more years of education.

The scores on aptitude tests in 1943 have but slight relationship to the responses on these items. In only one place is the regression coefficient significant: Those with higher aptitude scores are more likely to feel slightly better paid than they originally expected to be.

Since education and ability seem to be poor predictors of response to these seven items, what does determine whether persons claim to enjoy work? The answer seems to be in Table 14-5, which shows an almost perfectly monotonic relationship between average salary and response to these items. Persons who enjoyed their work and found it both challenging and interesting were those with the highest salaries. The ones who responded that they were better paid, that their work required the most independent judgment, and that they had the most responsibility and the best prospects for advancement compared with initial expectations were also better paid on the average. In most cases the difference between those who gave the highest response and the other groups is quite substantial, even though the number responding in the latter fashion was also large. Apparently, then, a man's salary has much to do with his attitudes toward his work or, conversely, a man's attitudes toward his work have much to do with his salary.

Education and Attitudes toward Life

As was mentioned at the beginning of this chapter, many persons expect much more from education than salable skills or success in careers. Some of these expectations may be manifest in such factors as participation in civic affairs, political persuasion, and attitudes toward social movements such as the youth revolution, toward society's concern with financial security, and toward the problem of racial segregation. To tap these areas, five questions (shown in Table 14-6) were asked, and the results are presented in Table 14-7. Most of these men always vote in local, state, and national elections; consider themselves middle-of-the-road to moderately conservative; and feel that young people have too much freedom, that most people have about the right amount of (or perhaps too much) concern for financial security, and that the races are integrating either at about the right pace or too rapidly.

Regression analyses of these items were performed to identify differences in attitude related to differences in education and in aptitude. The questions concerning politics, young people's free-

TABLE 14-6 *Questionnaire items on attitudes toward life*	3. *Please indicate with an X which of the following best describes your voting habits:*		
	Always vote in local, state, and national elections	☒	51-1
	Always vote in national elections, sometimes in state and local ones	☐	-2
	Usually vote in national elections	☐	-3
	Sometimes vote in national elections	☐	-4
	Seldom vote in any elections	☐	-5
	4. *Do you think of yourself as politically conservative or liberal?*		
	Very conservative	☐	52-1
	Moderately conservative	☒	-2
	Sometimes conservative, sometimes liberal	☐	-3
	Moderately liberal	☐	-4
	Very liberal	☐	-5

In this section we would like you to indicate your attitude about various social and economic problems. Please check the appropriate box and feel free to add additional explanation where necessary.

1. *Do you feel that young people today have too much freedom, too little, or about the right amount?*

Too much	☒	53-3
About right	☐	53-2
Too little	☐	53-1

2. *Do you feel that people today are too much concerned with financial security, too little, or what?*

Too much	☒	54-3
About right	☐	54-2
Too little	☐	54-1

3. *During the past 10 years or so, do you think that the pace of racial integration has been too fast, too slow, or about right—considering the welfare of the country as a whole?*

Too fast	☒	55-3
About right	☐	55-2
Too slow	☐	55-1

NOTE: The square corresponding to the most common response is marked with an X.

dom, financial security, and racial integration had significant education effects, but only the integration responses were significantly related to ability.

The voting-habits question had little variance, thus providing little opportunity to discriminate among the education groups.

	Number	Percent distribution	Mean salary
TABLE 14-7 **Response to questionnaire items on attitudes toward life**			
Voting habits			
1	3,860	77.4	15.0095
2	924	18.5	15.9208
3	98	2.0	16.3191
4	33	0.7	14.7070
5	71	1.4	15.5623
Political views			
1	420	8.5	15.4199
2	2,212	44.5	15.1846
3	1,540	31.0	14.8452
4	690	13.9	15.7035
5	107	2.2	17.5776
Amount of freedom			
1	71	1.4	15.3920
2	1,588	32.1	16.0161
3	3,293	66.5	14.7970
Financial security			
1	1,331	27.0	14.9470
2	1,790	36.3	15.9165
3	1,816	36.8	14.6153
Integration			
1	863	17.6	16.7969
2	1,972	40.2	15.4639
3	2,076	42.3	14.3111

Seventy-seven percent of the respondents indicated that they always vote in local, state, and national elections, and another 18.5 percent indicated that they always vote in national elections, but only sometimes in state and local elections. The overall average scale measure was approximately 1.3, which is near the "always-vote" side of the five-point scale. There were no discernible patterns of differences among the aptitude groups or the EDOCC categories.

The political philosophy question is related to education. A value of 3 on the scale indicates "sometimes conservative, sometimes liberal"; lower numbers indicate a more conservative persuasion, and higher numbers a more liberal one. The average value over the entire sample of 2.56 indicates an average somewhere between middle of the road and moderately conservative. The more educated respondents tend to be slightly more liberal than the less educated, although even the average of those in the highest education groups did not reach the middle-of-the-road category. The self-employed businessmen were noticeably more conservative than the others. The regression also indicates that the more educated teachers tend to be more liberal. It is interesting to note that the ability measure does not seem to predict responses to this item.

A majority of the respondents indicated a belief that young people today have too much freedom. This response was indicated by 66.5 percent of all respondents; the average response was 2.6 on a three-point scale. The regression analysis indicates a substantial relation with education, for there is a tendency for the more educated employees to be relatively closer to the "about-right" response. Teachers and self-employed professionals are the closest to the about-right position. Again, the ability measure has no apparent relationship.

There is a slight relationship between education and self-employed professionalism on the question concerning financial security. The average response was close to the about-right category. There is a very slight tendency for the more educated and self-employed professionals to feel that people today are too much concerned about financial security.

The racial-integration question has a strong relationship with education and also with ability and self-employment. The integration-is-proceeding-too-fast category was chosen by 42.3 percent of the high-ability self-employed men, but the about-right category was close behind with 40.2 percent. There is a slight tendency for the higher-aptitude groups to be closer to the about-right point than lower-aptitude groups. The relationship with education is monotonic for salaried employees; that is, the more educated groups are more likely to respond closer to the about-right category, whereas the less educated tend to be closer to the too-fast category. The self-employed businessmen tend to be slightly nearer the too-fast category. These results should be read in light of the fact that only 17.6 percent of this all-white sample responded that the pace of integration is too slow.

The average income for different responses (Table 14-7) shows no general pattern. The very liberal group, although few in number, have a substantially higher average salary than the other groups. The about-right category had a slightly higher average salary for the question about young people's freedom and financial security.

Those who believe that integration is taking place too slowly had a higher average salary.

Although these results generally indicated in Table 14-6 are true for all EDOCC and aptitude groups, there is a slight tendency for the more educated to be closer to the middle of the road in political views and to be closer to the middle of the scale on the questions about young people's freedom and racial integration. The higher aptitude groups are also closer to the middle of the road on young people's freedom and racial integration, but are slightly more likely to rate themselves as conservative.

Education and Attitudes toward Job Success

Although we cannot hope to disentangle the factors that lead to success in the work force, we have polled persons of varying success (or income) as to the factors they consider important. The items are shown in Table 14-8, and the results are presented in Table 14-9. The regression analyses in Table 14-1 show a number of strong relationships for different explanatory variables although none of the multiple correlations (except having a college degree) is high.

Overall, there is a strong tendency for respondents to consider performance and hard work to be the major factors contributing to success in their position; getting along with people and having a college diploma are ranked as very important, whereas being lucky is considered least important.

The average response was 4.4 on the five-point scale for one's own performace. The self-employed businessmen and professionals rank this item quite a bit higher than the salaried employees, and there is also a tendency for the higher aptitude and education

TABLE 14-8
Questionnaire items on attitudes toward job success

Below is a list of possible requirements for achieving success in a particular job or profession. Indicate on the scale where your own type of work should be ranked. That is, to what degree does success in your work depend on: (3 = average importance for success)

Your own performance	⑤	4	3	2	1	25
Having the right connections	5	4	③	2	1	26
Being able to get along with people	⑤	4	3	2	1	27
Being lucky or unlucky	5	4	3	2	①	28
Having a college diploma	⑤	4	3	2	1	29
Working hard	⑤	4	3	2	1	30

NOTE: The most common response is circled.

	Number	Percent distribution	Mean salary
TABLE 14-9 *Responses to questionnaire items on attitudes toward job succes*			
Own performance			
1	36	0.7	9.0764
2	67	1.4	9.9690
3	611	12.4	11.5320
4	1,334	27.0	13.9599
5	2,886	58.5	16.8198
Right connections			
1	920	19.0	15.9037
2	911	18.8	15.1177
3	1,595	32.9	15.2248
4	804	16.6	15.0765
5	622	12.8	14.5190
Getting along with people			
1	57	1.2	10.3632
2	107	2.2	12.9458
3	743	15.1	13.5613
4	1,620	33.0	15.3865
5	2,378	48.5	15.8694
Being lucky			
1	2,049	42.8	14.3135
2	940	19.6	15.3421
3	1,278	26.7	16.1031
4	326	6.8	16.8149
5	199	4.2	16.7712
College diploma			
1	828	17.2	14.2584
2	475	9.8	14.8062
3	1,280	26.5	15.6079
4	871	18.0	15.4279
5	1,372	28.4	15.5552
Working hard			
1	107	2.9	10.0377
2	140	2.9	11.3763
3	733	15.0	12.7895
4	1,343	27.4	14.3549
5	2,580	52.6	16.7918

groups to rank it higher than the less able or less educated. Teachers tend to think their own performance less important. The sample as a whole, however, ranked one's own performance very important; even the lowest aptitude or EDOCC groups had an average rank of more than 4.

There is a strong correlation between ability and the importance placed upon having the right connections. The more able persons rank connections less important than the less able. There is a slight but opposite relation with education.

The question of being able to get along with people had significant negative regression coefficients for ability, indicating that the more able tend to consider congeniality less important. However, the more educated as well as the self-employed professionals consider congeniality more important. This reversal seems to indicate that the most able consider ability sufficient, whereas the others consider congeniality an additional asset.

Luck is judged to be of below-average importance to all aptitude and EDOCC groups. There is a strong education effect, since the higher the education, the higher luck is rated, up to the graduate school level. The self-employed also rate luck more important than the salaried. There is no particular relationship between ability and belief in luck.

The importance of a diploma displays a striking effect. Those with more education consider a diploma much more important than those with less education. Self-employed professionals and teachers consider the diploma very important. The self-employed businessmen seem to think the diploma is relatively unimportant. The ability effect is quite small.

Hard work is considered important by nearly everyone in the sample. The more educated as well as the self-employed businessmen and professionals rate this higher than the less educated and the salaried. There is no discernible pattern for ability.

The respondents who placed great importance upon their own performance and hard work had substantially higher average salaries (Table 14-9); those who placed importance upon getting along with people and having a college diploma had slightly higher salaries on the average. There is also a slightly higher mean salary for those who think luck is important. The differences in mean salary for the responses to the question about having the right connections were very slight, but the lowest average salary is for the group who thought the right connections to be very important.

TABLE 14-10
Questionnaire
items on
attitudes toward
education

3. Based on your own personal experience, what do you think high schools and colleges should concentrate on? Indicate your choice by circling the appropriate number on the scale from 5 (very great importance) to 1 (very little importance).

	Great importance			*Little importance*		*Effects*
Basic skills (reading, mathematics, etc.)	⑤	4	3	2	1	67
General knowledge (history, literature, science, etc.)	5	④	3	2	1	68
Career preparation (vocational, professional, etc.)	⑤	4	3	2	1	69
Activities (school clubs, newspapers, sports, etc.)	5	4	③	2	1	70
Social awareness (current social problems, community action, etc.)	5	4	③	2	1	71

NOTE: The most common response is circled.

To summarize, this sample considers its own performance and hard work the most important factors in achieving success. Being educated and getting along with people are also considered important; having the right connections is deemed of little importance; and luck is considered hardly important at all. The self-employed rate most items higher than the salaried, except for the importance of a diploma. There is a tendency for the more educated salaried employees to rate all items higher than the less-educated salaried employees. The higher-ability respondents rate their own performance higher and the importance of contacts and luck lower than those of lower ability.

Education and Attitudes toward Education

Table 14-10 shows the questions asked to get an idea of what these men consider important in education. The results are presented in Table 14-11.

Overall, the sample considered basic skills to be most important for high schools and colleges to concentrate on. The average score was 4.7 on the five-point scale. The next most important item was career preparation, with a mean of 4.1. The mean response on general knowledge was approximately 3.8; for social awareness it was 3.4; and for extracurricular activities it was 2.7. Thus the sample considered the three R's most important.

The basic-skills item had no discernible pattern of responses

The multiple correlation of the item is the only insignificant correlation found for all 12 variables. All groups averaged over 4.6 on this item. Only one-half of 1 percent thought basic skills of little importance.

The general-knowledge item has a significant education effect:

TABLE 14-11
*Responses
toward
questionnaire
items on
attitudes
toward
education*

	Number	Percent distribution	Mean salary
Basic skills			
1	23	0.5	13.7591
2	49	1.0	15.4878
3	313	6.3	15.2990
4	717	14,4	14.3001
5	3,869	77.8	15.3842
General knowledge			
1	56	1.1	13.7289
2	240	4.8	14.6053
3	1,686	34.0	14.3015
4	1,748	35.2	15.0597
5	1,233	24.8	16.8074
Career preparation			
1	90	1.8	17.6643
2	187	3.8	19.5077
3	980	19.7	16.6765
4	1,253	25.2	15.3043
5	2,453	49.4	14.1440
Activities			
1	639	13.0	14.3441
2	1,203	24.3	15.0254
3	2,242	45.3	15.4388
4	641	13.0	15.6034
5	223	4.5	14.9870
Social awareness			
1	301	6.1	15.5967
2	605	12.2	15.5662
3	1,709	34.5	15.3468
4	1,426	28.8	15.0475
5	918	18.5	14.8050

The more educated a respondent, the more important he considers general knowledge. Teachers also value general knowledge more highly. Ability and self-employment do not show strong effects.

Career preparation was ranked in one of the two highest categories by nearly 75 percent of the respondents. There is a strong tendency for the more educated person to think career preparation is less important.

Nearly 70 percent of the respondents circled either the second or the third category for activities, indicating a tendency to think school clubs, newspapers, sports, and so forth, of middling or little importance.

Sixty-three percent of the respondents circled the third or fourth category for social awareness, attributing a middling to slightly more than middling importance to awareness of current social problems, community action, and so on. A negative relationship with ability was observed.

There is no particular salary differential on the basic-skills item, although the data show a slight tendency for those who think general knowledge more important to receive higher salaries. On both the career-preparation and activities items, the relationship between response and salary is curvilinear, with the extreme positions receiving lower salaries than the middle. The group that thought social awareness of very great importance had the lowest average salary.

The sample is fairly uniform in its attitudes toward education. The three R's are most important, with career preparation and general knowledge not far behind. Social awareness is considered of modest importance, and extracurricular activities of little importance. These attitudes have no relationship to aptitude. There is a tendency for the more educated to think general knowledge and activities more important and to consider career preparation and social awareness less important.

SUMMARY This sample represents a group of fairly successful men of above-average intelligence at the prime of their earning careers. The following briefly summarizes the answers to the questions we initially posed:

1   The more able persons are in fact more likely to receive more education than the less able, although a fairly sizable number of persons in the lowest aptitude group (about average for the population in

general) received college degrees and went to graduate school, and some entered the professions.

2 Those persons with more education do, on the average, receive larger salaries than those of equal ability but with less education. It is also true that for a given level of education, there is a tendency for the more able persons to receive larger salaries.

3 The sample as a whole enjoyed their work, especially those who were self-employed in business. The more educated persons found that their work was more challenging and more interesting and that it offered more chance for advancement than they expected when they started out in work, but they felt that they had somewhat less responsibility than they anticipated.

4 Although the sample as a whole is moderately conservative, there is a tendency for the more educated to be more nearly middle-of-the-road in politics and to be more likely to feel that young people have about the right amount of freedom, that people are not over-concerned about financial security, and that the pace of racial integration is about right.

5 A very large proportion of the sample felt that their own performance was the key to success. Persons with more education tended to consider the attainment of a college degree very important. They also considered having the right connections, congenial manners, and good luck important, but less so than the other factors.

6 Almost the entire sample felt that high schools and colleges should concentrate on the basic skills. The more educated persons tended to feel that general knowledge was more important and career preparation less important than those with less education. Education was not a significant factor in explaining the responses to the questions on extracurricular activities and social awareness.

Since ability was used as a controlling variable, we are in a position to make some comments about the effects of general ability on these variables. Aptitude as a whole is a less-forceful variable than education, although it has many significant effects after adjustment for education. As has been pointed out above, persons with higher aptitude scores tend to earn more money, given the same number of years of education. Persons with higher aptitude scores tend to feel that they are better compensated and are given less responsibility than they expected when they started out in business. They have slightly more middle-of-the-road views on integration than the less able. The more able consider their own performance important for success, but do not believe that having the right connections and congeniality are as important as those in the sample with lower aptitudes believe them to be. The more able are also less interested in the teaching of social awareness than those with lower ability scores.

Perhaps the most striking group in the study are the self-employed businessmen. Remembering that these men are those who are still self-employed in their forties, their salaries are substantially higher than the salaries of others with equivalent aptitude and education. They seem to enjoy their work more—much more. They are slightly more conservative politically and more likely to feel that integration is proceeding too quickly. They feel that all the factors contributing to success are important except for the college degree. Their beliefs about what high schools and colleges should accomplish do not seem to differ from those of the rest of the sample.

The self-employed professionals are better paid than others with equivalent ability and education except for the self-employed businessmen. The former tend to feel strongly on the questions concerning the use of independent judgment, having responsibilities, and opportunity for advancement. They also tend to feel that people are overly concerned with financial security. They rate their own performance, congeniality, hard work, and a college degree as being important. They do not differ from the sample as a whole in their views toward education.

The teachers in the sample receive substantially less income than others of equivalent aptitude and education. They tend to feel that they receive less compensation and have less opportunity for independent judgment, less responsibility, and less chance for advancement than they had expected when they began in their profession. Teachers do not seem to differ much from the sample in general in political and social views. However, they feel that a college degree is more important, and their own performance less important, than the rest of the sample. The only preponderance for teachers on attitudes toward education is their feeling that more emphasis should be placed on general knowledge.

Reference
Thorndike, Robert L., and Elizabeth P. Hagen: *Ten Thousand Careers*, John Wiley & Sons, Inc., New York, 1959.

Appendix A: Basic Data

by F. Thomas Juster

The chapters in this volume attempt to draw inferences about behavior from sets of observations about individuals—i.e., from samples of microdata. Many of the data sources used are relatively standard—the 1960 census 1/1,000 sample, the 1960–1961 BLS Survey of Consumer Expenditures, etc.—but a number of the samples analyzed in the volume represent nonrandom samples of individuals for whom a rich collection of information happened to be available. Much of the microdata that fit this category have been generated by researchers involved in the substantive work reported here and elsewhere. Because these samples are generally not representative of the population and are not widely known, they are described in some detail so that the reader can better understand and interpret the results reported above.

NBER-TH SAMPLE These chapters represent one of the first uses of what will come to be, in my judgment, one of the major bodies of data available for analyzing the returns to the quantity and quality of education. The sample has an interesting history. During World War II, the Army Air Force accepted volunteers for pilot, navigator, and bombardier training programs. The volunteers, who numbered some 500,000, had to pass the aviation cadet qualifying test with a score equivalent to that of the average college sophomore. Qualifiers were then given a battery of 17 tests measuring such abilities as mathematical and reading skills, physical coordination, reaction to stress, and spatial perception. Although these tests were modified during the war, a standard set of tests was used for 75,000 men during the period from July to September 1943.

In 1955 Professors Robert Thorndike and Elizabeth Hagen, of Columbia University Teachers College, undertook a study to determine the validity of these tests in predicting subsequent vocational

397

success. They selected a random sample of 17,000 of the 75,000 individuals tested during the July-to-September period. A very large fraction of the 17,000 people responded to the questionnaire—roughly 70 percent. Results of the original survey are published in Thorndike and Hagen (1959).

Thorndike and Hagen have shown that there were no significant differences in test scores between the civilian respondents in 1955 and the 75,000 volunteers tested on the same battery in 1943. When compared with the United States male population aged 18 to 26 in 1943, the air cadet group was more highly educated and recorded higher test scores; also, the tested group consisted of people willing to volunteer, which may be an important source of difference between the sample and the general population.

In 1968, the NBER contacted Professor Thorndike and learned that much of the basic information collected in the 1955 survey was still in existence. The mailing addresses for the entire sample of 10,000 were also available. The Thorndike-Hagen survey contains information on 1955 earnings, earnings for jobs held between separation from the service and the survey date, and some additional data on education and family background. However, the earnings data extended only to 1955; for many sample members only a few years of regular full-time earnings data are available after the completion of formal schooling. Hence the NBER decided to conduct a resurvey of the Thorndike-Hagen respondents.

Of the 10,000 (actually 9,600) respondents for whom we had 1955 addresses and who were in the Thorndike-Hagen 1955 follow-up study, we have managed to obtain detailed information from over 5,000 people on work and earnings history, educational attainment, family background, political and social attitudes, leisure-time activities, financial situation, and so forth.

The return rate for respondents who could be located is actually close to 70 percent in the NBER follow-up. Of the original 9,600, 300 had died by 1969; an additional 1,800 could not be located despite five separate follow-up attempts and an updating of addresses via the insurance and disability files of the Veterans Administration. Our basic sample was thus more like 7,500, with close to 5,100 completed forms being received.

The most accurate data on earnings from this sample are presumably those which relate to 1955 (from the Thorndike-Hagen study) and to 1969 (the actual mailing date of the NBER follow-up); data for other years are subject to error resulting from recall bias. Hence most of the chapters in this volume concentrate on the 1955 or, more generally, the 1969 earnings data.

SAMPLE BIAS As indicated above, the NBER-TH sample has more education than the population as a whole, as well as higher scores on an IQ-type test. Mean education in the sample is about 16 years, with a standard deviation of two years. Mean IQ is about 112 on a test for which the population mean is 100, and the standard deviation is 15. The sample is presumed to be almost entirely white as a result of segregation policies at the time and is heavily entrepreneurial: fully 20 percent of sample respondents are self-employed. Respondents are presumably less risk-averse than the population as a whole, as reflected both by their inclusion in a volunteer program and by the heavy proportion of entrepreneurially minded individuals. Mean 1969 income is roughly $18,000. Other relevant characteristics of the sample are described in the individual chapters in which the data are used. These include the chapter on education and screening by Taubman and Wales and the chapters by Hause, Wachtel, Solmon, and Beaton.

In the chapter by Hause, which uses the NBER-TH sample along with others, a number of observations were deleted. Hause eliminated independent proprietors, doctors, lawyers, teachers, and pilots and restricted the sample to those who were aged 44 to 47 in 1969. In addition, Hause eliminated respondents reporting poor health, those whose 1969 earnings were less than $500, and those whose 1969 income was more than three standard deviations from the mean, using the log of earnings for each educational level as the basis for the distributions. The final sample size in the Hause chapter was 2,316.

The Rogers Sample The Rogers sample is based on responses to a 1966 survey designed and carried out by D. C. Rogers. The modal group consists of Connecticut eighth graders tested for IQ in 1935. The age distribution is tight, with a standard deviation of 1.2 years. All earnings data are retrospective, obtained from the questionnaire. The 1965 figure is intended to be a reasonably precise measure of total earnings for the year. The 1960, 1955, and 1950 figures are full-time equivalent earnings based on inflated salary or wage-rate recall information.

The original sample contained 364 observations. By eliminating those reporting zero salary or wage for any year, those not working full time in 1965, those with a severe handicap, and three extreme observations (which were more than three standard deviations from the corresponding schooling means), the final sample size in the Hause paper is reduced to 343. These observations were rejected in order to reduce the extreme heteroscedasticity of individual earnings data that makes it difficult to estimate parameters of interest in small samples.

The Project Talent Sample

The Project Talent subsample is based on the responses of some 14,000 male high school juniors who took the Project Talent battery of tests in 1960 and who indicated positive earnings in 1966. For the calculations in the Hause chapter, respondents were eliminated who were still attending school, who worked only part time in 1966, who were farmers or in the military, or who reported poor health in 1960. Nonwhites were removed for separate analysis. For each of the five educational levels in the remaining observations, the mean and standard deviation of the log of 1966 earnings were computed; observations lying more than 2.75 standard deviations beyond the mean were discarded. The first group of criteria removed individuals who were not full-time members of the civilian labor force and specific groups whose earnings were heteroscedastic or subject to special influences. The second criterion eliminated observations in the extreme tails of the log-earnings distribution. This way of treating the data further reduces heteroscedasticity and is probably a low-cost way of improving the efficiency of the estimates (relative to no adjustments). The effective sample size was 8,840.

Missing independent variables were obtained either by assignment of modal class for discrete, nonordered variables or by estimation from subregressions using a flexible program written by A. L. Norman. No observation with more than five missing independent variables was used in subsequent calculations.

The Husén Sample

The Husén data are based on male third graders in Malmö, Sweden, who were given a series of four aptitude tests in 1938. Additional information was obtained from school and social records and a 1964 questionnaire (for which the response rate exceeded 80 percent). Information on earnings was obtained for 1968, 1964, 1959, 1954, and 1949 directly from archives containing a summary of data from individual income taxes. Thus these earnings are realized earnings rather than the full-time equivalent earnings reported in most of the other samples. No information was available on weeks worked per year or hours worked per week except for a questionnaire item that distinguished part-time and full-time workers in 1964. A rejection criterion for log of earnings exceeding 2.75 standard deviations of the corresponding mean (by schooling level) was applied and iterated once. Only respondents who answered the questionnaire were included in the analysis. The effective sample size is 455.

The "continental" schooling system, in which relatively few obtain high levels of formal schooling, prevailed when the Malmö third graders were tested.

The Consumers Union Sample

The Consumers Union panel was originated by the NBER for a study of consumer buying intentions (see Juster, 1964) and had also been used for a previous study of savings behavior (see Cagan, 1965). Panel members are above the national average in income and education. They are also meticulous, as indicated by their membership in Consumers Union and by their willingness to fill out long and complicated questionnaires. The response rates are exceptionally high for a mail survey—80 percent of the original panel responded to the first questionnaire.

The sample is certainly not representative of all United States households. Tables A-1 and A-2 compare the sample used in the Solmon chapter with all United States households, using education and income. College graduates predominate among sample households, and the income classes below $5,000 are small (although the income distribution is more similar to that of total United States households if the less-than-$3,000 income class is excluded). There

TABLE A-1
Comparison of education: Consumers Union sample and all United States households, 1957–1958, percent

Education	Consumers Union sample*	All U.S. households†
High school graduate or less	17.9	82.1
Some college	22.4	8.8
College graduate or more	59.7	9.2

*Excluding self-employed and not employed, incomplete questionnaires, and households with unusual gains or losses over $1,000 or with savings greater in absolute amount than 49 percent of income.

† Based on a sample survey of the labor force 18 to 64 years old in March 1957, U.S. Bureau of the Census (1959, p. 109).

		U.S. households†	
Income level	Consumers Union sample*	All	All excluding incomes less than $3,000
Less than $3,000	0.5	33.0	
3,000–3,999	1.7	11.1	16.6
4,000–4,999	4.7	12.4	18.5
5,000–9,999	59.2	35.1	52.4
10,000–14,999	26.3	6.4	9.6
15,000–24,999	6.3	1.6	2.4
25,000 and over	1.2	0.4	0.6

TABLE A-2 Comparison of income levels: Consumers Union sample and all United States households, 1958–1959, percent

* Excluding self-employed and not employed, incomplete questionnaires, and households with unusual gains or losses over $1,000 or with savings greater in absolute amount than 49 percent of income.

† Based on a sample survey of families and unrelated individuals in 1959 (U.S. Bureau of the Census, 1960, Table 5).

are also a disproportionately large number of teachers and government workers and a relatively small number of wage earners. Most of these distributional limitations may be avoided by breaking down the sample by income, education, occupation, and other characteristics. For example, although the sample has an average savings-income ratio much higher than that for all households, the difference in saving nearly disappears when differences in income are taken into account.

The data used for the Solmon study were obtained from the last of four questionnaires sent to the Consumers Union group. A doctoral student at Columbia University, Carl Jordan, processed the basic questionnaire data and was left with 6,291 observations; he then eliminated 64 observations containing errors, leaving 6,227. For the families on the original Jordan tape, some variables useful for the current study were obtained from previous questionnaires. It was necessary to eliminate 82 of these 6,291 observations for various reasons. Finally, the Jordan tape containing 6,227 observations was merged with the tape containing the additional variables (6,209 observations), and a tape with 6,056 observations was produced; the number of observations was smaller because only families appearing on both tapes were retained, and an additional 90 observations had to be eliminated because an income variable, supposedly identical on the two tapes, did not match.

An elaborate screening program was written in order to increase the accuracy of the savings estimates. Savings in 1959 was defined as the sum of changes in the value of assets between the end of 1958 and the end of 1959, minus the sum of changes in debt between 1958 and 1959, excluding capital gains or losses. Hence if an asset (or debt) was reported at the end of 1959 but nothing was reported for the end of 1958, the total amount of assets (debts) at the end of 1959 was presumably obtained during that year.

Since nonresponse could not be distinguished from a true zero, a screening program eliminated observations if an asset value for any component of financial and property saving appeared for 1959 but not for 1958. Exceptions were made for cases in which, despite the omission of the 1958 asset value, the respondent indicated that he had used personal records to respond—the implication being that in such a case a zero (blank) in 1958 really meant zero asset value. In other cases, a zero (blank) was presumed to indicate no response, and the observation was eliminated. A similar procedure was used if 1959 debt was reported but not 1958 debt.

This screening procedure was carried out for each component of savings; consequently, 1,818 observations were dropped, leaving 4,238. Too many observations were probably dropped, in that some people not indicating record use and having reported no assets or debts in a given category at the end of 1958 had, indeed, no 1958 asset or debt and had saved (dissaved) the entire end-1959 value during 1959. (However, if a zero appeared in both 1958 and 1959, the observation was not excluded.) The extra caution was employed in the screening procedure because it seemed better to reduce the sample size rather than run the risk of incorporating sizable errors in the savings data.

Thus the basic data tape used in the study contained 4,238 observations. Subsequently, additional observations were dropped for a number of reasons. We eliminated, for instance, those whose response to the educational-attainment question was unclear. Also eliminated were those families reporting husband's income or total family income of zero, as well as those with full savings (financial, property, and on-the-job training) equal to zero, since it was assumed that uniform zeros really meant nonresponse. The latter assumption would be invalid for any one asset or debt category, but the data used by Solmon obtained savings by aggregating across a large number of categories; it is hard to believe that a zero sum is a real number in such cases.

In nearly all cases extreme savings-income ratios reflect either unusual financial circumstances or errors; hence families reporting absolute values of the savings-income ratio in excess of 0.5 were eliminated, reducing the sample size from 4,238 to 3,387.

Several other questions arose with regard to pruning the sample further, in particular, the question of whether subgroups with special characteristics should be eliminated or analyzed separately. Three such groups were considered: (1) independent professionals and business proprietors (456), (2) 1959 house buyers (281), and (3) those with incomes under $3,000 or over $50,000 (20). (The figures in parentheses indicate the number of families in each group.)

In general, the effects on savings of groups 1 and 2 were studied by the use of dummy variables indicating whether the family head was self-employed or had purchased a home. The third group was small enough to be ignored.

References

Cagan, P.: *The Effect of Pension Plans on Aggregate Saving: Evidence from a Sample Survey,* National Bureau of Economic Research, New York, 1965.

Juster, F. T.: *Anticipations and Purchases: An Analysis of Consumer Behavior,* Princeton University Press for National Bureau of Economic Research, Princeton, N.J., 1964.

Thorndike, Robert L., and Elizabeth P. Hagen: *Ten Thousand Careers,* John Wiley & Sons, Inc., New York, 1959.

U.S. Bureau of the Census: *Statistical Abstract of the United States: 1959* (80th ed.), Washington, 1959.

U.S. Bureau of the Census: *Current Population Reports,* ser. P-60, no. 33, Jan. 15, 1960.

Appendix B: Mental-Ability Tests and Factors

by Paul Taubman and Terence Wales

The 17 tests used in obtaining the four factors discussed in the text are listed in Table B-1. A brief description of the tests appears in Thorndike and Hagen (1959, pp. 9–11), and a detailed discussion can be found through the entire book. From the titles and descriptions, it is clear that many of the tests measure different facets of the same ability. Rather than use all the tests or any arbitrary

TABLE B-1   *Factor loadings*

	Factor loading			
Ability test	*1*	*2*	*3*	*4*
Reading Comprehension	0.4123	0.0700	0.7186	0.0136
Mechanical Principles	0.0149	0.3522	0.7210	0.0247
Dial and Table Reading	0.6990	0.2566	−0.0129	0.3260
Spatial Orientation II	0.0658	0.1042	0.3117	0.6420
Spatial Orientation I	0.2217	0.1379	0.0311	0.7642
Numerical Operations I & II	0.7822	0.0597	−0.2183	0.1030
Speed of Identification	0.0500	0.1008	0.0643	0.7831
General Information—Navigator	0.4842	−0.1199	0.5605	0.1495
General Information—Pilot	−0.0811	0.0329	0.5874	0.3567
Mathematics B	0.7444	−0.0104	0.3514	−0.0717
Mathematics A	0.7464	−0.0469	0.3060	0.0571
Rotary Pursuit	−0.0304	0.6772	0.0453	0.0396
Two-Hand Coordination	−0.0385	0.6870	0.2703	0.0572
Complex Coordination	0.1251	0.7026	0.1877	0.2028
Aiming Stress	−0.0111	0.4128	0.0009	0.0093
Discrimination Reaction Time	0.3891	0.3800	0.0940	0.2636
Finger Dexterity	0.1974	0.5438	−0.1664	0.1253

SOURCE: All data in this table are from NBER-Thorndike sample.

subset, we used factor analysis to obtain measures of a few types of ability.

The basic idea in factor analysis is that any test contains information on one or more general abilities and on test-specific components. That is:

$$F = SC + u$$

where S is the set of scores, F represents the set of general abilities, and u is the test-specific components. Using the scores in each of the tests, it is possible to estimate C by imposing certain conditions on u. Estimates of the F can then be found from SC where the C are known as the factor loadings. Each F is, of course, just a weighted average of the test scores.[1] In some instances, however, the major weights in each average are attached to items that measure one type of attribute. The factor is then labeled by this attribute.

For the test scores in the NBER-TH data, the factor loadings for the four factors are given in Table B-1. Consider, first, the second factor, in which Rotary Pursuit, Two-Hand Coordination, and Complex Coordination all have loadings in excess of 0.65. In addition, Finger Dexterity, Aiming Stress, Discrimination Reaction, and Mechanical Principles have weights in the range of 0.35 to 0.54. The common element in all tests is coordination; consequently, we refer to this as the *complex coordination factor*. For the fourth factor the only important tests are Speed of Identification and Spatial Orientation I and II. Given the description of the Speed of Identification test, it seems clear that the fourth factor measures spatial perception and perhaps abstract reasoning.

Both these factors are easy to interpret or identify, whereas the first and third are somewhat more difficult. In the first factor the most important items with loadings of at least 0.69 are Numerical Operations, Mathematics A and B, and Dial and Table Reading, all of which are concerned with mathematics and quantitative skills. Unfortunately, secondary but still important weights (0.49 to 0.39) are accorded to Navigator—General Information, Reading Comprehension, and Discrimination Reaction Time. Although the navigator test emphasizes mathematical material, the other two

---

[1] Because the original test scores are standardized and then manipulated as correlation, all weights have to lie between plus and minus 1. The importance of each test in a factor is indicated by the absolute size of its loading coefficient.

	1955		1969	
Variable	*Coefficient*	*t-value*	*Coefficient*	*t-value*
Intercept	229	3.6	1356	4.4
Some college	54	4.1	193	4.3
B.A.	58	4.4	341	7.5
Some graduate	75	3.4	287	3.9
M.A.	51	2.5	351	5.1
Ph.D.	61	2.6	670	9.6
M.D.	300	6.9	494	3.8
Teacher	−162	1.3	490	0.1
Age (years)	8	4.1	−2	.3
Ability 2	23	1.5	69	1.3
Ability 3	33	2.2	107	2.1
Ability 4	50	3.4	144	2.9
Ability 5	84	5.7	279	5.5
Health	−33	4.4	−205	7.8
Single	−122	3.7	−237	2.2
Father, high school	26	2.5	108	3.1
Father, college	21	1.7	97	2.2
Biography 2	0.7	0.1	119	2.4
Biography 3	30	2.0	92	1.8
Biography 4	63	4.3	167	3.4
Biography 5	81	5.6	206	4.2
R^2	.10		.11	
Observations	3,500		3,700	

TABLE B-2 *Regression coefficients and t-values (Entire sample)*

NOTE: The dependent variable is monthly earnings in dollars. Education variables are zero-one dummies.
Ability i = value of 1 if individual is in ith mental-ability fifth and 0 otherwise.
Health = 1 if excellent, 2 if good, 3 if fair, and 4 if poor.
Single = value of 1 if individual is single and 0 otherwise.
Father, h.s. = value of 1 if father attended high school and 0 otherwise.
Father, college = value of 1 if father attended college and 0 otherwise.
Biography i = value of 1 if individual is in ith biography fifth and 0 otherwise.
SOURCE: NBER-Thorndike sample.

items do not; nevertheless, we treat this as a mathematical-ability test.

In the third factor, Reading Comprehension and Mechanical Principles have loadings in excess of 0.7; General Information—Pilot and General Information—Navigator have loadings of about

TABLE B-3 *Regression coefficients and t-values by occupation, 1969*

Variable	Professional, sales, and technical		Managers and owners		Blue-collar, white-collar, and service	
	Coefficient	t-value	Coefficient	t-value	Coefficient	t-value
Intercept	877	2.0	1781	3.6	866	4.6
Some college	86	1.1	95	1.2	32	1.5
B.A.	245	3.0	203	2.6	94	2.6
Some graduate	77	.7	180	1.5	158	1.8
M.A.	128	1.3	259	2.3		
Ph.D.	446	4.0	347	1.6		
M.D.	904	7.8				
LL.B.	584	5.8	66	2.0		
Teacher	−198	2.4				
Age (years)	6	.6	−2	.2	−.3	.1
Ability 2	103	1.5	30	.3	19	.7
Ability 3	110	1.6	23	.3	5	.2
Ability 4	130	1.9	90	1.0	55	2.0
Ability 5	30	4.4	225	2.6	30	.1
Health	−157	4.6	−257	5.6	−23	1.5
Single	−259	2.1	118	.5	−98	1.5
Father, high school	88	1.9	92	1.6	20	.9
Father, college	−84	1.5	157	2.2	−2	.1
Biography 2	105	1.6	91	1.1	−6	.2
Biography 3	48	.7	54	.6	43	1.4
Biography 4	40	.6	204	2.4	31	1.0
Biography 5	145	2.2	200	2.3	3	.1
Technical	82	1.1				
Sales	71	1.1				
Service					−46	1.9
White collar					−103	3.4
R^2	.21		.05		.04	
Observations	728		1085		208	

NOTE: See Table B-2 for an explanation of terms.

0.5; mathematics B and mathematics A have loadings of 0.35 and 0.30, respectively; and Spatial Orientation II has a loading of 0.31. In general, these tests encompass verbal ability, mathematical skills, reasoning, and mechanical principles. Since the first three items would be found in standard IQ tests, we have chosen to call this third factor *IQ*. However, it is important to note that Professor Thorndike believes that the first factor would correlate much more closely with IQ and should be named as such, while the third tends toward mechanical principles. The reader should keep this caveat in mind when examining our remarks about the importance of the different types of ability and when comparing the NBER-TH results with those of Wolfle-Smith.

Reference

Thorndike, Robert L., and Elizabeth P. Hagen: *Ten Thousand Careers,* John Wiley & Sons, Inc., New York, 1050.

Appendix C: Summary of Full Regression Equations of Log Earnings on Measured Ability and Background Variables

by John C. Hause

Regressions, for a single year, of the log of earnings on some ability measures and a more or less standard set of background variables are summarized in Table C-1 for the different samples and different schooling levels. The educational levels are not directly comparable for the different samples, and the coding should be checked in the main text. The scaling of the different ability tests makes direct comparison between samples meaningless, and the tests themselves would not be perfectly correlated. However, since earnings are expressed in logarithms, multiplying the ability coefficients by the standard deviation of the ability measure indicates the proportion (approximately) by which earnings are altered by this size of change in measured ability. This information is included in a number of tables in the main text.

The scaling and criteria used to produce dummy variables for high and low socioeconomic status differ greatly between samples and make comparison of coefficient magnitudes in the four samples meaningless.

TABLE C-1
Coefficients*
from full
regressions of
the logarithm of
earnings on an
ability measure
and background
variables

Education level	Sample size N	Ability† test	LNWK (log of weeks worked)	SCH (social class high)
Rogers (dependent variable: log of 1960 earnings)				
E_1	60	.024 (.35)		−.262 (.278)
E_2	117	.70 (.32)		.050 (.210)
E_3	51	.36 (.78)		.062 (.262)
E_4	68	.92 (.63)		−.106 (.174)
E_5	47	1.32 (.90)		.180 (.221)
Project Talent (dependent variable: log of 1966 earnings)				
E'_1	183	.02 (.16)	.489 (2.36)	.038 (.49)
E'_2	3853	.06 (3.24)	.488 (9.51)	.067 (4.00)
E'_3	1914	.00 (.03)	.514 (9.25)	.059 (2.44)

SCL (social class low)	RC (religion Catholic)	RJ (religion Jewish)	NM (not married)	S (southern U.S.)	PHLTH (serious illness since mid-teens)	PS (private school)	R^2
—.351 (.202)	.202 (.099)		—.473 (.180)			—.057 (.298)	.240
—.233 (.107)	.067 (.081)	.679 (.275)	—.045 (.132)			.072 (.134)	.165
.144 (.174)	.040 (.153)	.696 (.376)	—.744 (.390)			.556 (.238)	.298
—.119 (.182)	.114 (.139)	.170 (.270)	—.843 (.251)			.338 (.162)	.212
.020 (.222)	.566 (.210)	.636 (.245)	—.695 (.386)			.063 (.245)	.319

SCL (social class low)	RC (religion Catholic)	RJ (religion Jewish)	NM (not married)	S (southern U.S.)	PARS	PRVS	R^2
—.083 (1.20)	.042 (.67)	.203 (.88)	—.166 (2.53)	—.236 (2.74)	.023 (.11)	.026 (.09)	.136
—.046 (2.84)	.041 (2.57)	.050 (.91)	—.298 (21.3)	—.068 (3.57)	—.030 (.99)	.224 (3.59)	.149
.012 (.38)	.068 (2.45)	.093 (1.66)	—.320 (14.5)	—.095 (3.11)	—.017 (.42)	.001 (.02)	.156

TABLE C-1
(continued)

Education level	Sample size N	Ability† test	LNWK (log of weeks worked)	SCH (social class high)
Project Talent: (dependent variable: log of 1966 earnings) (continued)				
E'_4	793	—.03 (.56)	.702 (12.0)	.062 (1.49)
E'_5	2534	.06 (2.24)	.719 (34.3)	.038 (1.57)
NBER-Thorndike (dependent variable: log of 1969 earnings)				
E_1^+	489	.0267 (.0102)		—.059 (.092)
E_2^+	535	.021 (.011)		—.039 (.069)
E_3^+	900	.026 (.007)		.003 (.039)
E_4^+	211	.072 (.014)		—.011 (.086)
E_5^+	128	.044 (.024)		—.237 (.126)
E_6^+	53	.030 (.034)		—.356 (.148)

SCL (social class low)	RC (religion Catholic)	RJ (religion Jewish)	NM (not married)	S (southern U.S.)	PHLTH (serious illness since mid-teens)	PS (private school)		R^2
						PARS	PRVS	
.010 (.15)	.066 (1.38)	.132 (1.64)	−.330 (8.06)	−.082 (1.58)		−.052 (.76)	.165 (1.73)	.263
−.006 (.172)	.055 (1.92)	.027 (.67)	−.105 (4.98)	.038 (1.28)		−.069 (1.71)	−.031 (.00)	.376
−.034 (.040)	−.039 (.035)	.564 (.101)	−.180 (.077)	−.024 (.049)				.077
−.118 (.038)	.003 (.042)	.291 (.096)	−.058 (.081)	−.022 (.048)				.050
−.082 (.027)	.002 (.029)	.372 (.062)	−.167 (.059)	−.084 (.032)				.086
−.217 (.060)	.182 (.073)	.274 (.102)	−.176 (.128)	−.060 (.086)				.233
−.233 (.112)	.037 (.112)	.122 (.1578)	.118 (.208)	−.065 (.106)				.084
−.207 (.123)	.122 (.126)	.040 (.225)	−.420 (.230)	.129 (.159)				.216

TABLE C-1
(concluded)

Education level	Sample size N	Ability† test	LNWK (log of weeks worked)	SCH (social class high)
Husén Swedish sample (dependent variable: log of 1968 earnings)				
E_1^t	18	.392 (.607)		
E_2^t	235	.050 (.800)		−.138 (.161)
E_3^t	59	.219 (.379)		−.291 (.208)
E_4^t	66	.427 (.386)		.049 (.136)
E_5^t	51	.586 (.409)		.255 (.106)
E_6^t	21	.393 (.457)		−.018 (.157)

* Standard errors are in parentheses except for Project Talent, where the regression program gives t-values.

† Different ability tests are used for each major sample cohort. These are Rogers, IQ test scores; Project Talent, C004 (quantitative composite); NBER-Thorndike (a general-ability factor from Air Force test battery); and Husén, TST38 (total test score, 1938).

SOURCE: Author's computations are from data in the indicated samples.

SCL (social class low)	RC (religion Catholic)	RJ (religion Jewish)	NM (not married	S (southern U.S.)	PHLTH (serious illness since mid-teens)	PS (private school)	R^2
—.105 (.195)			—.112 (.241)		—.061 (.349)		.098
—.049 (.042)			—.163 (.072)		—.025 (.082)		.030
—.072 (.129)			—.121 (.394)		—.116 (.237)		.042
—.111 (.141)			—.277 (.157)		—.238 (.166)		.117
—.086 (.137)			—.071 (.161)		—.098 (.176)		.199
—.066 (.328)					—.049 (.239)		.056

Appendix D: The Concept of "Full Savings"

by Lewis C. Solmon

Before discussing reasons to expect particular relationships between education and savings, we must clarify our definition of *savings* and note the problems inherent in it. This study looks at savings behavior of a sample of families in 1959. The calculation of 1959 savings was initiated by deducting changes in nonhousing debt (during 1959) from changes in value of financial assets, excluding common stocks and mutual funds. To this was added the value of common stocks and mutual fund shares bought minus the value sold in order to determine additions to discretionary savings in the form of variable-price assets. The changes in variable-price assets due to appreciation or decline in value should not be considered saving or dissaving in the same sense as increases in other assets resulting from an individual's allocation of part of his income for that specific purpose. (The effects of unrealized capital gains or losses have been studied and was reported in Chapter 10.)

Savings in the form of real-property assets—namely, a change in value of nonhousing real estate and other assets valued over $1,000—is added to this concept of financial savings. Finally, mortgage principal repayments are taken into account. The action of repaying mortgage principal implies increased saving in the form of housing equity.

A number of other issues arise when an attempt is made to define savings completely. The appearance of a relation between savings, as conventionally defined, and schooling might be due to an actual relation between education and a more complete definition of savings, with the observed phenomenon due to systematic differences by education in the omitted portion of savings.

The problem can be illustrated by a simple case. Let full savings S_F equal the part included in the definition S_I plus the part excluded

S_E. Now, it is possible that the marginal propensities to save estimated using S_I decline with schooling E; i.e.,

$$MPS_I = a_1 - b_1 E \qquad (D\text{-}1)$$

Moreover, assume that had the marginal propensity to save in the form of S_E been estimated, the results would be the opposite; i.e.,

$$MPS_E = a_2 + b_2 E \qquad (D\text{-}2)$$

If $b_2 > b_1$, the true relationship between education and the marginal propensity to save would be positive if full savings could be quantified. Hence

$$MPS_F = a + bE \qquad (D\text{-}3)$$

The problem then becomes one of either increasing the fraction S_I/S_F or, at least, estimating the sign and magnitude of b_2 in order to present an inference about the full-savings–income relationship. Both of these paths are followed to some extent.

First, the definition used excludes changes in debt incurred for business, farm, or equipment. The study focuses on the effects of education rather than of occupation; whether debt is incurred in these forms is a function of the latter. In the regression estimates provided later, a control variable is introduced to account for families where the head is a business proprietor or independent professional. However, both business assets and business debt are omitted from the definition of savings. Since business assets are probably acquired in part by incurring debt and in part by reducing other forms of financial and property savings, those acquiring business assets should appear to be saving less than others. Although there is probably a systematic relationship between schooling and self-employment, this will not affect the savings-schooling relationship if a self-employment variable is used to control.

Although many people accumulate physical capital to help them earn income subsequently, another type of postschool capital accumulation is also taking place, namely, accumulation of human capital in the form of on-the-job training. Rather than allocating part of earned income for business equipment or financial assets an individual pays for on-the-job training by forgoing current income. Hence to adjust for savings in this form, not only must savings be augmented, but also a concept of full income is needed, one which includes income received and income forgone. Thus the first step is to separate *full* current income I^F into income received Y *plus* costs incurred (in terms of current income forgone) to obtain on-the-job training K. Mincer (1962, p. 54) uses the following approach to estimate on-the-job training costs:

Such estimates are obtained on the assumption that the rate of return is the same on each year's investment whether at school or on the job. In any given year after high-school graduation, those who go on to, or have graduated from, college would have earnings (Y_j), which equal earnings of high school graduates (X_j) plus the income earned on the differential investment in training made since graduation from high school, provided no further investment in training was incurred by them during year j. Costs of (incremental) training in year j are, therefore, measured by the difference between Y_j and X_j augmented by the (forgone) return on the previous (incremental) costs.

That is, Mincer shows that in any year j, training costs

$$K_j = X_j + \left(r \sum_{i=1}^{j-1} a_i K_i \right) - Y_j$$

$$a_i = \frac{1}{1 - (1/1 + r)^{n-j}} \tag{D-4}$$

where a_i is a correction factor for finite life and n is the length of working life.

It is now possible to define full savings, S_j^F as equal to saving in the traditional sense of accumulating financial and property assets S_j, plus earnings forgone to obtain training, that is, saving in the form of human capital K_j.

$$S_j^F = S_j + K_j \tag{D-5}$$

Furthermore, consumption C_j is a function of full income I^F:

$$C_j = a + b I_j^F \tag{D-6}$$

in the simplest form. From Eq. (D-4), full income equals measured income plus income forgone to obtain training:

$$I_j^F = Y_j + K_j \tag{D-7}$$

Substituting Eq. (D-7) in Eq. (D-6), we get

$$C_j = a + bY_j + bK_j \qquad \text{(D-8)}$$

Substituting further for C_j, we get

$$I_j{}^F - S_j - K_j = a + bY_j + bK_j$$

hence $\qquad S_j = -a + (1 - b)\, Y_j - bK_j \qquad \text{(D-9)}$

Mincer's data show that on-the-job training rises with formal educational attainment and declines with age. Certain tentative conclusions can be drawn from Eq. (D-9). In a group of people whose characteristics would lead us to predict equal amounts (or percentages) of total savings $(S_j{}^F)$, those with more schooling should have less savings as traditionally defined (S_j). Also, those who are older should have larger traditionally defined savings. In other words, since younger and more educated members of the labor force are saving more of their incomes in the form of investment in themselves, they probably will save correspondingly less in the form of financial assets and durables, other things being equal.

It has been argued in Chapter 10 that reasonable assumptions applied to traditional models of consumption and savings lead to the expectation that when savings are defined in the full-savings sense, more educated people *would* save more, as older members of the labor force do. The argument that includes investment in on-the-job training enables modification of these predictions. Since older workers invest less in on-the-job training, they should invest more in other forms of saving. Traditional assumptions lead to the prediction of more total saving as workers get older; hence empirically there should be a positive relationship between age and financial saving.

On the other hand, although it might be expected that more educated people save more in total, they also invest more in training, all else being equal. Thus it is unclear which way the relation between *financial* saving and education will go.

Mincer's estimates of investment in human capital (forgoing earnings to acquire on-the-job training) are for roughly the same period (1958–1959) as the data used for this study. His data permit calculation of a ratio, which we shall call d, for each age-education category of worker, d being that fraction of full income (received plus forgone) sacrificed in order to obtain on-the-job training. The Consumers Union panel sample we use contains husband's pretax (received) income, called *H,* which can be augmented to resemble full income by multiplying by 1 + *d* from the corresponding age-education group. The product of *d* times this full-income estimate is an estimate of earnings forgone in order to obtain on-the-job training. Hence savings should be augmented by $dH(1 + d)$ so as to incorporate investment in OJT, and family income should be increased by the same dollar amount in order to add to family income the forgone part of husband's income, thereby providing a measure of full family income. Since we are adding the same thing to both sides of the equation, the estimates will improve, partially for arithmetic rather than economic reasons. Moreover, since OJT varies with schooling, we can expect a more systematic relationship between education and saving when OJT is included. Lastly, this augmented model corresponds more to reality than one which omits OJT. The results were presented both with and without this adjustment for OJT.

Treatment of the acquisition of human capital differs somewhat from the previously described treatment of the acquisition of physical assets. In the latter case, our estimates are altered only to the extent that financial savings are reduced to acquire physical assets. In the former instance, the financial saving will be altered to the extent that financial assets are lower, or nonhousing debt higher, as a consequence of income forgone. However, on-the-job training is included in savings, while physical business assets are not. Moreover, income is adjusted only in the OJT case. This approach was chosen because of limitations of the data and the desire to highlight the effects of human capital. The result is that two equally educated people of the same age will be allotted equal saving in the form of OJT, but acquisition of business assets by one will be taken into account only by means of changes in financial saving and by the control variable for self-employment.

Two other components of saving have been excluded in these estimates. Changes in cash surrender value of life insurance were omitted, since there was evidence that this concept was not understood by many respondents, who appeared to confuse cash surrender value with face value. The variance of this variable was much larger than the variance of other components of saving. In the sample, mean saving in the form of increasing cash surrender value of life insurance did not vary systematically by schooling attainment, but remained in the 2 to 3 percent range of income. Of course, if the probability of confusing face value with the smaller cash surrender value declines with schooling, the true share of savings in this form would rise with education, given a constant reported share of income saved in this form. The evidence implies that if life insurance saving does vary with education, the correlation is positive.

The second omission is savings in the form of pension plans. If more educated people tend to have jobs with larger pension plans, then their omission tends to understate the positive relationship between full saving and education. Using figures from Cagan (1965, p. 34) and from the current study, both of which refer to the same data set, it can be shown that savings in the form of pension plans tend to rise with education.

Appendix Table D-1 shows that, overall, those covered by pensions save 32 percent more than those not covered and that the share of people covered rises with schooling. Together, these figures indicate that if pension-plan saving were included in saving, those with a high school education or less would increase saving by 17.35 percent; those with some college, by 18.96 percent; and those with four years or more, by 20.23 percent on the average. Hence pension saving would strengthen any positive correlation between schooling and saving.

TABLE D-1
Pension-plan coverage by schooling attainment

	High school or less	Some college	Four or more years of college
Fraction covered (adjusting Cagan's figures to include self-employed)*	0.5423	0.5925	0.6323
	Covered		Not covered
$\frac{\text{Saving (other than pension)}}{\text{Income}}$	0.087		0.078
$\frac{\text{Pension saving}}{\text{Income}}$	0.028		
$\frac{\text{Total saving}}{\text{Income}}$	0.115		0.078

*$\frac{0.115-0.077}{0.115}$ = 0.32; hence it was assumed that those covered saved 32 percent more than those not covered.

NOTE: Average savings increase due to pension coverage (according to schooling attainment) was obtained as the product of fraction covered (line 1) and the 32 percent.

SOURCE: Cagan (1965, p. 34) and the present study.

According to the above arguments and evidence, the omission of savings, in the form of both cash surrender value of life insurance and pension plans, tends to cause an understatement of any observed positive relationship between savings and education. The omissions are also troublesome when one tries to interpret patterns of responses to savings-attitude questions. The problem is whether more educated people considered their savings in these forms when responding. For example, it is uncertain whether the indication that a declining share of respondents save to provide for their old age as schooling level rises is due to less concern for old age, or to the realization that old age will be provided for by cashing in insurance and receiving a pension. That is, are pensions and life insurance considered part of savings? In interpreting the results, one must bear in mind that savings both in the form of cash surrender value of insurance and in the form of pension plans seem to rise with education.

One other general form of savings has been ignored so far. I refer to the accumulation of consumer durables. It is only the value of services obtained from durables during a particular period that should be considered consumption; the decision concerning whether to allocate savings to financial assets or consumer durables is really a portfolio decision.[1]

---

[1] These considerations lead to the prediction of a lower marginal propensity to consume, if properly measured, than those usually cited.

The "typical" United States value of the MPC is 0.75; of the APC, 0.88; and of the ϵ_y, 0.83. Permanent consumption has been estimated to be 0.9 of permanent income where C_P includes durable purchases. The relevant marginal propensity to consume dC/dY may be obtained from the following:

$$\frac{dC}{dY} = \frac{dY_p}{dY} \times \frac{dC}{dY_p} = \frac{dY_p}{dY} \times \frac{dC_S}{dY} \times \frac{dY}{dY_p} + \frac{dC_D}{dY} \times \frac{dY}{dY_p} \qquad \text{(D-10)}$$

The new subscripts on consumption C and income Y are S for service flows and D for durable purchases. Of course, $dC = dC_S + dC_D$. Equation (D-10) can be simplified to

$$\frac{dC_S}{dY} = \frac{dC}{dY} - \frac{dC_D}{dY} \qquad \text{(D-11)}$$

When substituting generally accepted values for dC/dY (0.75), dC_D/dY (0.15). and dY_p/dY (0.85), a value of the marginal propensity to consume service flows dC_S/dY is approximately 0.6. A question one would like to discuss is how education should influence this "MPC_S" or the analogous marginal propensity to save.

Other things being equal, purchase of a consumer durable will result in an instantaneous and roughly offsetting decline in financial-asset accumulations insofar as the purchase is debt financed. If a durable is purchased for X dollars and if debt increases by X dollars, the only effect on measured savings is the decline due to the debt increase. As the debt is paid off, however, savings will be larger because debt repayments are part of savings. If the durable asset is acquired for cash, measured savings will decline if financial assets are liquidated to obtain the cash.

Three types of consumer durables can be distinguished and are treated separately — housing, automobiles, and others. Following Cagan (1965), each nonhousing and nonauto consumer durable was valued at $300. An independent variable, value of consumer durables purchased, was inserted in the regressions. *Ceteris paribus,* as consumer-durable purchases increase, other savings should decline because of both the substitution of one method of deferring consumption for another and the fact that financial saving declines as durables are paid for or financed.

A similar result applies to automobiles, and so value of automobiles was inserted as a variable to explain savings as defined above. The greater the value of automobiles, the larger the auto-secured debt or the smaller the financial assets.

Purchasing a house has a similar, but probably larger, effect on savings as traditionally defined. House purchasers probably find themselves left with smaller financial savings and more need to purchase a variety of consumer durables than other savers. But a house purchaser whose other savings are low is not necessarily a person with little interest in, or desire for, savings. Hence several adjustments were made. First, those who had purchased homes in 1959 were eliminated altogether from the estimates. Then they were included, with a dummy variable inserted to control for whether a house had been purchased.

References

Cagan, P.: *The Effect of Pension Plans on Aggregate Saving: Evidence from a Sample Survey,* National Bureau of Economic Research, New York, 1965.

Mincer, Jacob: "On the Job Training: Costs, Returns, and Some Implications," *Journal of Political Economy,* vol. 70, part 2, pp. 50–79, Supplement: October 1962.

Appendix E: Ability Scores

by Albert E. Beaton

The members of the NBER-TH sample were tested in 1943 on a battery of 18 tests: Reading Comprehension, Mechanical Principles, Dial and Table Reading, Spatial Orientation I, Spatial Orientation II, Numerical Operations, Speed of Identification, General Information—Navigator, General Information—Pilot, Mathematics A, Mathematics B, Rotary Pursuit, Divided Attention, Two-Hand Coordination, Complex Coordination, Aiming Stress, Discrimination Reaction Time, and Finger Dexterity. For a description of the tests see Thorndike & Hagen (1959). These tests constitute a battery of the type of tests usually used for measuring aptitude for college admission plus other tests more specific to the role of Air Force pilot or navigator.

We wished to form a single measure of ability that would include as much information as possible from these tests. This is not to argue that ability is a single trait, but merely to devise a general index which is a composite of a number of different abilities. Any such composite obviously loses some of the information captured by the test scores.

To form the composite, we first computed a correlation matrix of the 18 tests and factor-analyzed the matrix using principal-components analysis with varimax rotation. The factor analysis indicated that the scholastic-type tests form one large factor, whereas the other tests fragmented into several small factors.

We then performed a principal-components analysis of the scholastic-type tests to form a single ability factor. The tests included were Reading Comprehension, Dial and Table Reading, Spatial Orientation I, Spatial Orientation II, Numerical Operations, Speed of Identification, and the Mathematics A and B tests. Because the Reading Comprehension test had a low floor—i.e., very low scores were impossible—a dummy variable was added

TABLE E-1
*Factor analysis and ability measures** *

Panel A: Means and standard deviations

Variable	Mean	Standard deviations
Reading Comprehension	22.6404	11.7236
Reading dummy	0.9841	0.1250
Dial and Table Reading	35.7257	8.8158
Spatial Orientation I	21.0812	6.4968
Spatial Orientation II	28.2426	5.5544
Numerical Operations	72.4753	22.1561
Speed of Identification	33.6293	7.0941
Mathematics B	16.2734	9.8541
Mathematics A	25.1058	17.0936

Panel C: Correlation coefficients

	Reading Comprehension	Reading dummy	Dial and Table Reading	Spatial Orientation I
Reading Comprehension	1.0000	0.2452	0.2962	0.2506
Reading dummy	0.2452	1.0000	0.0750	0.0580
Dial and Table Reading	0.2962	0.0750	1.0000	0.2758
Spatial Orientation I	0.2506	0.0580	0.2758	1.0000
Spatial Orientation II	0.1334	0.0400	0.3732	0.4006
Numerical Operations	0.1365	0.0200	0.5293	0.0451
Speed of Identification	0.1154	0.0512	0.2670	0.3523
Mathematics B	0.4999	0.1017	0.4492	0.1699
Mathematics A	0.4343	0.0994	0.4366	0.1916

Panel D: Factor loadings for first three factors

Principal components	I	II	III
Reading Comprehension	0.6011	0.2642	−0.4947
Reading dummy	0.2040	0.1188	−0.7088
Dial and Table Reading	0.7578	−0.0042	0.2585
Spatial Orientation I	0.4847	−0.5263	−0.2562
Spatial Orientation II	0.5424	−0.5960	0.0879
Numerical Operations	0.6152	0.2255	0.5051
Speed of Identification	0.4377	−0.6504	−0.0161
Mathematics B	0.7263	0.4359	0.0090
Mathematics A	0.7268	0.3135	0.0169

*The number of observations is 4,349.

Panel B: Latent roots		
Index	Root	Percent
1	3.1319	34.80
2	1.4783	51.22
3	1.1430	63.92
4	0.8529	73.40
5	0.6041	80.11
6	0.5190	85.88
7	0.4872	91.29
8	0.4225	95.99
9	0.3611	100.00

Spatial Orientation II	Numerical Operations	Speed of Identification	Mathematics B	Mathematics A
0.1334	0.1365	0.1154	0.4999	0.4343
0.0400	0.0200	0.0512	0.1017	0.0994
0.3732	0.5293	0.2670	0.4492	0.4366
0.4006	0.0451	0.3523	0.1699	0.1916
1.0000	0.2285	0.4474	0.1380	0.2124
0.2285	1.0000	0.1386	0.4500	0.4005
0.4474	0.1386	1.0000	0.0701	0.1395
0.1380	0.4500	0.0701	1.0000	0.5806
0.2124	0.4005	0.1395	0.5806	1.0000

such that a value of 1 was given to each person who did not score at the lowest possible level, and a score of 0 was attributed otherwise.

The results of this analysis are shown in Table E-1. The first panel of the table shows the means and standard deviations; the next presents the latent roots to indicate the relative size of the factors; and the third section contains the correlation coefficients. The factor loadings for the first three factors are shown in the remainder of the table.

The first factor accounts for nearly 35 percent of the variance of these tests. The factor loadings are high (>0.4) for all variables except the reading dummy variable. These loadings were used to compute the general-ability score.

The second factor is also interpretable as a contrast between the two mathematics tests against the spatial tests and the speed of identification test. The third factor is a contrast between the Numerical Operations and the Reading Comprehension tests.

Reference

Thorndike, Robert L., and Elizabeth P. Hagen: *Ten Thousand Careers,* John Wiley & Sons, Inc., New York, 1959.

Index

Ability (*see* Mental ability)
ACE (American College Entrance)
    examination, 55
Age, effect on earnings growth, 10
Age differences and crime, 35
Age-earnings profiles, 211–215
    (*See also* Obsolescence)
Alchian, Armen A., 339n.
American College Entrance (ACE)
    examination, 55
American Institutes of Research, 123n.
Anderson, G. Lester, 55
APC (average propensity to consume), 274,
    277
Aptitude:
    defined, 369
    scholastic (*see* IQ)
    (*See also* Mental ability)
Aptitude tests, 53
Arrest and prison data on education-
    crime relationship, 323–327
Arrow, K., 110
Ashenfelter, O., 96n, 127n.
Astin, A., 106
Attitudes:
    consumer, and savings behavior, 277–292
    toward education, effect of education on,
    40–41, 392–394

Attitudes:
    influence of education and ability on,
    38–41
    toward job success, effect of education
    on, 389–392
    toward life, effect of education on, 385–
    389
    and salary, effect of education and ability
    on, 365–396
Average propensity to consume (APC), 274,
    277

Background and ability variables,
    regression equations of log of earnings
    on, 411–417
Bancroft, Gertrude, 172n.
Barker, Richard W., 49, 51, 60, 63
Barzel, Yoram, 199n.
Beaton, Albert E., 25, 38, 365, 399, 427
Becker, Gary, 14n., 85n., 88, 90n., 95,
    96n., 109, 110n., 151n., 152, 158n.,
    176, 180n., 199, 205, 237, 261, 264,
    296n., 311, 314, 339n., 340n., 346n.,
    360n., 382n.
Behavior, effects of education on, 8, 24–25
Ben-Porath, Y., 207n.